The Rule of Law Under Threat

ELGAR STUDIES IN EUROPEAN LAW AND POLICY

Series Editor: Herwig C.H. Hofmann, *Professor of European and Trans-national Public Law, Faculty of Law, Economics and Finance and Robert Schuman Institute for European Affairs, University of Luxembourg.*

Elgar Studies in European Law and Policy is a forum for books that demonstrate cutting-edge legal and politico-legal analysis of the pertinent policies in a multi-jurisdictional Europe. The series is as relevant for academic reflection as for practical development of the matters addressed therein, such as policy relevance, its origins and the possibilities of future development. Books in the series take a multidisciplinary or multi-jurisdictional approach to the topics at their centers, with an aim to facilitating understanding of European law and policy matters and demonstrating their connectedness throughout jurisdictional levels. The series will provide coverage and analysis of various regulatory areas at the forefront of EU law and policy, including: the development of new European policy fields, issues of market regulation, economic and monetary matters and social dimensions of EU law.

For a full list of Edward Elgar published titles, including the titles in this series, visit our website at www.e-elgar.com.

The Rule of Law Under Threat

Eroding Institutions and European Remedies

Edited by

Robert Böttner

Assistant Professor of Public Law, Faculty for Law, Economics and Social Sciences, University of Erfurt, Germany

Hermann-Josef Blanke

Professor of Public Law, Public International Law and European Integration, Faculty for Law, Economics and Social Sciences, University of Erfurt, Germany

ELGAR STUDIES IN EUROPEAN LAW AND POLICY

 Edward Elgar

PUBLISHING

Cheltenham, UK • Northampton, MA, USA

Co-funded by
the European Union

Published by
Edward Elgar Publishing Limited
The Lypiatts
15 Lansdown Road
Cheltenham
Glos GL50 2JA
UK

Edward Elgar Publishing, Inc.
William Pratt House
9 Dewey Court
Northampton
Massachusetts 01060
USA

A catalogue record for this book
is available from the British Library

Library of Congress Control Number: 2024934603

This book is available electronically in the **Elgar**online
Law subject collection
http://dx.doi.org/10.4337/9781035330690

ISBN 978 1 0353 3068 3 (cased)
ISBN 978 1 0353 3069 0 (eBook)
Printed and bound by CPI Group (UK) Ltd, Croydon, CR0 4YY

Contents

List of contributors   vii
Preface   ix

1   The Rule of Law as a Fundamental Value of the Council of Europe, the European Union and in the Constitutional Traditions Common to the Member States   1
Juha Raitio

2   Measuring the Rule of Law: an Empirical Approach   14
Jacek Lewkowicz, Rafał Woźniak and Przemysław Litwiniuk

3   Post-accession Experience Regarding the Rule of Law   32
Herbert Küpper

4   The Fall of the Rule of Law and Democracy in Hungary and the Complicity of the EU   53
Gábor Halmai

5   Consequences of the Rule of Law Debates for the Accession Process of the States of the Western Balkan   76
Pavel Usvatov and Mahir Muharemovic

6   Are Judges Politicians in Robes? Comparative Aspects of the Recruitment and Election of Judges   99
Piotr Mikuli, Natalie Fox and Radosław Puchta

7   Rule of Law (Crisis) and the Principle of Mutual Trust   132
Konstantina-Antigoni Poulou

8   Questioning the Primacy of Union Law by National Constitutional Courts   154
Udo Bux

9   Political Strategies to Overcome the Rule of Law Crisis
      Taking into Account National Political Discourses – The
      Case of East Central European EU Member States   173
      *Astrid Lorenz, Jan Němec, Dietmar Müller, Madeleine
      Hartmann and Dorottya Vig*

10   The Rule of Law in the European Union and the Toolbox
      to Defend it: Article 7 TEU, Rule of Law Report and
      Dialogue, Budgetary Conditionality   196
      Jonathan Bauerschmidt

11   Article 7 TEU as 'Nuclear Option'? An Analysis of its
      Potential and its Shortcomings   219
      Robert Böttner and Nic Schröder

12   Financial Sanctions as a Remedy to Enforce the Rule of
      Law in Poland and Hungary   239
      Malte Symann

Index   256

Contributors

Jonathan Bauerschmidt, Member of the Legal Service at the Council of the European Union and Visiting Professor at Université Catholique de Louvain.

Robert Böttner, Assistant Professor at the Faculty for Law, Economics and Social Sciences at the University of Erfurt, Germany.

Udo Bux, Head of the European Parliament Liaison Office, Munich.

Natalie Fox, Jagiellonian University, Kraków.

Gábor Halmai, part-time Professor of Law at the European University Institute, Robert Schuman Centre for Advanced Studies, Florence and Professor emeritus at Eötvös Loránd University, Budapest.

Madeleine Hartmann, Doctoral researcher at Leipzig University.

Herbert Küpper, Director of the Institute for East European Law, Regensburg and lecturer in law at Andrássy University, Budapest.

Jacek Lewkowicz, Faculty of Economic Sciences, University of Warsaw.

Przemysław Litwiniuk, Warsaw University of Life Sciences.

Astrid Lorenz, Professor of the Political System of Germany and Politics in Europe at Leipzig University.

Piotr Mikuli, Jagiellonian University Kraków and Associate Member of the Centre for European Law and Internationalization at the University of Leicester.

Mahir Muharemovic, Rule of Law Programme South East Europe at the Konrad-Adenauer-Foundation, and University of Tuzla, Bosnia and Herzegovina (BiH).

Dietmar Müller, Postdoctoral researcher at Leipzig University.

Jan Němec, Postdoctoral researcher at Leipzig University.

Konstantina-Antigoni Poulou, University of Heidelberg.

Radosław Puchta, University of Białystok.

Juha Raitio, Professor of European Law, Faculty of Law at the University of Helsinki.

Nic Schröder, M.A. candidate, European and International Public Administration at Andrássy University, Budapest.

Malte Symann, attorney at law at Freshfields Bruckhaus Deringer.

Pavel Usvatov, Rule of Law Programme South East Europe at the Konrad-Adenauer-Foundation.

Dorottya Víg, Doctoral researcher at Leipzig University.

Rafał Woźniak, Faculty of Economic Sciences, University of Warsaw.

Preface

The rule of law is under attack, in Europe as well as in other parts of the world. Populist parties win large shares or even majorities in their countries' parliaments and form the government or at least part of a governing coalition. While blatant attacks on rule of law standards are obvious and easy to spot, others come in disguise and are more difficult to identify. The European Union as an integration project is among other things a community based on the rule of law. This is why the fulfilment of rule of law standards are an entry requirement for acceding to the Union as well as a fundamental value with which the Member States must comply during their membership. Still, we observe that to varying degrees the state of the rule of law within the Union's members is deteriorating. In order to counter these developments, it is important to reveal and understand the causes for these developments. This edited volume wants to contribute to this understanding.

The idea to this volume originated in the fall of 2022, when the two editors discussed different rule of law aspects with some of the persons eventually authoring chapters for this volume. It became clear that not only the symptoms and effects of deficits in the rule of law need to be discussed. Rather, it is also necessary to analyse where they originate. In doing so, country-specific contexts may need to be taken into account. At the same time, the view must be broadened from a purely legal perspective to an interdisciplinary analysis. The concept for this volume emerged from these discussions. Sadly, however, one of the editors did not live to see its completion. In January 2023, *Professor Dr. Hermann-Josef Blanke*, who had devoted a great deal of energy to compiling the contributions to this volume, passed away unexpectedly. This volume is dedicated to him and his academic legacy.

The book departs by mapping the rule of law as a common European value as it derives from different national and international contexts. It continues by exploring how to put a yardstick to this legal principle by explaining how rule of law standards may be put into numbers. This can help rendering the debate on actual and alleged deteriorations more objective. The following chapters look at the rule of law in the context of previous and future accessions in Eastern and South-Eastern Europe. On the one hand, this includes a view to countries of the so-called Eastern enlargement of the early 2000s, with a spotlight on Hungary as one of the recent and notorious cases of rule of law deficits within the European Union. In doing so, the book delves into national peculiarities that help sharpen the view on different perceptions of rule of law standards, which is helpful in shaping the responses to these deficits. On the other hand, another chapter will deal with how rule of law debates *within* the Union influence the discourse in and behaviour of countries eager to join the Union, which requires evidence from field research. These broader pictures are accompanied by analyses of specific details and problems concerning the 'attacks' on the rule of law, namely the principle of mutual trust, the appointment or election of (constitutional court) judges and the relationship between the Union and its Member States with regard to the principle of primacy of EU law, one of the building blocks of the Union's constitutional fabric. Finally, the book will look at ways to tackle rule of law deficits. This includes, on the one hand, political strategies that, as argued earlier, need to take account of specific national discourses on and perceptions of rule of law standards. On the other hand, the chapters explain the (legal) toolbox that the EU has at its disposal. This includes, in more detail, the Article 7 procedure as *the* (currently edgeless) constitutional tool and the new conditionality mechanism that approaches the issue from a pecuniary side.

Many people have contributed to the creation of this volume. Thanks are due to them. This includes, first and foremost, the authors who have dedicated themselves to this project. The editors would also like to thank our secretary *Christel Fliedner*, who took on a lot of organisational work, as well as *Felix Heinzel*, assistant at the chair, who devoted energy to the formal editing of the volume. Thanks are due also to Edward Elgar Publishing for including this edited volume in their publishing programme, and to *Luke Adams, Fiona Todd, Emily White*, and everyone else with Edward Elgar who helped conceptualize and shape the final outcome.

Robert Böttner, Erfurt
December 2023

1. The Rule of Law as a Fundamental Value of the Council of Europe, the European Union and in the Constitutional Traditions Common to the Member States

Juha Raitio

1. RULE OF LAW AS A VALUE IN THE CONTEXT OF THE EUROPEAN UNION AND THE EUROPEAN COUNCIL – ALLEGORY OF A TRINITY

Let's start by trying to define the concept of rule of law, although an attempt to define it is most likely controversial. In any case, the rule of law is associated with the deepest layers of law, the layer of moral considerations.[1] It represents the fundamental values of the Member States and relates, therefore, to both legal culture and legal norms.[2] Another starting point is that the rule of law is not only a formal principle. It is easy to point out, in this respect, that Article 2 TEU provides the authoritative context to interpret the rule of law in the framework of liberal democracy and the protection of human rights in an active civil society, in which citizens are equal before the law. In addition, there is reason

---

[1] Raitio, *The Principle of Legal Certainty in EC Law* (Kluwer 2003) at 301-304; Klami, *Methodological Problems in European and Comparative Law* (Helsinki University Press 1994) at 10-12.

[2] Tuori, *Ratio and Voluntas, The Tension Between Reason and Will in Law* (Ashgate 2011) at 208, *Tuori* has somewhat similarly separated the Constitution into explicit, written norms and constitutional culture, which refers to constitutional theories, concepts and principles, as well as ways of dealing with these, i.e. patterns of constitutional argumentation.

to highlight the procedure of Article 7 TEU[3] to oversee the integrity of values in accordance with Article 2 TEU.

Thus, the trinity of rule of law, liberal democracy and human rights form the legal-cultural level of EU law. This European "trinity of values" is not a novelty at all. For example, one can refer to the following citation from the German legal theorist *Radbruch*:

> Though democracy is certainly a praiseworthy value, the *Rechtstaat* is like a daily bread, the water we drink and the air we breathe; and the greatest merit of democracy is that it alone is adapted to preserve the *Rechtstaat*.[4]

A bit later *Hayek* has not only referred to this sentence by *Radbruch* but also added that democracy will not exist long unless it preserves the rule of law.[5]

One may also point out the so-called Copenhagen criteria and their connection to the rule of law in the same way as in the current Article 2 TEU. In 1993, the European Council clarified the conditions that countries seeking EU membership must fulfil. In accordance with these Copenhagen criteria, all European countries that adhere to the principles of freedom, democracy, human rights, respect for fundamental freedoms and rule of law may apply for membership.[6] Today, respecting the principle of rule of law as a condition for membership is manifested in Article 49 TEU so that any European State that respects and promotes values defined in Article 2 TEU can apply for EU membership.

So, it is only logical that in contemporary literature on EU law one can refer to the "thick" concept of rule of law, which contains both formal and material elements.[7] The protection of individual or human rights seems to strengthen the interpretation of "thick" rule of law.[8] This interpretation of the rule of law includes at least the following elements or objectives: legal order and

---

[3] See e.g. CFI, Case T-337/03, *Bartelli Gálves v The Commission*, EU:T:2004: 106, which concerned the procedure of Article 7 TEU.

[4] Radbruch, *Rechtsphilosophie* (K.F. Köhler 1950) at 357.

[5] Hayek, *The Constitution of Liberty* (Routledge & Kegan Paul 1960) at 248.

[6] See e.g. Jääskinen, *Euroopan Unioni, oikeudelliset perusteet* (Talentum 2007) at 61.

[7] See e.g. Pech, 'Promoting the rule of law abroad: on the EU's limited contribution to the shaping of an international understanding of the rule of law', in Kochenov and Amtenbrink (eds), *EU's Shaping of the International Legal Order* (CUP 2013) 108-129.

[8] See e.g. von Bogdandy, Antpöhler and Ioannidis, 'Protecting EU values, Rev-erse *Solange* and the Rule of Law Framework', in Jacab and Kochenov (eds), *The Enforcement of EU law and Values* (OUP 2017) 218-233 at 226.

stability; equality of application of the law; protection of human rights; and the settlement of disputes before an independent legal body.[9] However, there is a fear according to which the rule of law is in danger of becoming blurred as a concept and losing some of its expressiveness, if it is interpreted too broadly.[10] For example, *Raz* has warned against confounding the concept of rule of law with a wide range of values, principles or goals that are characteristic of a good legal system.[11] So how to tackle this fear of interpreting rule of law too broadly?

An answer is that a legal interpretation is always contextual in such a way that the concept of rule of law is not merely an ideal or unprecise rhetoric,[12] but its elements can be analyzed by studying relevant cases of law. Additionally, one can rely on the various lists of the elements of rule of law. From a wider European viewpoint, one can refer to the goals of the Council of Europe and take into account the expertise and views of the European Commission for Democracy through Law (the so-called Venice Commission) on the principle of rule of law. In its report, the Venice Commission lists the following factors included in the concept of rule of law:

- principle of legality, which refers to the transparency, accountability, democratic nature and pluralism of the legislative process
- legal certainty
- prohibition of arbitrariness of the executive powers
- access to justice in independent and impartial courts
- effective judicial review, which includes respect for fundamental and human rights, and

---

[9] McCorquodale, 'Defining the International Rule of Law: Defying Gravity?' (2016) 72 ICLQ, 277-304 at 284-285.

[10] Frändberg, 'Begreppet rättsstat', in Sterzel (ed), 31 Rättsstaten – rätt, politik, moral (1996) 21-41, at 22-23.

[11] Raz, *The Authority of Law, Essays on Law and Morality* (Clarendon Press 1979) p. 211.

[12] About rule of law as an unprecise ideal see e.g. ECJ, Case C-156/21, *Hungary v Parliament and Council*, EU:C:2022:97, para. 200: "In the first place, Hungary states that the rule of law is an ideal or, at most, a guiding standard, which is never fully achieved and respect for the rule of law should therefore be assessed in relative terms, since no State can claim to adhere to it perfectly. That ideal, which characterizes modern democracy, has developed in a complex way over the centuries, resulting, as is apparent from Study No 512/2009 of 28 March 2011 of the Venice Commission, entitled 'Report on the Rule of Law', in a complex concept which cannot be precisely defined and the substance of which is constantly evolving."

- equality before the law.[13]

The Commission's operating framework and the work of the Venice Commission have not been unimportant, because in January 2016 the Commission began a dialogue with Poland in accordance with the operating framework so that it referred to the Venice Commission's check list of rule of law due to problems related to the position of the Constitutional Court.[14] After that, there have been several cases in which the independence of the Polish court system has been under scrutiny.[15] It is important to note that the rule of law in Poland has also been under scrutiny in the European Court of Human Rights.[16]

The Venice Commission's interpretation of the rule of law has to a great extent been adopted by the EU institutions. For example, in the Commission communication dated 3 April 2019 the rule of law has been described by listing some sub-principles as follows:

> The rule of law includes, among others, principles such as legality, implying a trans-parent, accountable, democratic and pluralistic process for enacting laws; legal certainty; prohibiting the arbitrary exercise of executive power; effective judicial protection by independent and impartial courts, effective judicial review including respect for fundamental rights; separation of powers; and equality before the law. These principles have been recognised by the European Court of Justice and the European Court of Human Rights.[17]

One may also refer to the so called Conditionality Regulation,[18] wherein the rule of law is strongly connected to democracy and the requirement of the

---

[13] European Commission for Democracy Through Law (Venice Commission), 'Report on the Rule of Law', Report (2011), para. 41.

[14] European Commission, Recommendation (EU) 2016/1374 regarding the rule of law in Poland [2016] OJ L 217, 53-68, which has a reference to the Venice Commission's definition of the principle of rule of law in section 5 of the Introduction.

[15] See e.g. ECJ, Case C-216/18 PPU, *Minister for Justice and Equality v LM,* EU:C:2018:586; Case C-619/18, *Commission v Poland,* EU:C:2018:910; Case C-619/18 R, *Commission v Poland,* EU:C:2018:1021; Case C-619/18, *Commission v Poland,* EU:C:2019:531; Case ECJ C-558/18 & 563/18 *Miasto Lowicz,* EU:C:2020:234; Case ECJ C-824/18, *A.B.,* EU:C:2021:153 and Case C-204/21, *Commission v Poland,* EU:C:2023:442.

[16] See e.g. about judicial independence and access to the Court, *Grzeda v Poland,* App no 43572/18 (ECtHR, 15 March 2022).

[17] European Commission, 'Further strengthening the rule of law within the European Union', COM(2019) 163 final at 1-2.

[18] European Parliament and Council, Regulation 2020/2092 on a general regime of conditionality for the protection of the Union budget [2020] OJ L 433l, 1.

implementation of human rights.[19] The discourse concerning the concept of rule of law in the EU can, therefore, not be separated from the democracy that creates an environment of interpretation for the rule of law, the principle of the separation of powers[20] and the legal principles and human rights that legitimize the judicial system. In this context, the principle of rule of law is not merely a "rhetorical balloon", which can in a sense be filled up and include all that is deemed positive in law.[21]

2. THE ENGLISH AND THE GERMAN CONCEPT OF THE RULE OF LAW

Let's start by studying the various interpretations of the English concept of Rule of Law, which has originally been fairly formal and legal positivist with regard to its content.[22] For example for *Dicey*, the concept of rule of law meant that legislation was given undisputed priority compared to the discretion of the authorities.[23] He also found that in Great Britain, the unwritten Constitution was a result of the rights of private legal entities, which are typically various rights to freedom and whose realization is ensured by courts and whose content they also define with their interpretations in a way characteristic of a *common law* legal system.[24] *Dicey's* concept of rule of law included the requirement of equality in relation to legislation, which results in the fact that, like private individuals, officials also are under the jurisdiction of ordinary courts. The blurring of the difference between private and public law and preventing of administrative arbitrariness is central to *Dicey's* concept of rule of law.[25]

Collins has aptly highlighted the impact of various legal theoretical schools of thought on the content of the concept of the rule of law.[26] Legal positivists require that the constitutional state strictly adheres to the law in force and

---

[19] Regulation 2020/2092, *supra* note 18, recital 3.

[20] See e.g. ECJ, Case C-896/19, *Repubblika,* EU:C:2021:311, para. 54.

[21] Frändberg, (1996) *supra* note 10 at 22-23.

[22] Raitio, (2003) *supra* note 1 at 134-139; Tuori (2011) *supra* note 2 at 221-229.

[23] See e.g. Raitio, 'Does the concept of rule of law have any material content? A Nordic point of view' (2017) 24 Maastricht Journal of European and Comparative Law 6, 774-791.

[24] On the classic or traditional English concept of rule of law see: Dicey, *Introduction to the Study of the Law of the Constitution* (10th edn. Macmillan 1959), 183-205.

[25] MacCormick, *Questioning Sovereignty: Law, State and Nation in the European Commonwealth* (OUP 1999) at 44.

[26] Collins, 'Democracy and Adjudication', in MacCormick and Birks (ed), *The Legal Mind, Essays for Tony Honoré* (Clarendon Press 1986), 68-69.

emphasize the importance of a linguistic interpretation, i.e. one that relies on the wording of the legislation.[27] On the other hand, researchers known as "idealists" who are primarily bound to a natural justice interpretation tradition perceive the rule of law to also be a principle of substantive law, which aims to ensure the realization of the legal protection of citizens.[28] Thus, the English concept of Rule of Law seems to be relatively controversial. However, even though the formal concept of rule of law still has its supporters, *Dicey's* classic concept of rule of law is nevertheless already dated.[29]

Dworkin is a well-known researcher, who intertwines the concept of rule of law with substantive law content in addition to the aforementioned formal elements through rights belonging to individuals. *Dworkin's* legal theory gives a basis for seeing that outside a positivist legal interpretation characteristic of, for example, *H.L.A Hart*[30] and *Kelsen*,[31] there is also the possibility of a legally sound argumentation. *Dworkin's* premise was that the weakness of legal positivism was the rejection of the idea that private legal entities may have rights toward the state already before legislation has been enacted on these rights. In this sense, *Dworkin* strongly defends individual legal protection against the state.[32] The inclusion of material elements within the concept of rule of law,

---

[27] Raz, (1979) *supra* note 11, 217; Hart, *The Concept of Law* (2nd edn. Clarendon Press 1997), 155-184; Weber, 'Economy and Law', in Roth and Wittich (ed), *Economy and Society: An Outline of Interpretive Sociology* (Vol. 2, Bedminster Press 1968), 656-657.

[28] Dworkin, *Political Judges and the Rule of Law* (OUP 1980) at 259-287; Lyons, *Ethics and the Rule of Law* (CUP 1984) at 74-78.

[29] Bingham, *The Rule of Law* (Penguin books 2011) at 66-67, which contains the following apt description: "A state which savagely represses or persecutes sections of its people cannot in my view be regarded as observing the rule of law, even if the transport of the persecuted minority to the concentration camp or the compulsory exposure of female children on the mountainside is the subject of detailed laws duly enacted and scrupulously observed".

[30] Hart, (1997) *supra* note 27, 79-99: *H.L.A Hart* found that the law consists of valid legal norms that are in force and originated in the legislative process through legal procedures.

[31] Kelsen, *Pure Theory of Law* (University of California Press 1970) at 221-222; Kelsen, *Reine Rechtslehre*, (Österreichische Staatsdruckerei 1960) at 228. In *Kelsen's* legal theory, legal norms must be separated from moral or religious norms, because the validity of a legal norm may be derived from another superior norm.

[32] Dworkin, *Taking Rights Seriously* (Harvard University Press 1978) at xi and xiii. As a matter of fact, *Dicey's* emphasis that stresses legal protection in the concept of rule of law is somewhat similar.

which is characteristic of *Dworkin's* work has also received some support in continental European research.[33]

Furthermore, in the United Kingdom one should stress the protection of human rights in the context of interpreting the concept of rule of law. *Hood Phillips* already in the 1970s proposed that when Great Britain ratified the European Convention on Human Rights in 1951 as part of the concept of rule of law, the requirement of the realization of human rights was put forth at the same time. What is essential in *Hood Phillips'* interpretation is that he did not consider observing the concept of rule of law as a question limited to the interpretation of national law.[34]

It is relevant to compare the English Rule of Law to the one in Germany. It seems that the trinity between human rights, rule of law and liberal democracy enshrined by the Article 2 TEU resembles the modern German interpretation of the rule of law, namely *Rechtsstaat*.[35] After the Second World War, the German *Rechtsstaat* concept was developed toward emphasizing equality and democracy. One manifestation of this is *Habermas'* argument that the rule of law is possible only as a democratic rule of law.[36] After the war, the *Rechtsstaat* has become a concept that emphasizes social fundamental rights rather than a liberal concept that emphasizes individual freedoms. In addition, it has developed more into a substantive than a formal principle.[37] The legitimacy of modern law can be founded on the process according to which legislative amendments are implemented. In summary, in accordance with modern German legal thought, legislative procedure is regulated in the constitution, power belongs to the people and fundamental and human rights are adhered to in the rule of law. An active civil society, which is able to control the exercise of power by the state, functions in a modern state in which the rule of law prevails.

---

[33] Raitio, (2003) *supra* note 1 at 143-144; Hallberg, *The Rule of Law* (Edita 2004) at 15 and 70-90.

[34] Hood Phillips, *Constitutional and Administrative Law* (Fifth Edition, Sweet & Maxwell 1973) at 37, in which he states: "Nevertheless, there has a been a strong movement since the War – both within the Commonwealth and outside – to define fundamental or human rights, and such definitions or declarations have come to form an important part of a new international concept of 'the rule of law'."

[35] See e.g. Raitio, (2017) *supra* note 23 at 774-791.

[36] Tuori, (2011) *supra* note 2 at 63.

[37] Fernandez Esteban, *The rule of law in the European Constitution* (Kluwer Law International 1999) at 86.

3.   RULE OF LAW IN THE CASE LAW OF THE EUROPEAN COURT OF JUSTICE

Already before the principle of rule of law was separately mentioned in the EU Treaty, the European Court of Justice stated in 1986 in its *Les Verts* judgment that the, then European Economic Community, is a community of law because both its Member States and its institutions are under supervision aimed at compatibility between measures implemented by them and the document corresponding to the Constitution, i.e. the EU Treaty.[38] The *Les Verts* case essentially involved the implementation of the requirement for an effective judicial remedy in connection with an action for annulment. It was held in the judgment that the decision by the European Parliament may be appealed despite the fact that the European Parliament was not mentioned in the, then Article 173 EC (now Article 263 TFEU), concerning annulment. Rule of law thought is illustrated by the fact that all acts of the then EC institutions that produced legal effects had to be subject to judicial oversight.[39]

In contemporary EU law, however, the interpretation of rule of law is typically based on Article 2 TEU. As stated before and confirmed in Article 2 TEU, the EU legal concept of rule of law includes human rights as part of the same entity, which is aptly described by the following quote from the *Kadi* case:

> It is also clear from the case-law that respect for human rights is a condition of the lawfulness of Community acts (Opinion 2/94, paragraph 34) and that measures incompatible with respect for human rights are not acceptable in the Community.[40]

Therefore, there are indications in the case law of the Court of Justice of the European Union that the concept of rule of law includes certain material pre-requisites for legal decision-making.[41]

---

[38] ECJ, Case 294/83, *Parti écologiste "Les Verts" v European Parliament*, EU:C:1986:166, para. 23.

[39] See e.g. Joutsamo, Aalto, Kaila and Maunu, *Eurooppaoikeus* (Lakimiesliiton kustannus 2000) at 89; Hallberg, *Rule of Law, Prospects in Central Asia Rural Areas and Human Problems* (Edita 2016) at 92-93.

[40] ECJ, Cases C-402/05 and C-415/05 P, *Kadi and Al Barakaat International Foundation*, EU:C:2008:461, para. 284. Also correspondingly: ECJ, Case C-112/00, *Schmidberger*, EU:C:2003:333, para. 73.

[41] ECJ, Case 8/55, *Fédéchar*, EU:C:1956:7 and cases related to the concept of rule of law concerning EU law's external liability: ECJ, Case 5/71, *Schöppenstedt*, EU:C:1971:116; ECJ, Case 59/72, *Wünsche Handelsgesellschaft*, EU:C:1973:86;

As regards to the prerequisites of legal decision-making one should also point out the significance of the adequate reasoning so that the addressee of the decision is able to determine whether the decision contains a defect, allowing its legality to be challenged.[42] This demand of adequate reasoning can be linked to principles of sound administration, legal certainty as well as the rule of law. However, one may pose the question, whether the reasoning of the Court of Justice is always satisfactory from the perspective of various stakeholders or other courts. For example, in the *Ajos* case,[43] the Danish Supreme court did not accept the Court's reasoning in regards to discrimination on grounds of age in the context of the case. In that case, however, the Court has later stressed the importance to not infringe the obligations based on the preliminary rulings system outlined in Article 267 TFEU.[44]

However, it is important to note that many of the cases interpreting the rule of law concentrate on the independence of the judiciary and thus the system of the judicial review in a national context. Judicial review and its relation to the rule of law has not that clearly been stressed in the older case law, whereas in more recent case law the connection between judicial review and the rule of law has been expressed clearly in the wording of the reasoning.[45] For example, in *Rosneft* the Court stated as follows:

> It may be added that Article 47 of the Charter, which constitutes a reaffirmation of the principle of effective judicial protection, requires, in its first paragraph, that any person whose rights and freedoms guaranteed by EU law are violated should have the right to an effective remedy before a tribunal in compliance with the conditions laid down in that article. It must be recalled that the very existence of effective

---

ECJ, Case 20/88, *Roquette frères*, EU:C:1989:221; ECJ, Case C-152/88, *Sofrimport*, EU:C:1990:259 and ECJ, Case C-282/90, *Vreugdenhill*, EU:C:1992:124.

[42]   See e.g. ECJ, Case 69/83, *Charles Lux v Court of Auditors*, EU:C:1984:225, paras. 32-36.

[43]   ECJ, Case C-441/14, *Ajos*, EU:C:2016:278; Neergaard and Engsig, 'Activist Infighting among Courts and Breakdown of Mutual Trust? The Danish Supreme Court, the CJEU, and the Ajos Case' (2017) 36 Yearbook of European Law, 1-39; Nielsen and Tvarnø, 'Danish Supreme Court Infringes the EU Treaties by Its Ruling in the Ajos Case' (2017) 2 Europarättslig Tidskrift, 303-326 at 303: "In its judgment in the Ajos-case, the Court of Justice of the European Union (CJEU) upheld its findings in Mangold and Kücükdeveci. The Danish Supreme Court defied the CJEU and did the opposite of what the CJEU had held it was obliged to do."

[44]   See e.g. ECJ, Case C-385/17, *Hein,* EU:C:2018:1018, paras. 49-51.

[45]   ECJ, Case C-562/13, *Abdida*, EU:C:2014:2453, para. 45; ECJ, Case C-362/14, *Schrems*, EU:C:2015:650, para. 95 and ECJ, Case C-72/15 *Rosneft*, EU:C:2017:236, para. 73.

judicial review designed to ensure compliance with provisions of EU law is of the essence of the rule of law.[46]

The question concerning the independence and impartiality of the national courts typically comes to the fore in the framework of the preliminary rulings concerning the situation in Poland.[47] Yet, there are relevant cases from other countries as well, so one should not exaggerate the significance of the Polish cases.[48] For example, the protection of national identities in Article 4(2) TEU does not give right to national judiciaries to infringe the basic elements of the rule of law such as the independence of the judiciary. Additionally, it should be noted that the rule of law can be used as a legal argument in a court's proceedings, which has been stated by the European Court of Justice in the context of the Conditionality Regulation 2020/2092 as follows:

> Next, while it is true that Article 2(a) of the contested regulation does not set out in detail the principles of the rule of law that it mentions, nevertheless recital 3 of that regulation notes that the principles of legality, legal certainty, prohibition of arbitrariness of the executive powers, effective judicial protection and separation of powers, referred to in that provision, have been the subject of extensive case-law of the Court.

So, when the rule of law is interpreted so that the more specific case law of its sub-principles is taken into account one can reach plausible legal conclusions. However, even the principle of legal certainty can be analysed by its sub-principles, namely the principle of legitimate expectations (*Vertrauensschutz*),[49] principle of non-retroactivity[50] and other principles, which have a relative accurate scope of application compared to the rule of law.[51]

---

[46]   ECJ, Case C-72/15, *Rosneft*, EU:C:2017:236, para. 73.

[47]   See e.g. ECJ, Case C-216/18 PPU, *LM*, EU:C:2018:586; ECJ, Case C-619/18, *Commission v Poland*, EU:C:2018:910; ECJ, Case C-619/18 R, *Commission v Poland*, EU:C:2018:1021; ECJ, Case C-619/18 *Commission v Poland*, EU:C:2019:531; ECJ, Case C-558/18 and 563/18, *Miasto Lowicz*, EU:C:2020:234; ECJ, Case C-824/18, *A.B.*, EU:C:2021:153; ECJ, Case C-157/21, *Poland v Parliament and Council*, EU:C:2022.98 and ECJ, Case C-204/21, *Commission v Poland*, EU:C:2023:442.

[48]   See e.g. ECJ, Case C-896/19, *Repubblika*, EU:C:2021:311 and ECJ, Case C-156/21, *Hungary v Parliament and Council*, EU:C:2022:97.

[49]   See e.g. ECJ, Case 289/81, *Mavridis*, EU:C:1983:142, para. 21; CFI, Case T-571/93, *Lefebvre*, EU:T:1995:163 and ECJ, Case C-17/03, *VEMW*, EU:C:2005:362.

[50]   See e.g. ECJ, Case 98/78, *Racke*, EU:C:1979:14, paras. 15, 20.

[51]   See e.g. Raitio, (2003) *supra* note 1 at 187-263.

In the recent case C-204/21[52] the Court was called to assess a series of amendments to the laws, i.e. so called muzzle laws, on the judiciary adopted by Poland in 2019. These laws adopted new disciplinary offences and sanctions for judges and rules to prevent them from questioning the legitimacy and independence of any national court. These national measures infringed the Article 19(1) TEU, Article 47 of the EU Fundamental Rights Charter as well as Article 267 TFEU and thus the independence of the judiciary. While the case was pending in the Court, the Union blocked Polish funds under the Recovery and Resilience facility and made their release conditional on compliance with a series of milestones concerning judicial independence. This measure was effective, since Poland dismissed the controversial Disciplinary Chamber and substituted it with another Chamber of "Professional Liability", although it remains to be seen, whether this new Chamber really turns out to be a solution to the problems in Poland.

4.   RULE OF LAW AND THE FUTURE OF EUROPEAN VALUES – MUTUAL TRUST OR NOT?

EU citizens and national authorities should be able to trust in the realization of the rule of law in other Member States, so that the EU can act as a "region of freedom, law and security that does not have internal borders"[53] and that the internal market functions efficiently. This mutual trust among the Member States has also received an especially prominent role in Opinion 2/13 by the Court of Justice of the EU.[54] Similarly to the Court of Justice with regard to the trust among the Member States, one should emphasize that all of the Member States comply with Union law, especially with the fundamental rights recognized in EU law.[55] The concept of rule of law thus receives interpretive content in EU law only in connection to how democracy and fundamental rights are

---

[52]   ECJ, Case C-204/21, *Commission v Poland*, EU:C:2023:442.

[53]   European Commission, 'Why the principle of rule of law is decisively important for the EU', COM (2019) 158 final, para. 2.

[54]   ECJ, Opinion 2/13, *Accession of the European Union to the ECHR*, EU:C:2014:2454, paras. 168, 191, 192 and 258. The Court of Justice of the EU held that the planned agreement for the EU to join the European Convention on Human Rights is not in conformity with Article 6(2) TFEU or Protocol No. 8 to the EU Treaties, because, for example, it does not prevent the danger that the principle of mutual trust that exists among Member States in EU law can be infringed.

[55]   Ibid., para. 191.

realized and how the Member States can trust each other's legal systems.[56] Mutual trust can be seen to be a prerequisite for good governance.[57]

After the Opinion 2/13 the principle of mutual trust has caused academic debate about what it means and how it can be achieved.[58] According to Opinion 2/13, mutual trust can be associated with the specificities of European Union law. Namely, EU law is based on an independent source of law formed by framework agreements, which has primacy in relation to the Member States' law.[59] The key characteristics of EU law have formed a basis for the creation of a network of such principles, rules and legal relations which have a mutual dependency, which reciprocally binds the union itself and its Member States. The European Union is built on the understanding that each Member State shares several mutual values with all the other Member States, as described in Article 2 TEU. This starting point of mutually acknowledged values justifies that mutual trust can prevail between Member States. A legal structure as such also includes fundamental rights as they have been recognized in the EU Charter of Fundamental Rights, and which are interpreted in accordance with the Union's structure and objectives.[60]

President of the Court, Judge *Lenaerts* has had reason to emphasize that mutual trust does not mean "blind trust", but instead trust that must be earned and be based on the Member State complying with the level of human rights protection required by the EU.[61] Also in legal literature there has been the need

---

[56] Ibid., para. 191.

[57] Cramér, 'Reflections on the Roles of Mutual Trust in EU law', in Dougan and Currie (ed), *50 Years of the European Treaties, Looking Back and Thinking Forward* (Hart Publishing 2009) 43-61.

[58] See e.g. Bieber, "Gegenseitiges Vertrauen" zwischen den Mitgliedstaaten – ein normatives Prinzip der Europäischen Union?', in Epiney and Affolter (ed), *Die Schweiz und die Europäische Integration: 20 Jahre Institut für Europarecht* (Schulthess 2015), 37-55; Farturova, 'La Coopération Loyale vue sous le Prisme de la Reconnaissance Mutuelle: Quelques Réflexions sur les Fondements de la Construction Européenne' (2016) Cahiers de Droit Européen, 193-219: The connection between the principle of mutual trust and the principle of sincere cooperation or loyalty is one further argument to justify it.

[59] ECJ, Case 6/64, *Costa v ENEL,* EU:C:1964:66.

[60] Opinion 2/13, *supra* note 54, 166-171.

[61] Lenaerts, 'La vie après l'avis: Exploring the principle of mutual (yet not blind) trust' (2017) 54 Common Market Law Review, 805-840 at 838: *Lenaerts* emphasizes that, in terms of the efficiency of the principle of mutual trust and the protection of human rights, it is significant that the European Court of Human Rights, the Court of Justice of the European Union and national courts of justice engage in constructive dialogue. On the other hand, both the EU and member states must prepare trust-enhancing legislation, which maintains this mutual trust.

to emphasize the normative function of mutual trust.[62] So one may sum up, that the future of the European values lies in the mutual trust between Member States and that the concept of the rule of law indeed contains both formal and material elements.

---

[62] Bieber, (2015) *supra* note 58 at 38.

2. Measuring the Rule of Law: an Empirical Approach

Jacek Lewkowicz, Rafał Woźniak and Przemysław Litwiniuk

1. INTRODUCTION

The rule of law is a fundamental principle, which in a broad perspective refers to a state of affairs, in which everyone is subject to the law and is treated equally. It promotes virtues that are of high relevance for social, political and economic progress. In fact, the concept of the rule of law is composed of various kinds of institutional factors. Taking this into consideration, measuring the rule of law is associated with the challenges common for measuring institutions. However, even if the available indices have some drawbacks, they are still extremely valuable, given the opportunities they offer for empirical studies.

In this chapter, we bring the reader closer to the need and art of measuring institutions, with a particular focus on the rule of law. Appreciating the importance of practical examples, we focus on the design and scope of the following three indices of the rule of law: the Varieties of Democracy rule of law index, the Worldwide Governance Indicators rule of law index, and the World Justice Project rule of law index, which are the leading indicators given their vast application, as reflected in the available literature. The detailed description of the methodology, composition, as well as time and geographical scope of the indicators may be helpful in terms of using them consciously in social studies. Being aware of the advantages and disadvantages of the measures of the rule of law allows for a better research design, especially in case of interdisciplinary studies. Moreover, we provide some remarks on the observable changes in the rule of law worldwide in the recent decades to illustrate the current institutional context.

The chapter is organized as follows. The next section elaborates on the need of measuring the rule of law and draws the attention to some essential challenges in this respect. Then, we describe the selected indices of the rule of law and point out major differences between them, alongside with the implications for quantitative studies. The subsequent part of the chapter briefly presents the recent trends of the rule of law in a global perspective, whereas the last section concludes.

2. WHY MEASURE THE RULE OF LAW?

When elaborating on the issue of measuring the rule of law, a fundamental question arises – why it is worth to measure it at all? The answer, just like the question, is very straightforward. This approach enables for quantitative research on the rule of law, which is a powerful tool itself. It is claimed that some of the characteristics typically attributed to quantitative approach in social sciences cover *inter alia* the possibility to test hypotheses, objectivity, and staying value-free.[1] Importantly, given our focus, the development of indices like the measures of the rule of law contributes to bridging the quantitative-qualitative divide in social sciences.[2] It seems to be a very meaningful point of discussion, taking into consideration that both qualitative and quantitative methods in fields like law, economics or sociology, are applied in a rigorous way, providing opportunities for ground-breaking research. Moreover, it is also claimed that when doing research on the rule of law without a deep knowledge of quantitative and qualitative methods, the results can be simply erroneous.[3] Legal indicators, including the rule of law, not only serve as sources of knowledge, but they can be used as means of governing societies, *inter alia* because of the interest of policy makers in them.[4] This also opens the discussion about their validity and reliability.

Obviously, there are certain quality criteria for quantitative methods research that have to be met in order to get valid and interpretable results.[5] Awareness

---

[1]   Chui, 'Quantitative Legal Research' in McConville (ed), *Research Methods for Law* (Edinburgh University Press 2017) 48-71.

[2]   Shah and Corley, 'Building Better Theory by Bridging the Quantitative-Qualitative Divide' (2006) 43 Journal of Management Studies 8, 1821-1835; Wawro and Katznelson, 'Designing Historical Social Scientific Inquiry: How Parameter Heterogeneity Can Bridge the Methodological Divide between Quantitative and Qualitative Approaches' (2014) 58 American Journal of Political Science 2, 526-546.

[3]   Simion, 'Qualitative and Quantitative Approaches to Rule of Law Research' (2016) SSRN WPS, <http://dx.doi.org/10.2139/ssrn.2817565> accessed 1 December 2023.

[4]   Davis, 'Legal Indicators: The Power of Quantitative Measures of Law' (2014) Annual Review of Law and Social Science, 37-52 <https://doi.org/10.1146/annurev-lawsocsci-110413-030857> accessed 1 December 2023.

[5]   Bryman, Becker and Sempik, 'Quality criteria for Quantitative, Qualitative and Mixed Methods Research: A View from Social Policy' (2008) 11 International

of the nature of the data and the assumptions of considered quantitative apparatus (e.g. econometrics or machine learning) is key in the context of choosing the right approach given the research goal and research material. A clueless use of this kind of tools can be detrimental, because of misinterpretation of the output. A meaningful academic debate about measuring institutions provides us some essential guidelines, that obviously apply to the indices of the rule of law. Namely, measures of institutions should consider *de jure* and *de facto* dimensions, and be precise and objective.[6] What should be stressed here is that not only formal institutions matter, but also informal ones, as they influence the factual enforcement of regulations too.[7]

The rule of law is not a single institution, but a concept made up of multiple ones.[8] This is the key reason, why sometimes the measures of the rule of law are assessed as too broad or fuzzy.[9] What has to be noted, is that there is still an ongoing discussion on what the rule of law really means and there were developed valuable proposals on which dimensions should be included to improve the quality of the measures of the rule of law.[10] The next section discusses the details of some of the most popular and widely used indices of the rule of law.

3.   INDICES OF THE RULE OF LAW

3.1   The Varieties of Democracy Rule of Law Index

The V-Dem Institute, an independent research institute, is based at the Department of Political Science of the University of Gothenburg in Sweden. Varieties of Democracy (V-Dem) is a project of the V-Dem Institute dedicated for providing measures of democracy across countries. Besides the research programs and collaborations, the institute regularly publishes datasets containing the measures of democracy and other institutional or social factors

---

Journal of Social Research Methodology 4, 261-276; Jerrim and de Vries, 'The limitations of quantitative social science for informing public policy' (2017) 13 Evidence & Policy 1, 117-133; Deakin, 'The Use of Quantitative Methods in Labour Law Research: An Assessment and Reformulation' (2018) 27 Social & Legal Studies 4, 456-474.

  [6] Voigt, 'How (Not) to measure institutions' (2013) 9 Journal of Institutional Economics 1, 1-26.

  [7] Ibid.

  [8] Voigt, 'How to Measure the Rule of Law' (2012) 65 Kyklos 2, 262-284.

  [9] Voigt, (2013) *supra* note 6.

  [10] Voigt, (2012) *supra* note 8.

(V-Dem dataset[11]) and political parties characteristics (V-Party dataset[12]).[13] Although the V-Dem Institute is connected with the University of Gothenburg, the V-Dem Project includes over 3,700 academics, practitioners and country experts worldwide, many of whom affiliated at well recognizable universities. The beginning of the project dates in 2008, and 13 major versions of the V-Dem dataset have been published so far.[14]

The V-Dem dataset contains numerous democracy indicators. There are 4 types of indices, that is low-, mid- and high-level indices as well as the data gathered from external data sources (non-V-Dem products). The low-level indicators originate from the assessments by project managers, research assistants, country coordinators and country experts. The type of these indicators depends on whether being coded by one of the coding groups. Some of the offered indices are high-level or mid-level, that means being derived from low-level indicators.

The rule of law index from the V-Dem dataset was calculated basing on multiple variables. For the simplicity of presentation, we grouped them in three categories:

1. Compliance and independence: compliance with high court (V-Dem: v2juhccomp), compliance with judiciary (V-Dem: v2jucomp), high court independence (V-Dem: v2juhcind), lower court independence (V-Dem: v2juncind);
2. Government and administration: executive respects constitution (V-Dem: v2exrescon), rigorous and impartial public administration (V-Dem: v2clrspct), transparent laws with predictable enforcement (V-Dem: v2cltrnslw), access to justice for men (V-Dem: v2clacjstm), access to justice for women (V-Dem: v2clacjstw), judicial accountability (V-Dem: v2juaccnt);
3. Corruption: public sector corrupt exchanges (V-Dem: v2excrptps), public sector theft (V-Dem: v2exthftps), executive bribery and corrupt exchanges (V-Dem: v2exbribe), executive embezzlement and theft (V-Dem: v2exembez), judicial corruption decision (V-Dem: v2jucorrdc), judicial accountability (V-Dem: v2juaccnt).

---

[11] Coppedge et al., 'V-Dem Country-Year Dataset v13' (2023a) Varieties of Democracy (V-Dem) Project, <https://doi.org/10.23696/vdemds23> accessed 1 December 2023.

[12] Lindberg et al., 'Codebook Varieties of Party Identity and Organization (V–Party) V2' (2022) Varieties of Democracy (V–Dem) Project, <https://doi.org/10.23696 /vpartydsv2> accessed 1 December 2023.

[13] Available at <https://v-dem.net/data/>.

[14] Coppedge et al., 'V-Dem Organization and Management v13' (2023c) Varieties of Democracy (V-Dem).

These variables are type C indicators, which means they were coded by country experts.[15] The low-level indices are calculated using item response theory models, estimated using Bayesian approach. Within this ingenious approach, the notion of interest is derived from five country experts survey responses. It is assumed that each answer might be subjected to idiosyncratic, non-systematic error, therefore the answer is a sum of a latent value, common to all respondents and the noise.[16] Mid-level and high-level indices were derived using Bayesian factor analyses.[17] Within the approach, similarly as for the low-level indices, it is assumed that the notion of interest is a common factor for all the subcomponents. A consequence of the method is that the V-Dem index appears to be robust to outliers and especially advantageous in case of problems with subcomponents. *Coppedge et al.*[18] indicate the convergence problem with one of the subcomponents, namely transparent laws with predictable enforcement. It appears that it does not have any significant impact on the rule of law index quality, because of the two reasons. The first, although problematic, is that transparent law with predictable enforcement is only one out of 14 subcomponents in total. Secondly, robustness of the method with regard to outliers in (or even miscalculation of) some subcomponents constitutes an additional argument.

The V-Dem rule of law index quantifies "to what extent are laws transparently, independently, predictably, impartially, and equally enforced, and to what extent do the actions of government officials comply with the law".[19] The scale of the index runs from 0 (low) to 1 (high). The rule of law index, alike other indicators, is currently available for years 1789–2022 and covers almost all contemporary countries of the world. Additionally, the V-Dem dataset offers characteristics of no longer existing countries, for instance South Vietnam, German Democratic Republic, Kingdom of Piedmont-Sardinia or Landgraviate of Hesse-Kassel. A significant advantage of the V-Dem dataset lies in the fact that it offers not only point estimates of the index, but also confidence intervals, as well as standard deviations. Columns "Code low" and "Code high" denote lower and upper bounds of the highest posterior density

---

[15]   Coppedge et al., 'V-Dem Codebook v13' (2023b) Varieties of Democracy (V-Dem) Project at 30.

[16]   Pemstein et al., 'The V-Dem Measurement Model: Latent Variable Analysis for Cross-National and Cross-Temporal Expert-Coded Data' (2023) V-Dem Working Paper 21 at 3, <http://dx.doi.org/10.2139/ssrn.3595962> accessed 1 December 2023.

[17]   Coppedge et al., 'V-Dem Methodology v13' (2023d) Varieties of Democracy (V-Dem) Project at 7.

[18]   Coppedge et al., (2023) *supra* note 15 at 28.

[19]   Coppedge et al., (2023) *supra* note 15.

confidence interval. This interval is the one standard deviation confidence interval.

The values of the index can be compared across countries as well as over time. Importantly, global trends or tendencies seem to be meaningful. Between 2019 and 2020, a decrease of 0.2 observed for Brazil is statistically insignificant since the confidence intervals are overlapping. Reversely, an increase for Moldova is significant, since the value for 2020 lies outside the confidence interval of the 2019 estimate. In 2019 the adherence to the rule of law in Zimbabwe was comparable to Haiti since the confidence intervals are overlapping, whereas significantly lower than in Finland (separable confidence intervals). Table 2.1 presents an excerpt of the V-Dem dataset.

Table 2.1   *Excerpt of the V-Dem dataset*

Country	2019				2020			
	Estimate	Code low	Code high	Sd	Estimate	Code low	Code high	Sd
Brazil	0,64	0,54	0,73	0,60	0,62	0,52	0,72	0,60
Denmark	1,00	1,00	1,00	0,61	1,00	1,00	1,00	0,61
Finland	0,99	0,98	1,00	0,61	0,99	0,98	0,99	0,61
Haiti	0,13	0,08	0,19	0,60	0,13	0,08	0,19	0,61
Moldova	0,53	0,42	0,63	0,60	0,77	0,68	0,85	0,61
Venezuela	0,01	0,00	0,02	0,61	0,01	0,01	0,03	0,61
Zimbabwe	0,24	0,17	0,33	0,60	0,23	0,15	0,30	0,60

3.2   The Worldwide Governance Indicators Rule of Law Index

The Worldwide Governance Indicators[20] (WGI) is a project by the World Bank. It primarily aims at providing indicators of governance which is defined as "the traditions and institutions by which authority in a country is exercised".[21] The WGI indicators represent six dimensions of governance, that is: voice and accountability, political stability and absence of violence/terrorism, government effectiveness, regulatory quality, rule of law, and control of corruption. The indicators have been calculated by the World Bank since 1996.

---

[20]   Available at <https://info.worldbank.org/governance/wgi/>.
[21]   Kaufmann, Kraay and Mastruzzi, 'The Worldwide Governance Indicators: Met-hodology and Analytical Issues' (2011) 3 Hague Journal on the Rule of Law 2, 220-246 at 220.

Their high popularity led to annual publications of the updated versions of the dataset since 2002.

The WGI rule of law index is calculated using multiple data sources. The online appendix presents the representative sources. The 2022 WGI update, available at the time of writing, included multiple sources: Economist Intelligence Unit – Riskwire and Democracy Index, World Economic Forum – Global Competitiveness Report, Gallup World Forum, Heritage Foundation – Index of Economic Freedom, Institutional Profiles Database, Political Risk Services – International Country Risk Guide, US State Department – Trafficking of People Report, Varieties of Democracy Project – Liberal Component Index, Global Insight – Business Conditions and Risk Indicators. It should be noted that the list of sources is subjected to changes at data annual updates. The complete and actual list of data sources is available at the project's webpage.[22]

As indicated by *Kaufmann et al.*,[23] the WGI rule of law index is a perception index. It is based on the perceptions of households, firms, business information providers, non-governmental organizations, and some multilateral organizations. The rule of law index captures "perceptions of the extent to which agents have confidence in and abide by the rules of society, and in particular the quality of contract enforcement, property rights, the police, and the courts, as well as the likelihood of crime and violence".[24] The indisputable strength of having multiple kinds of data sources and surveyed agents comes with a price. *Kaufmann et al.*[25] define the disadvantage in terms of biases of the surveys' respondents. A household may perceive the current situation in the country differently than firms, and what is more, multilateral agencies or NGOs may focus on even other aspects of rule of law. A further consequence of the perception index lies in its subjectivity. *Kaufmann et al.*[26] raised the concern of to what extent these perceptions reflect the reality. On one hand, the perceptions offer to capture *de facto* rule of law, on the other hand however, these perceptions are subjective measures.

The WGI indices are cleverly calculated using the unobserved component model. The ingenuity of the approach arises from treating the rule of law as the common component present in all available data sources for a given country. Additionally, the method allows for different scales of the source subcomponents. The number of subcomponents is subjected to changes across

---

[23]   Kaufmann, Kraay and Mastruzzi, (2011) *supra* note 21 at 224.
[24]   Ibid. at 223.
[25]   Ibid. at 240.
[26]   Ibid.

publications, however, the index over-time comparisons should be unaffected. What is worth to emphasize, due to sources' publication frames and current data unavailability, some subcomponents are included as being lagged by one or two years. The methodology of the rule of law index calculation was presented in *Kaufmann et al.* (1999).[27] The method using the common latent factor approach seems to remain robust to idiosyncratic outliers in the subcomponents. As a result of this method, the rule of law index is a random variable with a standard normal distribution. Consequently, the range of values is approximately [−2.5; 2.5]. The higher the value, the higher the adherence to the rule of law.

The WGI rule of law index is available for over 200 countries, and at the time of writing, for the period 1996–2021. Table 2.2 presents an excerpt of the WGI rule of law dataset. Not only the point estimate of the index is published (column "Estimate"), but also the standard error of the estimate ("StdErr") and the number of data sources on which the estimate is based on ("NumSrc"). Column "Rank" contains values in the interval [0; 100] and indicates the relative position of a given country as compared to the rest, with 0 and 100 assigned to the countries with the lowest and the highest rule of law index value respectively. Columns "Lower" and "Upper" contain respectively lower and upper bounds of the 90% confidence interval of the rank.

Table 2.2   Excerpt of the WGI rule of law dataset

Country/ Territory	1996						2021					
	Estimate	StdErr	NumSrc	Rank	Lower	Upper	Estimate	StdErr	NumSrc	Rank	Lower	Upper
Hungary	0,91	0,18	9,00	79,40	68,34	86,43	0,53	0,14	12,00	69,71	59,62	75,96
Kazakhstan	-1,19	0,20	5,00	14,07	5,03	22,11	-0,49	0,14	11,00	34,13	24,52	44,23
United Kingdom	1,63	0,19	8,00	94,47	88,94	100,00	1,43	0,16	9,00	89,42	85,10	92,79

Kaufmann et al. present two possible approaches to interpret the index.[28] The first focuses on the point estimates, while the other uses ranks. The higher the estimate, the higher the extent to which the agents perceive the rule of law to be followed. For example, the point estimate for Kazakhstan for 1996 is −1.19, while for 2021 it is −0.49, indicating an improvement. *Kaufmann*

---

[27]   Kaufmann, Kraay and Zaido-Lobatón, 'Aggregating Governance Indicators' (1999) World Bank Policy Research Working Paper No. 2195, <http://documents .worldbank.org/curated/en/167911468766840406/Aggregating-governance-indic ators> accessed 1 December 2023.
[28]   Kaufmann, Kraay and Mastruzzi, (2011) *supra* note 21 at 232-236.

et al. suggest using confidence intervals alongside the point estimates.[29] The confidence interval is calculated as the estimate ± 1.64 times its standard error and represent the set of values statistically indistinguishable from the estimate. For Kazakhstan the confidence interval for 1996 is [−1.52; −0.86], while for 2021 is [−0.73; 0.25]. Separate (not overlapping) intervals indicate statistical differences of the estimates. In the same manner, a cross-country analysis can be performed. For the United Kingdom for 2021 the estimate is 1.43 with the confidence interval [1.16; 1.69]. Since the intervals for Kazakhstan and the United Kingdom are disjoint, we conclude on statistical difference between the point estimates.

A similar analysis of the rule of law perception in Hungary yields for 1996 the value of 0.91 and the value of 0.53 for 2021. It seems the that the confidence in the quality of contract enforcement, property rights, the police, the courts, and personal safety deteriorated over the period. Examination of the confidence intervals yields slightly overlapping intervals, that is for 1996 is [0.62; 1.20] and for 2012 is [0.30; 0.76]. *Kaufmann et al.* specify only a substantial overlap of the intervals as an indicator of statistical insignificance of the difference, without further clarification of the substantial overlap.[30] This is the reason, why we offer a method to identify substantial overlaps. The method consists of two steps. The first step requires calculation of a test statistic of the form:

$$T = \frac{Estimate_1 - Estimate_2}{\sqrt{\frac{StdErr_1^2}{N_1} + \frac{StdErr_2^2}{N_2}}}.$$

In the second step, the probability is as

$$Probability = 2*[1 - \Phi(|T|)],$$

in which $\Phi(|T|)$ denotes the cumulative distribution function of the standard normal distribution[31] of the absolute value of the test statistics T. If the calculated probability exceeds 10%, then substantial overlap of the confidence intervals should be concluded. Substantial overlap indi-

---

[29]   Ibid. at 231.

[30]   Kaufmann, Kraay and Mastruzzi, (2011) *supra* note 21.

[31]   The values of the cumulative distribution function of the standard normal distribution can be found using MS Excel function NORM.DIST(ABS(T);0;1;TRUE), R program function pnorm(abs(T)) or by using web calculator of the Stanford University at <https://web.stanford.edu/class/archive/cs/cs109/cs109.1192/demos/cdf.html> where x is the absolute value of the test statistic, *mu* = 0, *sd* = 1.

cates that the two point estimates are statistically equivalent. If substituting $Estimate_1 = 0.91$, $Estimate_2 = 0.53$, $StdErr_1 = 0.18$, $StdErr_2 = 0.14$, the test statistics is $T = 5.27$, while the probability is close to zero. Therefore, the confidence intervals for Hungary for years 1996 and 2021 overlap insubstantially indicating a significant deterioration of the rule of law perception.

Conveniently, for cross-country comparisons a percentile rank statistic is presented. The rank ranges from 0 (lowest) to 100 (highest). It is interpreted as a percentage of countries with lower perception of the rule of law. Both cross-country comparisons and time changes to the global average are possible with ranks. The convenience lies in the fact that the percentile 90% confidence intervals for ranks are already calculated. For instance, the rank for 2021 for Hungary is 67.71 with the confidence interval $[59.62; 75.96]$, while for the same year for the United Kingdom rank equals 89.42 with interval $[85.10; 92.79]$. The non-overlapping intervals indicate statistically higher perception of the rule of law in the United Kingdom in comparison with Hungary.

3.3   The World Justice Project Rule of Law Index

The World Justice Project (WJP) is an independent organization aiming mainly at providing reliable information about rule of law.[32] Its rule of law index has become one of the most important indices of its kind. The WJP has been publishing the data on the index since 2008. The Joint Research Centre of the European Commission audited the 2012, 2014, and 2021 editions so far.[33] The audits confirmed reliability of the WJP index.

The index is based on eight dimensions (composite factors), that each disaggregates to 44 components (sub-factors).[34] The eight composite factors are: constraints on government powers, absence of corruption, open government, fundamental rights, order and security, regulatory enforcement, civil justice, and criminal justice. The factors and sub-factors are derived from more than 500 variables codified upon two surveys that are held in 140 countries. The first survey is the General Population Poll that captures the perceptions of citizens. It had more than 154,000 households surveyed in total. Before 2012, the General Population Poll was aimed at citizens of three major metropolises in each country. Since 2012, this poll is intended to be nationally representa-

---

[32]   The data is available at <https://worldjusticeproject.org/rule-of-law-index/>.

[33]   Kovacic and Caperna, *Joint Research Centre Statistical Analysis of the World Justice Project Rule of Law Index 2021 (ROLI)* (Publications Office of the European Union 2022) <https://doi.org/10.2760/80392>.

[34]   World Justice Project, 'The World Justice Project Rule of Law Index 2022' (2022) at 15, <https://worldjusticeproject.org/rule-of-law-index/downloads/WJPIndex2022.pdf> accessed 1 December 2023.

tive.[35] The other survey is the Qualified Respondent's Questionnaire which is aimed at experts and academics from the fields of law or health, and those who interact with the government. The questions in this survey regard efficiency of judiciary, law regulations, enforcement, and reliability of accountability mechanisms.[36] For some countries, the number of the experts happens to be unsatisfactory, and this fact is reflected by high standard errors, which are unpublished. Once the data is gathered and verified, the raw survey responses are transformed using z-scores or the min-max transformation. The sub-factors, and subsequently the factors are aggregated using simple averages.[37] The WJP index components list is subjected to slight variation over time. Despite this fact, the index can be used for over-time comparisons.

The WJP defines the rule of law with the universal principles of accountability, just law, open government, as well as accessible and impartial justice. The principle of accountability means effective law to limit powers of the government and other agents, as well as enables verification and sanctioning of misconduct. The second principle reflects transparent and effective law, human rights, respect for property and contract rights. The third principle characterizes effectiveness of the government in providing efficient environments for all agents. Finally, the fourth principle covers the extent of appropriateness and completeness of justice. In general, the WJP's index measures the level of adherence to the rule of law, as defined by durable system of laws, institutions, norms, and community commitment that delivers accountable, clear and impartial law, open government, as well as accessible and impartial justice. The index ranges in the interval $[0;1]$, where 0 denotes low adherence and 1 denotes high adherence to the rule of law.

The WJP rule of law, in the 2022 edition, is available for 140 countries. The number of countries has increased since the first publication. In the currently available dataset, the first period contains the information on 97 countries, while for 2022 there are 140 countries included. The index is compiled and published every year with the exceptions for the 2012–2013 and 2017–2018 editions. The highest increases in the number of included countries were observed for 2016, 2019, and 2021 editions. The easily accessible information on sub-factors of the index seems to be advantage of the dataset. An excerpt of the World Justice Project is presented in Table 2.3.

---

[35] Ibid. at 185.

[36] Ibid. at 183.

[37] Botero and Ponce, 'Measuring the Rule of Law' (2011) SSRN WPS at 21, <http://dx.doi.org/10.2139/ssrn.1966257> accessed 1 December 2023.

Table 2.3   *An excerpt of the World Justice Project dataset*

Period	Argentina	Czechia	Kazakhstan	Mozambique	Myanmar	Slovakia
2012–2013	50,5	66,9	46,3	-	-	-
2014	50,3	67,5	46,7	-	40,6	-
2015	52,0	71,7	49,6	-	41,8	-
2016	55,4	74,6	50,3	-	43,5	-
2017–2018	58,2	73,8	51,4	-	42,1	-
2019	58,2	72,7	51,9	42,8	41,9	-
2020	58,0	73,1	52,3	41,3	41,9	-
2021	55,8	72,8	52,5	40,1	39,2	66,3
2022	54,9	73,2	52,8	39,6	36,2	65,7

The index under our consideration can be interpreted in both dimensions, that is across countries and in time. For instance, in every period the adherence to the rule of law in Argentina was higher than in Kazakhstan. A positive trend was observed in Kazakhstan over the entire period of 2012–2022, while in Argentina a positive tendency that started in 2014 collapsed into a negative trend after 2019. There is no clear tendency in the adherence to the rule of law in Czechia. Unfortunately, significance analysis cannot be performed to verify a hypothesis about stability of the index for Czechia. The World Justice Project report[38] and The World Justice Project Insights[39] offer cross-country comparisons, as well as regional and income group rankings. The unbalanced character of the dataset appears as a slight drawback. For instance, it is observed in the excerpt that the index for Mozambique covers the period of 2019–2022, for Myanmar: 2014–2022, and for the Slovakia: 2021–2022.

4.   COMPARISON OF THE RULE OF LAW INDICES

The three discussed indices are published by well-established and recognizable institutions. Despite representing the rule of law, the indices distinct in numerous dimensions. The differences result directly from the assumptions, methods, and strategies of compilation.

---

[38]   World Justice Project, (2022) *supra* note 34.
[39]   World Justice Project, 'The World Justice Project Rule of Law Index 2022 Insights. Highlights and data trends from the WJP Rule of Law Index 2022' (2022) <https://worldjusticeproject.org/rule-of-law-index/downloads/WJPIndex2022.pdf> accessed 1 December 2023.

First, the indices under our consideration are compiled on a basis of diverse sets of subcomponents. However, it is worth to stress that there is a common core of judicial components. These shared features consist of judicial independence, judicial impartiality, and timeliness of judicial decisions. Figure 2.1 presents the subcomponents common to all considered indices as well as the ones shared pairwise. Some idiosyncratic features included in the V-Dem rule of law index cover law transparency. Property rights, expropriation and respect for intellectual property are distinctive to the WGI indicator. Open government, fundamental rights and criminal justice components are specific to the WJP rule of law index.

Secondly, the described indices are based on surveys consisting of numerous questions about democracy and rule of law. Both V-Dem's and WJP's indices surveys only in-country agents, while the WGI index incorporates additional perceptions of multilateral, international institutions, or media providers. The V-Dem's index is calculated upon country experts' responses solely, while households alongside with experts are invited to produce the input for the WJP's index. The highest number of data sources characterize the WGI index, what is simultaneously its biggest strength and weakness. Having multiple data sources means assessing adherence to the rule of law from multiple angles. The disadvantage, in turn, is that various types of agents may focus on different aspects of the rule of law or even be biased. An opposite attitude of the V-Dem assures consistency across respondents, who as experts should identically identify aspects of democracy. Simultaneously, the V-Dem's approach does not offer as multi-angled perspective as the rest of the indices.

Thirdly, a direct consequence of the selection of data sources is the availability of information. The V-Dem rule of law index, based on in-country experts, offers the information for almost all contemporary countries, and covers the longest period. The in-country experts strategy appears to be less costly than the survey-based one. Furthermore, experts may quantify the adherence to the rule of law for more distant times. Surveys of households or firms consisting of the past might be hardly possible and quite likely to result in biased outcome due to assessing the past through the prism of the present circumstances. Consequently, the V-Dem database offers the information for 1789–2022 period, while the WGI and WJP datasets provide the information for the survey years only. What is more, the first edition of the WJP covers the two-year (2012–2013) period. The V-Dem approach of surveying five in-country experts falls short in countries with small population size and insufficient number of experts. For this reason, the WGI dataset covers much more small countries and territories than the V-Dem data set.

Another aspect that differentiates the indices under our consideration is their interpretation. They allow for cross-country comparisons, as well as for the ones over time. An inevitable consequence of using the unobserved

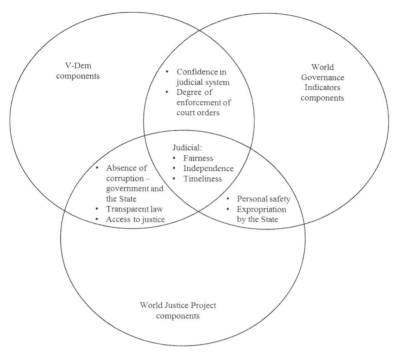

Figure 2.1   Components of the considered rule of law indices

components model in calculation of the WGI indicators is that in each year the global average is zero. Therefore, with no information of global trends, the over-time comparisons are interpreted to the global average for a given year. As observed by *Kaufmann et al.*, "there is little evidence of trends over time in global averages of our individual underlying data sources".[40] It appears to be contradictory to the WJP[41] concluding the global deterioration of the rule of law scores. Further analyses of the contemporary tendencies of rule of law indices are presented in the next section. The WJP and the V-Dem indicators offer the possibility of over-time tendencies and trends analyses. However, the superiority of these two indices over the WGI index cannot be concluded, because of one essential aspect of the WGI data set. The advantage lies in the confidence intervals that offer the possibility to verify whether an observed difference or a change over some periods is statistically significant. Statistical

---

[40]   Kaufmann, Kraay and Mastruzzi, (2011) *supra* note 21 at 232.
[41]   World Justice Project, (2022) *supra* note 39 at 49.

insignificance means that the two estimates are indistinguishable taking their standard errors into consideration.

Additionally, the robustness of the indicators due to changes in the set of subcomponents or even the subcomponents themselves is a complementary feature to those discussed above. The V-Dem and the WGI rule of law indicators appear superior in this context over the WJP indicator. As discussed in the respective subsections above, the WGI and the V-Dem are derived using the unobserved components model or the item response theory model, and therefore are less subject to any changes in individual components or the set of subcomponents. On the contrary, the WJP indicator is calculated as a plain average of the subcomponents, and thus its value is vulnerable to changes in subcomponents selection.

A further criterion in this comparison is the reproducibility and description of the methodology of the index derivation. For each and every indicator under consideration, methodological papers were published. The statistical audit of the WJP indicator was performed by the Joint Research Centre at the European Commission. Not only the methodology of the V-Dem was described in detail, but also the V-Dem Institute published the coder-level data alongside the core dataset. For the WGI rule of law indicator a set of input dataset as well as Stata codes were published. So in the context of external audit the three indices under consideration appear exact.

Finally, the three indices of the rule of law are popular among the scholars. Table 2.4 summarizes the dissimilarities between the indices, where one of the presented characteristics is the number of times the index was cited in the literature. We decided to search for publications using the indices in Google Scholar. It enables in-text search and unnecessarily returns only journal published articles.[42] The queries indicated the highest popularity of the WJP rule of law index. Additional battery of queries, focusing on publications since 2020, demonstrated moreover equal frequency of the three indices in the literature.

---

[42]   The queries were: "rule of law" AND "V-Dem"; "rule of law" AND "World Governance Indicators"; "rule of law" AND "World Justice Project".

Table 2.4   *Basic features of the indices under consideration*

	Rule of law index		
Characteristics	V-Dem	WGI	WJP
Question	To what extent are laws transparently, independently, predictably, impartially, and equally enforced, and to what extent do the actions of government officials comply with the law?	The extent to which agents have confidence in and abide by the rules of society, and in particular the quality of contract enforcement, property rights, the police, and the courts, as well as the likelihood of crime and violence.	Level of adherence to the rule of law defined by durable system of laws, institutions, norms, and community commitment that delivers accountability, clear and impartial law, open government, and accessible and impartial justice.
Data sources	Survey of in-country experts	Surveys of households, experts, multilateral organisations, media providers	Surveys of households and experts
Number of countries	370	214	141
Period	1789–2022	1996–2021	2012–2022
Interpretation	cross-country; over time changes; tendencies and trends	cross-country; over time changes versus global average; confidence intervals	cross-country; over time changes; tendencies and trends
Cited: Google Scholar	4770	7510	7690

5.   TRENDS IN THE RULE OF LAW

For the rule of law indices, the following approaches to the analysis of their dynamics can be pursued. The first assumes the analysis of the number of year-on-year decreases in rule of law across countries, while the other depends on a global trend approach. Figure 2.2 presents the share of countries, in which the adherence to the rule of law deteriorated in comparison to the previous year in the period of 2005–2022. The V-Dem index seems to moderately indicate global deterioration in the rule of law. Although the WGI index fluctuates

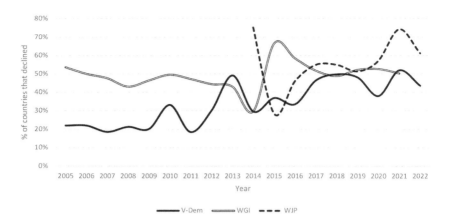

Figure 2.2   Percentage of countries, in which the adherence to the rule of law deteriorated in comparison to the previous year

around 50%, the serious decrease was observed since 2015 to 2017. A significant contraction was observed in the WJP index.

What has to be noted is that the indices are derived using dedicated surveys, therefore a certain level of uncertainty is always accompanying these estimates. The V-Dem and the WGI indices are published alongside their standard errors and confidence intervals. Using confidence intervals, it is possible to distinguish significant decreases out of all year-on-year changes. In the case of the WGI index, no more than 3% of significant decreases were observed in the period under consideration, although almost none since 2015. For the V-Dem index, significant deteriorations on yearly basis oscillate around 25% of all significant changes.

Interestingly, the search for a recent trend yielded no significant tendencies since 2020, neither globally nor in politico-geographic regions. What is more, a modest tendency to improve adherence to the rule of law is observed in a global dimension. This observation appears to be in line with the WJP[43] that concludes slow and instable changes in the rule of law adherence.

6.   CONCLUSIONS

The rule of law is a fundamental concept from the perspective of various legal systems. Naturally, its broad scope poses a challenge when it comes to meas-

---

[43]   World Justice Project, (2022) *supra* note 39.

uring this phenomenon for quantitative or comparative research. Importantly, given our focus, it has to be stressed that even if the indices measuring the rule of law have some imperfections due to availability of data (time and geographical range) or because of their design, they are of a very high significance for social scientists, as the indices allow for an entire branch of research bringing value-added in various dimensions, including recommendations for policy makers.

From the available indices of the rule of law, we selected the following three leading ones and described their details: the Varieties of Democracy (V-Dem) rule of law index, the Worldwide Governance Indicators (WGI) rule of law index, and the World Justice Project (WJP) rule of law index. Although they all touch upon different components of the concept of the rule of law, their common part covers some characteristics of judiciary – *inter alia.* independence, fairness and timeliness. The nuances in the design of these indicators of the rule of law should be considered when picking up the best fit in terms of the research goal or the nature of the data.

The levels of the rule of law observable in the recent years, for all the above mentioned indices, indicate that the rule of law, once achieved at a satisfactory degree, cannot be taken as granted, and continuous efforts for its benefit are required. Moreover, it still remains in question how to mitigate global or regional trends of deterioration of the rule of law spotted for the past years or how to support the very recent improvements.

3. Post-accession Experience Regarding the Rule of Law

Herbert Küpper

1. IN LIEU OF AN INTRODUCTION: SOME ICONOCLASTIC REMARKS

Did the 'new' Member States[1] slacken in their efforts to create and uphold the rule of law after their accession to the EU? Did they become lazy or overly complacent and let their achievements erode? Or did they erode, perhaps demolish their rule of law by purpose even? The short answer is a resolute "it depends".

If we are not satisfied with this short answer, we need to go deeper into details. To start with, we must have a closer look at the question(s) above. They insinuate that the new Member States possessed – or, depending on the perspective, practiced – a sufficient standard of rule of law at the time of accession. This underlying assumption is wrong. The new Member States did not function according to the rule of law when they joined the EU. At best, they struggled along on their path to establish some sort of rule of law.

To get at the truth of the matter, we must continue our iconoclasm. That the rule of law was at best deficient at the time of accession was no secret. In 2004, 2007 and 2013, the governments of the EU, the existing EU members and the states on the verge of accession knew that they did not meet the standards of a rule of law. They did not meet most of the Copenhagen criteria set as a yardstick for candidate countries in 1993. In each new Member State, the situation was somewhat different, but none of them could have been admitted to the EU if the Copenhagen criteria had been taken seriously. The rule of law

---

[1] For the purpose of this chapter, 'new' members are the formerly socialist countries that joined the EU in 2004 (Czechia, Estonia, Hungary Latvia, Lithuania, Poland, Slovakia, Slovenia), 2007 (Bulgaria, Romania) and 2013 (Croatia). The decisive factor is not the date of the accession because Cyprus and Malta as well joined in 2004 but are not considered 'new' Member States. The important factor is their Socialist past.

was a problem in practically all these states. If this is so, why were the new members allowed to join the EU? To cut a long story short: it was a political decision. In 2004, there was a general conviction that the time was ripe for admitting the Baltic and East Central European applicants, that the political damage of waiting until they would achieve the Copenhagen criteria would be graver than the damage done by allowing them in prematurely. That the damage of a premature accession was bigger than expected, had become obvious in 2007 so that Bulgaria and Romania, countries much further away from the Copenhagen criteria than Estonia, Czechia or Hungary had been three years previously, were allowed to join 'on probation'. Croatia's admission was a political decision, too. The EU and its members weighed the damage of prolonging the waiting period against the damage caused by a premature accession. Again, the scales tilted towards accession despite the fact that the rule of law was at best imperfect. As a trained lawyer, one may deplore this. But allowing a country to join the EU is first and foremost a political question, and giving a political rather than a legal answer is legitimate. Still, legitimate decisions, too, may produce unpleasant consequences.

2. WHAT IS THE RULE OF LAW?

When identifying the state of the rule of law in post-accession countries, we first need to agree on what the rule of law is. When we speak of rule of law here, we do not mean the specific common law principle but include equivalent continental European institutions such as '*Rechtsstaat(lichkeit)*' and '*légalité*'.

This rule of law is one of the fundamental values that the EU and all its Member States share (Article 2 TEU). A wide margin of appreciation exists about what that value may be. There probably is universal agreement that its very basics mean the absence of arbitrariness and that those in power, including the state, are bound by the rules that are valid for everybody. Beyond these basics, views and priorities differ. Nevertheless, it is obvious that the proliferating jungle of superbly chiselled doctrinal arabesques created by German-speaking academia is not the universally accepted rule-of-law idea. Nor does the centuries-old edifice of British-style rule of law with its many shortcomings, the defence of which has become so dear to common law academia, reflect the essence of the all-European idea.

Beyond the basic idea of rules binding everybody without arbitrariness, the ideas of what constitutes a rule of law vary – and do so legitimately – between epochs, countries, political worldviews and, finally, individuals with their different cultural, economic, or scholarly background. What may be considered good rule-of-law practice in England may count as a gross violation of the *Rechtsstaat* in Austria, the role of the permissible political element in a rule-of-law based public administration is defined differently in Scandinavia on the one hand and Mediterranean countries on the other.

In their rule of law dispute, some new Member States rely on this general ambiguity, arguing that they legitimately define their rule of law differently from the Commission or the Western European mainstream, sometimes adding that their rule of law was the genuinely 'European' article, as opposed to the 'degenerate' rule of law ideas that the EU and their Western members advocated. To make one point clear: a state practice violating the 'pan-European' core identified above, i.e. any state practice prone to arbitrariness and/or double standards for those in power, is not what European rule of law is about, even if we take into account that Europe harbours a variety of rule of law traditions with differing contents and that the EU working definition of the rule of law[2] includes more aspects than just the core of a lack of arbitrariness, aspects that occasionally lean more towards Western rather than Eastern European ideas and thus may lead to the EU applying double standards to the detriment of the new members' traditions. Nevertheless, when, to give two extreme examples, Hungary's government says that their habit of allowing a neo-feudal kleptocratic élite to keep what they amassed through less and less veiled corruption as long as they label their practices with a resentment-based ethno-nationalist ideology, this is just as much contrary to the basic pan-European idea of rule of law as are the assertions of Poland's PiS government that 'their' rule of law means that their alleged victory in the Polish war of cultures authorizes them to mould their – again resentment-based, clerical – ideas of throwing Poland back to an imaginary 19th century into a universally binding '*contrat social*' which prevails, if necessary, over formal law including the constitution. Reminding Hungary and Poland that aforementioned practices are contrary to the pan-European, including Hungarian and Polish, traditions of what constitutes a rule of law is therefore neither illegitimate nor the application of double standards.

To avoid ideological clashes over the 'true' rule of law, we will here limit the rule of law *à la Européenne* to a set of seemingly technical, yet pivotal elements: *inter alia*, the principle of legality including a transparent law-making process, separation of powers, absence of arbitrariness in executive action, protection by independent and impartial courts, non-discrimination and equality before the law.[3] We may add independent media as an efficient watch-dog. These elements demonstrate that a successful rule of law rests on the quality of

---

[2] For more detail, see fn. 3.

[3] These are the central rule-of-law elements listed in Article 2(a) of the Parliament and Council Regulation (EU, Euratom) on a general regime of conditionality for the protection of the Union budget [2020] OJ L 433I, 1.

the law including the quality of its application. The rule of law makes the law the measure of everything: socially relevant disputes are resolved on the basis of pre-formulated abstract rules. The sociological precondition is a general acceptance of the law – out of all systems governing social behaviour – as *the* central institution. This presupposes that society has by and large a positive image of, and institutional trust in, the law. This precondition – and now we come to the new Member States – is lacking in post-socialist states.

3.   THE LAW IN THE NEW MEMBER STATES

We must bear in mind that a positive and trustful image of the law is an exception in time and space. Most legal cultures regard the law as an instrument to govern, not as an instrument to protect the rights of the governed. This special role of the law, that Western European legal culture attributes to it as the basis of a system designed to avoid arbitrariness and create legal certainty, is the result of a rather lucky combination of several historical developments. Going far back in time, Roman law, unlike practically all other Mediterranean legal systems of the time, concentrated on private law, i.e. the horizontal rights of the private citizen, not on the vertical instruments of power such as public and criminal law. This heritage was preserved by the Catholic church which defined itself, *inter alia*, as a law-based institution, and it was developed by an academia who were, as a social group, essentially independent both from state and church. We can add many more elements, but this may suffice to give an idea of the rule of law in Western European legal culture. We have to stress the 'Western' in Western European legal culture because somewhat different traditions prevail in the East of our continent with its heritage of Byzantine law and Orthodox church(es). They attribute, to put it simply, more importance to the wise clemency that the pious ruler exercises in the individual case than to justice enshrined in general rules binding for all.[4] Eastern Orthodoxy searches material justice in the individual decision whereas Western legal culture believes in abstract and general rules as the materialisation of justice: material justice through law (Western Europe) v. material justice despite the law (Eastern Europe).

---

[4]   Brunner, 'Rechtskultur in Osteuropa: Das Problem der Kulturgrenzen', in Brunner (ed), *Politische und ökonomische Transformation in Osteuropa* (3rd edn. Berlin Verlag 2000), 111-132; Küpper, *Einführung in die Rechtsgeschichte Osteuropas* (Peter Lang 2005), 18-21, 26-28; Schlögel, *Die Mitte liegt ostwärts. Europa im Übergang* (Carl Hanser Verlag 2002); Soloviev, *Der Einfluß des byzantinischen Rechts auf die Völker Osteuropas* (Savigny-Stiftung für Rechtsgeschichte Romanistische Abtlg. 1959), 432-479.

In Western Europe, people are used to trust the law to carry at least a certain degree of material justice, and to debate about the justice of both old and new laws. In the new Member States, a much more cynical attitude prevails. The law is denounced as an instrument with which those in power rule, which they apply according to their interest and which, consequently, the citizens obey if it suits them and disobey if they think they can get away with it.[5]

What is the reason for this different attitude in 'old' and 'new' members? The *prima facie* answer is: the socialist past. Two to three generations under the rule of an ideology, which was even if we refrain from applying the rather cliché-like concept of legal nihilism,[6] highly derogatory of the law and its inner value, may have sufficed to imbue into the populations distrust and disrespect of the law. However, socialist legal cynicism is only the most recent layer on older traditions. The Eastern Greek-Byzantine half of our continent does not entertain too positive an image of the law as an instrument to create and further social justice. But also the Eastern half of Central Europe, i.e. the corridor of countries from Estonia to Croatia, despite belonging to Latin Western Europe and sharing the heritage of a positive image of the law, has had an ambivalent relationship to it. When in the 18th century the modern state and in the 19th century the present form of rule of law emerged in the region, these countries, with the partial exception of Hungary, were not independent but were modernized by foreign rulers in Berlin, Vienna and St. Petersburg (with the latter not being overly active in the modernisation department). This has resulted in an ambivalent relationship of these peoples to the institutions of state and law. The basic trust in 'their' law that Western European peoples could develop in the last centuries was impossible for the peoples of Eastern Central Europe to achieve because the law, however benign and modernizing it may have been at times, was not 'their' law but that of the Prussian, Austrian, or Russian rulers.

---

[5] For more detail, see e.g. Fekete, 'The Relevance of Studying Legal Cultures in Central and East Europe' (2019) Jahrbuch für Ostrecht, 161-164; Gajduschek, 'Wild East and Civilised West? Some indicators of legal culture in Hungary, Serbia and the Netherlands. An empirical comparative assessment' (2019) Jahrbuch für Ostrecht, 165-184; Fekete, 'Rights Consciousness in the CEE Region: Lessons from Earlier Studies' (2019) Jahrbuch für Ostrecht, 185-202; Vuković and Cvejić, 'Attitudes Towards the Rule of Law in Contemporary Serbia: A Coherent Legal Culture?' (2019) Jahrbuch für Ostrecht, 203-220; Matyasovszky-Németh, 'Taking Socio-Legal Studies Seriously: Some Comments on the Status of Social Rights in Hungary' (2019) Jahrbuch für Ostrecht, 221-234; Šipulová, 'ECtHR – Ally, Adversary, or Foe? The Attitudes of Judges Towards International Human Rights Law in the (Post-)Transitioning Area' (2019) Jahrbuch für Ostrecht, 235-250.

[6] On the post-socialist debate on bygone socialist legal nihilism see Luchterhandt, *Künftige Aufgaben der Ostrechtsforschung* (WGO-MfOR 1996), 159-175.

Socialist legal cynicism came on top of these older layers of estrangement. For the Soviet satellites, socialist law, too, was a foreign imposition. Only Yugoslavia and Albania chose the socialist path without intervention from Moscow, but there as well the socialist negation and depreciation of the law prevailed. Three decades of post-socialist development have not sufficed to overcome this legacy which is a heavy burden for the establishment of the rule of law. If the population does not accept the law as a positive value and an at least possible source of material justice, rule of law has little to build upon.

There are positive trends, too. After the end of socialism, there was a general enthusiasm for the rule of law because, unlike principles like democracy or social justice, the rule of law had always been negated officially by the socialist regimes. They had had 'socialist legality' but no rule of law. Consequently, the new self-definition as a rule of law – more precisely, as a *'Rechtsstaat'* because these countries translated the German and not the English expression into their languages – could symbolize better than anything else the breach with the old and the creation of a new system.[7] *'Rechtsstaat'* and 'rule of law' carried the promise of a better life. Furthermore, they served as a bridge to the pre-socialist past because the German *Rechtsstaat* doctrine had exercised its influence on the countries of Eastern Central Europe since the late 19th century. The post-socialist political debate defined their states of the interwar period, not always truthfully, as rule-of-law systems so that becoming a *Rechtsstaat* again would bring them back to their roots and thus right the wrongs that Soviet rule had inflicted on these states and their cultural identity. The 'return to Europe' and 'return to the own roots' went hand in hand with the question of the rule of law.

Parts of the legal and political elites were aware of the existing legal cynicism and tried to raise awareness of, and trust in, the law. There was a general hope that the quality of the law would improve under the new political circumstances. Joining the EU was generally seen as a way to create a law that could be trusted and build a legal system and culture that might serve as a sound basis for the future rule of law. An extreme case was Bulgaria where a substantial proportion of the population hoped that the EU would do away with the corrupt Bulgarian political elite and replace both them and the law they had enacted with 'untainted' European law.

---

[7] The one exception had been Yugoslavia where socialism had purported to create a socialist *'Rechtsstaat'*. As a consequence, the texts of post-socialist constitutions of Yugoslav successor states do not use the translation of the German *'Rechtsstaat'* but of the English "rule of law" because this better expresses the breach with their old system.

These exaggerated expectations were bound to, and did, fail. The EU did not do away with the ruling classes of the new members. EU law, being more often than not highly technical, may have raised the standards of legislatorial craftsmanship in the new members but certainly did not create legal systems of a higher quality of material justice. The EU had neither the competence nor the political will to interfere deeper into the new members than it interfered into the old ones. Thus, the structures in the new members were without external pressure to change. This was true before the accession because, as described above, the Copenhagen criteria were enforced only half-heartedly on the candidates. After the accession, the EU had no instrument at all to enforce higher standards of the rule of law. Even Romania and Bulgaria were beyond the reach of direct interventions of the EU when a special Cooperation and Verification Mechanism was in force.

Not all new members failed in shaping a rule of law. Generally speaking, there is a decreasing tendency from North to South. The Baltic republics have done rather well, Romania and Bulgaria as well as Hungary since 2010 and Poland since 2015 have major problems, and the new members in-between face sizeable shortcomings.

Nevertheless, in the populations' value system, the rule of law still carries higher acceptance in most new Member States than values like democracy or market economy. The reason probably is that general disappointment with democracy and the market is higher than with the rule of law.

4.   THE RULE OF LAW IN THE NEW MEMBER STATES: COURTS AND JUDGES

All this said, we will now turn to the development of the rule of law in the new Member States since their accession to the EU. As seen before, the rule of law was not complete when they acceded. Creating and maintaining the rule of law is not a one-time effort but a constant, every-day challenge. It is not enough to define the state as rule-of-law based in the constitution although enshrining the rule of law in the basic law may be helpful.[8] All new members enlist the rule of law in the constitutional text on the definition of the state. Their constitutional doctrine is aware of the fact that the rule of law is nothing static, but a process to be conducted every day, and that the *'Rechtsstaat'* covers a wide field.

In the first post-socialist decade, the constitutional courts of Hungary and Poland were especially active in applying the rule of law. The Hungarian court solved many cases on the basis of the general rule-of-law clause although more

---

[8]   The German Constitution (*Grundgesetz*) of 1949 does not identify the German state as a *'Rechtsstaat'* in its basic definitions in Article 20(1).

precise law such as basic rights was available. One reason might have been the positive associations that the rule of law carried among lawyers and the population, another that the vague rule of law provided a better basis for the decidedly 'activist' court that the Hungarian body was under its first president *Sólyom* (1990–1998).[9] The Polish court went even further, deriving an entire catalogue of basic rights – which was missing from the torso that the constitution was between 1992 and 1997 – from the rule of law, a practice which it continued, albeit to a somewhat more moderate extent, after the new constitution of 1997 with its extensive basic rights had been enacted.[10] Its Slovenian counterpart also applied the rule-of-law clause in the field of basic rights, though not to establish them (which was unnecessary because the constitution contains a fair enumeration) but to develop reliable criteria for their limitation as well as for the protection of acquired rights[11] – a doctrinal figure of the *Rechtsstaat* which also the Hungarian constitutional court used to torpedo substantial changes in the social system.[12] The Czech constitutional justices, to give a fourth example, instrumentalized in that period the rule-of-law clause mainly to fight – not without success – the extensive socialist legacy in legislative and legal culture such as retroactive laws, slovenly worded normative acts, excessive judicial formalism or selective application by the law by the public administration.[13] In the 1990s, the accession candidates seemed to be on a good path, at least if one looks at the constitutional courts. So: what went wrong?

Both old and new members have deficits in the rule of law, but the list of shortcomings is of a different quantity and quality in the new members. Mischiefs concern all pivotal elements of the rule of law.[14] The technical

---

[9] Brunner and Sólyom, *Verfassungsgerichtsbarkeit in Ungarn* (Nomos 1995), 46-55, 102-105; Győrfi, Kazai and Orbán, *Kontextus által világosan: A Sólyom-bíróság antiformalista elemzése* (L'Harmattan 2021); Küpper, *Die ungarische Verfassung nach zwei Jahrzehnten des Übergangs* (Peter Lang 2007), 43-47.

[10] Banaszak and Milej, *Polnisches Staatsrecht. Polskie prawo konstytucyjne* (C.H. Beck 2009), 27-31; Brunner and Garlicki, *Verfassungsgerichtsbarkeit in Polen* (Nomos 1999), 73-80.

[11] Šturm, *Komentar Ustave Republike Slovenije* (Fakulteta za podiplomske državne in evropske študije 2002), 12-13, 44-74.

[12] Küpper, 'Der Sparkurs der ungarischen Regierung auf dem Prüfstand des Verfassungsgerichts' (1996) Recht in Ost und West, 101-112.

[13] Bobek, Molek and Šimíček, *Komunistické právo v Československu* (Masarykova univerzita 2009); Brunner, Hofmann and Holländer, *Verfassungs-gerichtsbarkeit in der Tschechischen Republik* (Nomos 2001), 29-35. On the socialist legacy in legal culture in general see Jakab and Hollán, 'Die dogmatische Hinterlassenschaft des Sozialismus im heutigen Recht' (2005) Jahrbuch für Ostrecht, 11-40.

[14] See above section 2.

quality of many laws is poor,[15] the process of their adoption is in many states opaque. Public administration is paternalist, slow, tortuous and excessively formalist, and the poorly paid public servants tend to abuse their power vis-à-vis the citizens. In administrative practice, double standards and non-application of the law are wide-spread not only in connection with the omnipresent corruption but also to please those in power or just to tease those who are not. As a result, the law is applied by public authorities and quite often by the courts in a discriminatory manner. There is a sizeable bias in favour of members of the majority whereas rights of minorities are ignored and their duties unduly stressed. In the first two post-socialist decades, this affected mostly ethnic and sometimes religious minorities; a more recent target of anti-minority activism in the administrative and judicial application of the law are, *inter alia*, the various LGBTIQ groups. Sanctions tend to be milder or not at all pronounced or enforced against persons with political, social or economic power whereas persons of low social status experience "the utmost rigour of the law". One extreme example is the criminalization of homelessness in Hungary.

In the following, we will concentrate on a central institution in any *Rechtsstaat* and, at the same time, the most problematic power branch in most new members: the courts of law. The quality of the law in action largely depends on how the courts apply it. The absence of arbitrariness, the equality of the application of the law, and its binding force on those in power are a function of independent courts capable of administering the law at high professional standards. The equal, all-encompassing application of the law free of arbitrariness strongly relies on the independence of courts and judges. Courts are expected to apply the law according to its intrinsic rules,[16] i.e. without political, economic, religious, or other non-legal influences or bias. Many constitutions express this expectation with the formula that courts and/or judges are subject to the law only. In order to conform to this expectation, both courts and judges need to be independent. These two forms of independence are interdependent, but not identical. Classically, judicial independence is differentiated into an outer and an inner independence. This differentiation with its implication in legal sociology as well as in legal (constitutional) doctrine is a useful tool to analyse the independence of courts and judges in the new Member States.

---

[15]   Quite often, EU directives are translated verbatim and enacted as laws which results in poor quality because directives are not formulated for direct application but as a guideline for national law-makers.

[16]   The formulation and foundation of the law's intrinsic rules is the task of legal science, not of any state body.

There are two different scenarios in the new Member States: structural problems preventing judicial independence from working properly practically in all new Member States on the one hand and the intentional dismantling of judicial independence in Hungary and Poland on the other. Let's start with the latter.

4.1 Intentional Attack on Judicial Independence: Hungary and Poland

In Hungary and Poland, the nationalist-populist governments of Fidesz (in power since 2010) and PiS (between 2015 and 2023) have been abolishing judicial independence and trying to gain control over the courts as a central part of their politics. Their goals and methods differ, but both governments feel that independent courts and a true rule of law stand in the way of their political ambitions. The ambition of the Hungarian Fidesz is, to put it short, to get rich quickly. Since 2010, they have established a neo-feudal kleptocracy which allows the Fidesz leadership and their oligarch cronies to capture the state and plunder its resources. They gain popular acceptance by stressing an ideology of exclusive ethnonationalism and relating to a 'golden age' that never was, which appeals to a sufficient proportion of the electorate, and by establishing a clientelist system in which the leadership allots their clients sinecures. In Poland, PiS acts out of ideological conviction. They believe in what they preach and want to win their cultural war against the 20th and 21st centuries. They, too, relate to an imaginary past interpreted as 'golden'. All means were fair to win this war, including the replacement of the rule of law and independent courts with a system where the PiS' ideas of what is good and proper are supreme guidelines for all behaviour, public and private, in Poland. For the PiS leadership, corruption was not the central instrument for quick self-enrichment which it is for Fidesz leadership but much rather a tool for stabilizing their rule by buying the support of important stake-holders. Some reasons for the popular acceptance of these erratic political courses may be an underlying fear of losing national independence or the nation itself due to, *inter alia*, demographic processes (high mortality, low birth rates, significant emigration especially of the economically active strata).[17]

Due to a highly distorting electoral system, Fidesz has held a two-thirds majority in parliament since 2010 (with short interruptions) even when their

---

[17] For possible reasons in all post-socialist countries, see e.g. Fekete, 'On the Role of Public Sentiments in the Emergence of Post-Transitory Central European Constitutionalism' (2016) Jahrbuch für Ostrecht, 243-255; Krastev and Holmes, *The Light that Failed* (Allen Lane 2019); Küpper and Partlett, *The Post-Soviet as Post-Colonial* (Edward Elgar Publishing 2022), 111-237.

share of the vote was well under 50 per cent. With this majority, the government can and does modify the constitution *ad libitum*. In 2011, one year after their rise into power, Fidesz enacted an entirely new constitution.[18] The state organisation under the new constitution strongly resembles that of the old constitution, with seemingly minor changes. These changes concerned the appointments into state positions: the compulsory participation of the opposition, which under the old constitution was in operation with constitutional justices, was abolished,[19] all higher state positions require a maximum of a two third majority in parliament – which the mentioned distorting election laws provide Fidesz with. As a consequence, all institutions are staffed with loyal Fidesz partisans, reducing the system of checks and balances to a mere façade.[20]

The fact whether a given constitutional justice was appointed by Fidesz or another political power (in the case of justices appointed before 2010) was clearly visible in their decisions; since 2015, the court has been exclusively composed by Fidesz appointees.[21] The new constitution of 2011 renamed the Supreme Court into Curia (its name before 1949). Fidesz argued that the Curia was not identical with the former Supreme Court and, for this reason, the President of the old Supreme Court could not continue his office but parliament was to elect a new President of the Curia. In all formerly socialist countries, the supreme courts and their presidents are powerful institutions with considerable influence on the judicial practice in the entire country. Therefore, appointing the President of the Curia opened up channels of government influence on the judiciary. The former President of the Supreme Court complained before the European Court of Human Rights and won his case but nevertheless was not reinstalled in his old position.[22]

The next step to increase government influence on the judiciary was a constitutional amendment that awarded the National Judicial Office's President the power to transfer pending cases to another court. In practice, the President of the Office – *Tünde Handó*, wife of Fidesz' second-in-command

---

[18]   Hungary's Basic Law of 25 April 2011, as amended.

[19]   Küpper, *Ungarns Verfassung vom 25 April 2011* (Peter Lang 2012), 164-165.

[20]   Jakab, 'Informal Institutional Elements as Both Preconditions and Consequences of Effective Formal Legal Rules: The Failure of Constitutional Institution Building in Hungary' 82020) 68 American Journal of Comparative Law, 760-800. On the importance of capturing the control and integrity institutions for an authoritarian force on their way to unlimited state power, see Levitsky and Ziblatt, *How Democracies Die* (Penguin Random House 2018).

[21]   Szente, 'The Political Orientation of the Members of the Hungarian Constitutional Court Between 2010 and 2014' (2016) Constitutional Studies, 123-149.

[22]   *Baka v Hungary*, App no 20261/12 (ECtHR, 23 June 2016). The court awarded Mr. Baka EUR 70,000 in damages and EUR 30,000 in expenses.

József Szájer and member of the Fidesz inner circle – used that power to transfer cases with political implications or against one of the oligarchs to the Kecskemét Regional Court which boasted itself to be a loyal Fidesz partisan. Both the EU and the Hungarian legal professions protested against this gross violation of judicial independence. After six months, the government gave in and repealed the amendment.[23]

Another tool of the Fidesz government is intimidation. They applied it first as early as in 2010. When the, then still independent, Constitutional Court quashed a law important to Fidesz' leadership, Fidesz changed the constitution in less than a month, curtailing the powers of the Constitutional Court. It did not help the court that it quashed the law on technical grounds and even showed the government a constitutional way how to achieve their aim. In vain, the government was extremely irate and intent to demonstrate that their two-third majority enabled them to punish disobedient control institutions.[24] Intimidating courts was not limited to the Constitutional Court but extended to the judiciary at large including public prosecutors. In 2011, Fidesz reduced the pension threshold for judges and prosecutors from 70 to 62, sending several hundred judges and prosecutors into an early retirement on minimum pension. They argued that they wanted to get rid of the 'red judges' educated under the socialist system. This was merely a pretext because an analysis of these judges' case law does not reveal any leftist bias. The true reason was twofold: first, the Government demonstrated the judges that their tenure was not as safe as the constitution made believe and therefore they had better obey the government. Second, they vacated a large number of comparatively well-paid posts to feed their clients. Both the Constitutional Court and the European Court of Justice qualified this measure as illegal but only very few of the old judges were reinstalled in their positions.[25]

---

[23]   Hungary's Basic Law, Article 27(4) (1 April 2013–30 September 2013); Küp-per, (2012), *supra* note 19, 120-121, 159-161.

[24]   Constitutional Court decision 184/2010 (X. 28.) AB of 28.10.2010; Constitutional Amendment Act 2010:CXIX of 19 November 2010. The new constitution of 2011 continues the curtailed powers which László Sólyom, the former President of the Constitutional Court, described as 'an incurable wound on the Basic Law': Jakab, *Az új Alaptörvény keletkezése és gyakorlati következményei* (HVY-Orac 2011), 13-14.

[25]   Article 26(2)3 Basic Law. Act 2011:CXXXI of 14 October 2011 created a simplified procedure to appoint new judges on the many vacancies which was to facilitate the appointment of clients on judicial posts. ECJ, Case C-286/12, *Commission v Hungary*, EU:C:2012:687; Hungarian Constitutional Court, Decision 33/2012. (VII. 17.) AB of 17.7.2012.

In sum, the formal separation between the political powers and the courts has been reduced to a nice *mise-en-scène* to please the superficial eye of the rule-of-law beholder. The government with their two-thirds majority can, and does overcome every legal obstacle and reacts quite vengeful to any sort of opposition.

Compared to Hungary, the Polish PiS government used much more brutal methods to demolish the independence of the courts and the judiciary. In the case of the Constitutional Court, PiS used appointments, but unlike Fidesz in a blatantly illegal way. In 2015, the last pre-PiS parliament had elected three constitutional justices in the proper procedure; however, *Andrzej Duda*, the PiS President of the Republic refused to take their oath and thus prevented them from assuming office, which is an obvious violation of his duties and transgression of his powers. Instead, the new PiS parliament elected another three justices whom the PiS President installed. Since then, illegally appointed justices have sat in the Constitutional Court. That court has always decided in favour of the government. Consequently, the European Court of Human Rights no longer considers the Polish Constitutional Court a 'tribunal established by law'.[26] These Strasbourg decisions are not acted upon in Poland.

The same is true for the numerous decisions of the European Court of Justice declaring the Polish 'reforms' as contrary to European law, usually because the Polish measures violate the independence of judges and of courts as well as negate the supremacy of Union law.[27] The initiation of an Article 7-procedure and daily fines of 1 million EUR have had no effect either.

The Polish measures are too numerous to discuss in detail. Suffice to say that they have two core elements: staffing the higher courts with partisans, which started immediately after the elections in 2015, and intimidating the judiciary. For the latter, PiS has taken recourse to compulsory early retirement which may be undone by the head of state on an individual basis,[28] excessive rights of the Minister of Justice to decide on judicial careers, as well as a disciplinary chamber which may sanction any official or private behaviour of a judge which the government dislikes, e.g. requesting a preliminary ruling of the European Court of Justice. All PiS measures are about control. PiS can control Polish laws because they can re-write them in parliament and can control the constitution despite the lack of a two-thirds majority because their

---

[26]   *Xero Flor v Poland,* App no 4907/18 (ECtHR, 7 May 2021).

[27]   ECJ, Case C-204/21, *Commission v Poland*, EU:C:2023:442. The case summarizes the previous case law on Poland and finally declares the Polish 'reforms' a violation of Union law and rule of law values.

[28]   This violates, *inter alia*, judicial independence: ECJ, Case C-619/18, *Commission v Poland*, EU:C:2019:531.

Constitutional Court gives the constitution any interpretation the government wishes. But they cannot control Union law. Therefore, they oppose the validity of Union law in Poland and veil this endeavour to win control with the popular argument of restoring Polish sovereignty.[29]

The Hungarian interventions into judicial independence happened through appointments including court packing and thus were apparently legal, apart from Justice Baka's victory in Strasbourg and, arguably, the abolition of the National Judicial Office's power to reallocate cases. The Polish methods are often openly illegal and do not even try to create a veil of legality. One reason is that PiS, unlike Fidesz, held a simple, not a two-thirds majority in parliament and therefore could not redefine the rules the way Fidesz can. Another reason may be that where Fidesz is only interested in getting rich quickly and uses ideology as a means to gain voters, PiS is truly convinced of their cause and wants to reshape Polish life. As a tendency, Fidesz are kleptocrats and do not want courts and public prosecutors to stand in their corrupt ways whereas PiS are idealists who want courts to transport the content not of the law but of PiS ideology. Fidesz therefore chooses ways of least resistance including upholding a rule-of-law façade for their voters – social acceptance of the rule of law is still high in Hungary, albeit tarnished by cynicism – as well as for the sake of the EU. PiS, on the other hand, has an eschatological political agenda. In their perception of a cultural war, their programme counts more than 'formal' aspects like the rule of law or democracy. They seem to be supported in this by their loyal voters who cherish other values than the rule of law or independent courts.[30]

4.2 Structural Problems of the Court Systems of the New Member States

Given the North-South divide,[31] practically all new members still struggle to establish a judicial system that conforms to the requirements of the rule of law. A good example is Bulgaria: the vast majority of the amendments to its 1991 constitution concern the third power branch, the process is ongoing.[32]

---

[29] Matczak, '10 Facts on Poland for the Consideration of the European Court of Justice' (2018), Verfassungsblog, <https://verfassungsblog.de/10-facts-on-poland-for-the-consideration-of-the-european-court-of-justice> accessed 13 July 2023.

[30] Sadurski, "How Democracy Dies (in Poland)" (2018), 18/01, Sydney Law School Legal Studies Research Paper, <https://papers.ssrn.com/sol3/papers.cfm?abstract_id=3103491> paras 55-64.

[31] See above section 3.

[32] Schrameyer, "Die Verfassungsänderungen in Bulgarien", Jahrbuch für Ostrecht (2007), 339-372. The subsequent constitutional amendments, too, centre on

Another example: one of the largest political scandals in Romania in the last years was linked to the judicial sector. In 2018, the special prosecutor for corruption-related crimes, *Laura Kövesi*, was dismissed by the power elite including the Constitutional Court[33] for whom the efficiency of *Ms. Kövesi* posed an immediate threat.

4.2.1   Outer Independence

The classical tool to secure the outer independence of courts[34] is the separation of powers. It isolates the courts from the political powers (parliament, government, administration). Socialist systems were based on the unity of power. All state organs were obliged to further the political goal of creating socialism. Socialist court systems were administered by the ministries of justice and the supreme courts, with court presidents holding strong administrative competences. Courts, like all other state bodies, were supervised and guided by the party. This political oversight took different shades of intensity in time and place. Post-socialist constitutions enshrine the separation of powers and the outer independence of the courts, and sometimes of the judges. It is safe to assume that no country would have been admitted to the EU without this clause. The independence of courts nevertheless is under threat in some new Member States.

Courts and judges all over the world depend in multiple ways on other state powers, which may use this as an avenue of influence. The most important fields are judicial career decisions (appointment, promotion, transfer, disciplinary sanctions) on the level of the independence of the individual judge and the allotment of funds, infrastructure and investments on the level of the individual court. The seemingly obvious solution is to separate the judicial power strictly by transferring these decisions to that power branch.

Many post-socialist countries decided to install a judicial council[35] as a representative organ of the judiciary and, in some countries, the prosecution service. The role model was the Italian *Consiglio superiore della magistratura*. We can differentiate two types, depending on composition. If the majority of members is elected by the judges (and, where the council represents the pros-

---

courts and judges.

[33]   Constitutional Court decision no. 358 of 30 May 2018, defending the highly questionable dismissal decree of the Minister of Justice against a presidential veto.

[34]   We will not deal with the outer independence of judges because this question is much less problematic than their inner independence (section 4.2.2).

[35]   The Lithuanian council was created after Constitutional Court had declared unconstitutional the court administration and especially judicial career decisions by the executive power: Constitutional Court decision 16/98 of 21 December 1999.

ecutors as well, by that group), we have a 'genuine judicial council'. A body with less than half the membership having a mandate of the group they represent may be termed 'phoney judicial council'.

In all but one new Member States, judicial councils exist(ed):[36]

Table 3.1   Judicial Councils in the New Member States

State	Members		Powers			Remarks
	total	elected by judges + judges ex officio	career decisions	disciplinary sanctions	funding	
genuine						
Bulgaria	25	15	+	+	+	
Croatia	11	7	+	+	-	
Hungary	15	11	-	-	+	1997–2011
Latvia	15	10	+	-	+/-	statute
Lithuania	17	17	+	+/-	+/-	
Poland	25	17	+	-	-	
Romania	19	16	+	+	-	
Slovenia	11	6	+/-	-	-	
borderline						
Estonia	12	6	+	-	+/-	statute
Slovakia	18	9	+/-	-	-	
phoney						
--	not in new Member States, but in some candidate states					

At first sight, this looks promising. If we look beyond the mere figures at the post-socialist realities, we find deep discontent.[37]

In some countries, the judicial councils manage to shield the judicial careers and/or the court system from too immediate an influence by the executive and legislative powers. The price these court systems pay is the tutelage of the judicial council members over the judiciary. Judicial councils are dominated in most countries by the presidents of the mid-level and higher courts. As a result

---

[36] There is no council in the Czech Republic. The Hungarian council existed between 1997 and 2011. The Estonian and Latvian councils are not enshrined in the constitution but in statute.

[37] Kosař, 'Beyond Judicial Councils: Forms, Rationales and Impact Judicial Self-Governance in Europe' (2018) 19 German Law Journal, 1567-1612.

of pre-socialist and socialist traditions, Eastern European court presidents are powerful figures. They have a crucial say in judicial career decisions as well as the allotment of the funds that the court is given from the state budget. The judicial councils duplicate their power base. In South Eastern Europe with its strong clientelist traits, where even the socialist regimes worked on quasi-feudal mechanisms,[38] the judicial councils make it even easier for court presidents to turn 'their' courts into fiefs and demand loyalty from the judges employed there. Loyalty in this term does not denote political allegiance because court presidents rarely play an active role in politics. Loyalty encompasses, *inter alia*, the support of the president in inner-judicial structures (e.g. elections to the judicial council or other professional bodies), following the president's views on the proper interpretation of law and sparing the court president political embarrassment when deciding a case with political or material interests of the power elite. What may be a gain for the independence of the courts (because the other state powers have no immediate say) is a loss for the independence of the individual judge because professional and other pressure by court presidents or other judicial leaders tends to be more immediate and stronger than interventions by the political leadership. These mechanisms are particularly strong in Bulgaria and Romania, but can also be observed in Croatia, Slovenia or Slovakia. Croatia managed to mitigate to some extent the feudalizing effects of the judicial council by banning court presidents from membership in the council. In Hungary, where a judicial council existed between 1997 and 2011, the judiciary themselves brought complaints to this effect to the government during the drafting process of the new constitution of 2011. As a result, the judicial council did not make it into the new constitution.

In the Northern new Member States, the judicial councils do not contribute to the feudalization of the court system but reinforce the court presidents' power base by other mechanisms such as professional favouritism and nepotism. Court presidents organize with the help of the judicial councils inner-judicial power cliques for mutual assistance in career and other interests.

In some cases, the judicial councils could not prevent or counterbalance the influence that political actors exercise on the judiciary. This happens when the council has to share its powers. To give an example, the council in Slovenia proposes judicial appointments to parliament. Although the council

---

[38] Clientelism or (quasi-)feudalism in this sense denotes a system where the individual is allotted a clientelist status by the feudal masters. The individual owes loyalty and receives feeding. In South-Eastern Europe's socialism, the national and regional party leaders played the role of the feudal masters who granted and withdrew fiefs and sinecures. For more detail, see Roth and Zelepos (eds), *Klientelismus in Südosteuropa* (Peter Lang 2018).

assesses the professional and other qualities of the candidates, the decision in parliament is not just symbolic and opens up avenues for political considerations which the political parties make use of to promote the careers of their 'clients'.[39] Another reason is close contacts of members of the judicial council with political parties, which was identified e.g. in Slovakia as a major rule-of-law mischief. It is true that the constitutions of some new members including Slovakia forbid judges to be party members but this incompatibility has never prevented close political, clientelist or other ties between judges and parties. The Slovak council was not the main forum for these illicit bonds between judges (court presidents) and political decision-makers but its existence did not prevent them either.

The Czech Republic and, since 2011, Hungary grant the courts no self-administration. Courts are administered by other state organs. The Czech court administration is vested in the Ministry of Justice, the Presidents and Vice-Presidents of the Supreme Court and Supreme Administrative Court as well as the presidents of the lower courts. Career decisions lie in the hands of judges' representative bodies (judicial boards) in the various courts. The Ministry of Justice does not as a rule influence career decisions but can and sometimes does reward or punish individual courts by allotting a greater or smaller share of the judicial budget on them.[40] In Hungary, the judiciary opposed the continuation of the judicial council in the new constitution hoping for a restoration of the old system where the Ministry of Justice was responsible. However, the Fidesz government chose otherwise and established a special organ, the National Judicial Office. This office belongs not to the Ministry of Justice but to the Prime Minister's Chancellery, its first president was taken from the inner party circles.[41] Since then, there have been ongoing complaints from the judiciary that the National Judicial Office used its powers arbitrarily and in order to establish clientelist dependence among the judges.

In sum, the main reasons for a deficient outer independence of the courts are inadequate institutional arrangements, a lack of appropriate ethos in political bodies such as ministries of justice, and overall societal processes such as the refeudalization of the society at large which, naturally, do not spare the court sector with its larger number of quite well-paid sinecures. It is not easy to isolate the courts from overall trends, but a rule-of-law ethos can be achieved comparatively easily. The importance of such an ethos is exemplified by

---

[39]   CCJE, Reply CCJE REP(2007) 36, *Questionnaire for 2007 Opinion Concerning the Councils for the Judiciary, Reply by Slovenia*, Question 1.

[40]   CCJE, Reply CCJE REP(2007), *Questionnaire for 2007 Opinion Concerning the Councils for the Judiciary, Reply by Czech Republic.*

[41]   See above section 4.1.

countries like Germany, Sweden or the United Kingdom where the executive power possesses in principle far-reaching instruments of influence – taking just the law on the books relating to the independence of courts, neither of these countries would qualify for EU membership – but does not exercise them because "this is not done". However, such an ethos requires from political decision-makers self-restraint which is the one thing that political leaders in post-socialist countries lack. The deficiencies of the post-socialist political culture affect the outer independence of the courts, the system does not have any internalized brakes, checks and balances.

4.2.2   Inner Independence

The lack of inner independence of the judges is a problem typical of the new members. Inner independence is the willingness of the individual judge to decide only on the basis of the law as (s)he understands it, without listening to outside influences from the political sphere, wealthy parties or superior judges. This requires judges who are at the same time conscious of and critical about themselves.

In socialism, judges, next to notaries and, arguably, advocates, were the legal profession with the lowest prestige and income. Good law graduates hardly chose that career. Most conflicts of some social, economic or political relevance were decided by other forums so that courts and judges were left with petty civil and family matters[42] – and the vast area of criminal prosecution. Lawyers were educated not to question the state and political decisions and to apply the law verbatim. Passive, timid and overly obedient judges were system-compliant in a socialist state with its other mechanisms of handling conflicts.

The problem in the new Member States is that this type of judge continues to dominate. The old judges have educated their young colleagues joining the judicial service into this mentality. This was not too difficult because legal education has not been reformed after 1990 but continues the old forms of teaching the text but not the interpretation or spirit of the law. Furthermore, salaries and prestige of the judicial profession have risen but slowly, causing a counterselection in the recruitment of new judges. The judicial service of many new Member States still tends to attract mediocre rather than good law graduates. Many of these judges are aware of their deficient qualification, which contributes to their lack of inner independence.

---

[42]   Partial exceptions were Hungary and Yugoslavia since the 1960s and Poland since the 1980s.

As a result, many judges in the new Member States to this very day idolize the state (which is a problem especially for administrative judges[43]) and never question the legislator, apply the law textually instead of interpreting it adequately, shy away from material decisions and take refuge to excessive formalism and allowing parties to prolong procedures *ad infinitum*.[44] It is therefore easy for governments such as in Hungary or Poland to intimidate such judges, and governments everywhere to manipulate them ideologically, e.g. with nationalist rhetoric.

The lower the court the stronger is this problem. Higher judges are better qualified and less prone to belong to this type of 'authoritarian judge' but they, too, often lack a critical distance towards the state. Younger judges are less often 'authoritarian' than their older colleagues but find it difficult to assert themselves in the overall 'authoritarian' atmosphere in the courts. One problem has become better. In the two decades after the end of socialism, many judges did not accept professional criticism, insisting on their independence which allegedly immunized them from any, even scholarly criticism of their decisions. By now, judges and legal science have entered into a dialogue of discussing individual decisions under professional aspects.

The main reason for the survival of the 'authoritarian judge' is the lack of exchange of judicial staff after 1990. Courts were not in the centre of the socialist system. Therefore, they stood at the periphery of reform efforts during and after the post-socialist transition. The inner independence of judges is best where the old judges were examined and eventually dismissed after 1990: in Czechoslovakia/Czech Republic by way of lustration and in the Baltic states in the course of the decolonisation of their state apparatuses. These dismissals made way for new young and often well-educated lawyers and allowed gradually a more rule-of-law type of judge to emerge.

5.   CONCLUSION

The justice system in most new members does not conform to rule-of-law standards. In order to achieve outer independence, it would be necessary to shield the courts from interferences of the political sphere which again would require politicians to exercise self-restraint, and from overall societal trends.

---

[43]   Küpper, 'Nach dem Ende des Sozialismus: Wie baut man eine Verwaltungs-gerichtsbarkeit auf?', in Küpper and Himmelreich (eds), *Rechtsstaat durch Verwaltungs- gerichtsbarkeit: Deutschland, Ukraine, Kasachstan* (Peter Lang 2022), 55-144.

[44]   For a detailed description see Uzelac, 'Survival of the Third Legal Tradition' (2010) 49 Supreme Court Law Review, 377-396.

The latter seems hardly possible. The most pressing problem, however, is the lack of inner independence of judges. A better education of young (and perhaps older) judges, combined with higher pay and prestige and with positive role models, may help. But we are talking decades here. In the short run, there is little hope that the standards of judicial independence and thus the rule of law will rise.

4. The Fall of the Rule of Law and Democracy in Hungary and the Complicity of the EU

Gábor Halmai

1. INTRODUCTION

Hungary has received international attention as one of the first and most thorough political transitions after 1989, which, due to the negotiated 'rule of law revolution',[1] provided all the institutional elements of liberal constitutional democracy: rule of law, checks and balances and guaranteed fundamental rights. The characteristic of system change that Hungary shared with other transitioning countries was that it had to establish an independent nation-state, a civil society, a private economy, and a democratic structure all together at the same time.[2] Plans for transforming the Stalin-inspired 1949 Rákosi Constitution into a 'rule of law' document were delineated in the National Roundtable Talks of 1989 by participants of the Opposition Roundtable and representatives of the state party. Afterwards, the illegitimate Parliament only rubberstamped the comprehensive amendment to the Constitution, which went into effect on 23 October 1990, the anniversary of the 1956 revolution.

Twenty years later the same country became the first, and probably the model case, of backsliding into an illiberal system dismantling the rule of law. Both Freedom House and the Varieties of Democracy Project have tracked Hungary

---

[1] See the term used by the first Constitutional Court in its decision 11/1992. (III. 5.) AB.

[2] The terms 'single' and 'dual' transitions are used by *Adam Przeworski*. See Przeworski, *Democracy and the Market: Political and Economic Reforms in Eastern Europe and Latin America* (CUP 1991). Later, *Claus Offe* broadened the scope of this debate by arguing that post-communist societies actually faced a triple transition, since many post-communist states were new or renewed nation-states. See Offe, *Varieties of Transition: The East European and East German Experience* (MIT Press 1997).

as it has passed from a 'consolidated' liberal democracy in 2010 into the status of a 'hybrid regime'[3] or an 'electoral autocracy'.[4] The 2020 Rule of Law Index of the World Justice Project[5] ranked Hungary last out of 24 selected countries of the European Union, the European Free Trade Association (EFTA), and North America. The country is no longer a constitutional democracy able to ensure a peaceful rotation of power. Why was the EU, whose foundation is the values of democracy and the rule of law, unable to intercept the process for one of its own members? Hungary's transition into an authoritarian state was first and foremost facilitated by willing autocrats and fragile domestic democratic institutions, including the disproportional election system and easy amendment rule of the constitution. But the EU has also failed to force its Member State to comply with its original admission criteria (Article 49 TEU). This calls for a strong democratic opposition in the country, but also for self-reflection from the EU that, despite being built on the values of democracy and the rule of law, was unable to intercept the rise of authoritarianism in Hungary.

The current Hungarian state of affairs was made possible by the governing Fidesz party's 2010 electoral victory. Due to the disproportional electoral system, Fidesz, with a slight majority of the votes, received two-thirds of the seats. This allowed them to enact a new constitution without the votes of the weak opposition parties. Hungary, not even a Republic in its name anymore, according to the new Fundamental Law and proudly announced by Prime Minister *Orbán*, became an 'illiberal state', which abolished all checks on the government's power, like the independence of the Constitutional Court or ordinary judiciary, and does not guarantee fundamental rights, such as freedom of the media or religious freedom.

In other words, although Hungary became a liberal democracy on an institutional level after 1989, the consolidation of the system on a behavioural level was always very fragile. If one considers liberalism as not merely a limit on the public power of the majority, but also as a concept that encompasses the constitutive precondition of democracy – the rule of law, checks and balances, and guaranteed fundamental rights – then Hungary is not a liberal democracy

---

³   Csaky, 'Nations in Transit 2020 Dropping the Democratic Façade' (2020), Freedom House <https://freedomhouse.org/report/nations-transit/2020/dropping-democratic-facade> accessed 1 December 2023.

⁴   See the reports at <https://v-dem.net/publications/democracy-reports/> accessed 1 December 2023.

⁵   Andersen et al., 'Rule of Law Index 2020' (2020), World Justice Project <https://worldjusticeproject.org/sites/default/files/documents/WJP-ROLI-2020-Online_0.pdf> accessed 1 December 2023.

anymore. Ever since the victory of the current governing party, almost all public power is in the hands of the representatives of one party.

2.   THE RULE OF LAW 'COUNTER-REVOLUTION' OF 2010

Before the 2010 elections, most voters had grown dissatisfied not only with the government, but also with the transition itself, more than in any other East Central European country.[6] Fidesz fed these sentiments by claiming that there had been no real transitions in 1989–1990, and that the previous nomenklatura had merely converted its lost political power into economic influence, pointing to the previous two prime ministers of the Socialist Party, both of whom became rich after the transition owing to privatization. The populism of the Fidesz party was directed against all elites, including the elites who designed the 1989 constitutional system (in which Fidesz had also participated), claiming that it was time for a new revolution. That is why *Viktor Orbán*, the head of Fidesz, characterized the results of the 2010 elections as a "revolution of the ballot boxes." His intention with this revolution was to eliminate any kind of checks and balances and even the parliamentary rotation of governing parties. In the September 2009 speech, *Orbán* predicted that there was "a real chance that politics in Hungary will no longer be defined by a dualist power space. Instead, a large governing party will emerge in the center of the political stage [that] will be able to formulate national policy, not through constant debates, but through a natural representation of interests." *Orbán's* vision for a new constitutional order – one in which his political party occupies the centre stage of Hungarian political life and puts an end to debates over values – has now been entrenched in a new constitution, entered into force in April 2011.

Before 1 January 2012, when the new constitution came into effect, the Hungarian Parliament had been preparing a blizzard of so-called cardinal – or super-majority – laws, changing the shape of virtually every political institution in Hungary and making the guarantee of constitutional rights less secure. These legal regulations affect the rights on freedom of information, prosecutions, nationalities, family protections, the independence of the judiciary, the status of churches, functioning of the Constitutional Court and elections to Parliament. In the last days of 2011, the Parliament also enacted the so-called

---

[6]   In 2009, 51% of Hungarians disagreed with the statement that they are better off since the transition, and only 30% claimed improvements. In Poland, 14% and 23% in the Czech Republic reported worsening conditions, and 70% and 75%, respectively, perceived improvement. See European Commission, 'Eurobarometer 71, Public Opinion in the European Union Spring 2009' (2009).

Transitory Provision to the Fundamental Law, which claimed constitutional status and partly supplemented the new Constitution even before it went into effect. These new regulations had a bad impact on the political independence of state institutions, on the transparency of law making and on the future of human rights in Hungary.

On 11 March 2013 the Hungarian Parliament added the Fourth Amendment to the country's 2011 constitution, re-enacting a number of controversial provisions that had been annulled by the Constitutional Court. Requests were rebuffing by the European Union, the Council of Europe and the US government that urged the government to seek the opinion of the Venice Commission before bringing the amendment into force. The most alarming change concerning the Constitutional Court is that the amendment annuls all Court decisions prior to when the Fundamental Law entered into force. At one level, this makes sense: old constitution = old decisions; new constitution = new decisions. But the Constitutional Court had already worked out a sensible new rule for the constitutional transition by deciding that in those cases where the terminology of the old and new constitutions were substantially the same, prior decisions of the Court would still be valid and could still be applied. In cases, where the new constitution was substantially different from the old one, previous decisions would no longer be used. Constitutional rights are key provisions that are the same in the old and new constitutions – which means that, practically speaking, the Fourth Amendment annuls primarily the decisions that defined and protected constitutional rights and harmonized domestic rights protection to comply with European human rights law. With the removal of these fundamental Constitutional Court decisions, the government has undermined legal certainty with respect to the protection of constitutional rights in Hungary. These moves renewed serious doubts about the state of liberal constitutionalism in Hungary and Hungary's compliance with its international commitments under the Treaties of the European Union and the European Convention on Human Rights.

In April 2014, Fidesz, with 44.5% of the party-list votes, won the elections again, and due to 'undue advantages' for the governing party, provided by the amendment to the electoral system, secured another two-thirds majority. In early 2015 Fidesz lost its two-thirds majority as a consequence of mid-term elections in two constituencies, but they regained it after the April 2018 elections.

3. EU's TRADITIONAL TOOLS TO COPE WITH THE RULE OF LAW SITUATION IN HUNGARY

3.1 The Tavares Report: the Not Triggered Rule of Law Framework

This new constitutional system was the subject of a report for the European Parliament prepared by its Committee on Civil Liberties, Justice and Home Affairs (LIBE), adopted on 3 July 2013.[7] With its acceptance of the Tavares Report (named after *Rui Tavares*, a Portuguese MEP at that time) the European Parliament has called for a new framework for enforcing the principles of Article 2 TEU. The report calls on the European Commission to institutionalize a new system of monitoring and assessment.

The first reaction of the Hungarian government was not a sign of willingness to comply with the recommendations of the report, but rather a harsh rejection. Two days after the European Parliament adopted the report in its plenary session, the Hungarian Parliament adopted Resolution 69/2013 on "the equal treatment due to Hungary". The document is written in first person plural as an anti-European manifesto on behalf of all Hungarians: "We, Hungarians, do not want a Europe any longer where freedom is limited and not widened. We do not want a Europe any longer where the Greater abuses his power, where national sovereignty is violated and where the Smaller has to respect the Greater. We have had enough of dictatorship after 40 years behind the iron curtain." The resolution argues that the European Parliament exceeded its jurisdiction by passing the report, and creating institutions that violate Hungary's sovereignty as guaranteed in the TEU. The Hungarian text also points out that behind this abuse of power there are business interests, which were violated by the Hungarian government by reducing the costs of energy paid by families, which could undermine the interest of many European companies which for years have gained extra profits from their monopoly in Hungary. In its conclusion, the Hungarian Parliament calls on the Hungarian government "not to cede to the pressure of the European Union, not to let the nation's rights guaranteed in the fundamental treaty be violated, and to continue the politics of improving life for Hungarian families". These words very much reflect the Orbán-government's view of 'national freedom', the liberty of the state (or the nation) to determine its own laws: "This is why we are

---

[7] European Parliament, Resolution (EU) of 3 July 2013 on the situation of fundamental rights: standards and practices in Hungary (pursuant to the European Parliament resolution of 16 February 2012), 2012/2130(INI) [2013] OJ C 75.

writing our own constitution ... And we don't want any unsolicited help from strangers who are keen to guide us ... Hungary must turn on its own axis".[8]

Encouraged by the Tavares report, then-Commission President Barroso also proposed a European mechanism to be "activated as in situations where there is a serious, systemic risk to the Rule of Law".[9] Commission Vice-President Reding, too, announced that the Commission would present a new policy communication.[10]

Due to the pressure, the Hungarian government finally made some cosmetic changes to its Fundamental Law, doing little to address concerns set out by the European Parliament. The changes left in place provisions that undermine the rule of law and weaken human rights protections. The Hungarian Parliament, with a majority of its members from the governing party, adopted the Fifth Amendment on 16 September 2013. The government's reasoning states that the amendment aims to "finish the constitutional debates at international forum" (meaning the European Union). A statement from the Prime Minister's Office said: "The government wants to do away with those... problems which have served as an excuse for attacks on Hungary." But this minor political concession does not really mean that the Hungarian government demonstrated respect for the formal rule of law, as some commentators rightly argue.[11]

As none of the suggested elements have worked effectively in the case of Hungary, the European Commission proposed a new EU framework to the European Parliament and the Council to strengthen the rule of law in the Member States.[12] This framework is supposed to be complementary to Article

---

[8]   For the original, Hungarian-language text of Orbán's speech, entitled Nem leszünk gyarmat! [We won't be a colony anymore!], see Orbán, speech "Nem leszünk gyarmat!" (15 March 2012), <http://www.miniszterelnok.hu/beszed/nem _leszunk_gyarmat> accessed 1 December 2023. The English-language translation of excerpts from Orbán's speech was made available by Hungarian officials, see e.g. Spiegel, "The EU Soviet? Barroso takes on Orban", (2012), Financial Times: Brussels Blog, <http://blogs.ft.com/brusselsblog/2012/03/the-eu-soviet-barroso -takes-on-hungarys-orban/?catid=147&SID=google#axzz1qDsigFtC> accessed 1 December 2023.

[9]   European Parliament, Speech (EU), 13/684 Barroso, 'State of the Union address 2013' (1 September 2013).

[10]   European Parliament, Speech (EU), 13/677 Reding, 'The EU and the Rule of Law – What Next?' (4 September 2013).

[11]   von Bogdandy, 'How to Protect European Values in the Polish Constitutional Crisis' (2016) Verfassungsblog, <https://verfassungsblog.de/how-to-protect-euro pean-values-in-the-polish-constitutional-crisis/> accessed 1 December 2023.

[12]   European Commission, 'A new EU Framework to strengthen the Rule of Law', COM(2014) 158 final.

7 TEU and the formal infringement procedure under Article 258 TFEU, which the Commission can launch if a Member State fails to implement a solution to clarify and improve the suspected violation of EU law. As the Hungarian case has shown, infringement actions are usually too narrow to address the structural problem which persistently noncompliant Member States pose. This happened when Hungary suddenly lowered the retirement age of judges and removed from office the most senior ten percent of the judiciary, including many court presidents and members of the Supreme Court. The European Commission brought an infringement action, claiming age discrimination. The European Court of Justice in *Commission v. Hungary* established the violation of EU law,[13] but unfortunately the decision was not able to reinstate the dismissed judges into their original positions, nor could it stop the Hungarian government from further seriously undermining the independence of the judiciary and weakening other checks and balances with its constitutional reforms. Even though the Commission formulated the petition, the ECJ apparently wanted to stay away from Hungarian internal politics, or had an extremely conservative reading of EU competences and legal bases, merely enforcing the existing EU law rather than politically evaluating the constitutional framework of a Member State.[14] This was the reason that *Kim Lane Scheppele* suggested to reframe the ordinary infringement procedure to enforce the basic values of Article 2 through a systemic infringement action.[15]

The new framework allowed the Commission to enter into a dialogue with the Member State concerned to prevent fundamental threats to the rule of law. This new framework can best be described as a 'pre-Article 7 procedure', since it establishes an early warning tool to tackle threats to the rule of law, and allows the Commission to enter into a structured dialogue with the Member State concerned, in order to find solutions before the existing legal mechanisms set out in Article 7 are used. The Framework process is designed as a three-step procedure. First, the Commission makes an assessment of the situation in the member country, collecting information and evaluating whether there is a systemic threat to the rule of law. Second, if a systemic threat is found to exist, the Commission makes recommendations to the member country about how to

---

[13]   ECJ, Case C-286/12, *Commission v. Hungary*, EU:C:2012:687.

[14]   For the detailed facts of the case and the assessment of the ECJ judgment see Halmai, 'The Case of the Retirement Age of Hungarian Judges' in Nicola and Davies (eds), *EU Law Stories* (CUP 2017), 471-488.

[15]   Scheppele, 'EU can still block Hungary's veto on Polish sanctions' (2016) Politico <https://www.politico.eu/article/eu-can-still-block-hungarys-orban-veto-on-polish-pis-sanctions/> accessed 1 December 2023.

resolve the issue. Third, the Commission monitors the response of the member country to the Commission's recommendations.

The first step to use the new Rule of Law Framework was not taken against Hungary, but against Poland in early January 2016, and also Article 7 was triggered by the European Commission already in December 2017, even though the backsliding in Poland has only started in 2016, and has not yet reached the level of Hungary. The main reason for this difference was that the governing Fidesz party delivers votes to the European People's Party (EPP), the largest fraction at EP, while the Polish governing party, PiS belongs to the smaller fraction of the European Conservatives and Reformists.[16]

In June 2015, the European Parliament passed a resolution condemning *Viktor Orbán*'s statement on the reintroduction of the death penalty in Hungary and his anti-migration political campaign, and called on the Commission to launch the Rule of Law Framework procedure against Hungary.[17] But the Commission ultimately refused to launch the procedure with the argument that although the situation in Hungary raised concerns, there was no systemic threat to the rule of law, democracy and human rights.[18]

In December 2015, after the Hungarian Parliament in July and September enacted a series of anti-European and anti-rule of law immigration laws,[19] as a reaction to the refugee crisis, the European Parliament again voted on a resolution calling on the European Commission to launch the Rule of Law Framework. The Commission continued to use the usual method of infringement actions, finding the Hungarian legislation in some instances to be incompatible with EU law (specifically, the recast Asylum Procedures Directive 2013/32/EU) and the Directive 2010/64/EU on the right to interpre-

---

[16] See this conclusion in Kelemen, 'Europe's Other Democratic Deficit: National Authoritarianism in Europe's Democratic Union' (207) 52 Government and Opposition, 211-238.

[17] European Parliament, Press release (EU), "Hungary: MEPs condemn Orbán's death penalty statements and migration survey", 10 June 2015, <https://www.europarl.europa.eu/news/en/press-room/20150605IPR63112/hungary-meps-condemn-orban-s-death-penalty-statements-and-migration-survey> accessed 1 December 2023.

[18] European Parliament, Press release (EU), "Hungary: no systemic threat to democracy, says Commission, but concerns remain", 2 December 2015, <https://www.europarl.europa.eu/news/en/press-room/20151201IPR05554/hungary-no-systemic-threat-to-democracy-says-commission-but-concerns-remain> accessed 1 December 2023.

[19] Halmai, 'The Invalid Anti-Migrant Referendum in Hungary' (2016), Verfassungsblog, <https://verfassungsblog.de/hungarys-anti-european-immigration-laws/> accessed 1 December 2023.

tation and translation in criminal proceedings.[20] This was the first time that the Commission has alleged a violation of the Charter of Fundamental Rights in an infringement action.[21]

---

[20] Regarding the asylum procedures, the Commission was concerned that there was no possibility to refer to new facts and circumstances in the context of appeals and that Hungary was not automatically suspending decisions in case of appeals – effectively forcing applicants to leave the territory before the time limit for lodging an appeal expired, or before an appeal has been heard. Regarding rights to translation and interpretation, the Commission was concerned that the Hungarian law fast-tracked criminal proceedings for irregular border crossings, which did not respect provisions of the Directive on the right to interpretation and translation in criminal proceedings, which ensures that every suspect or accused person who does not understand the language of the proceedings is provided with a written translation of all essential documents, including any judgments. Also, the Commission expressed its concerns about the fundamental right to an effective remedy and a fair trial under Article 47 EUCFR. There were concerns about the fact that under the new Hungarian law dealing with the judicial review of decisions, in the event that an asylum application is rejected, a personal hearing of the applicant is optional. The fact that judicial decisions taken by court secretaries (a sub-judicial level) that lack judicial independence also seems to be in breach of the Asylum Procedures Directive and Article 47 of the Charter. European Commission, Press release IP 15/5228, 'Commission opens infringement procedure against Hungary concerning its asylum law', 10 December 2015, <http://europa.eu/rapid/press-release_IP-15 -6228_en.htm.> accessed 1 December 2023.

[21] See this option as one of three scenarios using the Charter as a treaty obligation in Hoffmeister, 'Enforcing the EU Charter of Fundamental Rights in Member States: How Far are Rome, Budapest and Bucharest from Brussels?' in von Bogdandy and Sonnevend (eds), *Constitutional Crisis in the European Constitutional Area. Theory, Law and Politics in Hungary and Romania* (Hart Publishing 2015). According to *Hoffmeister* in the first scenario, a Charter right is further specified by EU secondary law. For example, Article 8 of the Charter on the protection of personal data lies at the heart of Directive 95/46/EC which largely harmonizes the rules on data protection in Europe. In the second scenario, the Charter right is not underpinned by specific EU legislation. That is the case, for example, with Article 10(1) of the Charter on the freedom of thought, conscience and religion. According to *Armin von Bogdandy* and his colleagues, national courts could also bring grave violations of Charter rights, such as freedom of the media in Article 11 to the attention of the CJEU by invoking a breach of the fundamental status of Union citizenship in conjunction with core human rights protected under Article 2 TEU. The idea behind this proposal is that the EU and Members States can have an interest in protecting EU citizens within a given member state. See von Bogdandy et al., 'A Rescue Package for EU Fundamental Rights - Illustrated with Reference to the Example of Media Freedom' (2012) Verfassungsblog, <http://

3.2   The Sargentini Report: Triggering the Article 7 Procedure

After many years of hesitation, on 12 September 2018 the European Parliament
– the first time ever – launched Article 7 TEU proceedings against a Member
State's government. The MEPs by 448 votes for to 197 against and with 48
abstentions adopted the report prepared by *Judith Sargentini* denouncing the
many violations of EU values by *Viktor Orbán*'s government. With the adoption of the Sargentini report the unequal treatment of the two rogue Member
States had changed, mostly due to the fact that 115 out of the 218 MEPs of
EPP also voted against the *Orbán* government. The change of EPP's view on
Orbán has been foreseen after the unexpected announcement of EPP's leader,
Manfred Weber, who was considered earlier as one of the main supporters
of *Orbán*, to support the report. After the parliamentary vote *Weber* even
challenged leaders of the Member States in the Council to take a stance on
Orbán's domestic policies, after MEPs "did their job" in triggering the Article
7 process.[22]

In his speech, prior to the vote, *Orbán* threatened the then European
Parliament with a new composition after the 2019 elections, when anti-migrant
populist parties can even have the lead, and form the European Commission:
"We need a new European Commission that is committed to the defence of
Europe's borders."[23] This threat must have been one of the reasons for the
majority of EPP that despite their vote for the Sargentini report they did not
want to kick out *Orbán's* Fidesz from the party family before the 2019 parliamentary elections. Even though the EP elections did not bring the expected
victory of the populists, and EPP at least suspended Fidesz' membership, the
commitment of the newly elected European institutions[24] did not make it more
likely that the Council, with the necessary four fifths majority, will follow

---

verfassungsblog.de/ein-rettungsschirm-fr-europische-grundrechte/> accessed 1
December 2023. The following debate initiated by the editors of the piece featured
comments by *Michaela Hailbronner, Daniel Halberstam, Dimitry Kochenov,
Mattias Kumm, Peter Lindseth, Anna Katharina Mangold, Daniel Thym, Wojciech
Sadurski, Pál Sonnevend, Renáta Uitz* and *Antje Wiener.*

[22]   Khan, 'Weber challenges European leaders over Hungarian rights' (2018)
Financial Times, <https://www.ft.com/content/e353ba68-b993-11e8-94b2-17176f
bf93f5> accessed 1 December 2023.

[23]   Ibid.

[24]   Besides the fact that *Frans Timmermans*, who was instrumental to trigger
Article 7 against both Poland and Hungary, did not get the rule of law portfo-
lio in the current Commission, in her first speech in the European Parliament
Commission President *Ursula von der Leyen* stated regarding these procedures that
"We must all learn that full rule of law is always our goal, but nobody's perfect."

the proposal of the Parliament by determining the existence of a clear risk of a serious breach by Hungary of the values on which the Union is founded. The corrective arm of Article 7, which can lead to sanctions against the Member State, including the suspension of the voting rights of the representative of that government in the Council, can even be vetoed by any Member State.[25]

This scepticism has been confirmed by the fact that the first Council hearing occurred on 16 September 2019, more than one year after the parliamentary decision thanks to the Finnish presidency. The Parliament was denied the opportunity to present its reasoned proposal with the Commission being asked instead to provide a factual update on the relevant infringement procedures against Hungary.

But this parliamentary resolution came too late, several years after the *Orbán* government's actions already represented a "clear risk of a serious breach of the values on which the Union is founded". Launching Article 7 meant also too little, because besides the important political function of naming and shaming Hungary as a violator of EU values, the chances to reach the corrective arm of the procedure are extremely low.[26] Hence, one can argue that instead of Article 7 alternative means from the toolkits of the EU may be more effective.[27] Infringement actions as alternatives did not really work so far in the case of Hungary, but cutting off EU structural funds for regional development or other

---

See Rettmann, 'Von der Leyen signals soft touch on migrants, rule of law' (2019), EUobserver, <https://euobserver.com/news/145504> accessed 1 December 2023.

[25] The votes on the Sargentini report have shown that besides the Polish government, which already committed itself to veto any possible sanctions against Hungary, there were other governments, which would be reluctant to vote for sanctions, for instance that of the UK.

[26] See the same assessment of the vote by Carrera and Bárd, 'The European Parliament Vote on Article 7 TEU against the Hungarian government, Too Late, Too Little, Too Political?' (2018), CEPS, <https://www.ceps.eu/publications/euro pea n-parliament-vote-article-7-teu-against-hungarian-government-too-late-too-little> accessed 1 December 2023.

[27] *Klaus Bachmann* argues for using alternative tools instead of Article 7. See Bachmann, 'Beyond the Spectacle: The European Parliament's Article 7 TEU Decision on Hungary' (2018) Verfassungsblog, <https://verfassungsblog.de/beyond -the-spectacle-the-european-parliaments-article-7-teu-decision-on-hungary/> accessed 1 December 2023.

forms of assistance as a value conditionality approach[28] have just started to be implemented.[29]

4.   VALUE CONDITIONALITY AS A NEW INSTRUMENT – WITH COMPROMISES

During the EU's long and mostly unsuccessful struggle to bring *Viktor Orbán*'s government into compliance since he came to power in 2010, occasionally the European Commission has put on hold some EU funding to Hungary. This happened in 2013 after the Hungarian Parliament enacted the Fourth Amendment to the new Fundamental Law, finally dismantling the Constitutional Court and other checks and balances on governmental power. But the official reason for this suspension was not the grave violation of the rule of law, but some alleged irregularities in the way development subsidies had been managed by Budapest.[30]

Real financial sanctions were proposed against Hungary (and Poland) in mid-August 2016 by two German MEPs. *Ingeborg Grässle*, a Christian-Democrat MEP and the head of the Parliament's committee on budgetary control suggested: "There needs to be stronger rules for the disbursement of funds … Countries that don't respect EU laws, or countries that don't participate enough in the resettlement of migrants or the registration of refugees, should be deprived of funds." Vice-President of the Parliament, the Liberal *Alexander Graf Lambsdorff*, singled out Poland and Hungary as net recipients of EU funds that have been flouting EU values by saying: "The federal government must ensure, when the EU budget is reviewed this

---

[28]   For a detailed analysis of this possibility see Halmai, 'The Possibility and Desirability of Rule of Law Conditionality' (2019) 11 Hague Journal on the Rule of Law, 171-188.

[29]   Council, Press release, 'Rule of law conditionality mechanism: Council decides to suspend EUR 6.3 billion given only partial remedial action by Hungary', 12 December 2022, <https://www.consilium.europa.eu/en/press/press-releases/2022/12/12/rule-of-law-conditionality-mechanism/> accessed 1 December 2023. See some examples of an emerging literature about the topic: Pohjankoski, 'Of Carrots and Sticks: Constitutional Limits to Rule-of-Law Conditionality', in Rosas, Raitio and Pohjankoski (eds), *The Rule of Law's Anatomy in the EU* (Hart Publishing 2023), 157-170, and Miklóssy, 'Tackling EU Conditionality with the Hungarian Legal Manoeuvres', in Rosas, Raitio and Pohjankoski (eds), *The Rule of Law's Anatomy in the EU* (Hart Publishing 2023), 171-187.

[30]   'Brussels suspends funding to Hungary over alleged irregularities' (2013) Financial Times, <https://www.ft.com/content/9b85c228-04f1-11e3-9e71-00144f eab7de> accessed 1 December 2023.

fall, that EU countries that are net recipients, such as Poland and Hungary, show more solidarity in [on] the issue of refugees and also respect European values."[31] Similarly, then-Austrian Chancellor, *Christian Kern* said that "If countries continue to duck away from resolving the issue of migration, they will no longer be able to receive net payments of billions from Brussels," arguing that "solidarity is not a one-way street."[32] Also, French presidential candidate *Emmanuel Macron* stated that "You cannot have a European Union which argues over every single decimal place on the issue of budgets with each country, and which, when you have an EU member which acts like Poland or Hungary on issues linked to universities and learning, or refugees, or fundamental values, decides to do nothing."[33] *Vivian Reding*, MEP and former EU Commissioner for justice and fundamental rights declared: "This would be the most effective way to influence the behaviour of a government like the Polish one – making a link with the money. It's the only thing they understand."[34]

---

[31] Schiltz, 'Deutschland ist Zahlmeister in Europa' (2016) Die Welt, <http://www.welt.de/politik/ausland/article157586134/Deutschland-ist-Zahlmeister-in-Europa.html> accessed 1 December 2023. Hungary has received enormous EU cohesion funds sums during the period *Orbán* has been in power. The country has received as much as 6-7% of its GDP as inflows from the various cohesion and structural funds of the Union since 2010. This has generated an average GDP growth of around 3%, which according to a KPMG study commissioned by the government, would have been zero without the EU transfers. This means that without the cohesion and structural fund transfers, Hungary would have no autonomous economic growth. See Pogátsa, 'The Political Economy of Illiberal Democracy' (2017) Social Europe, <https://www.socialeurope.eu/the-political-economy-of-illiberal-democracy> accessed 1 December 2023. That is why it is nothing but political propaganda when *Viktor Orbán* claims that Hungary does not need EU money. See his interview in the Hungarian Public Radio: Orbán, 'Magyarország nincs rászorulva senkinek a pénzére' (22 December 2017), <http://hvg.hu/gazdasag/20171222_orban_magyarorszag_nincs_raszorulva_senkinek_a_penzere> accessed 1 December 2023.
[32] 'Austria calls for less money for EU states opposing refugee distribution' (2017) Deutsche Welle, <http://www.dw.com/en/austria-calls-for-less-money-for-eu-states-opposing-refugee-distribution/a-37848662>, accessed 1 December 2023.
[33] Bertrand, 'France's Macron wants sanctions on Poland, others, for violating EU principles' (2017) Euronews, <http://www.euronews.com/2017/04/28/france-s-macron-wants-sanctions-on-poland-others-for-violating-eu-principles> accessed 1 December 2023.
[34] Stearns, 'Europe's Eastern Rebels Expose Next Fault Line for EU Leaders' (2017) Bloomberg, <https://www.bloomberg.com/news/articles/2017-07-30/europe-s-eastern-rebels-expose-next-fault-line-for-eu-leaders> accessed 1 December 2023.

Gajus Scheltema, then-ambassador of the Netherlands to Hungary, referring to the Hungarian government in an interview claimed: "The argument over what happens with our money is indeed growing ever fiercer. We can't finance corruption, and we can't keep a corrupt regime alive."[35]

First-hand proof of governmental corruption, also mentioned in the Sargentini report, has been provided by OLAF, the EU's anti-fraud office, following an investigation in Hungary, which found serious irregularities related to street-lighting contracts awarded to a company that had been owned by *Orbán's* son-in-law, *István Tiborcz*. OLAF has called on the European Commission to claw back more than EUR 40 million of EU funds spent on lighting projects.[36] But since Hungary was among the eight Member States that declined to take part in the EU prosecution service, which was created in 2017, the criminal investigation of the matters depends on the Hungarian prosecutor's office, led by Fidesz loyalist. Hence, one obvious measure would be to oblige Hungary to join the EU prosecutor service if it wants to continue to receive EU funds.

In 2017 the European Parliament linked the monitoring of EU funds in Hungary with the government's disrespect of EU values and policies, for instance on migration and refugees. After a debate on Hungary at the plenary session on 26 April 2017, the Parliament stated in a resolution that "recent developments in Hungary have led to a serious deterioration in the rule of law, democracy and fundamental rights, which is testing the EU's ability to defend its founding values".[37] Therefore, the resolution calls for: "a) the launching of Article 7(1). MEPs instruct the LIBE Committee to draw up a formal resolution for a plenary vote, b) the Hungarian Government to repeal laws tightening

---

[35] <http://hungarianspectrum.org/2017/08/31/ambassador-scheltema-we-mustnt-keep-a-corrupt-regime-alive/> accessed 1 December 2023.

[36] Rankin, 'Orbán allies could use EU as cash register, MEPs say' (2018) The Guardian, <https://www.theguardian.com/world/2018/feb/12/orban-allies-could-use-eu-as-cash-register-meps-say> accessed 1 December 2023.

[37] The resolution was adopted by 393 votes to 221 with 64 abstentions, which means some members of European Peoples Party (EPP), the party group of Fidesz, did not vote against the resolution. *Manfred Weber*, the president of the EPP-group also harshly criticized the Lex CEU. According to its press-release "the EPP wants the CEU to remain open, deadlines suspended and dialogue with the US to begin". The EPP also stressed that "NGOs are an integral part of any healthy democracy, that they represent the civil society and that they must be respected". See EPP, Press release, 'Prime Minister Orbán to comply with EU laws and EPP values following meeting with EPP Presidency', 29 April 2017, <http://www.epp.eu/press-releases/prime-minister-orban-to-comply-with-eu-laws-and-epp-values-following-meeting-with-epp-presidency/> accessed 1 December 2023.

rules against asylum-seekers and non-governmental organizations, and to reach an agreement with US authorities, making it possible for the Central European University to remain in Budapest as a free institution, and finally c) the European Commission to strictly monitor the use of EU funds by the Hungarian Government".[38] The Commission's Reflection Paper on the Future of EU Finances, published on 28 June 2017, states: "Respect for the rule of law is important for European citizens, but also for business initiative, innovation and investment, which will flourish most where the legal and institutional framework adheres fully to the common values of the Union. There is hence a clear relationship between the rule of law and an efficient implementation of the private and public investments supported by the EU budget."[39]

The German Government went even further regarding the latter call of the Parliament by suggesting to link receipt of EU cohesion funds to respect for democratic principles.[40] The proposal was drafted explicitly with the situation in Poland in mind, as it has been allocated a total of EUR 86 billion from various EU cohesion funds for the period 2014–2020 and would, under normal circumstances, expect substantial funds in the next budget cycle as well.[41] Germany, together with Austria and Italy, has also repeatedly argued that spending conditionality should be used to discourage Member States' non-compliance with the EU migration and asylum acquis, in particular with the Council's refugee relocation plan.[42]

---

[38] European Parliament, Press release, 'Fundamental rights in Hungary: MEPs call for triggering Article 7' (17 May 2017), <http:// www.europarl.europa.eu/ news/ en/ press -room/ 20170511IPR74350/ fundamental -rights -in -hungary -meps -call-for-triggering-article-7> accessed 1 December 2023.

[39] European Commission, 'Reflection Paper on the Future of EU Finances', COM(2017) 358 final.

[40] Eder, 'Berlin looks into freezing funds for EU rule-breakers' (2017) Politico, <http://www.politico.eu/article/poland-rule-of-law-europe-germany-berlin-looks -into-freezing-funds-for-eu-rule-breakers/> accessed 1 December 2023.

[41] See e.g. the data available here: European Commission, '2014-2020 Cohesion Policy Overview', <https:// cohesiondata .ec .europa .eu/ > accessed 1 December 2023. Poland has for instance been allocated ESIF funding of EUR 86 billion representing an average of EUR 2,265 per person over the period 2014-2020. See Pech and Scheppele, 'Rule of Law Backsliding in the EU: Learning from Past and Present Failures to Prevent Illiberal Regimes from Consolidating within the EU' (2017) 19 Cambridge Yearbook of European Legal Studies, 3-47.

[42] AFP, 'Germany supports cutting EU funds to countries that refuse refugee quotas' (2015) Business Insider, <https://www.businessinsider.com/afp-germany -backs-cutting-eu-funds-to-states-that-refuse-refugee-quotas-2015-9> accessed 1 December 2023; Wintour, 'Austria Threatens EU Funding Cuts over Hungary's Hard Line on Refugees' (2017) The Guardian, <https:// www .theguardian .com/

Also *Günther Öttinger*, the German budget commissioner of the former European Commission, said that EU funds could become conditional after 2020, depending on the respect for the rule of law.[43] Similarly, Commissioner *Jourová* argued for such a new conditionality requirement: "We need to ensure that EU funds bring a positive impact and contribute more generally to promote the EU's fundamental rights and values. That is why I intend to explore the possibility to strengthen the 'fundamental rights and values conditionality' of EU funding to complement the existing legal obligations of Member States to ensure the respect of the Charter when implementing EU funds."[44] In October 2017, *Jourová* linked again EU funds to rule of law, by saying that "[w]e need to make better use of EU funds for upholding the rule of law. ... In my personal view we should consider creating stronger conditionality between the rule of law and the cohesion funds."[45] On 23 November 2017, *Hans Eichel*, co-founder and former chairman of G20, former Minister of Finance of Germany, and *Pascal Lamy*, former European Commissioner, also on behalf of former European Commissioners *Franz Fischler* and *Yannis Peleokrassas* sent an open letter to *Jean-Claude Juncker*, then President of the European Commission, asking the European Commission to temporarily suspend payment of all EU funding to Hungary, with the exception of funding provided directly by the Commission, i.e. without the intermediary role of the Hungarian government.[46]

Similarly, a policy paper of the Centre for European Reform suggests that for more serious breaches, the Commission could suspend disbursement of funds, and step up monitoring and verification. In doing so, it would have to

---

world/ 2017/ mar/ 08/ austria -calls -for -less -funding -for -eu -countries -refusing -refugees> accessed 1 December 2023; Oliphant, 'Italy Threatens Hungary: EU Countries Who Reject Migrant Quota Should Have Funding Cut' (2016) Daily Express, <accessed 1 December 2023.https:// www .express .co .uk/ news/ world/ 720470/ Funding -cut -European -Union -Hungary -REJECT -migrant -quota -Italy -Matteo-Renzi> accessed 1 December 2023.

[43]   Maurice, 'Commission hints at political conditions for EU funds' (2017) EUobserver, <https://euobserver.com/institutional/138063>, accessed 1 December 2023.

[44]   European Commission, Speech 17/403 Jourová, '10 years of the EU Fundamental Rights Agency: a call to action in defence of fundamental rights, democracy and the rule of law' (28 February 2017).

[45]   Zalan, 'Justice commissioner links EU funds to "rule of law"' (2017) EU observer, <https://euobserver.com/political/139720> accessed 1 December 2023.

[46]   <http://hungarianspectrum.org/2017/11/28/open-letter-to-jean-claude-juncker/> accessed 1 December 2023.

ensure that the poorer regions and vulnerable groups did not suffer disproportionate harm from measures designed to have an impact on governments
that ignore EU values and the rule of law. Funding, the Centre recommends,
could be directed away from governments and go directly to enterprises or be
disbursed by civil society organizations[47] – if there are still such independent
organizations, I would add.

On the other hand, former Commission President *Juncker* said that net
recipients of EU funds may resent being penalized financially for actions that
net contributors could carry out with impunity. Therefore, he expressed concerns about tying the rule of law to structural funds, which he claimed could
be "poison for the continent", and "divide the European Union".[48] Even after
the Commission decided to trigger the Article 7 (1) procedure against Poland,
which put the country on a path that could ultimately lead to sanctions, *Juncker*
said that he preferred that the EU and Poland hold "sensible discussions with
each other, without moving into threatening gestures."[49]

In mid-February 2018, the European Commission published its
Communication on a new, modern Multiannual Financial Framework for
a European Union that delivers efficiently on its priorities post-2020 as a contribution to the Informal Leaders' meeting.[50] The Communication points out
that "as part of the public debate, it has been suggested that the disbursement of
EU budget funds could be linked to the respect for the values set out in Article
2 of the EU Treaty and in particular to the state of the rule of law in Member
States". At the same time the German government has circulated a draft white
paper to other EU Member States proposing to link cohesion funds to respect
for EU solidarity principles.[51] Germany wants more of the EU's next multiannual budget to be tied to respect for core EU policies and values, including the

---

[47] Selih, Bond and Dolan, 'Can EU Funds Promote the Rule of Law in Europe?'
(2017) Centre for European Reform.

[48] Eder, 'Juncker: German plan to link funds and rules would be "poison"'
(2017) Politico, <http://www.politico.eu/article/juncker-german-plan-to-link-fu
nds-and-rules-would-be-poison/> accessed 1 December 2023.

[49] Mischke, 'Juncker rejects cutting EU funds to Poland' (2018) Politico,
<https:// www .politico .eu/ article/ eu -commission -president -jean -claude -juncker
-rejects-cutting-eu-funds-to-poland/> accessed 1 December 2023.

[50] European Commission, Press release IP 18/745, 'EU long-term budget
after 2020: European Commission sets out options – and their consequences'
(14 February 2018), <http:// europa .eu/ rapid/ press -release_IP -18 -745 _en .htm>
accessed 1 December 2023.

[51] Brunsden and Khan, 'Germany wants EU to reward states for taking migrants'
(21 February 2018) Financial Times, <https://www.ft.com/content/abb50 ada-166
4-11e8-9376-4a6390addb44> accessed 1 December 2023.

rule of law and migration. This plan would be a big departure from traditional uses of the structural funds, which have had a heavy focus on infrastructure projects as well as education and training for EU nationals. The Polish government attacked the plan, "because it could lead to limitation of member states' rights guarded by the EU Treaty".[52]

The usual argument against such kind of financial sanctions is that it would punish the people of Hungary (or Poland for that matter), instead of their leaders, pushing them further away from the EU, and into the arms of their illiberal governments.[53] Also, academic critics point out that the proposal, if implemented, could undermine the European citizens' union by leaving behind those citizens who have the misfortune to live in a members state with an authoritarian national government.[54] But why not consider the scenario that those regions and citizens taken hostage by their own elected officials, and who do not want to suffer due to the loss of EU funds because of their authoritarian leaders, will be emboldened to stand up against such governments, and vote them out of office, probably even if the election system isn't fair, as is the case in Hungary now. A proof that the European Union is still important for the Hungarian voters is the result of a poll conducted right after the European Parliament's vote to trigger Article 7 in which 56% of the respondents answered "yes" when asked if the European Parliament's decision on the Sargentini report was fair, and just 24% responded "no". Some 53% of the respondents said the negative vote was only about the Hungarian government, while more than 12% saw it as being about the whole country, and 16% thought it was about both.[55]

---

[52]   Peel, Khan and Politi, 'Poland attacks plan to tie EU funds to rule of law' (19 February 2018) Financial Times, <https://www.ft.com/content/d6ef7412-157c-11e8-9376-4a6390addb44> accessed 1 December 2023.

[53]   See this argument by *Danuta Hübner*, Chair of the European Parliament's Committee on Constitutional Affairs. Hübner, 'Euroviews. View: EU must not surrender to illiberal forces' (2017) Euronews, <www.euronews.com/2017/12/29/view-eu-must-not-surrender-to-illiberal-forces> accessed 1 December 2023. Similarly, former Commissioner *László Andor* argues that as a consequence of political conditionality, poorer regions would suffer because of their illiberal governments; see <http://www.progressiveeconomy.eu/sites/default/files/LA-cohesion-final.pdf> accessed 1 December 2023.

[54]   Müller, 'Geld nur bei Wohlverhalten: Sind politische Bedingungen der EU-Strukturfonds die Lösung für Ungarn und Polen?' (2017) Der (europäische) Föderalist, <http://www.foederalist.eu/2017/05/kein-geld-regelbrecher-politische-bedingungen-eu-strukturfonds-ungarn-polen.html> accessed 1 December 2023.

[55]   Cuddy, 'Exclusive poll: What do Hungarians think of the European Parliament's vote to trigger Article 7?' (2018) Euronews, <https://www.euronews.com/

Outside the scope of an Article 7 procedure, Prime Minister *Orbán* claims that linking EU funds to political conditions goes against the EU treaties.[56] But one can argue that the Common Provisions Regulation 1303/2013[57] that regulates the European Structural and Investment Funds (which combines five funds, including the Cohesion Fund) requires governments to respect the rule of law as a condition for receiving money.[58] Article 6 of the Regulation requires governments to ensure that funds are spent in accordance with EU and national law. The provision reads: "Operations supported by the ESI Funds shall comply with applicable Union law and the national law relating to its application." Some scholars argue that the Regulation should expressly specify the rule of law as forming part of "applicable Union law".[59] Of course the Regulation can relatively easily be amended, but I do not think that is even necessary to acknowledge that the rule of law, as part of Article 2 TEU, is applicable primary Union law. In my view, if a Member State does meet these requirements, it does not fulfil the legal conditions of the funds, and consequently cannot get them. Independent courts can be considered as essential institutions conditions, and one could certainly raise the question whether the captured courts in Hungary (or again in Poland for that matter) qualify as 'courts' under Article 19 TEU.[60]

2018/09/13/exclusive-poll-what-do-hungarians-think-of-the-european-parliament-s-vote-to-trigger-artic> accessed 1 December 2023.

[56] "The EU is based on treaties, and there is nothing in there that would create this possibility [of linking funds to the rule of law]," *Viktor Orbán* said in an interview. See Zalan, 'Trouble Ahead' (2018) Berlin Policy Journal, <https://berlinpolicyjournal.com/trouble-ahead/> accessed 1 December 2023.

[57] Parliament and Council, Regulation (EU) 1303/2013 laying down common provisions on the European Regional Development Fund, the European Social Fund, the Cohesion Fund, the European Agricultural Fund for Rural Development and the European Maritime and Fisheries Fund and laying down general provisions on the European Regional Development Fund, the European Social Fund, the Cohesion Fund and the European Maritime and Fisheries Fund and repealing Council Regulation, 2013, OJ L 347, 320.

[58] For a similar argument see Butler, 'To Halt Poland's PiS, Go for the Euros' (2017) LibertiesEU, <https://www.liberties.eu/en/news/to-halt-polands-pis-go-for-euros>.

[59] Waelbroeck and Oliver, 'Enforcing the Rule of Law in the EU: What can be done about Hungary and Poland?' (2018) Blog Droit Européen, <https://blogdroiteuropeen.com/2018/02/09/enforcing-the-rule-of-law-in-the-eu-what-can-be-done-about-hungary-and-poland-part-ii-michel-waelbroeck-and-peter-oliver/> accessed 1 December 2023.

[60] ECJ, Case C-64/16, *Associação Sindical dos Juízes Portugueses*, EU:C:2018:117, suggests that the EU principle of judicial independence may be relied upon

According to the Commission's Delegated Regulation (EU) No 240/2014 on the European code of conduct on partnership in the framework of the European Structural and Investment Funds,[61] the governments of the member states must closely cooperate with "bodies representing civil society at national, regional and local levels throughout the whole programme cycle consisting of preparation, implementation, monitoring and evaluation" (recital 2). They should also "examine the need to make use of technical assistance in order to support the strengthening of the institutional capacity of partners, in particular as regards small local authorities, economic and social partners and non-governmental organisations, in order to help them so that they can effectively participate in the preparation, implementation, monitoring and evaluation of the programme" (Article 17(1) of the Regulation).

Finally, in May 2018 the European Commission proposed a new Conditionality Regulation[62] with the purpose to condition the distribution of EU money in compliance with the rule of law, so that EU money no longer funded national authoritarian governments such as Hungary's. But the law-making process changed the regulation to become much harder to trigger and more limited in what it can reach. In fact, the term 'rule of law' is not even included in the regulation's current title. This first 'compromise'[63] in September 2020 was a consequence of Germany's effort to protect Fidesz member of the European People's Party's (EPP) fraction in the European Parliament, partly because of the strong economic interests of Germany in Hungary, such as the German car industry. The Hungarian and the Polish governments wanted to get rid of the conditionality regulation altogether and threatened to veto the EU's Multiannual Financial Framework – the next seven-year budget of the Union – and the Recovery plan package, which

---

irrespective of whether the relevant national measure implements EU law. About the innovative nature of the judgment see Ovádek, 'Has the CJEU Reconfigured the EU Constitutional Order?' (2018) Verfassungsblog,<https://verfassungsblog .de/ has -the -cjeu -just -reconfigured -the -eu -constitutional -order/ > accessed 1 December 2023.

[61]   Commission Regulation (EU) 240/2014 on the European code of conduct on partnership in the framework of the European Structural and Investment Funds, 2014, OJ L 74, 1.

[62]   COM(2018) 324 final.

[63]   Pech (@ProfPech), "Have received copy of Council presidency 'compromise' text re Commission's proposed new #ruleoflaw conditionality mechanism first put forward in 2018 (why this isn't made public is beyond me) My quick verdict: more of a sabotage attempt than a compromise text (quick thread)", Twitter/X, 29 September 2020, <https:// twitter .com/ ProfPech/ status/ 1310854116919463936?s=20> accessed 1 December 2023.

aimed at healing the damages caused by the COVID-19 pandemic. The threat of veto changed the political mood in the EU; the determined position of the Netherlands, the Nordic countries, and the European Parliament pushed the German presidency to soften its initial conciliatory attitude towards Hungary (and Poland). Thanks to this push, the budgetary conditionality was adopted. Even though it does not explicitly protect the rule of law, it does protect the Union budget in cases when funds have already been misspent.

Although the subject of blackmail through veto has disappeared with the adoption of the Conditionality Regulation, the European Council made another compromise on 10 December 2020,[64] again brokered by the German Presidency with the Hungarian and the Polish government(s). Even though the Conclusion is non-binding, it certainly has effects, practically suspending the application of the Regulation by allowing Member States to challenge it before the CJEU. On March 10, 2021 as expected, the Hungarian government (along with its Polish counterpart) challenged the Regulation.[65] This provided the opportunity for the Hungarian 'mafia state' to keep misusing EU funds for the benefit of *Orbán's* oligarchs and his own family and avoid the triggering the Regulation before the 2022 parliamentary elections.

Indeed, although on 16 February 2022 the ECJ dismissed all the claims of the Hungarian (and the Polish) government(s),[66] and in early March also the European Council finalized the guideline binding the Commission as to how to apply the Regulation, the Commission only triggered the conditionality mechanism on 27 April 2022, after Fidesz won its fourth consecutive parliamentary election, again with a two-third majority. Surprisingly, on 18 September 2022 the Commission proposed to suspend 65% of three targeted cohesion funds, and also requested the implementation of 17 key measures regarding compliance with important corruption and rule of law requirements. Additionally, Hungary has to meet 10 conditions, partly on judicial independence in order to receive the allocated money under the Recovery Fund (RRF). This meant that the Hungarian government would have lost all recovery money for good should no agreement have been reached with the Commission by the end of 2022 about the implementation of these 27 'super milestones'. On 30 November the Commission assessed that the Hungarian government had not fulfilled its

---

[64] Council, Note (EU), EUCO 22/20 about the European Council meeting of 10-11 December 2020.

[65] Bayer, 'Hungary and Poland to Brussels: See you in court' (2021) Politico, <https://www.politico.eu/article/hungary-poland-to-brussels-see-you-in-court/> accessed 1 December 2023.

[66] See ECJ, Case C-156/21, *Hungary v. Parliament and Council*, EU:C:2022:97, and ECJ, Case C-157/21, *Poland v. Parliament and Council*, EU:C:2022:98.

promise to implement the 17 anti-corruption measures, hence it recommended to the Council to suspend EUR 7.5 billion of the country's Cohesion Funds. Although the Hungarian government has not complied with the 10 rule of law requirements, the Commission approved Hungary's Recovery Plan, but proposed to the Council to put a freeze on an additional EUR 5.8 billion from Hungary's 2022 allocation under the RFF, due to the remaining concerns.[67] On 12 December 2022 the Council with a qualified majority blocked EUR 6.3 billion of the three Cohesion Funds to Hungary instead of the EUR 7.5 billion proposed by the Commission, and has approved the RFF money on the condition of satisfying the milestones. But until these are met in full first, Hungary cannot access its entire EUR 5.8 billion in Recovery Funds.

Additionally to these suspensions, and the one mentioned earlier because of the non-compliance with certain provisions of the Charter of Fundamental Rights, Hungary has been cut off from the Horizon Europe and the Erasmus+ programmes, as a consequence of university privatization. According to estimates all these mentioned suspensions make up at least EUR 28.7 billion.[68]

5.   CONCLUSION

This chapter tried to prove that the rule of law backsliding in Hungary happens in a non-democratic system with authoritarian tendencies. The last nine years of this development have shown that the EU's traditional mechanism of the infringement procedure did not work, neither the triggered Article 7 procedure nor the most recent attempts of the outgoing European Commission on the EU Rule of Law Toolbox[69] published on 3 April 2019 and the Rule of Law Review Cycle[70] announced on 17 July 2019, not to speak about the mentioned

---

[67]   Scheppele, Kelemen and Morijn, 'The Good, the Bad and the Ugly: The Commission Proposes Freezing Funds to Hungary' (2022) Verfassungsblog, <https://verfassungsblog.de/the-good-the-bad-and-the-ugly-2/> accessed 1 December 2023.

[68]   Scheppele and Morijn, 'Frozen' (2023) Verfas-sungsblog, <https://verfassungsblog.de/frozen/> accessed 1 December 2023.

[69]   European Commission, 'Initiative to strengthen the rule of law in the EU', <https://ec.europa.eu/info/policies/justice-and-fundamental-rights/upholding-rule-law/rule-law/initiative-strengthen-rule-law-eu_en> accessed 1 December 2023. About the assessment of this Communication see Pech and Kochenov, 'Strengthening the Rule of Law within the European Union. Diagnoses, recommendations, and what to avoid' (June 2019) RECONNECT Policy Brief.

[70]   European Commission, 'Good administration', <https://ec.europa.eu/tran sp arency/regdoc/rep/1/2019/EN/COM-2019-343-F1-EN-MAIN-PART-1.PDF> accessed 1 December 2023. For the critique of this follow up Communication see Pech et

rather decreased commitment of the new European Commission to force the governments to end the breach of European values.

I think that to keep the vision of Europe as a value community, it is inevitable to enforce the joint values of the rule of law, democracy and fundamental rights in every Member State. For this reason, the more consequent use of certain traditional tools, such as infringement procedures also for the breach of values enshrined in Article 2 TEU, or even triggering Article 7 for that matter are important, because if democracy is hijacked, courts are captured, rights are threatened and the EU is disrespected by a Member State government, the sincere cooperation guaranteed in Article 4(3) cannot be guaranteed. But at the same time, new means of value conditionality should also be activated, such as cutting funds for member states that do not comply with certain basic institutional requirements of the rule of law. Unfortunately, the newly introduced economic conditionality mechanism is burdened with a number of bad compromises, but this seems to provide the only hope for the discontinuation of the unprincipled protection of Hungary's autocratic government and the start of serious enforcement of the values of democracy, the rule of law, and fundamental rights that make up the EU's ideological foundation. Otherwise, the EU is doomed to fail as a value community, and may fall apart altogether as a result.

al., 'The Commission's Rule of Law Blueprint for Action: A Missed Opportunity to Fully Confront Legal Hooliganism' (2019) Verfassungsblog, <https://verfassungsblog .de/the-commissions-rule-of-law-blueprint-for-action-a-missed-opportunity-to-fully -confront-legal-hooliganism/> accessed 1 December 2023.

5. Consequences of the Rule of Law Debates for the Accession Process of the States of the Western Balkan

Pavel Usvatov and Mahir Muharemovic[1]

1. INTRODUCTION: THE RULE OF LAW CHALLENGE IN EU ENLARGEMENT

The EU is a community based on the rule of law, and the rule of law has become increasingly central to the European Union's enlargement policy and accession process in the recent years.[2] However, effectively promoting rule of law compliance and values has posed challenges not only in candidate countries but also in the EU itself.

During the two enlargement rounds in 2004 and 2007 to Central and Eastern Europe (CEE) and South Eastern Europe (SEE)[3] the focus was predominantly on the adoption of the EU acquis,[4] with less emphasis on practical implementation and enforcement. This led to a discrepancy in some states between extensive and fairly rapid legal harmonisation and the substantive and material internalisation and implementation[5] of the reforms. Following accession, this

---

[1]   The views expressed in this article are those of the authors and do not necessarily represent those of their affiliated institutions.

[2]   See e.g. Article 2.1(a)(i) and Annex II of Regulation (EU) No 231/2014 establishing an Instrument for Pre-accession Assistance (IPA II) [2014] OJ L 77/11.

[3]   2004: Republic of Cyprus, Czech Republic, Estonia, Hungary, Latvia, Lithuania, Malta, Poland, Slovakia and Slovenia; 2007: Bulgaria and Romania.

[4]   Ognjanoska, 'Promoting the Rule of Law in the EU Enlargement Policy: A Twofold Challenge (2021) 17 CYELP, 237 ff. at 243.

[5]   *Martin Mendelski* distinguishes between "*de jure* rule of law" and "*de facto* rule of law" (italics in original) where the ladder includes the judicial capacity and impartiality, which is part of the implementation. See Mendelski, 'The EU's Pathological Power: The Failure of External Rule of Law Promotion in South Eastern Europe' (2015) 39 Southeastern Europe, 318-346 at 321 ff.

has manifested itself in rule of law backsliding in some of the new Member States, such as Hungary since 2010 and Poland since 2015, which has sparked a debate on the rule of law throughout the EU that refuses to end. Some authors speak more generally of a 'democratic backsliding' which also includes the rule of law in other young Member States, e.g. in Czech Republic under *Andrej Babiš* from 2017 to 2021[6] or in Slovenia 2015.[7] The modest improvements that Romania had achieved at the formal reform level in the years following its accession to the EU in 2007 were partially reversed under *Victor Ponta* between 2012 and 2015,[8] and the persistent problems regarding the independence of the judiciary[9] and the implementation of ECtHR judgments[10] continue to preoccupy both the Court and the ECJ.

Learning from previous accession processes, the EU has given greater priority to the strengthening of the rule of law in the countries of the Western Balkans (Albania, Bosnia and Herzegovina, Kosovo, Montenegro, Northern Macedonia and Serbia) in the 2011 Enlargement Strategy.[11] A year later the Commission had presented a new approach to enlargement including a "new [more demanding] approach to judiciary and fundamental rights and justice".[12] In 2014 so-called "safeguard clauses" for chapter 23 "on judiciary and fun-

---

[6]   Hanley and Vachudova, 'Understanding the illiberal turn: democratic back-sliding in the Czech Republic' (2018) 34 East European Politics 3, 276-296. But cf. Bakke and Sitter, 'The EU's Enfants Terribles: Democratic Backsliding in Central Europe since 2010' (2022) 20 Perspectives on Politics 1, 22-37.

[7]   Bugaric and Kuhelj, 'Slovenia in crisis: A tale of unfinished democratization in East-Central Europe' (2015) 48 Communist and Post-Communist Studies 4, 273-279.

[8]   Tanasoiu, 'Romania in the EU: Political developments and the rule of law after accession' in von Bogdandy and Sonnevend (eds), *Constitutional Crisis in the European Constitutional Area* (Hart 2015), 184 ff.

[9]   See for example Joined Cases C-83/19 et al., *Asociaţia "Forumul Judecătorilor din România"*, EU:C:2021:393, and Press Release 82/21, available at <https:// curia .europa .eu/ jcms/ upload/ docs/ application/ pdf/ 2021 -05/ cp210082en .pdf> accessed 1 December 2023.

[10]   Romania has not implemented 113 leading ECtHR judgments (60% in the past 10 years) and performs very poorly overall, with over 500 of the ECtHR's 1357 judgments against RO not implemented, see Violations 1959 – 2022, ECtHR statistics, <https://www.echr.coe.int/documents/d/echr/stats_violation_1959_2022 _eng>, and <https://hudoc.exec.coe.int/> accessed 1 December 2023.

[11]   This new approach focusing on the rule of law reforms in the Western Balkan countries was introduced with the Enlargement Strategy 2011, see European Commission, 'Enlargement Strategy and Main Challenges 2011-2012', COM(2011) 666, among others "5. Conclusions and Recommendations", no. 5.

[12]   COM(2012) 600 final, para. 1 and 2.

damental rights" and chapter 24 on "justice, freedom and security" of the Framework have been introduced.[13] The safeguards provide for these chapters "to be opened early in the process and closed at the end", for creation of "comprehensive reform action plans, which are required as opening benchmarks", an introduction "of 'interim benchmarks' to further guide the reform process" and of "closing benchmarks only set once substantial progress made across the board, including on track records of implementation on the ground". Finally, it calls for "safeguards and corrective measures, for example the updating of benchmarks and [...] a mechanism to stop negotiations on other chapters if progress on chapters 23/24 lags behind".[14]

The Western Balkan (WB) countries hoping to join the EU have struggled to make progress on meeting EU requirements in that regard. In practice, progress towards achieving the goals of the rule of law is still quite limited. Even the "frontrunner" countries Montenegro and Serbia have made little advancement on required reforms.[15] Some of the main rule of law challenges include weak judiciaries and problems with judicial independence, judicial efficiency, corruption, and organised crime.[16]

Considering this situation in the WB countries and the fact that the EU faces problems with the rule of law even in its own Member States, many EU countries are increasingly sceptical about extending membership to the WB countries.[17] The rule of law debate within the EU and the "enlargement fatigue" did not go unnoticed there.

---

[13]   COM(2014) 700 final.

[14]   An example of benchmarking in practice can be found in Bajić and Marić, 'EU's benchmarking within chapters 23 and 24 in accession negotiations with Serbia: Effects and challenges' (2018) European Fund for the Balkans, <https://epi .org.mk/post/11103?lang=en> accessed 1 December 2023.

[15]   See European Commission, 'A more credible, dynamic, predictable and political EU accession process - Commission lays out its proposals' (5 February 2020) Press release IP 20/181, <https:// ec .europa .eu/ commission/ presscorner/ detail/en/IP_20_181> accessed 1 December 2023.

[16]   See European Court of Auditors, 'EU support for the rule of law in the Western Balkans: despite efforts, fundamental problems persist' (2022) Special Report, 01/2022, para. 57, <https:// www .eca .europa .eu/ Lists/ ECADocuments/ SR22_01/ SR _ROL -Balkans _EN .pdf> accessed 1 December 2023. See also Haider, 'Rule of Law Challenges in the Western Balkans' (2019) Governance and Social Development Resource Centre, <https://gsdrc.org/publications/rule-of-law -challenges-in-the-western-balkans/> accessed 1 December 2023.

[17]   Böttger and Maugeais, 'Countering the Rule of Law Backsliding in the Western Balkans' (2021) 11 ÖGfE Policy Brief, <https:// www .oiip .ac .at/

2.   PERCEPTION OF THE RULE OF LAW DEBATE IN THE WESTERN BALKANS

The consequences of the rule of law debate in the EU have so far led to the new *formal* approach to the accession process mentioned above. The substantive, i.e. factual, changes and adjustments to rule of law projects and reforms in the region are still under discussion.[18] The consequences for the further accession process in terms of *substantial* changes depend on whether and what de facto impact the rule of law debate and the new requirements have in the Western Balkans.[19] The perception and reception of the debate in the region is therefore important for the development of a strategy (see below section 4. 'Conclusion').

In assessing the perception of the EU rule of law debate in the Western Balkans, we need to distinguish between the population and state institutions and decision-makers. The impact of the debate on the population has not yet been measured or studied. The population surveys focus on local social, economic, and political issues in the region, on perceptions of the EU as a whole (which are not improving in most countries, especially in the former Yugoslavia[20]). The rule of law issues in the EU have also not played a major role in the WB media.[21]

In this part we focus on the perceptions of decision-makers in the judiciary, in administrative authorities and of government and parliamentary staff dealing with rule of law issues. Their opinions are not usually published. However, in

---

publikation/ countering -the -rule -of -law -backsliding -in -the -western -balkans -by -katrin-boettger-dominic-maugeais/> accessed 1 December 2023.

[18]   The essential content of the – once again – "new methodology" from 2020, which provides for so-called 'accelerated integration' and a 'phasing-in' approach, remains unclear as well, COM(2020) 57 final.

[19]   The no less important discussion on the consequences of the debate for enlargement (or its halt) on the part of the EU is not part of this chapter.

[20]   The percentage of respondents who "tend to trust" the EU is in Albania 77%, Kosovo 63%, Bosnia and Hercegovina 57%, Montenegro 54%, North Macedonia 48% and Serbia 32%, figures extracted from Standard Eurobarometer 99 (Spring 2023), <https://europa.eu/eurobarometer/surveys/detail/3052> accessed 1 December 2023.

[21]   Rare examples include <https:// analiziraj .ba/ i -clanice -eu -imaju -problema -s -vladavinom -prava/> ("EU members have problems with the rule of law too", 1 October 2020) or <https://balkans.aljazeera.net/news/world/2022/2/16/sud-eu -protiv -poljske -i -madjarske -mehanizam -novcane -kazne -opravdan> ("EU court against Poland and Hungary: Penalty mechanism justified", 16 February 2022), both accessed 1 December 2023.

our day-to-day work, we hold numerous confidential conversations, closed discussion groups and workshops on rule of law topics in all countries of the region. Therefore, this chapter is based not only on the analysis of publications on the topic and the application of deductive methods, but also on our empirical experience from the last five years of work in the region.[22]

The main commonality between all the interlocutors[23] is that most of them have at least heard of the EU rule of law debate regarding Poland and especially Hungary. Often the knowledge is superficial ("some issues with the independence of judiciary" or "appointment of judges"). We have not met anyone with an in-depth knowledge of the details except for a few lawyers or experts on Poland and Hungary and rule of law, specifically on constitutional law.

The opinions we have heard range from honest, but rather restrained criticism of rule of law backsliding to ignoring the EU debate to misusing the concept of the rule of law and redefining it for political purposes. Often the perception and the resulting approach is a mixture of all three. Finally, despite the differences in opinions, perceptions and personal involvement, there is a great similarity in the results of political and practical actions: The improvements in the rule of law in all Western Balkans states have been, if at all, formal in nature and have not led to substantive changes.[24] However, acceptance of the formal accession requirements was always high.

Those who honestly criticise the backsliding in Poland and Hungary are mostly not (yet) in decision-making positions, many of them working in

---

[22] Personal communication (names, locations and dates of workshops or dialogues) cannot be published for reasons of confidentiality. Quotations that are not footnoted are from the personal communication. For more information, please contact the authors.

[23] In 2022, ca. 300 lawyers, public officials and other legal experts participated in workshops and conferences organised by the KAS Rule of Law Programme South East Europe in Albania, BiH and Serbia. Confidential discussions were held with five to ten high-ranking officials per country in Albania, BiH, Serbia, Montenegro and Kosovo.

[24] In that regard we agree with the European Court of Auditors, 'EU action has contributed to reforms, but has had little overall impact on progress in the rule of law' (2022) Special Report: EU support for the rule of law in the Western Balkans: despite efforts, fundamental problems persist, 25 ff., <https://www.eca.europa.eu/Lists/ECADocuments/SR22_01/SR_ROL-Balkans_EN.pdf> accessed 1 December 2023. All WB countries continue to be classified as "hybrid regimes" (or are in transition between an authoritarian and a democratic state), see <https://freedomhouse.org/countries/nations-transit/scores>, accessed 1 December 2023, and below.

projects funded by the EU or other donors to promote the rule of law and democracy. Their stance coincides with the opinions of critics within the EU, especially in the countries with which they cooperate. They are the minority. Thus, the focus will be on the two remaining categories: those who ignore the debate or do not perceive it as a problem, and those who take it further and redefine the rule of law for their own purposes.

2.1   Ignoring the Debate

One way of dealing with the debate is not to engage with it at all. This is true for the majority of decision-makers in most WB countries we spoke to, namely in Albania, Bosnia and Herzegovina (BiH), Northern Macedonia and to some extent Kosovo and Montenegro. As frontrunner countries, Montenegro and Serbia have been scrutinised more closely than other WB countries, which is why the experts and decision-makers there are better informed. In Serbia, interlocutors are more inclined to discuss the issue due to the proximity to and political dialogue with Hungary.

There are several reasons for ignoring the rule of law debate:

First, many interlocutors realise that the rule of law debate in the EU has already resulted in stricter accession criteria, introduction of benchmarks and stricter conditionality before the accession negotiations have been opened. The WB countries, except for Montenegro and Serbia, have not experienced any change regarding the requirements, so they do not expect further consequences for the process.

Second, the EU has disappointed the expectations of WB candidate countries several times in the past.[25] The prevailing opinion is that it is not the rule of law but the domestic politics of the EU Member States (e.g. Bulgaria's blockade regarding North Macedonia or Albania) and the geopolitical situation that are decisive. Especially after Ukraine and Moldova were granted candidate status before Bosnia and Herzegovina, which has been waiting since February 2016 (not to mention Kosovo, which is "hopelessly waiting for mere visa liberalisation"), the EU "cannot sell that accession is a merits-based process".[26]

---

[25]   Jean-Claude Juncker 2014: "... there will be no enlargement of the European Union for the next five years", <https:// ec .europa .eu/ commission/ presscorner/ detail/ en/ IP_14_984>. After North Macedonia signed the Prespa Agreement in 2018 and changed its state name, partly under pressure from France, the same France blocked the opening of accession negotiations in 2019, https:// www .bbc .com/news/world-europe-50100201.

[26]   This opinion is very widespread in WB countries and is openly expressed even by politicians, see e.g. <https://www.rferl.org/a/balkan-eu-membership-summit

Third, despite the backsliding, the rule of law situation in Poland and even in Hungary is perceived (sic) as better than in the WB states. As long as rule of law standards in the WB have not even reached the level of these two countries, despite all the problems and differences between them, and the formal benchmarks of the accession framework are met, many interlocutors in the WB countries see no need to engage with the EU rule of law debate at home. They do not expect any consequences of the debate for their own actions as their countries are not yet EU Member States.

Fourth, the WB countries are busy with debates regarding internal issues as well as the EU accession and the acquis conditions they must fulfil. The issues in Poland or Hungary seem far away (except for Serbia), and the prevailing opinion is that WB countries only have to introduce formal reforms to comply with chapters 23 and 24 of the acquis.

Fifth, there are many contentious legal issues that attract more attention in WB countries, including the way the EU deals with migration at its borders and the Member States undermining EU rules, e.g. regarding push-backs (Croatia), Frontex (Italy, Greece), border controls in the Schengen area (Covid, migration control) or the violation of Maastricht criteria by Member States. The so-called 'what-aboutism' is strong among decision-makers in the WB region.

In Albania, for example, the prevailing belief is that the country and thus the decision-makers have done a lot to comply with the acquis (this is also where public support for EU accession is strongest[27]). This is true for the formal changes that have been introduced, e.g. the ongoing vetting process for judges and prosecutors in Albania, but it must be said that the reforms have not yet had any significant positive impact overall.[28] In North Macedonia and Montenegro, on the other hand, despite all the formal reforms the rule of law

---

-frustration/31912243.html>; <https://www.brusselstimes.com/244437/western-bal kans-frustrated-as-ukraine-gets-eu-candidate-citizenship-within-months>.

[27] 92% of the respondents in public surveys think that EU accession would be a "good thing". Moreover, 42% expect accession by 2030 (2021 survey: 39% expected accession by 2025!), while in Serbia 40% believe that their country's accession will never happen. Data extracted from the Balkan Public Barometer 2023 by Regional Cooperation Council, <https://www.rcc.int/balkanbarometer/ results/2/public> accessed 1 December 2023.

[28] In Albania, only 1% of respondents in public surveys "totally trust" the judiciary, 19% "tend to trust", while 74% "trust less" or "not at all". Regarding the duration and cost of proceedings, enforcement and transparency, between 0 and 1% attest the judiciary an "excellent" or "very good" and, depending on the category, 10 to 15% a "good". Between 64% and 72% rate these services as poor or very poor, <https://www.rcc.int/balkanbarometer/results/2/public> accessed 1 December 2023.

situation is [rightly] perceived as being worse than in any EU country, and they would like having at least the level of functionality like in Poland. In Bosnia and Herzegovina, there are so many internal problems and dysfunctionalities that any EU debate that does not directly concern BiH is not of much interest there. In Serbia, the problems in Poland and Hungary are partly seen not as a problem of these countries, but as a problem of Brussels limiting the autonomy of these Member States.

2.2   (Re)definition of the Term and Misappropriation of the Acquis

The term 'rule of law' was already mentioned in the Maastricht Treaty from 1992 (preamble), has been part of the *acquis communautaire* since 2002,[29] and it is enshrined in the Article 2 TEU. The European Commission created a "compelling working definition"[30] of the term on the basis[31] of the decisions of the European Court of Justice, the European Court of Human Rights, and the communications of the Venice Commission:

> "Under the rule of law, all public powers always act within the constraints set out by law, in accordance with the values of democracy and fundamental rights, and under the control of independent and impartial courts. The rule of law includes, among others, principles such as legality, implying a transparent, accountable, democratic and pluralistic process for enacting laws; legal certainty; prohibiting the arbitrary exercise of executive power; effective judicial protection by independent and impartial courts, effective judicial review including respect for fundamental rights; separation of powers; and equality before the law."[32]

However, there is no uniform and complete definition of the term "rule of law" in the treaties or other legal documents. The lack of a positive legal definition can be (mis)understood as a major weakness of the concept and an invitation

---

[29] CE Parliamentary Assembly Resolution 1290 (2002).

[30] Pech and Grogan. 'Meaning and Scope of the EU Rule of Law' (30 April 2020) RECONNECT, June 2020, at 24, <http://dx.doi.org/10.2139/ssrn.4100123> accessed 1 December 2023

[31] European Commission, 'A new EU framework to strengthen the Rule of Law', COM(2014) 158 final, Annex 2, 2-3. See also Press Release IP 14/237, <https://ec.europa.eu/commission/presscorner/detail/en/IP_14_237> accessed 1 December 2023.

[32] European Commission, 'Further strengthening the Rule of Law within the Union - State of play and possible next steps', COM(2019) 163 final, 2. See also Council of Europe (Venice Commission), 'Report on the Rule of Law', CDL-AD(2011)003rev, 10-13.

to an arbitrary and illiberal interpretation.[33] This invitation is readily accepted by some and falls on fertile ground in systems that traditionally have legal positivist and formalist approach to the law.[34] The aforementioned "working definition" is most openly challenged in Serbia, in the Republika Srpska of BiH, in North Macedonia and in Montenegro, i.e. in the countries of the former Yugoslavia. In Albania and Kosovo there seems to be more readiness to accept the "working definition", at least when it comes to the formal compliance with it. Nevertheless, in all above-mentioned countries the term "rule of law" is often interpreted in a very formalistic way.[35]

The independence of the judiciary, for example, is seen as a purely formal concept, implying the isolation of judges from the public by prohibiting them from being politically active (e.g. being a member of a political organisation or party, expressing political opinions, etc.[36]), speaking in public, or engaging in "improper conduct", which is a very broad term and can include statements on social media that are not even related to their work. Such restrictions have a chilling effect on the judiciary and lead to the withdrawal of judges and also other public servants from civil society life, resulting in less trust among the population and less transparency.[37] At the same time problems such as (but not limited to) the judges' insufficient freedom of decision (e.g. deviating from decisions of higher instances or from opinions of more influential colleagues), work overload that limits decision-making capacity and leads to poor quality of judgments, lack of privacy in shared offices, a strict and intimidating code

---

[33] See the different forms of "critique" ("illiberal", "double standard", "juris-tocracy", and "Doctrine of the Holy Crown") and counterarguments in Pech and Grogan, (2020) *supra* note 30 at 44 f.

[34] Exemplary for BiH see the Expert Report on Rule of Law issues in Bosnia and Herzegovina (so-called "Priebe Report"), paras. 20 and 21; *Mendelski* (2015) *supra* note 5 came to the same conclusion already in 2015.

[35] Elbasani, 'International Promotion of Rule of Law: Facing Connections between Patronage, Crime, and Judiciary Corruption' in Esch and van Zijverden (eds), *Rule of Law Reforms in the Western Balkans* (Aspen Institute 2018) 32-37 at 36; on formalism in the judiciary see Uzelac, 'Survival of the Third Legal Tradition?' (2010) Supreme Court Law Review, 377-396.

[36] The constitutions of most WB countries contain such provisions: Article 143 in Albania, Article 106(1) in Kosovo, Article 54 in Montenegro, Article 100 in North Macedonia, Article 55 in Serbia.

[37] In the region, 28% of respondents "totally distrust" and 35% "tend not to trust" the judiciary; 22% say the transparency is "very poor" and 33% rate it as "poor". The worst results are in Northern Macedonia, Albania, BiH and Montenegro, the best in Kosovo, see <https://www.rcc.int/balkanbarometer/results/2/public> accessed 1 December 2023.

of conduct or disciplinary procedures that are too easy to initiate are not addressed. These issues are often not even considered within the definition of the rule of law.

In none of the WB countries is the rule of law considered a benchmark for legislative procedures. "Principles such as legality, implying a transparent, accountable, democratic and pluralistic process for enacting laws" are widely ignored. The executive has appropriated as much power as it could, not only during the Covid 19 pandemic.[38] Numerous legal acts continue to be issued as executive orders or decrees without any parliamentary or public participation. Alternatively, they are passed in an abbreviated or accelerated legislative procedure in parliaments, which are degraded to organs of acclamation.[39]

One of the most common justifications for the executive enacting regulations and implementing parliamentary fast-track procedures is the claim that the amendments are necessary to meet the requirements of the acquis, the EU ("Brussels") or the European courts, which supposedly need to be implemented urgently. It is often claimed that the regulations are only a copy of EU legislation, so that no standard parliamentary procedure is necessary or useful since European regulations cannot be amended anyway. Due parliamentary procedure apparently does not fall under the concept of the rule of law from the perspective of the actors. At the same time, such fast-track procedures are rarely or never criticised by the EU.[40]

---

[38] The pandemic had a very negative impact on the fragile political system in region overall, see Huszka and Lessenska, 'Viral vulnerability: how the pandemic is making democracy sick in the Western Balkans' (8 December 2020) ECFR, <https://ecfr.eu/publication/viral-vulnerability-how-the-pandemic-is-making-democracy-sick-in-the-western-balkans/> accessed 1 December 2023; Country-specific analysis in Esch and Palm (eds), *The Covid-19 pandemic in the western Balkans: consequences and policy approaches* (Aspen Institute 2020), <https://www.aspeninstitute.de/wp-content/uploads/2020-The-Covid-19-Pandemic-in-the-Western-Balkans.pdf> accessed 1 December 2023.

[39] For a comprehensive overview of all WB countries, see the study by the Westminster Foundation for Democracy, *Parliamentary Boycotts in the Western Balkans* (2022), <https://www.wfd.org/sites/default/files/2022-05/wfd-wb-boycotts.pdf> accessed 1 December 2023. E.g. in BiH, "[t]he legislature … has been reduced to a debate club …", Blagovčanin, 'The Rule of the Cartel' (2020) Transparency International, 8; Bieber, 'A presidential decision' [in Serbia] (26 October 2022) BiEPAG, <https://biepag.eu/blog/a-presidential-decision/> accessed 1 December 2023.

[40] Even in the case of EU Member States, the problem of a high number of fast-track procedures and government emergency ordinances is only addressed in the rule of law reports as "other institutional issues related to checks and balances"

Finally, the fact that the primacy of EU law, including rule of law, in certain areas is questioned by some national constitutional courts or governments, is also interpreted by many interlocutors as a weakness of the European rule of law system. The idea of uniformity of EU law and the concept of the rule of law is hard to sell when individual EU Member States have their own interpretations of the rules. It does not help that the very specific decisions of the German Federal Constitutional Court (e.g. the PSPP judgment of May 5, 2020[41]) or authorities in other Member States are taken out of context and misrepresented or misinterpreted by the decision-makers in WB states. The 'double standard' argument is already there and difficult to refute with legal arguments.[42] It is even more difficult to explain why, for example, judges or prosecutors in the WB countries have to be appointed by a special High Judicial Council, while such an institution does not even exist in Austria, Germany or Sweden where the sometimes quite political appointments are widely accepted.

3.   SHORTCOMINGS IN THE DEBATE: INSTITUTIONS AS AGENTS OF RULE OF LAW

The rule of law debate in the EU focuses almost exclusively on the justice sector and mostly leaves out one crucial element of the rule of law system: the institutions. Meanwhile, most interactions between citizens and the state take place at or with administrative authorities, most legal acts against citizens and most violations of their rights occur through the public administration and its institutions. Only a part of it ends up in the courts, and a much smaller part still is referred to the higher courts and the Constitutional Court. It can be argued that a well-functioning public administration would significantly relieve the judiciary in administrative law cases and beyond and improve the rule of law in a country more efficient than is possible through judicial reforms alone.[43] Nevertheless, substantial (i.e. not just formal) reforms and especially capacity

---

and not as a significant rule of law problem as we see it, see e.g. for Romania: European Commission, C SWD(2022) 523 final, para. IV.

[41]   German Federal Constitutional Court, Judgment of the Second Senate of 5 May 2020, 2 BvR 859/15 (= BVerfGE 154, 17-152). The English version is available at <https://www.bundesverfassungsgericht.de/SharedDocs/Entscheidungen/EN/2020/05/rs20200505_2bvr085915en.html>.

[42]   *Pech* and *Grogan* merely question the "credibility" of the critique of double standards because of the "illiberal" intentions of the critics; see Pech and Grogan, (2015) *supra* note 30 at 57.

[43]   We do not want to downplay the important role of the judicial reforms, but the lack of substantial reforms in the institutions undermines the efforts.

building in institutions other than the judiciary and the police (in a broader sense) are not the focus, if they take place at all.[44]

Despite the mention of the need of "well-functioning and stable public administration built on an efficient and impartial civil service" in the opening statement for accession negotiations of the ministerial meeting regarding Serbia,[45] as an example, the crucial chapters 23 and 24 of the acquis are still heavily focused on the judiciary and the police. Chapter 23 makes just a passing mention that "reliable institutions are required *to underpin a coherent policy of prevention and deterrence of corruption*",[46] without giving them any independent significance. Chapter 24 only mentions the need for "a strong and well-integrated administrative capacity" but limits it to "law enforcement agencies and other relevant bodies".[47] Other than that only "financial institutions" (chapters 9 and 17), an "institutional framework" for the implementation and monitoring of EU funds (chapter 22) and an "external audit institution" (chapter 32) have been included in the acquis. An analysis of the opened negotiation chapters with Montenegro and Serbia, especially (but not limited) to chapters 23 and 24, also shows that institutions outside of the judiciary, police in a broader sense (including border control, migration, visa issues, etc.), budgetary issues and outside the area of anti-corruption and anti-discrimination

---

[44] Only 2014 the "public administration reform" was included in the "fundamentals first" approach, European Commission, 'Enlargement Strategy and Main Challenges 2014-15', COM(2014) 700 final. So far, there are no established standard indicators in this regard, but a set of standards developed within the SIGMA framework, OECD, 'The Principles of Public Administration' (2017). In none of the WB countries the implementation of key processes is happening in practice with a few exceptions in specific areas, see OECD, 'Government at a Glance: Western Balkans' (2019) at 31, <https://www.oecd-ilibrary.org//sites/b2d01687-en/index.html?itemId=/content/component/b2d01687-en#tab005> accessed 1 December 2023.

[45] Accession Document, AD 1/14, CONF-RS 1 (21 January 2014), para. 37, <https://data.consilium.europa.eu/doc/document/AD%201%202014%20INIT/EN/pdf> accessed 1 December 2023. The same paragraph also states that "[m]ore specifically, this will require the necessary capacity and structures for the sound management and efficient control of EU funds", which raises the question of whether the ministerial meeting was only concerned about funds or about institutional capacity in Serbia in general.

[46] Emphasis added.

[47] In eleven chapters the term 'administrative capacity' is being mentioned, e.g. regarding the regulation of agriculture (chapter 11), of fiscal interests like taxation (chapter 16) and budget (chapter 33) or environmental protection (chapter 27) according to the EU policies etc.

are not central to the reforms, if they occur at all.[48] It seems that the authors of the documents assume that the large rest of public administration dealing with the daily life of citizens (health, education, transport, housing, emergency management, etc.) is functioning well enough in WB states.

The consequences of paying not enough attention to institutional development can be seen in all WB countries: overall 61% of respondents in public surveys in the region assess the law enforcement as *ineffective*,[49] 62% *do not trust* local authorities,[50] and only 31% are satisfied with the public services.[51] The surveys on government effectiveness[52] reflect the low efficiency and effectiveness of the public institutions. In-depth investigations show that the authorities and institutions not only provide inadequate services, but in some cases do not function (see below).

3.1   The Rule of Informal Institutions

Historically, the WB region has experienced a great deal of change, including the formation and dissolution of states, political and legal systems, ideologies, institutions, social classes and tribal structures. Nevertheless, certain social practices have not changed. In the face of these drastic ideological and legal changes, people have relied more on informal social networks of relatives, friends and clans for security than on the instruments of the rule of law.[53] When traditions and customs are firmly established, they can have a significant

---

[48]   See <https://www.mei.gov.rs/eng/documents/negotiations-with-the-eu/access ion-negotiations-with-the-eu/negotiating-positions/> for the open chapters and negoti- ation positions in Serbia and <https://www.eu.me/en/negotiating-chapters/> for Mon- tenegro, both accessed 1 December 2023.

[49]   The proportion of respondents who consider law enforcement to be ineffec- tive is 82% in Albania, 76% in North Macedonia and 69% in BiH. <https://www .rcc.int/balk anbarometer/results/2/public> accessed 1 December 2023.

[50]   The proportion of respondents who do not trust local authorities is 78% in BiH, 68% in North Macedonia, and 63% in Montenegro, <https://www.rcc.int/balk anbarometer/results/2/public> accessed 1 December 2023.

[51]   The proportion of respondents who are satisfied with the public services in BiH is 22%, in North Macedonia and Montenegro 26% each, <https://www.rcc.int/ balk anbarometer/results/2/public> accessed 1 December 2023.

[52]   Percentile rank in 2021 for BiH was 13,46 (2019: 27,88); Kosovo: 42,79; North Macedonia: 50; Albania: 53,37; Montenegro: 53,85; Serbia: 55,77; Net- herlands: 97,12. Data extracted from <https://info.worldbank.org/governance/wgi/> accessed 1 December 2023.

[53]   European Commission, 'Closing The Gap Between Formal And Informal Institutions In The Balkans', https://cordis.europa.eu/project/id/693537.

impact on people's lives. It is likely that those who have more influence in society are treated better by the authorities than those who have less power. Moreover, long-standing social norms are often interpreted and enforced by those with more authority. Montenegro and Albania are among historical examples, where society was highly fragmented and suspicious of centralised power. It was made up of kinship groups, clans, and tribes, and lacked the elements of centralization.[54]

The socialist regimes managed to destroy parts of these links and structures through collectivisation and terror (esp. Albania), but after the fall of the socialism some of them experienced a revival. In addition, many of the networks created during the socialist period are still intact, as reflected in the continuity within political parties, elites and economic groupings in all countries of the region.[55] "Lustration of public officials who were active in the time of one-party rule in the countries of the Western Balkans, essentially did not take place."[56]

In addition to the historical development and pre-socialist traditions, the experience of a dense system of informal social relations, arbitrary decision-making and corruption that characterised everyday life under state socialism has deeply shaped the societies in the WB countries. "In state socialism, corruption was a structural necessity to all spheres of daily life".[57] As in earlier times, the official rules were supplemented by an informal code of mafia-like loyalties. The socialist informal institutions and rules do matter still up to this day.[58]

The result of this development is a vicious circle: where the state and its institutions are corrupt, unreliable or perhaps non-existent, society turns to 'private providers' such as clans, mafia-like structures or other informal

---

[54] For an example of development in Albania see Elsie, *The Tribes of Albania: History, Society and Culture* (I.B. Tauris 2015).

[55] For example, the current president of Republika Srpska, *Milorad Dodic*, began his career in 1986 as the chairman of the Laktaši Municipal Council. *Sali Berisha*, the former prime minister of Albania (2005-2013), used to be a secretary of the communist party and a personal physician to *Enver Hoxha* (Albania's communist chief of state until 1985).

[56] Hatschikjan, Reljić and Šebek (eds), *Disclosing hidden history: Lustration in the Western Balkans* (CDRSEE 2005) at 16.

[57] Swirek and Pospech, 'Escape from arbitrariness: Legitimation crisis of real socialism and the imaginary of modernity' (2021) 24 European Journal of Social Theory 1, 140-159.

[58] A general analysis, but also fruitful for the Balkans, is provided by Chavance, 'Formal and informal institutional change: the experience of postsocialist transformation' (2008) 5 The European Journal of Comparative Economics 1, 57-71.

authorities for protection and security.[59] In such situations, formal rules
become 'myths' that people believe they have to follow, but which have
little substance in reality. "They serve to legitimise ways in which tasks are
carried out, even while these ways may diverge greatly from how things are
supposed to be done, according to the [formal] rules".[60] The natural outcome
of these informal structures and networks is, in turn, corruption, which is one
of the main challenges that WB citizens face in their daily lives. The system
is proving to be self-sustaining. Although respondents in public surveys rank
corruption third among the burning issues in the region after economic issues
(unemployment and cost of living),[61] they actively engage in corrupt activities.[62] Corruption in the broadest sense, bribery and nepotism have become an
integral part of the culture in the Western Balkans, especially when it comes
to public administration, health care or education. Very often, bribery is the
result of poor work by public bureaucracies or limited access to quality public
services.[63] This 'incompetence' of the civil service is again the result of nepotism and patronage in the recruitment of civil servants.[64] The vicious circle
continues as such 'bad systems' attract even more corrupt people to them,
which further corrupts the whole system.

The importance of the informal sector in the WB region is reflected in its
economic impact. In 2022, the EU Commission estimated its economic role in
Bosnia and Herzegovina at up to 33%, in North Macedonia as much as 38%,
in Albania around 33%, and in Montenegro at 24.5% of GDP.[65] In Kosovo, the

---

[59] Fukuyama, *Political Order And Political Decay: From The Industrial
Revolution To The Globalization Of Democracy* (Farrar, Straus and Giroux 2014)
at 114.

[60] Giddens, Duneier, Appelbaum and Carr, *Essentials of Sociology* (W.W.
Norton & Company 2019) at 361.

[61] Center for Insights in Survey Research, *2022 Western Balkans Regional
Survey* (IRI 2022) at 17.

[62] Regional Cooperation Council, 'Balkan Barometer 2020', <https://www.rcc
.int/balkanbarometer/>.

[63] See, for example, the journalistic testimony of Aljović, 'Korupcija, mito i nep-
otizam postali sastavni dio kulture na Zapadnom Balkanu' (4 May 2021) AlJazeera,
<https://balkans.aljazeera.net/teme/2021/5/4/umjesto-nulte-tolerancije-protiv-korup
ciji-na-balkanu-postoji-tolerancija-na-korupciju> accessed 1 December 2023.

[64] Ibid.

[65] BiH: SWD(2022) 336 final, 55; North Macedonia: SWD(2022) 337 final,
53; Albania: SWD(2022) 332 final, 55; Montenegro (2019 report, newer reports do
not show exact figures): SWD(2019) 217 final, 47.

informal economy accounts for more than a third of total employment,[66] and in Serbia still for about 13.2%.[67]

3.2   Captured and Extractive Institutions

The consequence of the informality rule in institutions is the so-called 'state capture'.[68] Political elites control access to all public institutions and thus the allocation of public funds and resources, including regulatory and judicial bodies. They "enable a misuse of public resources, generate irresponsible public spending, and, as a consequence, a high level of corruption".[69] In his analysis of the situation in Bosnia and Herzegovina, *Blagovčanin* speaks of "the rule of the cartel".[70] The findings of the European Fund for the Balkans[71] are consistent with this assessment:

"The most recent history of Western Balkan politics is full of examples which point to direct involvement of government officials in electoral fraud, corruption, abuse of

---

[66]   SWD(2022) 334 final, 64.

[67]   SWD(2022) 338 final, 74. In the 2018 report, the Commission estimated the share of the informal economy at around 30% of GDP, SWD(2018) 152 final, 43.

[68]   "… state capture is not just widespread corruption. Rather, its essence lies in a distinct network structure in which corrupt actors cluster around parts of the state allowing them to act collectively in pursuance of their private goals to the detriment of the public good", Fazekas and Tóth, 'From Corruption to State Capture. A New Analytical Framework with Empirical Applications from Hungary' (2016) 69 Political Research Quarterly 2, 320 ff. See also Richter, 'Der Wolf im Schafspelz: Illegitime Herrschaft durch State Capture in Nachkriegs- und Transitionsgesellschaften' (2017) 6 Zeitschrift für Friedens- und Konfliktforschung 2, 174-206. *Maarten Lemstra* illustrates the phenomenon with the example of Serbia, see Lemstra, 'The destructive effects of state capture in the Western Balkans' (September 2020) Clingendael Policy Brief, Clingendael Institute, at 2 ff. See also the report by Transparency International, Examining State Capture [Western Balkans and Turkey], 2020, <https://www.transparency .org/en/publications/examining-state-capture>. Some authors argue that 'capture' has penetrated much further into society, including NGOs, trade unions, business actors and the media, Cvetičanin, Bliznakovski and Krstić, 'Captured states and/or captured societies in the Western Balkans' (2023) Southeast European and Black Sea Studies (2023), DOI: 10.1080/14683857.2023.2170202.

[69]   The European Fund for the Balkans, *Extractive Institutions in the Western Balkans* (Paper Series 2016) at 8.

[70]   Blagovčanin, *The Rule of the Cartel* (Transparency International Bosna i Hercegovina 2020).

[71]   The European Fund for the Balkans, (2016) *supra* note 69 at 9.

power and authority, conflict of interest, blackmail, wiretapping, and criminal activity, but also in the nomination and appointment of public prosecutors and judges. These are all activities that are directed toward insuring this privileged access. The preference for non-democracy is, therefore, a consequence of the preference for privileged access to extractive public institutions."

Captured institutions tend to be extractive, meaning that a small elite holds all the power and makes decisions that primarily benefit and enrich themselves, without regard for the wider population. The existence of extractive institutions endangers the very fundamentals of rule of law and democracy, among others elections. Elections in the WB therefore became a farce.[72] *Blagovčanin* further elaborates that in hybrid regimes (and all WB countries are classified as such), corruption is present in the electoral process due to the manipulability of the system.[73] To maintain their power, incumbents use unethical and illegal tactics, such as buying votes, giving public sector jobs to their supporters, and awarding public contracts to companies with close ties to the ruling elites. These companies then provide resources to the ruling party's campaigns. In the consequence, separation of powers, checks and balances, an independent and impartial judiciary, equality before the law, i.e. all the cornerstones of the modern concept of the rule of law, become illusions. When public (state) institutions are "captured" by political elites, the rule of law is also hijacked and accountability is a non-existing concept.

3.3   The Low Trust Problem

During the Covid 19 pandemic, the issue of trust in public institutions became not only an important, but to some extent a systemic issue, even in the established democracies of the most developed countries. One of the striking findings was the correlation between citizens' refusal to be vaccinated and their lack of trust in the government.[74] Although the perception of mistrust has increased due to the omnipresence of the issue in the media, the problem of diminishing trust in political leadership and institutions has been discussed earlier, e.g. on the occasion of the rise of populism in the US and Europe.[75] In the context of developments in post-socialist societies, the question of trust has

---

[72] Ibid.; Blagovčanin, (2020) *supra* note 70.

[73] Ibid. at 13.

[74] See e.g. Bajos et al., 'When Lack of Trust in the Government and in Scientists Reinforces Social Inequalities in Vaccination Against COVID-19' (2022) 10 Frontiers Public Health, <https://doi.org/10.3389/fpubh.2022.908152>.

[75] See e.g. Alhan, Guriev et al., 'The European Trust Crisis and the Rise of Populism' (2017) Brookings Papers on Economic Activity, 309-382.

been examined in detail before.[76] In the WB region, the war experience adds up to the legacies from the socialist regimes.[77]

While EU Member States are concerned about the declining trust of their citizens, people in the countries of the Western Balkans are still significantly behind the trust level of their peers in the EU.[78] Meanwhile, the level of trust is substantial because there is a strong correlation between a high level of trust in the society and a low level of corruption[79] as well as between trust and levels of rule of law.[80] There is also "a strong negative relationship between perceived corruption and confidence in government".[81]

The positive effect of trust is that confident citizens are more likely to have a favourable opinion of their democratic systems, take part in political activities, and be involved in civic organisations. Countries with a higher trust level tend to have more effective democratic systems, more open market, higher economic growth, and less criminal activity and corruption.[82]

---

[76] The number of publications on this topic is overflowing, e.g. Mishler and Rose, 'Trust, Distrust and Skepticism: Popular Evaluations of Civil and Political Institutions in Post-Communist Societies' (1997) 59 The Journal of Politics 2, 418-451; Sapsford and Abbott, 'Trust, confidence and social environment in post-communist societies' (2006) 39 Communist and Post-Communist Studies 1, 59-71; Different approach (communist legacies being not decisive) by Epperly, 'The Myth of the Post-Communist Citizen' (2019) 43 Social Science History 2, 297-317.

[77] On differences between former Yugoslavia and other post-soviet states and Soviet Union see Dimitrova-Grajzl and Simon, 'Political Trust and Historical Legacy: The Effect of Varieties of Socialism' (2010) 24 East European Politics and Societies 2, 206-228.

[78] OECD, *Government at a Glance: Western Balkans* (2019) at 126; Golubović, Džunić and Golubović, 'Trust In Political Institutions In Western Balkan Countries' (2015) 13 Law and Politics 1, 13-21.

[79] Rothstein, *The quality of government: corruption, social trust, and inequality in international perspective* (2011) at 150.

[80] Muharemović, *Social (Dis-)Trust and The Plague of Corruption in the Western Balkans: The Rule of Law as the Victim* (Konrad Adenauer Stiftung, 2021).

[81] OECD, (2019) *supra* note 78 at 126.

[82] Rothstein, (2021) *supra* note 79 at 147.

4.   CONCLUSION: MATERIALITY AS
A CONSEQUENCE FOR THE ACCESSION
PROCESS

As mentioned in the introduction, the "new methodology" as one of the results from the rule of law debate in the EU has already been enshrined in the nego-tiating frameworks for Northern Macedonia and Albania 2020. Montenegro and Serbia have subsequently opted in. The criteria are thus set. However, we are not very optimistic that their formal fulfilment will lead to more and better rule of law in the region, and instead not to further formal reforms and the creation of empty institutional shells. As an example, in Serbia, over the past two decades, almost every government has carried out some formal reforms in the judiciary (the last one is still underway), which, with the commendable exception of reducing the backlog of cases,[83] have not led to substantive improvements. In Albania, Montenegro and in North Macedonia the changes were just formal in nature and did not (yet) lead to any improvements.[84] In BiH there was no reform at all due to the dysfunctionality of the legislative powers and institutions in the last years. The "governments in the Western Balkans have managed to combine a formal commitment to democracy and European integration with informal authoritarian practices",[85] reporting only superficial progress, with no real improvements for citizens or democratic governance.[86]

The crucial question is whether and what consequences will be drawn for the *substantive* implementation of the acquis from the lessons learned from the

---

[83]   Between 2016 and 2018, "almost 1 million cases were cleared from the backlog and efficiency measures were extended to courts covering more than 82% of the Serbian population", European Court of Auditors, (2022) *supra* note 24 at 22 nr. 37; for details see European Commission, 'Serbia 2018 Report', COM(2018) 450 final at 17.

[84]   The lack of progress is reflected in public surveys on trust in the judiciary, which is lowest in Northern Macedonia (13% tend to trust, 2% fully trust), Albania (19% tend to trust, 1% fully trust), and BiH (28% tend to trust, 5% fully trust). The figures are consistent with transparency and other categories, <https://www.rcc.int/balkanbarometer/results/2/public>.

[85]   European Court of Auditors, *EU support for the rule of law in the Western Balkans: despite efforts, fundamental problems persist* (Special Report, 01/2022), para. 06.

[86]   See Soyaltin-Colella, *The EU Accession Process, Chinese Finance and Rising Corruption in Western Balkan Stabilocracies: Serbia and Montenegro* (Routledge 2022); Richter and Wunsch, 'Money, power, glory: the linkages between EU conditionality and state capture in the Western Balkans' (2019) 27 Journal of European Public Policy 1, 41-62.

regressions in the rule of law in some EU countries, but also from the failures seen in the WB countries so far.

One of the inherent, systematic problems is in the reform approach itself: Compliance with the acquis requires the alignment of not only the political and economic, but also the institutional framework in the WB countries with the EU model. Until now, the EU did not pay much attention to the substantial implementation of the formally introduced reforms. The analysis of EU reports (SWDs) for 13 post-socialist countries, now EU Member States, shows that little attention has been paid to informality.[87] The current accession methodology and negotiation frameworks do not address the informal aspect of the transition either.

The introduction of purely formal reforms is possible and already underway. However, countries need to adapt not only their legislation but also the de facto modus operandi to EU standards, and are required to do so as quickly as possible. This leads to a copy-and-paste approach, where standards, institutional architecture and façades are planted in societies and traditional structures where they are foreign bodies. In academia, this problem has been addressed many times. For example, "… when Slovenia implemented reforms, it did it in a very particular way: as an uncritical model-taker of policy models from the West. This mimicry was done in a fairly top down, bureaucratic way, creating institutions without deep enough roots in society, and without necessary trial and error style usually needed for successful evaluation of proposed reforms."[88]

Slovenia was not an exception but the rule,[89] as almost all institutional and legal changes in the WB region follow the models of (different!) EU Member States entering into partnerships with or advising WB countries.[90] This approach has not changed, although research and experience have shown that "European Union's strategy of transposing formal rules from one environ-

---

[87] Mujarić and Kumalić, 'Formal and Informal Institutions in Policy – Evidence from South East Europe' in Gordy and Efendic (eds), *Meaningful reform in the Western Balkans: Between formal institutions and informal practices* (Peter Lang 2019), 147-167 at 148.

[88] Bugaric and Kuhelj, (2015). *supra* note 7 at 274.

[89] Many authors argue that the accession conditionality not only did not have a positive impact but had a "pathological effect" on the development in the region, see Mendelski, (2015) *supra* note 5; see also Soyaltin-Colella, (2022) *supra* note 86; Richter and Wunsch, (2019) *supra* note 86.

[90] For example, the High Judicial Councils are reminiscent of the French *Conseil supérieur de la magistrature* (CSM), the public notary's office in Serbia and Northern Macedonia, regulated and established after a very tough process, followed the German model, etc.

ment to another can be viewed as having been unsuccessful".[91] One striking example is the establishment of the High Judicial Councils (HJC). *Mendelski's* research from 2015 showed that "[r]ather than being guarantors of judicial independence and the rule of law, most judicial councils from SEE evolved into politicized, unaccountable, and non-transparent bodies that tended to undermine the rule of law... It could be argued that judicial councils, rather than improving judicial independence, just opened up a different channel of political influence."[92] In the last years the situation improved slightly in some countries, but not significantly.[93]

The first consequence should be to rethink the formalistic approach and to diversify the emphasis on judiciary.[94] The material implementation of the reforms and their functioning in real life must be the yardstick and not just the passing of another law or creation of another institution.[95] Only in this way can the decision-makers be held accountable and perhaps they would refrain from mere 'window-dressing'. To achieve this, the 'more the better' and the scattergun approach should be replaced by a strategic, qualitative reform process. In doing so, the urgent (and not only those considered important) needs of the population are to be given greater consideration and priorities are to be adjusted. The everyday problems of people in WB countries do not necessarily coincide with the ideas in Brussels, Berlin or Paris.[96] Mostly they are more basic and less ideological, the level of "self-actualisation" of *Maslow's*

---

[91]   Gordy and Efendic, 'Engaging Policy to Address Gaps Between Formality and Informality in the Western Balkans' in Gordy and Efendic, (2019) *supra* note 87, 7-19 at 12.

[92]   See Mendelski, (2015) *supra* note 5 at 336, with further references.

[93]   An improvement can be seen in Albania due to the reform of the High Judicial Council in 2019 and the ongoing vetting process involving international experts. In other countries, e.g. in BiH, no improvements can be seen, European Court of Auditors, (2022) *supra* note 24 at 23 box 2; regarding Montenegro, 31 box 6 and 35 para. 61.

[94]   Damjanovski and Kmezić, 'Europeanisation and Institutionalisation of EU Rules in the Western Balkans' in Gordy and Efendic, (2019) *supra* note 87, 21-64 at 29.

[95]   This approach is also necessary to build trust as it is related "not to what takes place on the input side of the representational democratic system, but to what happens at the output side", Rothstein, (2021) *supra* note 79 at 151.

[96]   The poverty in the WB region is still very high with a headcount ratio at *national* poverty lines >21%, see <https://databank.worldbank.org/source/world-development-indicators>. The EU accession means 'economic prosperity' for 40% and 'freedom to study and/or work in EU' for 29% of the respondents, while 'gender equality' receives 6%, <https://www.rcc.int/balkanbarometer/results/2/public>.

hierarchy of needs has not yet been reached for the vast majority of citizens in the Balkans.[97]

The second consequence is that a comprehensive analysis of regulations and institutions already in place in every WB country needs to be conducted in order to find out what areas need to be prioritized. It is very possible that the eye of the needle is not the judiciary or the police, but other institutions. Not every rule or institution needs to be harmonised or replaced at this stage of the accession process, especially those that function quite well in a formal or even informal way. This, of course, cannot always be in line with the goals of the EU, for which, for example, security and police are particular priorities. The problem is that not everything can be done at once.

The third consequence is to understand that reforms cannot succeed against informal networks and institutions. They are key to meaningful reform and need to be studied and considered in order to reduce institutional capture. We agree with the OECD: "Informal practices, if not factored into the design of public policy or regulated, may weaken formal institutions and citizen trust in them. This could create a vicious circle that ultimately wears out the social contract necessary for stability."[98] The undeniably important fight against corruption must not lead to institutional dysfunctionality.[99]

The fourth consequence is that public services need to be "democratised" in all areas, especially in the daily life of citizens and local government, and not only in the areas formally prioritised first by the acquis (see the first consequence). Such democratisation of institutions can only be successful if the problem of trust is solved, which requires the involvement of citizens at a broad level. The involvement of civil society was envisaged under IPA II, but the results are not yet visible and the main focus on EU-friendly NGOs and organised groups should be reconsidered. Finally, the glaring lack of free,

---

[97] Only 18% of respondents in the region are satisfied with their job opportunities, 22% with their economic situation, 24% with the safety, 27% with the health services, 30% with the education, <https://www.rcc.int/balkanbarometer/results/2/public>.

[98] OECD, *Multi-dimensional Review of the Western Balkans* (2021) at 90.

[99] This happened in Albania, for example, where the vetting process led to an exodus of judges and prosecutors and widespread obstruction of the judiciary over a five-year period. The Supreme Court backlog alone was still at around 35,000 cases by the end of 2022. "The average length for a case at appeal level is 893 days. However, at Tirana Appeal Court, the average length for a criminal [sic] case is 5 820 days", European Commission, SWD(2022) 332 final at 21. Some courts continue to operate with 50% of the staff. Trust in the judiciary has almost fallen back to the level before the vetting process began, see *supra* note 28.

independent and objective media as part of civil society needs to be urgently
and effectively addressed.

6.   Are Judges Politicians in Robes? Comparative Aspects of the Recruitment and Election of Judges[1]

Piotr Mikuli, Natalie Fox and Radosław Puchta

1.   INTRODUCTION

To tackle the question of whether judges are essentially politicians, one must delve into the considerations surrounding the political aspects of power. The definitions of the concept of politics vary depending on whether we are dealing with a formal, functional or behavioural view. We know from *Aristotle* that it is about the art of governing the state. More recent definitions emphasise the role of reconciling various perspectives and aligning interests. We also link politics with the pursuit of power in every social entity, clarifying its inherent nature. If politics is the making of authoritative decisions that significantly affect society, then the courts' and judges' activities are political.

Nevertheless, contemporary perspectives on the functioning of the rule of law emphasise the separation of the dispensation of justice from other legal forms of state action.[2] Therefore, the separation of powers requires that state functions be dispersed and entrusted to different bodies. As is well known, the

[1]   The chapter is partly based on research conducted by Piotr Mikuli, funded by the Polish National Agency for Academic Exchange (NAWA) conducted at the University of Glasgow in 2022. The research has been also supported from the Priority Research Area 'FutureSoc' under the Strategic Programme Excellence Initiative at Jagiellonian University.

[2]   See *inter alia* Beverley McLachlin, 'Judicial Independence: A Functional Per-spective' in Mads Andenas and Duncan Fairgrieve (eds), *Tom Bingham and the transformation of the law: a liber amicorum* (OUP 2009); Shimon Shetreet (eds), *The Culture of Judicial Independence: Rule of Law and World Peace* (Martinus Nijhoff Publishers 2015); Laurent Pech, 'The Rule of Law as a Well-Established and Well-Defined Principle of EU Law' (2022) HJRL14, 107-138.

role of the courts varies in separation of power doctrines. For *Montesquieu*, judges were supposed to be 'the mouth that pronounces the words of the law', whose role was only to decide individual cases based on the language of the laws. The modern state regulates so many areas of social life that it is impossible to regulate these issues unambiguously. Therefore, in applying the law, the courts must interpret it, hence leading to an increasing role for the judiciary because of the creation of the judge's interpretation of the law, which resembles law-making.

This contemporary role of the courts and so-called judicial activism is, of course, controversial. It is said that judges do not have sufficient democratic legitimacy to participate in law-making. The law-making role of the judiciary, which originates primarily in the judicial review of legislation, including statutes, is nuanced in the various theories that refer to departmentalism or continuous democracy. These concepts assume that, in the modern state, many bodies, including the courts, not only the parliament, are involved in creating legal norms. The courts' vital role in determining the content of the law can lead to describing judges as politicians in robes. Nevertheless, the active role of the courts in controlling the legislature can also be justified by, on the one hand, the system of checks and balances and the necessity to restrain the legislature (in this sense, the courts become the guardian of the rule of law), here with the primary aim of protecting the constitutional norm; on the other hand, the independence and impartiality of the judiciary as a desirable feature legitimises the considerable powers of the courts in modern states. In this sense, all fit into the mechanism of a certain balance in the state, where the political decision is nuanced by the professional factor.

The hallmark of judges' actions should be professionalism and impartiality, which are essential for the legitimacy of judicial power, and which cannot be provided by mere democratic legitimacy analogous to the democratic electoral legitimacy of the legislature and executive.

The rule of law emphasises the independence of the judiciary and impartiality of judges by separating courts and judges from current politics. In this sense, when talking about the judiciary, we want to distance it from politics, which is understood somewhat differently than in those general definitions given earlier, that is, from current involvement in political disputes and current ideas about governance, from partisanship.

Taking these considerations into account, we address the issue of judicial appointments in the contemporary state. In our chapter, we consider both the courts of general jurisdiction, including apex courts and constitutional courts. Because of the limited length of the study, we will not refer to the appointment process in special courts, including administrative courts, which appear in some constitutional systems.

## 2.	JUDGES IN COURTS OF ORDINARY JURISDICTION

Obviously, there is no common consensus on the best procedure to appoint judges.[3] The process of selecting candidates for judicial offices plays a key role in ensuring the independence of the judiciary,[4] a huge diversity of judicial appointment systems exists.[5] Each lawmaker is searching for its own way to combine the principle of judicial independence with other constitutional values, such as judicial professionalism, accountability and the representativeness of the judiciary. Sometimes, different systems are used at the same time for different levels of the judiciary: when judges of general jurisdiction courts are supposed to be selected based solely on their qualifications and merit, which presupposes a rather technocratic process, a more politicised mechanism is adopted to choose candidates for apex or constitutional courts.

---

[3]	"There is, however, no agreement in international law as to the method of [judicial] appointment. In this field, a certain degree of discretion is left to individual States, provided that the selection be always based on the candidates' professional qualifications and personal integrity. (…) international standards do not explicitly determine which body within a State has the power to appoint judges or the exact procedure to be followed. However, it is important to bear in mind that any appointment procedure must guarantee judicial independence, both institutional and individual, and impartiality, both objective and subjective. This requirement derives from the principle of separation of powers and of checks and balances, which constitute indispensable safeguards to this end'. See 'International Principles on the Independence and Accountability of Judges, Lawyers and Prosecutors" (Practitioners Guides No. 1, 2007) <https://www.refworld.org/pdfid/4a7837af2.pdf> accessed 29 August 2023.

[4]	Because the ECtHR has already clearly enlightened the process of appointing judges, here regarding its fundamental implications for the proper functioning and the legitimacy of the judiciary in a democratic state governed by the rule of law, this necessarily constitutes an inherent element of the concept of 'establishment' of a court or tribunal 'by law', and an interpretation to the contrary would defy the purpose of the relevant requirement. To establish whether a court can be considered 'independent' within the meaning of Article 6(1) ECHR, regard must be given, *inter alia*, to the manner of appointment of its members, which pertains to the domain of the establishment of a 'tribunal'. See App. No. 26374/18, *Guðmundur Andri Ástráðsson v Iceland*, [2020], para. 218-234.

[5]	See Anna Dziedzic, 'Selection of Judges' in Rainer Grote, Frauke Lachenmann and Rüdiger Wolfrum (eds), *Max Planck Encyclopaedia of Compar-ative Constitutional Law* (OUP 2020) [online].

Nevertheless, some trends can be noticed, not only within the European legal space, but also worldwide.[6]

When it comes to the judges of general jurisdiction courts and apex courts other than constitutional courts, one can distinguish the three most common models of judicial appointments. First, the competence to appoint judges remains the domain of the institutions or institutions pertaining to political power (the so-called political model). This competence could then be exercised either by a single state organ (being a part, alternatively, of the executive or legislative branch) or by one state organ 'with the advice and consent' of another one. Second, judicial appointments may formally remain in the hands of the political power, but the latitude of the latter in selecting a nominee is limited by an independent factor, here in the form of specialised bodies such as appointments commissions or judicial councils. When common-law jurisdictions tend towards judicial appointment commissions (the so-called appointment commission model), civil law jurisdictions rely rather on judicial councils (the so-called judicial council model). In addition to these key models, several other, far less common, models could be identified, among them, for example, the so-called transitional model, which is when a political body with formally unlimited nominating powers accepts a kind of self-restraint, and – from the opposite side of the scale – the so-called co-option model, which is when appointments of new judges lie solely in the hands of the incumbent judges.

Historically, judicial appointments belonged to the prerogatives of the executive. Judges were officials appointed by a monarch who was acting alone or on the advice of their ministers.[7] The royal assent was intended to be a source

---

[6]   According to the Council of Europe's recommendations, "The authority taking decisions on the selection and career of judges should be independent of the executive and legislative powers. With a view to guaranteeing its independence, at least half of the members of the authority should be judges chosen by their peers. However, where the constitutional or other legal provisions prescribe that the head of state, the government or the legislative power take decisions concerning the selection and career of judges, and independent and competent authority drawn in substantial part from the judiciary (…) should be authorized to make recommendations or express opinions which the relevant appointing authority follows in practice". See Committee of Ministers of the Council of Europe, *Judges: Independence, Efficiency and Responsibilities*, Recommendation CM/Rec(2010)12 adopted by the Committee of Ministers of the Council of Europe on 17 November 2010 and explanatory memorandum, Council of Europe Publishing 2011, paras 46-47 <https://rm.coe.int/cmrec-2010-12-on-independence-efficiency-responsibilites-of-judges/16809f007d> accessed 29 August 2023.

[7]   See Alan P. Obe, 'Power and Judicial Appointments. Squaring the impossible circle' in Erika Rackley and Graham Gee (eds), *Debating Judicial Appointments in an Age of Diversity* (Routledge 2017), 33.

of legitimacy for judges, as well as a guarantee of their independence vis-à-vis other state officials. In modern times, this prerogative has passed into the hands of either the President of the Republic (in countries with a presidential or hyper-presidential model of government) or the government, particularly the minister responsible for court administration (in parliamentarian democracies). In the United Kingdom, the Lord Chancellor used to monopolise this process (which was highly secretive and informal) before the country switched into the independent appointment commission model in 2005. Nowadays, however, because of, among other factors, the principle of separation of powers, it would be hard to justify any monopoly of a single political body in the selection of judges. The single-body appointment mechanism continues to be used for constitutional judges' appointments when the chambers of a parliament select those who are then supposed to control the legislation (e.g., Germany, Poland). As far as judges of ordinary courts are concerned, a model that requires the consent of at least two political bodies belonging to different branches of government appears to be far more common, above all in countries with a presidential system.

Undoubtedly, the constitutional mechanism applied in the US Constitution at the level of federal courts has become exemplary. According to Article II, Section 2, Clause 2, of the US Constitution (so-called 'Appointments Clause'), the President shall nominate and 'by and with the advice and consent of the Senate' appoint Justices of the Supreme Court. The same procedure is used to fill judgeships in the lower federal courts created by Congress, that is, for district and circuit judges.[8] The procedure consists, therefore, of three steps: the presidential nomination of a candidate, his/her approval by the Senate and, finally, the formal commission by the President. No specific requirements for a nominee have been established by the Constitution, which is why the appointing authority enjoys relatively broad discretionary powers.[9] In practice, federal judgeships are filled by people who have received appropriate legal training and gained relevant experience in the legal profession. To avoid Senate refusal, the President usually holds informal consultations with leading

---

[8]   See paras 44 and 133 of the U.S. Code.

[9]   Theodore W. Ruger, 'The Judicial Appointment Power of the Chief Justice' (2004), 7 U. Pa. J. Const. L, 341: "Judicial authority is thus rendered more democratic because the discretion to choose judges lies in the political arena. This fundamental constitutional bargain – judges generally insulated from public pressure but chosen with popular input – is a key component of the standard theoretical defence of judicial review against accusations of excessive 'countermajoritarianism'. So important is this up-front public input that the Constitution does not vest appointment authority in just one elected body, but instead bifurcates the power between the President and the Senate".

congressmen. The Office of White House Counsel, the Department of State, Justices of the Supreme Court (above all, the Chief Justice) and the American Bar Association,[10] among others, are also involved in these informal consultations and preselection of an appropriate candidate. However, a key role in the procedure for appointing federal judges is played by the Senate Committee on the Judiciary and, at least in cases of district judges, the nominee's home state senators who receive a 'blue slip' that they return to the Committee, indicating if they are going to support a presidential nomination.[11] It is up to the Committee's chairman to finally decide whether and when to convene a plenary meeting of the Committee to publicly hear a candidate. If a presidential nominee receives positive votes from a majority of the Committee's members, he will be voted by the full Senate by a simple majority of the senators present and voting.[12] At the end of this procedure, the President signs a nominee's commission.

This two-body political mechanism of judicial appointment was transplanted, frequently with modification, in other countries, above all in Latin America. For example, the Brazilian Constitution provides for similar procedures for judicial appointments at the highest level of the judiciary. Justices of the Supreme Federal Court, Superior Court of Justice, Superior Labour Court and Superior Military Court are commissioned by the President of the Republic after their nominations have been approved by the Federal Senate.[13] Candidates to the Supreme Federal Court are freely chosen by the President of the Republic because they do not have to fulfil any specific conditions, except for being knowledgeable in law and having an unblemished reputation.[14]

---

[10] Since 1953, the American Bar Association's Standing Committee on the Federal Judiciary has been conducting independent peer evaluations of the professional qualifications of nominees to the federal courts.

[11] This custom gives nominee's home state senators a *de facto* veto over presidential nomination. See Brannon P. Denning, 'The "Blue Slip": Enforcing the Norms of the Judicial Confirmation Process' (2001) 10 BORJ, 75.

[12] However, before voting on the nomination, the debate on the candidate must be closed, for which a three-fifths majority is required. Since 2017, the only exception concerns Supreme Court nominations. In such cases, 51 votes are sufficient to end the debate.

[13] See Articles 101, 104 and 123 of the Constitution of the Federative Republic of Brazil of 5 October 1988. In the case of justices of the Supreme Federal Court and Superior Court of Justice, approval must be adopted by the absolute majority of the Federal Senate.

[14] Except for the refusal of the Senate to approve five presidential nominees at the beginning of the Brazilian Republic (in 1894), no President has seen his nominee rejected since then. See Maria Angela de Santa Cruz Oliveira Jardim and

The scope of presidential discretion is limited in the case of other superior courts. For example, a major part of nominees to the Superior Court of Justice (two-thirds) and Superior Labour Court (four-fifths) are to be selected by the courts themselves among lower-level judges. The remaining part is filled by lawyers and prosecutors who are also preselected by the courts. Thus, the freedom of action of the political authority is circumscribed by professional preselection. At the same time, however, the President freely selects candidates to the Superior Military Court from among certain categories of military officers, auditor judges, prosecutors and lawyers.

Cooperation between presidents of the republic and parliaments is also needed, for example, in Argentina. The Justices of the Supreme Court of Argentina are appointed by the President of the Nation with the consent of the Senate. Before the 1994 Constitutional Reform, the Argentinian Senate validated presidential nominations with a simple majority vote. To exclude partisanship, the new Argentinian Constitution provides that approval shall be passed by a qualified majority of two-thirds of senators who are present during a public meeting convened for this purpose.[15] As far as lower court judges are concerned, the Argentinian appointment system has shifted into a kind of mixed model, where not only two political bodies, but also a judicial council, are involved in the appointment process. The judges of lower federal courts are appointed by the President of the Nation based on a binding proposal submitted by the Judicial Council (*Consejo de la Magistratura*) and with the consent of the Senate that is given during a public meeting. The creation of the Judicial Council[16] in 1994 was a result of a long history of a highly politicised, secretive judicial appointment process. The legal concept was transplanted from European constitutional territory to 'depoliticise' the process of electing lower judges. For each vacancy, the Council proposes a *terna vinculante*, that is, a three-person, rank-ordered list of candidates from which the President may appoint one person. Each recommendation should be supported by two-thirds of the Council members before being sent to the President. This high majority requirement impedes the executive from pushing through its preferred candidates. The selection process aims to be transparent (opened to the public) and objective (evaluation standards must be predetermined).

Another way of circumscribing political discretion during the judicial appointment process is to create an independent commission that is competent in selecting candidates in an open and inclusive way. This model, as men-

---

Nuno Garoupa, 'Choosing Judges in Brazil: Reassessing Legal Transplants from the United States' (2011) 59 Am. J. Comp. Law 2, 529.
[15]   See Article 99(4) of the Constitution of the Argentine Nation.
[16]   However, the Council did not start its operations until 1998.

tioned above, was adopted in 2005 in the United Kingdom.[17] As a result of the Constitutional Reform of 2005, the Judicial Appointments Commission for selecting candidates for judicial posts in England and Wales was established. Similar institutions have also been created in Scotland and Northern Ireland. The committees are composed of judges who do not have a majority, representatives of other legal professions and lay persons.[18] The selection panels that they convene for selecting specific candidates for the recruitment process also have a mixed composition. The influence of representatives of the executive, that is, the Lord Chancellor or the national executive, is currently limited. As for judicial offices in the higher courts, the Lord Chancellor's participation in the procedure for selecting the final candidate for a vacancy is maintained. This also applies to the nomination procedure of Lord Chief Justice. Formally, the appointment to the positions of Lord Chief Justice, Heads of Divisions of the High Court and of Lords of Appeal is similar to that of judges of the Supreme Court (see below). This means that the monarch issues the act of appointment with the recommendation of the Prime Minister, and the latter acts on the advice of the Lord Chancellor.

As far as judges of the Supreme Court of the United Kingdom are concerned, the political model was abandoned in 2005. According to Article 26(3) of the Constitutional Reform Act 2005, the Prime Minister must recommend for an office of the President of the Supreme Court, the Deputy President of the Court and justices of the Court any person who is selected as a result of the convening of a special selection commission,[19] and may not recommend any

---

[17]   See Simon Shetreet and Sophie Turenne, *Judges on Trial: The Independence and Accountability of the English Judiciary* (2nd edn CUP 2013), 102-178; Graham Gee and others, *The Politics of Judicial Independence in the UK's Changing Constitution* (Cambridge University Press 2015), 159-173.

[18]   For instance, the Judicial Appointments Commission for England and Wales is composed of 15 members. The Chairman of the Commission is a lay member. Of the 14 other Commissioners, six must be judicial members (including two tribunal judges) two must be professional members (each of which must hold a qualification listed below but must not hold the same qualification as each other) five must be lay members, one must be a nonlegally qualified judicial member. See sec. 4-8 of the Judicial Appointments Commission Regulations 2013.

[19]   Section 27 of the Constitutional Reform Act 2005 and the Supreme Court (Judicial Appointments) Regulations 2013 specify that the commission must have an odd number of members and no less than five in number. In a case of appointment as a justice of the Court, the selection commission must consist of the President of the Court (who is to be the chairman of the selection commission), a member of the Judicial Appointments Commission, a member of the Judicial Appointments Board for Scotland, a member of the Northern Ireland Judicial

other person. When a vacancy arises, it is up to the Lord Chancellor to convene such a commission within the time frame specified in the law. The legislation does not prescribe a concrete procedure that a selection commission must follow. In practice, each selection commission determines on its own how to operate, here subject to guidelines made by the Lord Chancellor. However, some critical rules must be obeyed. First, the process before the commission results in selecting only one candidate. Second, a candidate needs to meet the qualifications set out by law.[20] This election must be on merit only. Obviously, no member of the commission can be selected for the appointment. Third, in making selections, the commission must ensure that the justices will have knowledge and experience of practice in the law of each of parts of the United Kingdom. After the selection stage is completed by the commission, the Lord Chancellor either approves the result, rejects it or requires the commission to reconsider.[21] The Lord Chancellor must give the commission reasons in writing for rejecting or requiring reconsideration of a selection. If the Lord Chancellor rejects a selection, then the commission is obliged to choose a different person. In the case of requiring reconsideration, the commission may select the same person or a different one.[22] If the Lord Chancellor approves the person selected by the commission, the Prime Minister must then recommend that person to the monarch for appointment.

Continental jurisdictions instead rely on a judicial council that is competent for not only judicial appointments, but also for exercising other functions related to the protection of judicial independence, such as the disciplinary responsibility of judges, organisation of the judiciary or management of public funds allocated to the judiciary. This council, called the Supreme Council of Judiciary (*Conseil supérieur de la magistrature*), was created for the first time in France in 1883 as a body that could enforce the disciplinary responsibility

---

Appointments Commission and a senior UK judge nominated by the President. When the selection commission is convened to choose a candidate for the President of the Supreme Court Presidency, the outgoing President may not be a member of the commission. In these circumstances, in principle, it may be the Deputy President of the Supreme Court.

[20] According to Article 25(1) of the Constitutional Reform Act 2005, a person is not qualified to be appointed a judge of the Supreme Court unless he has (at any time) held high judicial office for a period of at least two years, been a qualifying practitioner for a period of at least 15 years, satisfied the judicial appointment eligibility condition on a 15-year basis or been a qualifying practitioner for a period of at least 15 years.

[21] See Article 20 of the Supreme Court (Judicial Appointments) Regulations 2013.

[22] See ibid., Article 22.

of magistrates.[23] In 1946, the Council became an autonomous constitutional body. Its current structure stems from the constitutional reform adopted in 1995. Two separate panels have been created: the first one for judges' cases and the second one with jurisdiction over prosecutors. As far as judges are concerned, the Supreme Council of the Judiciary makes proposals (*propositions*) for the appointment of judges of the Cassation Court, as well as chief judges in lower courts, namely the first presidents of court of appeal and presidents of trial court (*tribunal judiciaire*). Applications for these posts are simultaneously sent to the Council and the Minister of Justice, but the initiative belongs to the Council. For each appointment, once candidates' files have been examined, the Council makes a proposal that is submitted to the President of the Republic. Judicial posts other than those mentioned above are filled after the Council's consent (*avis conforme*). In the latter cases, the Council gives its opinion on the proposals made by the Minister of Justice.[24] In principle, however, candidates for judicial offices of the lowest grade are recruited from the top graduates (*auditeurs*) of the National School of Judiciary (*École supérieure de la magistrature*);[25] meanwhile, judgeships of the higher grade are filled based on seniority and merit, here according to a promotion table prepared by a special promotion committee.[26] At the end of the selection process, decrees on appointments or promotions are issued by the President of the Republic.[27]

Judicial councils have also been created in many other countries. The scope of powers of such councils, as well as their composition and functioning, differ from one jurisdiction to another. As far as judicial appointments are concerned, one can find councils that have a decisive role and those that only make proposals submitted to the executive. Italian judges are appointed through competitive examinations.[28] Once the exam is passed, the High Council of Judiciary (*Consiglio superiore della magistratura*)[29] approves a ranking list

---

[23]   In fact, at that time, the Supreme Council of Judiciary consisted of all chambers of the Cassation Court assembled to hear disciplinary cases concerning magistrates.

[24]   See Article 65(4) of the Constitution of the French Republic (1958) and Article 15 of the Organic Law No 94-100 on the Supreme Council of the Judiciary (1994).

[25]   See Article 26 of the Ordonnance No. 58-1270 introducing the Organic Law on the Status of the Magistrates (1958).

[26]   See ibid., Articles 27 and 34.

[27]   See Piotr Mikuli, Natalie Fox, Radosław Puchta (eds.), *Ministers of Justice in Comparative Perspective* (Eleven International Publishing 2019).

[28]   See Article 106(1) of the Constitution of the Italian Republic (1947).

[29]   The Italian High Council of Judiciary is a body that has a mixed composition. It comprises the President of the Republic (as its chairman), the First

(*graduatoria*) and decides on the appointments of those with the best results. Appointment decrees are issued by the Minister of Grace and Justice within 10 days of receipt of the Council's resolution.[30] A new judge is obliged to take part in an 18-month theoretical and practical internship. Once the internship is completed and the candidate's aptitude for exercising judicial functions has been confirmed, the Council assigns this individual a vacant judicial post.[31]

In Poland, all judges of all categories and levels of the judiciary are appointed by the President of the Republic on the motion of the National Council of the Judiciary.[32] Although a relevant constitutional provision is drafted in an imperative manner stating that judges 'shall be appointed' by the President of the Republic,[33] the recent constitutional practice demonstrates that the Council's

---

President of the Cassation Court, the Prosecutor General in this Court, 20 members elected by all ordinary judges belonging to the various categories and 10 members elected by the Parliament at a join meeting of the two Chambers by a three-fifth majority. See Article 104 of the Constitution of the Italian Republic (1947), as well as Articles 22 and 23 of the Organisation and Functioning of the High Council of Judiciary Act (1958).

[30]   See ibid., Article 12.

[31]   The Italian High Council of Judiciary has significant powers concerning not only judicial recruitment, but also judicial career (assignments, transfers, promotions), as well as judges' disciplinary responsibility. See Article 105 of the Constitution of the Italian Republic (1947).

[32]   The Polish National Council of Judiciary was created in 1989 as one of the elements of the Polish democratic transition. According to Article 187(1) of the Constitution of the Republic of Poland (1997), the Council is comprised of 25 members, among whom the First President of the Supreme Court, the Minister of Justice, the President of the Supreme Administrative Court, a representative of the President of the Republic, 15 judges chosen among judges of the Supreme Court, common courts, administrative courts and military courts, four members chosen by the Sejm from among deputies and two members chosen by the Senate from among senators. From 1989 to 2018, those elective judicial members of the Council were elected autonomously by competent assemblies of judges. As a result of the 'Reform of the Judiciary' adopted at the turn of 2017 and 2018, all 15 judges who are members of the Council are currently elected by the Sejm (the lower chamber of the Polish parliament), which is in clear violation of the principle of separation of powers. It was the main reason why, in 2022, the Great Chamber of the European Court of Human Rights clearly pointed out that 'the fundamental change in the manner of electing the NCJ's judicial members, considered jointly with the early termination of the terms of office of the previous judicial members (…), means that its independence is no longer guaranteed'. See *Grzęda v Poland* ECHR 43572/18 [2022], para. 322.

[33]   See Article 179 of the Constitution of the Republic of Poland (1997).

motion is not binding in the sense that the President of the Republic may reject it without giving any reason. Some argue that, because judicial appointments constitute one of the presidential prerogatives,[34] this competence is treated as a personal power of the President of the Republic and a sphere of their exclusive responsibility. Such an interpretation is intended to make the judicial review of presidential appointments impossible, even if those appointments have been issued because the Council was established unlawfully.

In some democratic countries, there is neither an independent appointment commission nor a judicial council. Hence, a competent political authority (usually the government) formally has a free hand while appointing judges. However, to preserve the independence of the judiciary, a kind of self-restraint has been imposed. In Germany, judges officially play no part in the appointment of federal judges (*Bundesrichter*).[35] Judges of the German federal supreme courts[36] are chosen jointly by the competent federal minister (namely, the Federal Minister of Justice or the Federal Minister of Labour and Social Affairs[37]) and a committee responsible for the election of judges (*Richterwahlausschuss*).[38] The composition of such a committee is purely political; it consists of 32 members, 16 of whom are competent ministers of the *Länder* (*ex officio* members),[39] and the other 16 are members elected by the Bundestag in accordance with the proportional representation principle at the beginning of the Chamber's term of office (elective members).[40] If there is a vacancy in one of the supreme federal courts, a meeting of the Judicial Election Committee is then convened, which is chaired by a relevant federal minister. Both the federal minister and Committee members may present a candidate for the vacant post. A nominee is chosen by the Committee in a secret ballot, with a simple majority of the votes cast. Nevertheless, the

---

[34] Which means that a presidential official act on judicial appointment does not need to be countersigned by the Prime Minister. See Article 144(3) of the Constitution of the Republic of Poland (1997).

[35] See Piotr Mikuli, Natalie Fox, Radosław Puchta, (2019) *supra* note 27.

[36] Namely, judges of the Federal Court of Justice, Federal Administrative Court, Federal Finance Court, Federal Labour Court and Federal Social Court.

[37] Although the Federal Minister of Justice is the competent federal minister with respect to the Federal High Court of Justice, Federal Administrative Court and Federal Finance Court, the Federal Minister of Labour and Social Affairs has nominating powers in cases of appointing judges of the Federal Labour Court and Federal Social Court.

[38] See Article 95(2) of the Basic Law of the Federal Republic of Germany (1949).

[39] Usually, they are state ministers of justice.

[40] See Articles 2-5 of Election of Judges Act (1950).

federal minister has *de facto* veto power. Only when the minister agrees with the decision of the Committee does the minister apply to the Federal President for the appointment of the person elected, which, in practice, is a mere formality. In this highly politicised procedure, a form of self-restraint is that the competent federal minister may, either on their own initiative or that of a member of the Judicial Election Committee, request a judicial appointment council (*Präsidialrat*) of the court concerned for a written opinion on the candidate. This council is a body of judicial self-government that is established in each federal court.[41] Although a judge cannot be appointed or elected until an opinion of the *Präsidialrat* has been given,[42] such an opinion is not legally binding for the appointing authority. In practice, however, the candidature of a person who has obtained a negative assessment from the *Präsidialrat* is not presented for the appointment. A similar self-restraint mechanism exists in Sweden, where permanent salaried judges are appointed by the government.[43] There is, however, the Judges Proposals Board (*Domarnämnden*), which is an independent governmental agency under the Ministry of Justice, and which has existed since 2008. It deals with all matters concerning the appointments of permanent judges and submits proposals of judges to the government. Usually, the president of the court with the vacancy interviews candidates and then submits comments to the Board. Proposals submitted to the government shall be motivated and may not be appealed. For each vacancy, the Board indicates at least three candidates who are best suited for the post. The final decision belongs instead to the government.

On the opposite side, there is the so-called co-optation model, which gives the judiciary a decisive role in selecting new judges. This model is especially used when it comes to lower judge appointments. In Japan, for example, while Justices of the Supreme Court are appointed and reviewed through a political process, career judges of the inferior courts are appointed by the government from a list of persons nominated by the Supreme Court for the 10-year term of office.[44] The governmental appointment of lower court judges is a mere

---

[41] See Article 49 of Status of Judges Act (1972). The *Präsidialrat* of the Federal Court of Justice is comprised of the president of that court (acting as chairman), his permanent deputy, two members elected by the Court presidium from among its members and three further members. *Präsidialräte* of other federal supreme courts are comprised, for each of them, of the president of the court concerned (acting as chairman), the president's permanent deputy, one member elected by the court presidium from among its members and two further members. See Article 54(1) of Status of Judges Act (1972).

[42] See ibid., Article 57(3).

[43] See Article 6, Chapter 11 of the Instrument of Government (1974).

[44] See Article 80 of the Constitution of Japan (1946).

formality. In practice, the Supreme Court Secretariat has control over their appointments. However, the Secretariat evaluates not only the aptitude of a candidate to be a judge,[45] but also how the individual performs based on their duties. Because of this, the Japanese judicial appointment process has been criticised as resulting in the extensive dependency of lower court judges for the Supreme Court.[46] It is quite similar in South Korea, where the Chief Justice and Justices of the Supreme Court are appointed by the President of the Nation with the consent of the National Assembly,[47] but other judges are appointed by the Chief Justice with the consent of the Council of Supreme Court Justices[48] for the 10-year renewable term of office. They are also assigned to their posts by the Chief Justice.[49] The Judicial Personnel Committee was established as an advisory group for the Chief Justice to plan and coordinate personnel issues. Also, in Brazil, at the trial level, the process of selecting judges is entirely administrated by the judiciary, with no executive participation whatsoever. At the appellate level, the executive only appoints one-fifth of the seats and the judiciary itself appoints all the remaining appellate court seats. As a result, the majority of appellate court seats are filled by career federal judges who are promoted by seniority or merit. Candidates for the one-fifth of appellate court seats are chosen from among lawyers and prosecutors by federal regional courts themselves and then submitted to the President of the Republic.[50]

---

[45] In Japan, they are generally appointed as lower court judges those who have served as an assistant judge for at least 10 years (a career system), but there is also a way where judges are appointed from practising attorneys (also having at least 10 years of the professional experience).

[46] See Daniel H. Foote, 'The Supreme Court and the Push for Transparency in Lower Court Appointments in Japan' (2011) 88 Wash. U. L. Review 6, 1745; Takayuki Il, 'Japan's Judicial System May Change, But Its Fundament Nature Stays Virtually the Same? Recent Japanese Reforms on the Judicial Appointments And Evaluation' (2013) 36 Hastings International and Comparative Law Review 2, 459.

[47] As far as justices other than the Chief Justice are concerned, the Chief Justice first submits to the President's recommendations for appointments, which also grants him a great influence on the Supreme Court composition.

[48] This Council consists of all Supreme Court justices, including the Chief Justice.

[49] See Article 104 of the Constitution of the Republic of Korea (1948).

[50] See Maria Angela de Santa Cruz Oliveira Jardim and Nuno Garoupa, (2011) *supra* note 14.

Table 6.1   *Models of Judicial Appointments*

Model	Chief Characteristic	Example	Pros	Cons
'Political Model'	– competence to appoint judges remains the domain of a state body or bodies pertaining to political power	– the United States of America (where federal judges are appointed by the President 'by and with the advice and consent' of the Senate)	– some may argue that there is a high level of the judicial legitimacy as a result of the fact that judicial appointments are made by a democratically elected body	– a high level of the politization of the judicial appointment procedure – risk that political beliefs of a nominee prevail over her/his professional ability during the appointment process
'Transitional Model'	– political body with formally unlimited nominating powers accepts a kind of self-restraint	– Germany (where the competent federal minister appoints judges to the federal courts/ tribunals in cooperation with the Council for the appointment of judges, the Presidium Councils of the courts are also involved in the procedure. The Federal President makes a formal nomination.)	– participation in the appointment procedure of an additional body may constitute an element of merit in a purely political appointment procedure	– In practice, the nomination process may still remain highly politicised
'Appointment Commission Model'	– judicial appointments formally remain in the hands of the political power, but the latitude of the latter in selecting a nominee is limited by a judicial appointment commission	– the United Kingdom (where the judicial appointments commissions have been established)	– such appointment commission is supposed to ensure the merit-based selection of candidates who are then presented to the political authority for appointment	– the political authority retains some influence over the outcome of the selection process carried out by the judicial appointment commissions.

Model	Chief Characteristic	Example	Pros	Cons
'Judicial Council Model'	– an independent state body called 'Judicial Council' plays a decisive role in selecting candidates and appointing judges	– France (where all judicial posts are filled by the President of the Republic, but it is up to the Supreme Council of Judiciary to make proposals for the appointments to higher judicial posts and to give its consent for appointments to lower judicial posts)	– as professional judges may in some constitutional systems make up the majority of council's members, they preserve a decisive voice during the selection of candidates, which should ensure the merit-based assessments of future judges – due to its mixed composition, judicial council may become an area of the cooperation between all branches of the state power in the field of the administration of justice as well as judicial training and career	– politization of the composition or functioning of a judicial council may undermine the independence of the entire judiciary
'Co-Option Model'	– appointments of new judges lie solely in the hands of the incumbent senior judges	– Japan (where the Supreme Court Secretariat plays a decisive role in selecting candidates for appointments to lower courts)	– strengthening of the judiciary independence in result of the lack of influence of the political power on judicial appointments and judicial career	– impairing of the accountability of the judiciary towards the people and its representative bodies – risk of an extensive dependency of lower court judges towards the Supreme Court

Source: Authors' original elaboration.

3. CONSTITUTIONAL COURT JUDGES

The methods of electing Constitutional Court judges from a comparative perspective allow us to see the form of election and correlated decision of the legislature regarding the duration of the functions considered relevant to the question of the independence of Constitutional Court members. An analysis of the functioning of each state organ can be conducted regarding the aspects of its independence. Systemically, three aspects of this issue can be identified – that is, the independence of the formal, functional or behavioural approach – while the phenomenon of the interaction of these dimensions in practicing the functioning of the authority can be seen.

The scope of competence of the judicial or *quasi*-judicial body that controls the hierarchical structure of the legal order determines the role of its judicial personnel substrate for the proper functioning of the rule of law. Adopting a specific model of constitutional review in each system determines the legal status of judges. In political systems with a dispersed model of judicial review of legislation, the analysis of the presented issue should also consider the factors that determine the position of judges adjudicating in courts of a general jurisdiction. Therefore, it can be taken as an axiom that this relationship is based on the assertion that the competence and jurisdictional monopoly of a Constitutional Court with a broad scope of cognition implies, at the same time, the need for a specific legal framework to guarantee the proper undertaking of judicial actions by Constitutional Court judges. A significant role in implementing the theoretical assumptions of the 'Kelsen model' was used by Austria, which is the 'homeland' of the concept of judicial protection of constitutionality in Europe. The creation of this centralised model was based on the strong belief that the competence to review the constitutionality of legislation cannot be entrusted to all judicial bodies. Thus, it was recognised that, in view of the supremacy of the Constitution, with the need to provide an effective means of protecting its role in the legal system and protect the rights of the individual from state interference, it is necessary to create a single-instance jurisdictional body that is located outside the ordinary court system, such as the Constitutional Court.

The literature indicates that the model of founding the composition of the Constitutional Court is an important circumstance in describing the legal significance of the Constitutional Court.[51] In each political system, the model that has been adopted can be analysed on two levels. First, it determines the

---

[51] See, e.g., Katalin Kellemen, 'Appointment of Constitutional Judges in a Comparative Perspective – With a Proposal for a New Model for Hungary' (2013) 54 Acta Juridica Hungaria 5.

pro futuro relations between the appointing entity and individual members of the Constitutional Court. In other words, the procedure adopted for the election of judges implies their legal status. Second, the procedural conditions for the decision-making act of electing a constitutional judge may be conditioned by other constitutional determinants, such as the monarchical form of government, the indirect election of the President as an executive or the federal shape of the state. The composition of the Constitutional Court should attempt to strike a balance between the requirement of adequate legitimacy and ensuring the independence of Constitutional Court judges. The question of legitimacy is related to the basic function of the Constitutional Court: to review the constitutionality of legal acts, that is, primarily laws. This is why, in many countries, both in Western Europe and in the new democracies established on the ruins of the former Eastern Bloc, parliament plays an important role in the nomination process. The constitutions of European countries have most often assumed a strong parliamentary influence when it comes to the selection of constitutional judges, which has probably been influenced by the recognition that parliament should have a significant influence on creating a body to challenge its decisions. Nevertheless, because of the special role of constitutional judges, in some countries, the power to appoint them has been divided between different state bodies. The broad influence of the parliamentary body on the selection of judges is supposed to be a kind of compensation for the immanent feature of the Constitutional Court, which is nowadays not only a negative legislator, but also plays the role of co-creator of law because of the specificity of a legal act, such as the Constitution. The decisions of the Constitutional Court, as it were, enter the sphere of politics, so the problem of legitimacy to undertake these tasks is a key issue. Notwithstanding the relatively significant participation of the legislative authority in the nomination process, it is possible to distinguish three basic models for the appointment of Constitutional Court judges. The criterion for division is the number of bodies participating in the process of creating the composition of the Constitutional Court and its constitutional position. Thus, it is possible to indicate (1) a model with an exclusive or dominant role for the parliament, (2) a model with a dominant role for the executive and (3) a mixed model in which there are multiple actors in the electoral process. In the mixed model, however, two subtypes can be distinguished, in which the authorities can make appointments (a) independently of each other or (b) on a cooperative basis.[52]

---

[52] See also Natalie Fox and Piotr Mikuli, 'W poszukiwaniu optymalnego modelu wyboru sędziów sądu konstytucyjnego' in Jerzy Ciapała and Przemysław Mijal (eds.), *Wokół wybranych problemów konstytucjonalizmu. Księga jubileuszowa Profesora Andrzeja Bałabana* (Wydawnictwo Sejmowe 2017).

Italy played an important pioneering role in constructing mechanisms to ensure the constitutionality of the entire legal order.[53] The Constitutional Court of the Italian Republic *(Corte Costituzionale della Repubblica Italiana)* was created by the Italian Constitution of 1947 as a constitutional body *(organo costituzionale)* as a way to overcome the legacy of totalitarianism. The procedure for the election of 15 judges involves a group of functionally and competently independent actors acting in the legislative, executive and judicial spheres. This solution is a procedural expression of the principle of the separation and balance of powers, which is binding, although not at the textual level. One third of the composition is nominated by the President of the Republic by his decree, which is countersigned by the Prime Minister, one third is elected by the Parliament sitting in a joint session of both chambers by secret ballot by a qualified majority of two thirds of the members of the Assembly and, after a third vote, by a majority of three fifths of the members of the Assembly,[54] and the remaining one third of the composition is elected by the higher ordinary and administrative judiciary.[55] More precisely, three judges are appointed by the Court of Cassation, one by the Council of State and one by the Court of Auditors. The separation of nominating powers is important if only because of the *Corte Costituzionale* jurisprudence signalled in the literature, which determines the scope and manner in which the various organs in the state perform their tasks, for example, regarding the constitutional position of the President in relation to the other organs of the executive power. At the same time, it is important to bear in mind the special legal status of the President as one of the actors involved in the process of appointing the judges of the Court. The President is elected by both chambers of parliament with the complementary participation of regional delegations. In turn, the participation of regional delegates is the only guarantee that their interests are safeguarded by the newly elected judges of the Court. Furthermore, the literature recognises the special role of the head of state in controlling the Constitution as its guardian.

---

[53]   Title VI, Chapter I of the Constitution of the Italian Republic of 1947 is devoted to the Constitutional Court (Articles 134-137), Title IV (Articles 101-113) is devoted to the judiciary and organisation of justice.

[54]   The Chamber of Deputies *(La Camera dei deputati)*, here as the lower chamber, and the upper chamber, which is the Senate, hold joint sittings. To prevent the *Corte Costituzionale* from obstructing its work, parliamentary practice has adopted an extra-constitutional mechanism for the exercise of the Italian Parliament's creative function, taking the form of a separate process for the election of Constitutional Court judges. This separation takes into account the political conditions of the multiparty system, namely that the opposition (parliamentary minority) has the possibility to elect two of the five vacant judicial positions.

[55]   See Article 135 of the Constitution of the Italian Republic of 1947.

In Spain, representatives of three powers are involved in the process of electing the 12 judges of the Constitutional Court. However, the formal act of appointment is carried out by the monarch, who is outside the classical separation of powers. Nevertheless, this prerogative of the monarch is only ceremonial in nature because the monarch is bound by the requests of those directly involved in the appointment procedure of the Constitutional Court. Moreover, the literature points out that the *Cortes Generales* as Parliament influences the appointment of 10 of the 12 judges, but this view does not seem to take into account the guarantee under Article 2 of the Spanish Constitution of respect for the autonomy rights of nationalities and regions.[56] Thus, the internal division of powers of a creative nature has normative significance, which must be sought primarily in the differentiation of interests pursued by the various actors involved in the election of judges. Turning to the parity analysis, four judges are elected at the request of the Congress of Deputies four more at the request of the Senate, two judges at the request of the government and two judges at the request of the General Council of the Judiciary. Importantly, the Spanish Constitution provides for a qualified majority for the election of a judicial candidate by Congress and the Senate (three-fifths of the statutory composition). This prevents the nomination of judges by a specific parliamentary majority.[57] The election of constitutional judges in the Kingdom of Spain, which is two-tiered in the formal sphere and disjointed in the sphere of competence, significantly strengthens the guarantee of their independence while maintaining a balance of interests in the composition of the Constitutional Court. It is also not insignificant that the final – in the formal sense – act of appointment is carried out by the monarch, whose constitutional role is described as moderating.

The procedure for electing judges of the Austrian *Verfassungsgerichtshof* only partially takes into account the federal nature of the state because the Constitution makes the Federal President the mandatory decision-making body of the process.[58] The appointment process requires the fusion of two correlated elements in the form of the cooperation of the legislature and the federal gov-

---

[56] This is caused by the relations of the executive as an emanation of the parliamentary majority. See Luis Moreno, 'Federalization and Ethnoterritorial Concurrence in Spain' (1997) 27 Publius 4, 65.

[57] See Victor Ferreres Comella, 'The Spanish Constitutional Court: Time for Reforms' in Andrew Harding and Peter Leyland (eds.), *Constitutional Courts. A Comparative Study* (CUP 2009).

[58] Giving an important role to the President of the Federation in Austria in the process of selecting judges must consider the President's political position, which in the sphere of exercising powers is completely dependent on the activity of the federal government.

ernment with the President and the means of initiating the judicial selection procedure in the form of an application by an authorised entity. At the same time, the Austrian model can be qualified as a mixed model with executive dominance. Although Article 147 of the Austrian Basic Law of 1920 provides for parity in the form of a half-sharing of potential judicial positions between the legislature and executive, it is impossible not to see the predominance of the federal executive in the nomination process because of the mandatory participation of the President. At the same time, the judicial community's lack of participation in selecting judges is symptomatic. Regarding the peculiarities related to Austria's federal character, two aspects can be decoded at the normative level. First, the Constitution reserves the criterion of the place of residence of the members of the Constitutional Court. It is envisaged that it will be necessary to elect judges (members) whose place of residence is outside the federal capital, which is explicitly defined by quotas in the Constitution. The rationale for this solution was presumably to take into account local needs, including the preservation of plurality in the composition of the Austrian Constitutional Court. Second, the Federal Council, being an emanation of the interests of the Länder, is an active participant in the appointment process.[59] At the same time, it should be emphasised that only three out of the twelve members (one out of the six deputy members) of the Austrian Constitutional Court are elected at the request of this legislative body.

The constitutional system of the Federal Republic of Germany can serve as an example of the extensive influence of the federal character of the state on the procedure for appointing judges of the Constitutional Court. This relationship becomes apparent at several moments in the process of completing the personnel substrate of the *Bundesverfassungsgericht*. First, an obligatory participant – alongside the Federal Parliament (*Bundestag*) – in the act of selecting judges is the Federal Council (*Bundesrat*), as an emanation of the representation of the Länder. The German legislature divides the creative powers between the *Bundestag* and *Bundesrat* (eight judges in each).[60] As a result, the guarantee

---

[59] This nature of the Federal Council can be decoded directly from the provisions of the Federal Basic Law. See Articles 35-36 of the Austrian Basic Law (1920).

[60] The *Bundesverfassungsgericht* consists of two senates, each of which has eight judges. See Article 2(1), (2) of the German Federal Constitutional Court Act in the version of 1 August 1993 (Federal Law Gazette I p. 1473), last amended by Article 4 of the Act of 20 November 2019 (Federal Law Gazette I, 1724), hereinafter referred to as the 'German Federal Constitutional Court Act 2019'. Half the membership is elected by the Bundesrat (the upper house of the German legislature), the other half by a special committee of the Bundestag (the lower house). To be elected, a judge must secure a two-thirds majority of votes cast; this rule

system is designed to ensure the relatively permanent equality of these two organs in the act of selecting judges for the Federal Constitutional Court. Thus, the activity of the Bundesrat is intended to protect the federal character of the state while guaranteeing, in the long term, respect for the Constitutional Court's rulings in cases involving individual federal subjects. Second, political and geographic pluralism is expressed in the qualified two-thirds majority with which the act of electing the Federal Council is adopted.

The judges of constitutional courts are most often appointed for a fixed term, unlike those of courts of general jurisdiction.[61] Such a vision seems to be related to a belief in the important role of the Constitutional Court, where the rotation of judges is important, rather than to some preservation of a unique line of jurisprudence. Undoubtedly, the independence of the adjudicating body is conditioned by the absence of systemic mechanisms for making the personal substrate dependent on the body that creates it. Thus, the tenure of office while common prohibition of re-election determines freedom from pressure in the adjudicatory activity of judges.[62]

Differences emerge both in terms of the length of the term of office, the method of appointment and the permissibility of re-election to the position. For instance, in Italy,[63] France[64] and Spain,[65] the constitutions indicate the duration of the term of office numerically, which is nine years. In Italy, judges are appointed without age limits, but they come from among the most experienced lawyers, judges of the higher ordinary and administrative courts, lawyers with at least 20 years of experience and university professors of law. The term of office is long – it lasts nine years from taking the oath, but the judge cannot be appointed for another term. Members of the Constitutional Council in France are also appointed for a nine-year term, with one-third of them renewed every three years.

In Austria, judges serve until they reach the retirement age of 70.[66] Turkey once had a similar practice with judges elected for lifelong terms however, the

---

has generally prevented any party or coalition from determining the court's composition.

[61] However, for example Austria maintains the system where judges are appointed until reaching the retirement age. Similarly, Turkey once had a similar practice, but currently, constitutional judges there are elected for 12-year terms.

[62] On the term of office and the functions performed by it, see Marek Zubik, *Status prawny sędziego Trybunału Konstytucyjnego* (Biuro Trybunału Konstytucyjnego 2011).

[63] Article 135(3) of the Italian Constitution (1947).

[64] Article 56 of the French Constitution (1958).

[65] Article 159(3) of the Spanish Constitution (1978).

[66] Article 147(6) *in fine* of the Austrian Basic Law (1920).

current system involves 12-year term. In Germany, on the other hand, constitutional judges have a fixed term of 12 years, but nevertheless, with a retirement age censure of 68 years.[67] This approach somewhat deviates from the concept of a fixed term of office for an individual member.

In the countries of Central and Eastern Europe, we can also observe various solutions regarding the election of constitutional judges, but to a large extent, the method of selecting constitutional judges was inspired by solutions adopted in countries with established democracies. Parliament appoints the entire composition of the Constitutional Court in Poland, Hungary,[68] Croatia[69] and Slovenia.[70] In other countries of the region, the model of dividing appointments between different bodies has been adopted (e.g., in Bulgaria: four judges are appointed by the National Assembly, four by the President and four by a joint meeting of judges of the highest court instances (i.e. General Assembly of the judges of the Supreme Court of Cassation and the Supreme Administrative Court);[71] in Romania: three judges are appointed by the lower chamber of parliament – the Chamber of Deputies, three by the Senate and three by the

---

[67] Article 4(1) in connection with Article 4(3) of the German Federal Constitutional Court Act 2019. Justices of the German Federal Constitutional Court shall be retired upon request without proof of their incapacity for office if they have held the post of Justice of the Federal Constitutional Court for at least six years and they have reached the age of sixty-five. Article 98(3) Pt 1 of the German Federal Constitutional Court Act 2019.

[68] The Hungarian Constitutional Court consists of 15 members, each elected for twelve years by a two-thirds majority of the votes of the unicameral body of the Parliament (National Assembly). See Article 24(4) *ab initio* of the Hungarian Constitution (2011).

[69] The Constitutional Court of the Republic of Croatia consists of 13 judges elected by the Croatian *Sabor* for an eight-year term. The election is made from eminent lawyers, especially judges, prosecutors, advocates and university professors of legal sciences.

[70] The Constitutional Court of the Republic of Slovenia consists of nine judges elected from among professional lawyers by the National Assembly on the proposal of the President of the Republic.

[71] Article 147(1) of the Constitution of the Republic of Bulgaria (1991). The Constitutional Court elects a Chairman of the Court with a three-year term of office. The Chairman may be re-elected. Eligible for membership at the Constitutional Court are Bulgarian citizens with no other citizenship who meet the requirements of Article 147(3) of the Constitution of the Republic of Bulgaria (1991), i.e. being lawyers of high professional experience. The justices are not subject to an age restriction.

President of the Republic)[72] or a mixed model (e.g., in the Czech Republic by the President with the consent of the Senate;[73] in Albania three judges are appointed by the President of the Republic, three are elected by the Assembly and three by the High Court).[74]

The attempt to create a single optimal and universal model for the selection of constitutional judges is, in principle, doomed to failure. The individual elements shaping the constitutional adjudicating body's position in constitutional courts are determined, *inter alia*, by systemic conditions (unitary state, federation), political tendencies (e.g., strong decentralisation process), historical aspects (e.g., role of the monarch in the appointment of judges) or constitutional tradition. It is also important to note the differences in the length and manner in which the term of office of the members of the Constitutional Court is determined. In principle, each model, apart from having some advantages, also has significant disadvantages. Election by parliament can result in an overpoliticised election, separation between the various authorities and the election of candidates who will only represent the interests of the current superiors of the various authorities and, in a model requiring some co-option, lead to decision-making paralysis, resulting in the absence of a judge for a very long period. The latter danger is also very real in a situation where a qualified majority in the parliamentary chamber is required to fill a vacancy in the Constitutional Court. On the one hand, the inclusion of parliamentary opposition in the electoral process can be viewed a positive here; on the other hand, the lack of consensus may prevent elections from taking place.

---

[72] Article 142(3) of the Romanian Constitution (1991). The Constitutional Court consists of nine judges, appointed for a term of office of nine years, that cannot be prolonged or renewed and shall be renewed by one third of its judges every three years, in accordance with the provisions of the Court's organic law. Article 142(2) in connection with Article 142(5) of the Romanian Constitution (1991).

[73] Article 84(2) of the Constitution of the Czech Republic (1992). The President of the Republic selects a candidate whose name is then sent, through the Office of the President of the Republic, to the Senate with a request to express its consent to her/his appointment as a Justice of the Constitutional Court.

[74] The Constitutional Court in Albania is composed of nine members who remain in office for nine years without the right to be reappointed. The composition of the Constitutional Court shall be renewed every three years by one-third of its composition, in accordance with the procedure provided by law. Article 125 of the Albanian Constitution (1998), Amending Law 115/2020, dated 30 July 2020 and Article 7 on the Organization and Functioning of the Constitutional Court of the Republic of Albania, No 8577, dated 10 February 2000.

In light of the above, looking at the solutions operating in contemporary states, a certain modifying element affecting an increase of the authority of the Constitutional Court may be the introduction of a procedure for electing a judge by assuming the idea of political and social pluralism of its formation. This trend is particularly evident in federal states or in highly decentralised states, where the interests of the administrative units of the state are taken into account directly (e.g., Austria, Germany) or indirectly (e.g., Italy). However, attaching great importance to the social or ideological background of judicial candidates also poses an important risk: it may lead to the reinforcement of the public's perception that a judge should uphold certain interests rather than be guided primarily by their legal knowledge and experience in the process of interpreting the Constitution.[75]

4. CONCLUSION

The process of judicial appointments is about safeguarding a fundamental principle, namely guaranteeing the independence of the judiciary both in organisational and individual terms. In this sense, the appointment procedure must be correlated with ensuring legitimacy, which is not a simple reflection of democratic legitimacy. Therefore, it becomes a question of selecting those who will be impartial and professional; it would seem to be a desirable solution to include people from outside the judicial community in the bodies that are making nomination decisions. Therefore, the model of a mixed judicial council, rather than a strictly judge-only composition, seems attractive. In our opinion, however, the aim is not, by including politicians to some extent as well, to increase democratic legitimacy; rather, it is to ensure that the selection is as objective as possible, where different rationales are expressed and balanced. This also has some reference to constitutional judges. The dominant role of parliament in the appointment process was linked to the fact that it is constitutional judges who will challenge parliament's legislative decisions, so it is parliament that perhaps should have a say in determining their composition.

In the search for an optimal model of appointing ordinary and constitutional judges, it is worth looking not only at the body formally making appointments, but also at the entire decision-making sequence. In relation to ordinary judges, we have emphasised the role of independent bodies comprised not only of judges but also of lay persons or representatives of other legal professions.

---

[75] Natalie Fox and Piotr Mikuli (eds.), 'W poszukiwaniu optymalnego modelu wyboru sędziów sądu konstytucyjnego in Jerzy Ciapała and Przemysław Mijal,' *Wokół wybranych problemów konstytucjonalizmu. Księga jubileuszowa Profesora Andrzeja Bałabana* (Wydawnictwo Sejmowe 2017).

Table 6.2   Composition and method of appointment of Constitutional Court judges

Country and Constitutional Court/ Tribunal	Composition	Term in office	Form of election / Appointing entity
Austria Verfassungsgerichtshof (VfGH)	14 (including the President and the Vice President) + six substitute members	indefinite period, until mandatory retirement at 70 years	Federal President by his decree countersigned by the Prime Minister upon request: – Federal Government (President, Vice-President, six constitutional judges and three substitute members) – National Council (*Nationalrat*) three constitutional judges and two substitute members – Federal Council (*Bundesrat*) three constitutional judges and one substitute member
Germany Bundesverfassungsgericht (BVerfG)	16	term of office ends after 12 years or when the retirement age of 68 is reached. Justices may not be re-elected	Half of the 16 Justices of the Federal Constitutional Court are elected by the Federal Parliament (*Bundestag*), and half by the Federal Council (*Bundesrat*). A two-thirds majority vote of their composition is required to elect constitutional judges

Country and Constitutional Court/ Tribunal	Composition	Term in office	Form of election / Appointing entity
Italy Corte Costituzionale	15 + 16 lay judges for constitutional responsibility	9 years (not renewable)	– one-third nominated by the President of the Republic by his decree countersigned by the Prime Minister – one-third elected by the Parliament sitting in a joint session of both chambers by secret ballot by a qualified majority vote of two-thirds of the members of the Assembly and, after a third vote, by a majority vote of three-fifths of the members of the Assembly – one-third elected by the higher ordinary and administrative judiciary (three judges appointed by the Court of Cassation, one by the Council of State and one by the Court of Auditors) Lay judges are selected by lot from a list established by Parliament
Spain Tribunal Constitucional	12	9 years (not renewable)	The formal act of appointment is carried out by ceremonial prerogative of the monarch: – four judges elected at the request of the Congress of Deputies – four judges elected at the request of the Senate – two judges at the request of the government – two judges at the request of the General Council of the Judiciary Importantly, the Spanish Constitution provides for a qualified majority for the election of a judicial candidate by Congress and the Senate (three-fifths of the statutory composition)

Country and Constitutional Court/ Tribunal	Composition	Term in office	Form of election / Appointing entity
Turkey Anayasa Mamkemesi	15	elected for a term of 12 years and shall retire at the age of 65	Grand National Assembly elects: 1) two Justices with a secret voting from among three candidates to be nominated for each vacant position by and from among the president and members of the Court of Accounts 2) one Justice from among three candidates nominated by the heads of the bar associations from among self-employed lawyers President of the Republic selects: 3) three Justices from the Court of Cassation 4) two Justices from the Council of State among three candidates nominated for each vacant position by their respective General Assembly amongst its presidents and members 5) three Justices, at least two of which must be law graduates, from three candidates nominated for each vacant position by the Council of Higher Education amongst Professors in the fields of law, economics and political sciences of higher education institutions and who are not members of the Council itself 6) four Justices from among high-level bureaucrats, attorneys, senior judges and prosecutors, and rapporteurs of the Constitutional Court with experience of at least five years

Country and Constitutional Court/ Tribunal	Composition	Term in office	Form of election / Appointing entity
France Conseil Constitutionnel	9 +former Presidents of the Republic	9 years with one-third of them renewed every three years	The members are appointed by the President of the Republic – three judges and the presidents of each of the Houses of Parliament (the President of the National Assembly – three judges, and the President of the Senate – three judges respectively). The nominees have to be accepted by an appropriate commission in both houses of Parliament
Poland Trybunał Konstytucyjny	15	9 years (not renewable)	Elected individually by the first chamber of Parliament (Sejm) from among persons with 'outstanding legal knowledge' by an absolute majority vote in the presence of at least half the statutory number of deputies. Candidates are presented by a group of at least 50 MPs or the Presidium of the Sejm (Speaker of the Sejm and deputy speakers). The Presidium makes its decisions by a majority of votes (in the form of resolutions). In the event of an equal number of votes, the vote of the Speaker of the Sejm prevails
Hungary Alkotmánybíróság	15	12 years	National Assembly (unicameral body of the Hungarian Parliament) with qualified majority (a two-thirds majority vote of of all deputies). Members of the Constitutional Court shall be nominated by Parliament's standing committee for constitutional issues

Country and Constitutional Court/ Tribunal	Composition	Term in office	Form of election / Appointing entity
Croatia Ustavni Sud	13	8 years	The procedure for electing a judge of the Constitutional Court is instituted by a competent committee of the Croatian Parliament which publishes an invitation in the Official Gazette 'Narodne novine' to judicial institutions, law faculties, the chamber of attorneys, legal associations, political parties, and other legal persons and individuals, to propose candidates for the election of one or more judges of the Constitutional Court. An individual may also propose himself/ herself as a candidate. The competent committee submits to the Croatian Parliament (Sabor), together with its proposal, a list of all the candidates who comply with the conditions for being elected judge of the Constitutional Court. Members of the Croatian Sabor vote for each proposed candidate individually with a two-thirds majority vote of the total number of deputies
Slovenia Ustavno sodišče	9	9 years (not renewable)	Constitutional judges are elected on the proposal of the President of the Republic by the National Assembly. Any citizen of the Republic of Slovenia who is a legal expert and has reached at least 40 years of age may be elected a Constitutional Court judge

Country and Constitutional Court/ Tribunal	Composition	Term in office	Form of election / Appointing entity
Bulgaria Конституционният съд на	12	9 years (not eligible for reelection or reappointment)	One third of constitutional judges is elected by the National Assembly; one third is appointed by the President and one third is elected by the General Assembly of the judges of the Supreme Court of Cassation and the Supreme Administrative Court. The members of the Constitutional Court are renewed every three years from each quota
Romania Curtea Constituţională	9	9 years (cannot be prolonged or renewed)	Three constitutional judges are appointed by the first chamber of parliament – the Chamber of Deputies, three by the Senate and three by the President of the Republic. The Constitutional Court is renewed by one third of its judges every three years, in accordance with the provisions of the Court's organic law

Country and Constitutional Court/ Tribunal	Composition	Term in office	Form of election / Appointing entity
Czech Republic Úvodní strana	15	10 years	Constitutional judges are appointed by the President of the Republic and shall be confirmed by the Senate. President should propose the name of a potential candidate, which is then submitted to the second chamber of the Parliament, the Senate. The President needs the approval of a simple majority of senators (votes of more than half of those present) to appoint his nominee
Albania Gjykata Kushtetuese	9	9 years (without the right to be reappointed)	Three constitutional judges are appointed by the President of the Republic, three are elected by the Assembly and three judges are elected by the High Court. The Assembly elects the Constitutional Court judges by no less than three-fifth majority of its members. If the Assembly fails to elect the judge within 30 days of the submission of the list of candidates by the Justice Appointment Council, the first ranked candidate in the list shall be deemed appointed. The composition of the Constitutional Court shall be renewed every three years to one-third thereof, in accordance with the procedure determined by law

Source: Authors' original elaboration.

Regarding constitutional judges, for example, solutions could be considered in which the role of the opposition is strengthened by establishing a qualified majority for selecting judges by parliament or assigning nominations to different bodies. In the latter case, it would be worthwhile to consider including not only the bodies of both political forces but, for example, judicial councils or ombudsmen in the process.

7. Rule of Law (Crisis) and the Principle of Mutual Trust

Konstantina-Antigoni Poulou

1. INTRODUCTION

The qualification of mutual trust as a leading term of EU law dates back to the Opinion 2/13 on the EU's accession to the ECHR, in which the ECJ inferred from the principle of mutual trust that Member States, when implementing Union law, "may be required to presume that fundamental rights have been observed by the other Member States, so that not only may they not demand a higher level of national protection of fundamental rights from another Member State than that provided by EU law, but, save in exceptional cases, they may not check whether that other Member State has actually, in a specific case, observed the fundamental rights guaranteed by the EU."[1] Since then, much ink has been spilled over the operation of mutual trust in the Area of Freedom, Security and Justice (AFSJ) and its limitations in times of rule of law crisis, particularly vis-à-vis fundamental rights. However, the legal nature and limits of the principle of mutual trust under EU primary law remain uncharted territory. So is the relationship between the notions of mutual trust (crisis) and rule of law (crisis).

In view of the above, this chapter seeks to shed some light on the rationale, scope and limits of the mutual trust principle and its relationship to rule of law. To this aim, the first section examines the foundation of the mutual trust principle, namely the EU values enshrined in Article 2 TEU. The second section unravels the mystery surrounding the legal nature of mutual trust and delivers an overarching definition: It is argued that mutual trust constitutes a legal principle with binding effects that go beyond those of an "ordinary" legal principle. Rather, it is a constitutional principle of EU law that permeates the entire European legal order and pertains both to the cooperative relationship

---

[1] ECJ, Opinion 2/13, *Accession of the European Union to the ECHR*, EU:C: 2014:2454, para 192.

between the EU and its Member States (vertical dimension) and the cooperation between requesting/issuing and requested/executing Member State (horizontal dimension). It will then be demonstrated that the outer limits of the mutual trust principle are not contingent on the different fields of EU action but are prescribed by EU primary law. Finally, the interconnection between the rule of law crisis and the mutual trust crisis will be pointed out. The chapter concludes with some final remarks.

2.   EU VALUES: THE FOUNDATION OF THE MUTUAL TRUST PRINCIPLE

The EU is based on the fundamental premise that its Member States share a set of values, including respect for human dignity, freedom, democracy, equality, the rule of law and respect for human rights (Article 2 TEU). The common commitment to EU values, particularly to the rule of law,[2] "implies and justifies the existence of mutual trust between the Member States that those values will be recognized and, therefore, that the law of the EU that implements them will be respected".[3] The mere fact that Member States are bound by Article 2 TEU seems to justify the derivation of the principle of trust.[4] The underlying rationale is thus the (alleged[5]) congruence of national legal systems as well as the incorporation of EU values in them.[6] In this sense, the homogeneity of values[7] and the creation of a common European legal space are perceived to be indispensable for the EU integration,[8] and justify its qualification as a Union of

---

[2]   Cf. also Kulick, 'Rechtsstaatlichkeitskrise und gegenseitiges Vertrauen im institutionellen Gefüge der EU' (2020) 75 Juristenzeitung, 223–231, at 224.

[3]   ECJ, Opinion 2/13, *supra* note 1, para. 168.

[4]   Huber, 'Europäische Verfassungs- und Rechtsstaatlichkeit in Bedrängnis' (2017) 56 Der Staat, 389–414, at 404; Rizcallah, *Le principe de confiance mutuelle en droit de l'Union européenne* (Bruylant 2020), 266, para. 406 refers to the "lecture axiologique" of trust.

[5]   See Kullak, *Vertrauen in Europa* (Mohr Siebeck 2020), 106 f.

[6]   von Bogdandy, 'European Law Beyond Ever Closer Union Repositioning the Concept, its Thrust and the ECJ's Comparative Methodology' (2016) 22 ELJ, 519–538, at 534; the hypothesis that all Member States share indeed the European values constitutes an illusion, Rizcallah, (2020) *supra* note 4, 282 f., para. 441 f.

[7]   Further Levits, 'Die Europäische Union als Wertegemeinschaft' in Jaeger (ed), *Europa 4.0?* (Jan Sramek 2018), 245 f.; Schorkopf, *Homogenität in der EU* (Duncker & Humblot 2000), 69 f.

[8]   von Bogdandy, (2016) *supra* note 6, at 520; similarly, Calliess, 'Europa als Wertegemeinschaft' (2004) 59 Juristenzeitung, 1033–1045, at 1034 f.

values.[9] However, it is notable that the interconnection between EU values and mutual trust was only (explicitly[10]) established in 2014 in Opinion 2/13 of the ECJ. This delay can be explained if one considers the original perception of the EU primarily as an economic union and the absence of a dogmatic approach of the concept of trust by the EU institutions.[11]

Given that a definition of EU values is nowhere to be found in the Treaties, Member States are granted with a wide discretion in interpreting their exact content.[12] While it holds true that the bedrock of EU values are the values on the respective national legal systems, nonetheless they have emerged in a specific historical-cultural context and are, therefore, extremely subjective and context-related.[13] In view of their anchoring in EU primary law, EU values have an autonomous meaning, which can be further concretized by way of a qualitative comparison of the constitutions of the Member States.[14] They are legally binding both for the EU[15] and the Member States,[16] which is why national legal structures are subject to the (legal) standards of Article 2 TEU beyond the limitations set by Article 51(1) of the EU Charter of Fundamental

---

[9]   Calliess, (2004) *supra* note 8, at 1041 f.; von Bogdandy, 'Tyrannei der Werte? Herausforderungen und Grundlagen einer europäischen Dogmatik systemischer Defizite' (2019) 79 ZaöRV, 503–551, at 512; Voßkuhle, *Die Idee der Europäischen Wertegemeinschaft* (Klaus Bittner 2018), 38.

[10]   See, however, the Convention relating to extradition between the Member States of the European Union [1997] O.J. C191/13 20; Programme of measures to implement the principle of mutual recognition of decisions in criminal matters [2001] O.J. C12/10 10.

[11]   Rizcallah, (2020) *supra* note 4, 254, paras. 388 f.

[12]   Potacs, 'Balancing Values and Interests in the Art. 7 TEU Procedure' (2018) Die Verwaltung, 159–167, at 161; similarly, Bobić, 'Constructive Versus Destructive Conflict: Taking Stock of the Recent Constitutional Jurisprudence in the EU' (2020) 22 CYELS, 60–84, at 69; Mlynarski, *Zur Integration staatlicher und europäischer Verfassungsidentität* (Mohr Siebeck 2021), 132 f.

[13]   Speer, 'Die Europäische Union als Wertegemeinschaft – Wert- und rechtskonformes Verhalten als konditionierendes Element der Mitgliedschaft' (2001) DÖV, 980–987, at 981.

[14]   Regarding the concretisation of EU values in the *acquis communautaire* cf. Boekestein, 'Making Do With What We Have: On the Interpretation and Enforcement of the EU's Founding Values' (2022) 23 GLJ, 431–451, at 441 f.

[15]   Articles 3(1) and 21 TEU.

[16]   Articles 7 and 49(1) TEU.

Rights (EUCFR).[17] Hence, Article 2 TEU forms – if not defines – the identity of the EU and can be regarded as an eternity clause of EU law.[18]

A further issue pertains to the justiciability and extent of binding nature of Article 2 TEU,[19] especially in classic sovereignty-related areas of the Member States, such as the organization of the courts. Several Member States refute these suppositions by insisting on the enforcement of their own national values in areas that lie outside the scope of EU law.[20] Such cases demonstrate a fundamental structural imbalance in the EU Treaties, which, on the one hand, attach crucial importance to EU values – and, thus, indirectly to the principle of mutual trust – but on the other hand confer very limited competences to the EU for enforcing the values enshrined in Article 2 TEU.[21]

---

[17] ECJ, Case C-156/21, *Hungary v Parliament and Council*, EU:C:2022:97, para. 232; Case C-157/21, *Poland v Parliament and Council*, EU:C:2022:98, para. 264; Brauneck, 'Rettet die EU den Rechtsstaat in Polen?' (2018) NVwZ, 1423–1429, at 1428; Klamert and Kochenov, 'Article 2 TEU' in Kellerbauer, Klamert and Tomkin (eds), *The EU Treaties and the Charter of Fundamental Rights: A Commentary* (OUP 2019), para. 4.

[18] Schorkopf, 'Der Wertekonstitutionalismus der Europäischen Union' (2020) 75 Juristenzeitung, 477–485, at 482.

[19] Cf. Boekestein, (2022) *supra* note 14, at 444 f.; von Bogdandy, 'Principles of a systemic deficiencies doctrine: How to protect checks and balances in the Member States' (2020) 57 CMLRev., 705–740, at 705, 712, 716; Kochenov, 'Biting Intergovernmentalism: The Case for the Reinvention of Article 259 TFEU to Make It a Viable Rule of Law Enforcement Tool' (2015) 7 HJRL, 153–174, at 165; Kochenov, 'The Acquis and Its Principles: The Enforcement of the "Law" versus the Enforcement of "Values" in the European Union' in Jakab and Kochenov (eds), *The Enforcement of EU Law and Values* (OUP 2017), 10 f.; Mader, 'Enforcement of EU Values as a Political Endeavour: Constitutional Pluralism and Value Homogeneity in Times of Persistent Challenges to the Rule of Law' (2019) 11 HJRL, 133–170, at 137; Spieker, 'Defending Union Values in Judicial Proceedings. On How to Turn Article 2 TEU into a Judicially Applicable Provision' in von Bogdandy et al. (eds), *Defending Checks and Balances in EU Member States* (Springer 2021), 244.

[20] Schorkopf, (2020) *supra* note 18, at 483.

[21] Kochenov, 'EU Law without the Rule of Law: Is the Veneration of Autonomy Worth It?' (2015) 34 YEL, 74–96, at 79; Priebus, 'The Commission's Approach to Rule of Law Backsliding: Managing Instead of Enforcing Democratic Values?' (2022) 60 JCMS, 1684–1700, at 1686 f.; Wouters, 'Revisiting Art. 2 TEU: A True Union of Values?', 5 EP (2020), 255–277, at 260.

3.   DEFINING MUTUAL TRUST

3.1   Main Characteristics: An Interdisciplinary Approach

Mutual trust has predominantly been perceived as an extra-legal concept or a political objective with only marginal legal significance.[22] However, an interdisciplinary approach that incorporates insights regarding the concept of trust from sociology – which traditionally examines cooperation systems in complex social structures and institutions – will underline the main character-istics of mutual trust.[23]

First of all, the mutual trust principle is distinguished by a tripartite structure, in which subject A entrusts subject B with an object C or in that A trusts that B will perform the behaviour C.[24] In the context of EU law, Member States as such can be perceived as legal systems, whereas EU institutions, national courts and authorities as institutional structures that can mutually grant and receive trust.[25] However, in EU cooperation relationships the object of trust is twofold and encompasses what will hereinafter be referred to as *abstract* and *specific* trust: On the one hand, the abstract (systemic) trust pertains to the overall capability of national legal systems to uphold and enforce EU law.[26] This trust is premised on the equivalence of the legal systems and the quali-tative equivalent regulations in force, which can equally guarantee the lawful

---

[22] Bieber, '"Full Faith and Credit" als Verfassungsregel im Verhältnis der EU-Mitgliedstaaten?' in Lorenzmeier and Folz (eds), *Recht und Realität* (Nomos 2017), 56; Franzius, 'Europäisches Vertrauen? Eine Skizze' (2010) HFR, 159–176, at 163; Willems, 'Mutual trust as a term of art in EU criminal law: revealing its hybrid character' (2016) EJLS, 211–249, at 234.

[23] Similarly, Marin, '"Only You": The Emergence of a Temperate Mutual Trust in the Area of Freedom, Security and Justice and Its Underpinning in the European Composite Constitutional Order' (2017) EP, 141–157, at 155; Rizcallah, (2020). *supra* note 4, 191 f.; Weilert, 'Vertrauen ist gut. Ist Recht besser?' in Weingardt (ed), *Vertrauen in der Krise. Zugänge verschiedener Wissenschaften* (Nomos 2011), 108 f.; Willems, *The Principle of Mutual Trust in EU Criminal Law* (Hart Publishing 2021), 11 f.

[24] Hardin, *Trust and Trustworthiness* (Russel Sage Foundation 2002), at 7, 9; Sztompka, *Trust: A Sociological Theory* (CUP 1999), at 55; in the legal discourse see also Kullak, (2020) *supra* note 5, at 8; Willems, (2016) *supra* note 22, at 239.

[25] Willems, (2022) *supra* note 23, 170; Wischmeyer, 'Generating Trust Through Law? Judicial Cooperation in the European Union and the "Principle of Mutual Trust"' (2016) 17 GLJ, 339–382, at 345.

[26] See e.g. ECJ, Case C-159/02, *Turner*, EU:C:2004:228, para. 25; Case C-491/10 PPU, *Aguirre Zarraga*, EU:C:2010:828, para. 70.

application of EU law in their territory.[27] On the other hand, the specific trust relates to the compliance with EU law of the issuing/requesting Member State in the context of a *specific* cooperation relationship. In this case, "compliance with EU law" refers both to the implementation and the lawful application of EU law.[28]

Second, mutual trust aims at reducing the complexity[29] in cooperation relationships that arises from any differences in the legal systems of the Member States. Indeed, the presumption of trust enables the effective pursuit of common interests, such as combating transnational crime, protecting the external borders of the EU and ensuring the stability of the financial system. Third, mutual trust always entails a level of risk, wherein the party granting trust can only anticipate the protection of its interests by the party receiving its trust. Within the European legal order, assuming risk implies that EU law is *expected* to be lawfully applied in the Member States. Consequently, the level of trustworthiness assigned to the Member States depends on their actual compliance with EU law, particularly with Article 2 TEU which, as mentioned above, constitutes a *sine qua non* for establishing trust in cooperation relationships.[30]

The fourth characteristic of mutual trust lies in its inherent possibility of being rebutted, i.e. in its conditional nature.[31] The recipient of trust can potentially betray the trust relationship, meaning that trust cannot be limitless or unconditional. Rather, it can be unilaterally revoked.[32] At EU level, this implies that the presumption of EU law compliance can occasionally be frustrated, so that a regime of blind trust cannot be justified.[33] Even so, the principle of mutual trust can only be rebutted if a certain threshold is met, depending on the specific circumstances of each case. Against this backdrop, in the context of EU law a distinction needs to be made between the two objects of trust: The rebuttal of the abstract (systemic) trust in the capability of

---

[27] Kaufhold, 'Gegenseitiges Vertrauen: Wirksamkeitsbedingung und Rechtsprinzip der justiziellen Zusammenarbeit im Raum der Freiheit, der Sicherheit und des Rechts' (2012) Europarecht, 408–431, at 422.

[28] Cramér, 'Reflections on the Roles of Mutual Trust in EU Law' in Dougan and Currie (eds), *50 Years of the European Treaties: Looking Back and Thinking Forward* (Hart Publishing 2009), 53; Prechal, 'Mutual Trust Before the Court of Justice of the European Union' (2017) EP, 75–92, at 83.

[29] Hartmann, *Europäisierung und Verbundvertrauen* (Mohr Siebeck 2015), 28 f.

[30] Ronsfeld, *Rechtshilfe, Anerkennung und Vertrauen – die Europäische Ermit-tlungsanordnung* (Duncker & Humblot 2015), 219.

[31] Willems, (2016) *supra* note 22, at 236.

[32] Weilert, (2011) *supra* note 23, 108, 115; Wischmeyer, (2016) *supra* note 25, at 347.

[33] Cf. Wischmeyer, (2016) *supra* note 25, at 347.

national legal systems to uphold EU law, particularly Article 2 TEU, presupposes cases of serious and repeated violations of EU law. Conversely, the presumption of compliance with the applicable EU law provisions (specific trust) in a specific cooperation relationship (e.g. execution of a European Arrest Warrant) can always be rebutted based on objective evidence pointing to the unlawful actions of the concerned Member State.[34] In such cases, although the presumption of trust is rebutted in this specific context, the *abstract* (systemic) presumption that EU law is generally upheld in the legal order of the concerned Member State is maintained. Finally, trust is reciprocal, meaning that Member States are motivated to respond to cooperation requests from other Member States, ensuring compliance with the relevant EU law provisions. This incentive is due to the fact that they may themselves be in the position of the requesting Member State in the future.[35]

3.2   Definition of the Mutual Trust Principle

In view of the above, this paper proposes the following definition of the mutual trust principle: Mutual trust constitutes a constitutional legal principle of EU law with normative content. It aims to address the complexity arising from any differences in national legal systems by dictating that Member States – and, where applicable, EU institutions[36] – fulfil their cooperation obligations following a dual, rebuttable presumption. Firstly, Member States are required to presume that all national legal systems are equally capable of upholding and enforcing EU law. The rebuttal of this presumption is subject to a high threshold, only attainable in cases of serious and repeated breaches of EU law. Secondly, the executing/requested Member State must presume that the issuing/requesting Member State has lawfully applied the relevant EU law provisions in the specific cooperation scheme. This presumption is subject to a lower threshold and can be rebutted based on objective evidence. If neither presumption is rebutted, two negative obligations follow for the executing/requested Member State, namely the obligation to refrain from demanding a higher national level of fundamental rights protection in its territory and to

---

[34]   Cf. Warin, 'A Dialectic of Effective Judicial Protection and Mutual Trust in the European Administrative Space: Towards the Transnational Judicial Review of Manifest Error?' (2020) 13 REALaw, 7–31, at 23 f., according to whom the national courts of the executing Member State may review the transnational act adopted by the issuing Member State in case of an obvious violation of EU law by the latter.

[35]   Ronsfeld, (2015) *supra* note 30, 218.

[36]   See *infra* section 3.3.3.

abstain from re-evaluating the issuing/requesting Member State's actual compliance with EU law.

3.3   In Search of a Legal Basis in EU Primary Law

The main argument against the qualification of mutual trust as a legal principle of EU law is the lack of its explicit anchoring in the Treaties.[37] This section will, therefore, explore and trace its appropriate legal basis in EU primary law, thereby highlighting its constitutional significance within the multilevel constitutional legal order of the EU.

3.3.1   Article 2 TEU

The ECJ consistently emphasizes that the community of values, as indicated by Article 2 TEU, implies and justifies the existence of mutual trust between the Member States.[38] The connection drawn between Article 2 TEU and the principle of mutual trust implies that compliance with the former constitutes a substantive prerequisite for the latter's existence.[39] However, Article 2 TEU does not impose any positive obligations on Member States, in the sense of attaining a specific level of EU values protection, let alone can it establish concrete obligations for Member States in their cooperation relationships.[40] The introduction of the non-regression principle by the ECJ regarding the protection of EU values,[41] does not impose a duty of mutual trust among Member States; rather, it prohibits any national measures that would undermine the EU values, and refers, therefore, to the vertical relationship between the EU and its Member States. Consequently, a normative connection between the principle of trust and Article 2 TEU must be rejected.[42]

---

[37]   Maiani and Miglionico, 'One principle to rule them all? Anatomy of mutual trust in the law of the Area of Freedom, Security and Justice' (2020) 57 CMLRev., 7–44, at 13; Ostropolski, 'The CJEU as a Defender of Mutual Trust' (2015) 6 NJECL (2015), 166–178, at 166.

[38]   Settled case law since Opinion 2/13, *supra* note 1, para. 168.

[39]   Klamert and Kochenov, (2019) *supra* note 17, para. 9; Kullak, (2020) *supra* note 5, 204.

[40]   Klamert and Kochenov, (2019) *supra* note 17, para. 5.

[41]   ECJ, Case C-896/19, *Repubblika*, EU:C:2021:311, para. 64; critical Scholtes, 'Constitutionalising the end of history? Pitfalls of a non-regression principle for Article 2 TEU' (2023) 19 EuConst, 59–87, at 68 f.

[42]   On Article 2 in combination with Article 7 TEU as an appropriate legal basis, albeit without any further argumentation see von Bogdandy and Ioannidis, 'Das systemische Defizit – Merkmale, Instrumente und Probleme am Beispiel der Rechtsstaatlichkeit und des neuen Rechtsstaatlichkeitsaufsichtsverfahrens'

3.3.2   Article 4(2) TEU
A further potential legal basis that warrants examination is Article 4(2)
TEU. It is argued that the principle of equality among Member States prohibits them from imposing their own values and legal assessments, thereby
preventing them from re-evaluating choices made by other Member States.[43]
Consequently, a refusal to cooperate or a re-evaluation would amount to a violation of the principle of equality among Member States.[44] Two points should
be raised in this regard: First, the wording of this provision does not introduce
a positive obligation of mutual trust between Member States.[45] Second, Article
4(2) TEU imposes an obligation solely on the EU to respect the national identities of its Member States, thereby referring to the vertical relationship between
the EU and its Member States.[46]

3.3.3   Article 4(3) TEU
The principle of mutual trust is rooted in the principle of sincere cooperation
enshrined in Article 4(3) TEU,[47] as indicated by their parallel structure.[48]

(2014) ZaöRV, 283–328, at 284; on Article 2 in combination with Article 3 TEU
as an appropriate legal basis see von Danwitz, Der Grundsatz des gegenseitigen
Vertrauens zwischen den Mitgliedstaaten der EU' (2020) Europarecht, 61–89, at
79 f., who, however, neglects the fact that Article 3 TEU binds only the EU and
not the Member States.
    [43]   Lenaerts, 'La vie après l'avis: exploring the principle of mutual (yet not
blind) trust' (2017) 54 CMLRev., 805–840, at 807 f.; critically, Ladenburger, 'The
Principle of Mutual Trust between the Member States in the Area of Freedom,
Security and Justice' (2020) ZEuS, 373–407, at 382.
    [44]   Lenaerts, (2017) *supra* note 43, at 808.
    [45]   Classen, 'Die Gleichheit der Mitgliedstaaten und ihre Ausformungen im
Unionsrecht' (2020) Europarecht, 255–269, at 262.
    [46]   Klamert, 'Article 4 TEU' in Kellerbauer, Klamert and Tomkin (eds) (2019)
supra note 17, para. 19.
    [47]   ECJ, Case C-284/16, *Achmea*, EU:C:2018:158, para. 58; Blobel and Spath,
'The tale of multilateral trust and the European law of civil procedure' (2005)
30 EL Rev., 528–547, at 535; von Bogdandy and Spieker, 'Reverse Solange
2.0: Die Durchsetzung europäischer Werte und die unions- und strafrechtliche
Verantwortung nationaler Richter' (2020) Europarecht, 301–332, at 330; Closa,
'Reinforcing EU Monitoring of the Rule of Law' in Closa and Kochenov (eds),
Reinforcing Rule of Law Oversight in the European Union (CUP 2016), 17;
Gerard, 'Mutual Trust as Constitutionalism?' in Brouwer and Gerard (eds),
*Mapping Mutual Trust: Understanding and Framing the Role of Mutual Trust in
EU Law* (EUI 2016), 76; Spieker, (2022) *supra* note 19, 259; of different opinion,
Ladenburger, (2020) *supra* note 43, at 382.
    [48]   Similarly, Kullak, (2019) *supra* note 5, 205 f.

Article 4(3) TEU pertains to the horizontal relationship between Member States, imposing a duty of cooperation when fulfilling obligations arising from EU law.[49] The principle of mutual trust complements this duty by prescribing *how* this cooperation should take place, introducing a rebuttable presumption of compliance with EU law in the horizontal relationships between Member States. This interpretation is supported not only by the explicit connection of the principle of sincere cooperation to "mutual respect" between Member States and the EU in Article 4(3) TEU[50] but also by recent case law of the ECJ.[51]

Furthermore, this section argues that, similar to the principle of sincere cooperation, the mutual trust principle also has a vertical dimension,[52] which is, however, of limited significance, since questions concerning the allocation of competences are mainly addressed by the principle of conferral. Firstly, with regard to the trust of the EU towards its Member States, EU institutions trust that Member States uphold EU values, particularly the rule of law and EU fundamental rights, and thus refrain in principle from scrutinizing their actual compliance. However, if EU values are not upheld in the Member States, the foundation of trust is compromised. In this context, the European Commission confirmed in its Communication on the protection of the Union's budget in case of generalized deficiencies regarding the rule of law in the Member States that the ongoing rule of law crisis in certain Member States has eroded the foundation of mutual trust, prompting the proposal of appropriate EU measures.[53] In this regard, the rule of law conditionality mechanism[54] reflects the broken trust of the EU towards Member States that violate its core values. Nonetheless, the principle of mutual trust retains its normativity: The presumption that all Member States respect the rule of law and sufficiently protect the financial interests of the EU is still applicable. Financial sanctions can only be imposed in case of a breach of the rule of law that directly affects the protection of the Union's financial interests. Conversely, the principle of mutual trust would be violated if the rule of law conditionality regulation introduced

---

[49] ECJ, Case 42/82, *Commission v France*, EU:C:1983:88, para. 36; Case C-116/11, *Bank Handlowy and Adamiak*, EU:C:2012:739, para. 6.

[50] Cf. Gerard, (2016) *supra* note 47, 77.

[51] Case C-17/19, *Bouygues travaux publics and Others*, EU:C:2020:379, para. 40.

[52] In favour of the vertical dimension of mutual trust, albeit without further argumentation, Spieker, (2022) *supra* note 19, 259; Willems, (2021) *supra* note 23, 175; see also ECJ, Case C-831/18 P, *Kommission v RQ,* EU:C:2020:481, para. 81, in which the ECJ acknowledges the existence of mutual trust between the Commission and the national authorities.

[53] COM (2018) 324 final, 1.

[54] [2020] OJ L 433I/1.

an *ex-ante* conditionality mechanism, requiring Member States to demonstrate their adherence to the rule of law prior to the allocation of EU funds.

Another manifestation of the vertical dimension of mutual trust is the presumption that national courts fulfil all requirements to refer a question to the ECJ for a preliminary ruling under Article 267 TFEU.[55] However, this presumption is refuted if a final judicial decision from a national or international court concludes that the judge constituting the referring court does not meet the criteria of being an independent and impartial tribunal established by law within the meaning of Article 19(1), subparagraph 2 TEU.[56] Once again, mutual trust is conditional in this context.

Lastly, the trust granted by the Member States towards the EU primarily concerns the cooperative relationship between national constitutional courts and the ECJ. The presumption applies that EU institutions exercise their conferred powers as dictated by the Treaties and, thus, act in accordance with EU law. Based on this rebuttable presumption, national constitutional courts refrain from scrutinizing whether competences are exercised in line with the Treaties and whether the essential content of fundamental rights is protected by EU institutions.[57]

3.4   Limits

As previously discussed in the context of the interdisciplinary approach, the principle of mutual trust can be refuted under specific circumstances. However, the ECJ has occasionally addressed these conditions for rebutting mutual trust in a somewhat inconsistent manner in its case law. Therefore, the purpose of this section is to outline the doctrinal underpinnings of the limitations of mutual trust.

3.4.1   Article 7(2) TEU

It is well established that the violation of EU values is primarily addressed by Article 7 TEU, which outlines the consequences in the event of a collapse of the foundation of mutual trust. Similarly, the preamble of the Framework Decision on the European Arrest Warrant explicitly states that a serious and

---

[55] ECJ, Case C-132/20, *Getin Noble Bank,* EU:C:2022:235, para. 69.

[56] Ibid., para. 72.

[57] Similarly, Kahl, '§ 27 Vertrauen (Kontinuität)' in Kube, Morgenthaler and Seiler (eds), *Leitgedanken des Rechts* (C.F. Müller 2013), para. 29; Kirchhof, 'Die Rechtsarchitektur der Europäischen Union' (2020) Neue Juristische Wochenschrift, 2057–2063, at 2059; Lenaerts, 'Kooperation und Spannung im Verhältnis von EuGH und nationalen Verfassungsgerichten' (2015) Europarecht, 3–28, at 6, 10.

persistent breach of EU values by a Member State, confirmed by a Council decision under the procedure of Article 7(2) TEU, leads to a general suspension of mutual trust towards that Member State.[58] This has been reiterated by the ECJ in its case law concerning the rule of law.[59] However, the possibility of a general suspension of the principle of mutual trust towards the violating Member State, upon the issuance of a Council decision under Article 7(2) TEU, should apply universally and extend beyond the mechanism of the European Arrest Warrant.[60] Given that the Council decision under Article 7(2) TEU serves as substantial evidence that EU values are systematically violated in a Member State, neither the transnational effect of the acts issued in that Member State nor the assumption that EU law and especially the fundamental rights have been observed can be justified. This signifies a complete breakdown of the systemic trust in the overall capacity of the legal system of the concerned Member State to uphold and enforce EU law. Against this backdrop, the procedure outlined in Article 7(2) TEU indicates the absence of the foundation of mutual trust towards the violating Member State and thus establishes a clear limit to the principle of mutual trust.

3.4.2 European Public Policy Clause based on Article 2 TEU

It is important to clarify that the limit imposed by Article 7(2) TEU, in the form of a general suspension of the principle of mutual trust, does not imply that violations of EU values below this threshold cannot result in a one-time, case-specific suspension of mutual trust.[61] By its very nature, mutual trust can be rebutted if there are indications of an erosion of its foundation in a specific case. Thus, if a violation of an EU value can be established in the context of a particular cooperation request based on objective evidence, the presumption of compliance with EU law should be rebutted. However, even in such cases, the systemic trust in the overall capacity of the legal system of the Member State concerned to uphold and enforce EU law is maintained. One way to achieve this is through the development of a European public policy clause anchored in Article 2 TEU and the introduction of a uniform standard against

---

[58] [2002] OJ L 190/1, Recital 10.

[59] ECJ, Case C-168/13 PPU, *F.*, EU:C:2013:358, para. 49; Case C-216/18 PPU, *Minister for Justice and Equality*, EU:C:2018:586, paras. 70, 72; Joined Cases C-354/20 PPU and C-412/20 PPU, *Openbaar Ministerie*, EU:C:2020:1033, para. 57.

[60] See also Kullak, (2020) *supra* note 5, 172.

[61] Cf. Canor, 'My brother's keeper? Horizontal Solange: An ever closer distrust among the peoples of Europe' (2013) 50 CMLRev. 383–422, at 399.

which all cooperation requests would be assessed.[62] This would effectively block transnational acts that violate fundamental legal principles of the EU. The refusal to cooperate would then occur after an individualized examination by the requested Member State, assessing the extent to which a value of Article 2 TEU is violated based on its concretization in the *acquis communautaire*.[63] However, it is essential to consider that while EU fundamental rights concretize the values of Article 2 TEU, there is a risk of circumventing Article 51(1) EUCFR, whose scope – contrary to that of Article 2 TEU – does not extend to cases with no connection to EU law.[64] This concern can be addressed by considering solely violations of the essence of fundamental rights[65] as a possible limitation to the mutual trust principle in the context of the European public policy clause.[66] Thus, even an isolated violation of EU values that falls below the threshold of Article 7(2) TEU should serve as a limit to mutual trust and result in a one-time, case-specific suspension.

3.4.3   National Constitutional Identity Clause

An important aspect that merits further examination pertains to the potential role of the national constitutional identity clause, as outlined in Article 4(2) TEU, as a possible limit to the principle of mutual trust under EU primary law. This clause serves as a counterweight to mutual trust in cases where the EU values of Article 2 TEU and the non-regression principle are not violated, but the fundamental structures of a particular Member State's constitutional order establish a higher (minimum) level of protection compared to Article 2 TEU or accord constitutional significance to a value not explicitly enshrined therein. The objective of this section is to examine whether the constitutional pluralism protected by Article 4(2) TEU imposes a limit on the principle of mutual trust

---

[62]   Sceptical on the enforceability of Article 2 TEU: Bonelli, 'Infringement Actions 2.0: How to Protect EU Values before the Court of Justice' (2022) 18 EuConst, 30–58, at 44 f.

[63]   On the distinction between values and *acquis communautaire* see Kochenov, (2017) *supra* note 19, at 12 f.

[64]   von Bogdandy and Spieker, (2020) *supra* note 47, at 304.

[65]   Brkan, 'The Concept of Essence of Fundamental Rights in the EU Legal Order: Peeling the Onion to its Core' (2018) 14 EuConst, 332–368, at 338 f.; Wendel, 'Mutual Trust, Essence and Federalism – Between Consolidating and Fragmenting the Area of Freedom, Security and Justice after *LM*' (2019) 15 EuConst, 17–47, at 25 f.

[66]   Cf. Kullak, (2020) *supra* note 5 at 168; Spieker, (2021) *supra* note 19 at 257; similarly, Kaufhold, '§ 48 Grundsätze der gegenseitigen Anerkennung und des gegenseitigen Vertrauens' in Kahl and Ludwigs (eds), *Handbuch des Verwaltungsrechts* (C.F. Müller 2021), para. 77.

when the requested Member State's legal system establishes a lower threshold for the violation of an EU value or protects a value not mentioned in Article 2 TEU as constitutionally significant.

National constitutional courts often interpret Article 4(2) TEU as a safeguard against the absolute supremacy of EU law over national constitutional law, which grants them the right to refuse the application of EU law if they deem it to violate the national constitutional identity within their jurisdiction.[67] However, it is important to note that the constitutional identity clause does not establish an inviolable core of sovereignty that Member States can invoke unilaterally.[68] Instead, it imposes an obligation on EU institutions to strike a balance between the primacy of EU law and the protection of national constitutional identity, guided by the principle of proportionality.[69] If this balancing exercise results in an encroachment on the national constitutional identity of a Member State, two scenarios arise: either the relevant EU measure will be struck down as invalid or the Member State concerned will be exempted from following the relevant EU obligation that violates Article 4(2) TEU.[70]

In view of the above, can a Member State invoke its national constitutional identity in the meaning of Article 4(2) TEU, in order to be exempted from a cooperation obligation arising from EU law? In other words, can Article 4(2) TEU pose a limit to the principle of mutual trust? Firstly, addressing this question requires a distinction between fully harmonized and non-harmonized (or partly harmonized) areas of EU law. In fully harmonized areas, the practical effectiveness of EU law in relation to the protection of EU fundamental rights has already been considered by the EU legislator. Consequently, Member States cannot request a higher level of protection in their territory

---

[67]   See e.g. Ludwigs, '§ 44 Verwaltung als Teil der nationalen Identität' in Kahl and Ludwigs (eds) (2021) *supra* note 66, paras. 5 f.; Spieker, 'Framing and managing constitutional identity conflicts: How to stabilize the *modus vivendi* between the Court of Justice and national constitutional courts' (2020) 57 CMLRev. 361–398 at 383; further see Pracht, *Residualkompetenzen des Bundesverfassungsgerichts* (Mohr Siebeck 2022), at 280 f.

[68]   von Bogdandy and Schill, 'Die Achtung der nationalen Identität unter dem reformierten Unionsvertrag' (2010) ZaöRV, 701–734, at 725; Martinico, 'Taming National Identity: A Systematic Understanding of Article 4.2 TEU' (2021) 27 EPL, 447–464, at 453; Pernice, 'Der Schutz nationaler Identität in der Europäischen Union' (2011) 136 Archiv des öffentliches Rechts, 185–221, at 194 f.; ECJ, Joined Cases C-357/19 et al., EU:C:2021:1034, *Euro Box Promotion*, EU:C:2021:1034, para. 249; Case C-430/21, *RS*, EU:C:2022:99, para. 70.

[69]   Klamert, (2019) *supra* note 46, para. 21.

[70]   von Bogdandy and Schill, (2010) *supra* note 68, at 726.

and thus demand to be released from their duty to cooperate on that ground.[71] In non-harmonized (or partly harmonized) areas of EU law, Member States have more flexibility to tailor the rules according to their constitutional values. However, this flexibility should not contradict other EU values[72] or undermine the unity and effectiveness of EU law.[73] The evaluation of whether value-driven regulatory choices jeopardize the unity and effectiveness of EU law falls within the exclusive jurisdiction of the ECJ, as stipulated in Article 19(1) TEU. Given that the principle of mutual trust is intertwined with the effectiveness of EU law, the prospects for successfully invoking Article 4(2) TEU to challenge mutual trust are rather limited. Besides, the practical importance of Article 4(2) TEU diminished by the overlap between the values protected under the national constitutional clause and those enshrined in Article 2 TEU.[74] Consequently, objections raised by national constitutional courts could be framed as concerns regarding a potential violation of Article 2 TEU and could be addressed through the aforementioned European public policy clause. This approach would enable national courts to actively contribute to the development of a solid foundation for the principle of mutual trust by integrating their national assessments into the European understanding of EU core values.[75] It can be, thus, reasonably concluded that Article 4(2) TEU can only be invoked as a limitation to the principle of mutual trust in highly exceptional circumstances.[76]

---

[71]   ECJ, Case C-399/11, *Melloni*, EU:C:2013:107, paras. 57 f.; Lenaerts, (2015) *supra* note 57, at 21; Millet, 'Successfully Articulating National Constitutional Identity Claims: Strait Is the Gate and Narrow Is the Way' (2021) 27 EPL, 571–596, at 576.

[72]   ECJ, Case C-399/09, *Landtová*, EU:C:2011:415, paras. 41 f.

[73]   ECJ, Case C-168/13 PPU, *F.*, EU:C:2013:358, paras. 51 f., 74; Anagnostaras, 'Solange III? Fundamental rights protection under the national identity review' (2017) 42 EL Rev., 234–253, at 248.

[74]   von Bogdandy and Schill, (2010) *supra* note 68, at 713; Spieker, (2020) *supra* note 67, at 389.

[75]   Grabenwarter, Huber, Knez and Ziemele, 'The Role of the Constitutional Courts in the European Judicial Network' (2021) 27 EPL, 43–62, at 54 f.; Schnettger, 'Article 4(2) TEU as a vehicle for national constitutional identity in the shared European legal system' in Calliess and van der Schyff (eds), *Constitutional Identity in a Europe of Multilevel Constitutionalism* (CUP 2019), at 13 f.; Spieker, (2020) *supra* note 67, at 391.

[76]   von Bogdandy and Schill, (2010) *supra* note 68, at 716; Millet, (2021) *supra* note 71, at 584 f.; Pernice, (2011) *supra* note 68, at 216; on a different position see Sáenz Pérez, 'Constitutional identity as a tool to improve defence rights in European criminal law' (2018) 9 NJECL, 446–463, at 450 f.

4.   EXCEPTIONS UNDER EU SECONDARY LAW

In addition to the limitations specified in EU primary law, further exceptions to the principle of mutual trust can be introduced in EU secondary law through provisions outlining grounds for refusal of recognition or execution of a trans-national administrative act.[77] In such cases, these exceptions to the principle of mutual recognition also serve as exceptions to the underlying principle of mutual trust, even if no breach of the foundation of trust in the sense of non-compliance with EU law has taken place.

5.   THE RULE OF LAW CRISIS AS A CRACK IN THE FOUNDATION OF MUTUAL TRUST

Rule of law[78] is explicitly laid down in Articles 2[79] and 49(1) TEU regarding the accession of a state to the EU. The European understanding of the rule of law encompasses the core requirements, which are common to all democratic constitutional states and requires that state power be exercised in accordance with the constitution and the applicable laws, as well as subject to judicial review by independent courts.[80] The requirements arising from the rule of law principle are legally binding both for the EU and the Member States.[81] Recently, in its *ASJP*[82] judgment, the ECJ contributed to the operationalization of the European rule of law principle,[83] by emphasizing that Article 19(1)

---

[77]   Similarly, Kaufhold, (2021) *supra* note 66, para. 75; Kullak, (2019) *supra* note 5, at 109.

[78]   Englisch: *Rule of Law*; Französisch: *état de droit*; Griechisch: κράτος δικαίου.

[79]   Cf. Classen, 'Rechtsstaatlichkeit als Primärrechtsgebot in der Europäischen Union – Vertragsrechtliche Grundlagen und Rechtsprechung der Gemeinschaftsgerichte' (2008) Europarecht, 7–21, at 7; further Payandeh, 'Das unionsverfassungsrechtliche Rechtsstaatsprinzip' (2021) 61 Juristenzeitung, 481–489, at 482.

[80]   ECJ, Case 294/83, *Les Verts v European Parliament*, EU:C:1986:16, para. 23; von Bogdandy and Ioannidis, (2014) *supra* note 42, at 288; Classen, (2008) *supra* note 79, at 8; Tsourdi, 'Asylum in the EU: One of the Many Faces of Rule of Law Backsliding?' (2021) 17 EuConst, 471–497, at 476 f.; Voßkuhle, 'Rechtsstaat und Demokratie' (2018) Neue Juristische Wochenschrift, 3154–3158, at 3154.

[81]   Payandeh, (2021) *supra* note 79, at 484.

[82]   ECJ, Case C-64/16, *Associação Sindical dos Juízes Portugueses (ASJP)*, EU:C:2018:117.

[83]   See Schorkopf, (2020) *supra* note 18, at 480, according to whom the ECJ has transformed the rule of law into a legally subsumable and enforceable norm.

TEU concretizes the value of the rule of law.[84] The latter inherently entails the requirement for an effective judicial control.[85] This requirement is not limited by Article 51(1) EUCFR, but applies to all national judicial systems, insofar as they are called to rule upon areas covered by EU law and decide on questions of application or interpretation of EU law.[86] In that sense, the independence of the national courts must also be ensured.[87] Consequently, the design of national judicial systems and the guarantees of independence are assessed under EU law.[88]

Although EU values form the foundation of mutual trust and no ranking between them can be inferred from Article 2 TEU,[89] there is a close(r) connection particularly between the value of the rule of law and mutual trust:[90] Given the very limited number of enforcement and sanction mechanisms at EU level, the enforcement of EU law mainly depends on the way its primacy is guaranteed in the Member States.[91] The existence of trust regarding compliance of national legal systems with the requirements arising from the rule of law constitutes, therefore, a prerequisite for further EU integration.[92] At the same time, the mutual trust principle imposes a rebuttable presumption of respect of the rule of law, in the sense of the lawful application of the applicable law. It follows that compliance with the rule of law requirements by the Member

---

[84] ECJ, Case C-64/16, *supra* note 82, para. 32. In the same vein, the value of democracy mentioned in Article 2 TEU is concretised by Article 10(1) TEU, according to which the functioning of the EU is based on the principle of representative democracy, cf. ECJ, Case C-502/19, *Junqueras Vies*, EU:C:2019:1115, para. 63; C-418/18 P, *Puppinck and others v Commission*, EU:C:2019:1113, para. 64; C-718/18, *Commission v Germany*, EU:C:2021:662, para. 124.

[85] ECJ, Case C-64/16, *supra* note 82, para. 36.

[86] Ibid., paras. 29, 33 f.; Bonelli and Claes, 'Judicial serendipity: how Portuguese judges came to the rescue of the Polish judiciary' (2018) 14 EuConst, 622–643, at 630 f.; Pech and Platon, 'Judicial independence under threat: The Court of Justice to the rescue in the ASJP case' (2018) 55 CMLRev., 1827–1854, at 1832 f.

[87] ECJ, Case C-64/16, *supra* note 82, paras. 41 f.

[88] On this subject Pech and Scheppele, 'Is the Organisation of National Judiciaries a Purely Internal Competence?' (2018) Verfassungsblog, <verfassungsblog.de/is-the-organisation-of-national-judiciaries-a-purely-internal-competence/> accessed 1 December 2023.

[89] Levits, (2019) *supra* note 7 at 247.

[90] Cf. Lenaerts, 'Upholding the Rule of Law through Judicial Dialogue' (2019) 38 YEL, 3–17, at 7.

[91] Similarly, von Bogdandy, 'Vertrauen im europäischen Rechtsraum' in Kadelbach (ed), *Verfassungskrisen in der EU* (Nomos 2018), 34.

[92] Ibid., 33; COM(2014) 158 final, at 2.

States is an indispensable functional condition for the principle of mutual trust.[93]

5.1 Rule of Law Crisis Framed as Mutual Trust Crisis

Considering that Article 2 TEU is the foundation of mutual trust, it logically follows that systematic violations of EU values erode this trust among the Member States and endanger the smooth cooperation in the EU.[94] More specifically, the systemic trust in the overall capacity of national legal systems of lawfully applying and enforcing EU law heavily depends on the extent to which Member States have established a national judicial system in conformity with the requirements of Article 19(1) TEU.[95] The existence of an independent judiciary constitutes an indispensable condition for mutual trust between the Member States.[96] The rebuttal of this systemic trust takes gradually place through repeated and systemic violations of the value of the rule of law. In this sense, the rule of law crisis simultaneously points towards a crisis of mutual trust.[97]

5.2 The Systemic Deficiencies Doctrine

However, the term "rule of law crisis" is only suitable to describe Member State actions in relation to the rule of law principle.[98] It is, thus, of purely descriptive nature without any legal implications.[99] The derivation of concrete

---

[93]   See also Payandeh, (2021) *supra* note 79, at 489.

[94]   von Bogdandy, (2019) *supra* note 9, at 515; Voßkuhle, (2018) *supra* note 80, at 3155.

[95]   Similarly, Ronsfeld, (2015) *supra* note 30, 253 f.; Schmidt, *Verfassungsaufsicht in der EU* (Nomos 2021), 48; COM(2013) 160 final, 2.

[96]   Kochenov and Morijn, 'Augmenting the Charter's Role in the Fight for the Rule of Law in the European Union: The Cases of Judicial Independence and Party Financing' (2021) 27 EPL, 759–780, at 770; Pech and Scheppele, 'Illiberalism Within: Rule of Law Backsliding in the EU' (2017) CYELS, 3–47, at 11; Zinonos, 'Judicial Independence & National Judges in the Recent Case Law of the Court of Justice' (2019) 25 EPL, 615–636, at 631 f.

[97]   In this sense cf. Kube, 'Vertrauen im Verfassungsstaat' (2021) 146 Archiv des öffentliches Rechts, 494–519, at 503; Kulick, (2020) *supra* note 2, at 224; Ladenburger, (2020) *supra* note 43, at 386; Ronsfeld, (2015) *supra* note 30, 248.

[98]   Further Schmidt, (2011) *supra* note 95, 34 f.

[99]   Ibid., 49; Schmidt and Bogdanowicz, 'The infringement procedure in the rule of law crisis: How to make effective use of Article 258 TFEU' (2018) 55 CMLRev., 1061–1100, at 1081.

legal consequences with regards to the mutual trust is rather due to another legal concept, namely that of the systemic deficiency in relation to the rule of law.[100]

The core question pertains to the point in time at which one can trace a rule of law crisis in a Member State. National legal systems provide for different levels of protection of fundamental rights, institutional bodies and even regulations, thereby guaranteeing the European diversity in the meaning of Article 4(2) TEU and setting outer limits to EU action. Corrective measures or interventions on the part of the EU in the legal structures of Member States must therefore be limited to exceptional cases of serious violations of the EU values. The concept of systemic deficiencies is designed precisely for this aim, namely to doctrinally capture the legal situation, in which the violations of EU values are so serious, that the existence of systemic trust in the legal structures of the concerned Member State can no longer be assumed. Systemic deficiencies can not only justify the introduction of EU measures,[101] but also constitute a potential reason for refusing cooperation requests between Member States.

Although the term 'systemic deficiencies' is difficult to define,[102] it does not cover expected, "normal" violations of law in a legal system,[103] but only extreme situations of erosion of the rule of law through pertinent, serious violations.[104] This approach is also endorsed by the Commission in its Communication on a new EU Framework to strengthen the Rule of Law, by pointing out that when the mechanisms established at national level to secure the rule of law cease to operate effectively, they pose a threat to the rule of law.[105] In its subsequent proposal for a regulation on the protection of the Union's budget in case of generalized deficiencies as regards the rule of law in the Member States, the Commission defines systemic deficiencies as "a widespread or recurrent practice or omission, or measure by public authorities which affects the rule of law".[106] Systemic deficiencies in relation to the rule of law can, therefore, be summarized as a qualified breach of EU law.[107]

---

[100] von Bogdandy and Ioannidis, (2014) *supra* note 42, at 283 f.; similarly, Schmidt and Bogdanowicz, (2018) *supra* note 99, at 1082.

[101] von Bogdandy, (2019) *supra* note 9, at 523; Mader, (2019) *supra* note 19, at 156.

[102] Cf. von Bogdandy and Ioannidis, (2014) *supra* note 42, at 298.

[103] Luhmann, *Ausdifferenzierung des Rechts* (Suhrkamp 1981), 115: normative expectations are maintained even in the case of their (isolated) disappointment.

[104] von Bogdandy and Ioannidis, (2014) *supra* note 42, at 284.

[105] COM(2014) 158 final, 5.

[106] COM(2018) 324 final, Article 2(b).

[107] Schmidt, (2021) *supra* note 95, at 65; see also Wunderlich, 'Von der Rechtsgemeinschaft zur Verweigerungsunion?' (2019) Europarecht, 557–577, at 577.

A starting point for a doctrinal approach of the legal concept of systemic deficiencies is Article 7 TEU, which assumes a clear risk of a serious (and persistent) breach of Article 2 TEU, in conjunction with the principles of conferral and procedural autonomy of the Member States, according to which the latter are generally responsible for upholding the rule of law as well as for remedying violations under national law.[108] The EU is, therefore, entitled to take targeted measures to remedy the corresponding deficits in the Member States only in extreme cases of systemic breaches of EU values, in which the corrective mechanisms and national measures in place prove to be inadequate to eliminate these threats.[109]

Furthermore, in their vertical dimension, i.e. regarding the relationship of the EU vis-à-vis the Member States, systemic deficiencies in relation to the rule of law can justify the imposition of EU measures in extreme situations on the basis of Article 7 TEU.[110] In their horizontal dimension, i.e. regarding the relationship between the Member States, systemic deficiencies can lead to the rebuttal of the principle of mutual trust and the suspension of intergovernmental cooperation. Due to the interdependence[111] of the national legal systems and the comprehensive cooperation obligations in different areas of law, it is highly likely that systemic deficiencies in one Member State can have negative effects in the territory of another Member State.[112] In this respect, the existence of systemic deficiencies in relation to the rule of law presupposes not only legal structures that undermine the rule of law in the Member State concerned in the sense of a qualified illegality (internal dimension), but also the triggering of negative effects on the legal systems of the other Member States (external dimension), resulting in the endangerment of a smooth inter-

---

[108] With reference solely to Article 7 TEU see von Bogdandy and Ioannidis, (2014) *supra* note 42, at 292.

[109] von Bogdandy, (2020) *supra* note 19, at 715 f.

[110] von Bogdandy and Ioannidis, (2014) *supra* note 42, at 292; also Wendel, 'Rechtsstaatlichkeitsaufsicht und gegenseitiges Vertrauen' (2019) Europarecht, 111–132, at 125 refers to the "protective function" of systemic deficiencies.

[111] Hillion, 'Leaving the European Union, the Union way: A legal analysis of Article 50 TEU' (2016) 8 EPA, 1–12, at 6.

[112] Closa, (2016) *supra* note 47, 18; Fisicaro, 'Rule of Law Conditionality in EU Funds: The Value of Money in the Crisis of European Values' (2019) 4 EP, 695–722, at 698; Toggenburg and Grimheden, 'Managing the Rule of Law in a Heterogeneous Context: A Fundamental Rights Perspective on Ways Forward' in Closa and Kochenov (eds) (2016) *supra* note 47, at 149.

state cooperation.[113] The erosion of EU values shakes the EU to its core, even threatening its existence.[114]

6.   CONCLUSION

In conclusion, this extensive examination has shed some light on the concept of the mutual trust principle within the EU legal order. Based on the shared values enshrined in EU primary law (Article 2 TEU), such as democracy, freedom, and the rule of law, mutual trust underpins the EU's cooperative framework both in its horizontal and vertical dimension: It relies on the presumption that these values will be respected in the Member States' territory when entering cooperation schemes dictated by EU law. While EU values are legally binding for both the EU and its Member States, the lack of a precise definition in the Treaties leaves Member States with a substantial discretion in interpreting their exact content. Nevertheless, the values enshrined in Article 2 TEU carry an autonomous meaning and underpin the identity of the EU. The disjuncture between the importance attributed to EU values and the limited competencies granted to the EU institutions for their enforcement poses a significant challenge.

A key point is the definition of mutual trust, which draws from an interdisciplinary approach. It elucidates the intricate nature of this principle, encompassing both an abstract and a specific object of trust. The former (abstract trust) refers to the overall capability of national legal systems to uphold and enforce EU law, relying on the equivalence of legal systems and regulations in place. The latter (specific trust) pertains to the compliance with EU law by the requesting Member State within specific cooperation relationships. In any case, however, trust is not unconditional; it can be rebutted when a specific threshold is reached. In this sense, it is essential to find both the legal basis and limits of mutual trust in EU primary law. While Article 4(3) TEU constitutes the legal foundation of mutual trust, Articles 2, 7(2) TEU, and, in extreme cases, Article 4(2) TEU set its outer limits.

Against this backdrop, the crisis of EU values, such as the rule of law crisis in some Member States erodes the foundation of mutual trust. This erosion is reflected in the concept of systemic deficiencies regarding the rule of law. The existence of such systemic deficiencies can function as the basis for EU intervention under Article 7 TEU and may also lead to the suspension of intergovernmental cooperation among Member States, thereby highlighting the

---

[113] Schmidt and Bogdanowicz, (2018) *supra* note 99, at 1082.
[114] von Bogdandy, (2020) *supra* note 19, at 719.

substantial consequences of the collapse of mutual trust. In this sense, the rule of law crisis can also be framed as a mutual trust crisis.

All in all, this section underscores the intricate interplay between mutual trust, EU values, and the rule of law crisis. Upholding the mutual trust principle is imperative for the unity and integrity of the European Union. To this end, the principle of mutual trust will reach its full potential only if it rests on a solid foundation, which in turn must be co-shaped both by national and European actors.

8. Questioning the Primacy of Union Law by National Constitutional Courts

Udo Bux[1]

1. PRIMACY, PRECEDENCE, SUPREMACY – DYNAMICS RESULTING FROM THE CO-EXISTENCE OF LEGAL ORDERS

The issue of primacy of EU law over national law of EU Member States has been a topic in political discourse ever since the concept was developed by the Court of Justice of the European Communities more or less 60 years ago. The debate on primacy of EU law regularly gains momentum when a case of conflicting national and EU law receives public attention and the conflicting national, even national constitutional law, shall step back. When recently Austria started a discussion on whether the use of cash should be enshrined in the constitution,[2] the European Commission was quick to retaliate: Such an operation would be useless as cash is protected by 'overriding' EU law. Member States had transferred their monetary sovereignty to the EU when the euro was introduced. Monetary issues were therefore exclusive responsibility of the EU.[3]

When the Second Senate of the German Federal Constitutional Court (FCC) in its judgment of 5 May 2020 refused to accept the validity of a decision of the Governing Council of the European Central Bank, the interested public immediately perceived it as if the FCC was challenging the primacy of EU law over German domestic law. Although, according to the FCC, the ruling was not

---

[1] The opinions expressed in this text are those of the author and do not reflect the views of the European Parliament or its members.

[2] <https://www.politico.eu/article/austria-chancellor-karl-nehammer-cash-use-constitution/> accessed 1 December 2023.

[3] Selmayr, 'Bargeld ist durch die EU-Verfassung geschützt - Mitgliedstaaten haben keine Währungssouveränität' (11 August 2023) KURIER, <https://kurier.at/meinung/gastkommentar/bargeld-ist-durch-die-eu-verfassung-geschuetzt/4025 54 852> accessed 1 December 2023.

about *primacy*, but about an *ultra vires* review (points 111 and 234) this caused uproar in the academic and political discussion: In the aftermath of the judgment, the European Parliament committees on Constitutional Affairs and on Legal Affairs held public hearings[4] and academic authors heavily criticized the FCC.[5] The European Commission was alarmed and even filed an infringement procedure against Germany,[6] supported by the German Federal Government (against itself, meaning against the FCC). In its judgment of 5 May 2020, the FCC had used three times the word 'precedence' (not 'primacy'),[7] whereas the term 'primacy' was used in the order of the Second Senate of the FCC of 6 July 2010 (*PSPP*)[8] in the English version of the text. Later, the First Senate of the FCC used 'precedence' instead in its order of 6 November 2019 (*right to be forgotten II*).[9] Also, 'primacy', 'precedence',[10] and 'supremacy'[11] can be found in rulings of both the European Court of Justice (ECJ) and the German FCC dating back to the 1970s.

---

[4]   AFCO committee: <https://www.europarl.europa.eu/committees/en/juri-afco - hearing-on-the-consequences-of/product-details/20200714CHE07441>;
   JURI committee: <https://www.europarl.europa.eu/committees/en/workshop -on-the-principle-of-primacy-of-/product-details/20220517WKS04201>

[5]   Sarmiento and Weiler, 'The EU Judiciary After Weiss: Proposing A New Mixed Chamber of the Court of Justice' (2 June 2020) Verfassungsblog, <https:// verfassungsblog.de/the-eu-judiciary-after-weiss/> accessed 1 December 2023.

[6]   Ruffert, 'Verfahren eingestellt, Problem gelöst? - Die EU-Kommission und das Bundesverfassungsgericht' (7 December 2021) Verfassungsblog, <https:// verfassungsblog.de/verfahren-eingestellt-problem-gelost/> accessed 1 December 2023.

[7]   German FCC, Judgment of the Second Senate of 5 May 2020, 2 BvR 859/15 et al., available at <https://www.bundesverfassungsgericht.de/e/rs20200505 _2bvr085915en.html>.

[8]   German FCC, Order of the Second Senate of 6 July 2010, 2 BvR 2661/06,available at <https://www.bundesverfassungsgericht.de/e/rs20100706_2bvr266106en.html>

[9]   German FCC, Order of the First Senate of 6 November 2019, 1 BvR 276/171, available at <https://www.bundesverfassungsgericht.de/e/rs20191106_1bvr027617en .html>

[10]   ECJ, Case 61/79, *Denkavit*, EU:C:1980:100, paras. 5 and 12; Case 224/97, *Ciola*, EU:C:1999:212, paras. 2 and 26.

[11]   ECJ, Case 14/68, *Walt Wilhelm and others v Bundeskartellamt*, EU:C:1969:4, para. 5; CFI, Case T-362/04, *Minin*, EU:T:2007:25, para. 101.

2.   ORIGINS AND SOURCES OF PRIMACY

2.1   The Principle of *pacta sunt servanda*

Primacy of EU law is not laid down in the Treaties (TEU/TFEU);[12] it is a legal principle of the European Communities ever since. Following the entry into force of the Treaty of Lisbon on 1 December 2009, the EU now has legal personality and has acquired the competences previously conferred on the European Community. Community law has become EU law. The principle of the primacy is also referred to as 'precedence'[13] or 'supremacy'[14] of EU law in the literature. It has been developed from sovereign nations' respect for the *pacta sunt servanda* principle which they obey amongst themselves as a fundamental principle of (international) law (Article 26 of the Vienna Convention on the Law of Treaties).[15] It can be described as the "idea that where a conflict arises between an aspect of EU law and an aspect of law in an EU Member State (national law), EU law will prevail."[16]

As the principle of primacy of EU law is not laid down in the EU Treaties (only as part of a non-binding declaration annexed to the Treaties), it might be politically unwise to mention it all the time, *as if it were written in the Treaties*. Those were meant to have a 'supranational' nature from the start. In this context, another provision of the Vienna Convention should be mentioned: Article 27 provides that a State may not invoke the provisions of its internal law as justification for its failure to perform a treaty unless there has been a manifest error regarding the competence to conclude said treaty in accordance with Article 46 of the Convention (which rarely ever applies).

---

[12] Opinion of the Council Legal Service of 22 June 2007, contained in Declaration No. 17 concerning primacy annexed to the Treaty of Lisbon: "At the time of the first judgment of this established case law … there was no mention of primacy in the treaty. It is still the case today."

[13] Ziller, *The primacy of European Union Law* (European Parliament 2022), PE 732.474, at 9.

[14] Kumm, 'The Jurisprudence of Constitutional Conflict: Constitutional Supremacy in Europe before and after the Constitutional Treaty' (2005) ELJ, 262 ff. at 294–295.

[15] UNTS, vol. 1155, at 331. All EU Member States except France and Romania are party to the Convention.

[16] EUR-Lex database, Glossary of summaries, 'Primacy of EU law (precedence, supremacy)' <https://eur-lex.europa.eu/EN/legal-content/glossary/primacy-of-eu-law-precedence-supremacy.html> accessed 1 December 2023.

2.2   No Uniform Terminology

On the EU level, the term 'primacy' is used as 'primauté' in French, 'primacía' in Spanish, 'primato' in Italian, and 'Vorrang' in German. Previously, different terms had been used in the English (e.g. 'precedence' or 'supremacy'). *Jacques Ziller* in a study for the European Parliament[17] points out that in the French version of the *Costa v E.N.E.L.* judgment of 15 July 1964,[18] the term 'prééminence' was first employed, rather than 'primauté'; it was only later that the stronger word 'primauté' was added as a keyword in the tables of the ECJ Reports. In the English version of the judgment it was translated to 'precedence' (not 'primacy') in the digital version of the judgment, which can still be found on the EUR-Lex database. At that time, it was an original concept and did not mean anything other than 'supremacy' of the Community law. From the start of the three Communities, the three founding treaties provided for institutions and specific procedures designed to guarantee the application of EU law in a much more effective way than with most international treaties known so far, unlike the UN Charter, for example, which does not entail the obligation to accept the jurisdiction of the International Court of Justice. Since the first Treaty of 18 April 1951, participation in this European Coal and Steel Community automatically meant that Member States accepted the jurisdiction of the Court of Justice and thus 'primacy of EU law'. In 1951, a smart way had to be found to ensure participation of the founding Six and to avoid saying *expressis verbis* "any new rule issued by the new High Authority will even overrule your constitution!". Enshrining the principle in the Treaties would have endangered the whole of *Jean Monnet's* project.

2.3   Decentralised Enforcement of Union Law

It is a historical fact that European Community and later EU institutions do not have direct power over national authorities of its Member States. This innovative concept was the *very nature* of the new community of states designed in the Paris and Rome Treaties in the mid-20th century. Still, the EU of today has no enforcement administration of its own, no army, no police. "The sole force of the European Community law is the force of law."[19] In order to take effect, the citizens and national authorities (judges, politicians, civil servants

---

17   Ziller, (2022) *supra* note 13 at 9.
18   ECJ, Case 6/64, *Flaminio Costa v E.N.E.L.*, EU:C:1964:66.
19   Rodríguez Iglesias, 'Judicial Protection of the Citizen under European Law' in Markezinis (ed), *The coming together of the common law and the civil law* (Hart 2000), 195-213; Louis, 'Le droit communautaire, cinquante ans après' in

etc.) have to accept and respect the principle in day-to-day business and on many occasions, acting of their own free will. Since the Treaty of Lisbon, Article 4 (3)(2) TEU therefore provides: "Member States shall take any appropriate measure ... to ensure fulfilment of the obligations ... resulting from the acts of the institutions of the Union." This means a duty of Member States to implement provisions of Union law so as to ensure fulfilment of obligations contained therein.[20]

The founding Treaties of the Communities and later the Union also opted for a system under which enforcement of EU law was left in principle to the national courts.[21] This means, a national legal dispute may be brought before the European Courts only where it comes within the scope of EU law and only if this is permitted under the conditions prescribed by the Treaties. Also, the European Courts have to respect those limits conferred to them by the Treaties.[22]

2.4   Enforcement by the Courts

Because of the idea of a decentralised enforcement of the new law *sui generis,* the EEC Treaty (1957) established the procedure for failure to fulfil an obligation (now Article 258 TFEU). It gave the supranational predecessor of the European Commission the unique power to find that a Member State has failed to fulfil its primary or secondary law obligations. On the flip side of the coin is that Member States had to be protected from abuse by the High Authority by the possibility of bringing action against its acts (or for failure to act) (now Article 263 TFEU).

It was against this background that the *Costa v E.N.E.L.* judgment was handed down in 1964, which was at the time harshly criticised especially by the French government. It was a judgment in the framework of a preliminary reference procedure (now Article 267 TFEU).[23] Article 267 TFEU can be seen as *the* key for upholding primacy of European law by the Court of Justice: any

---

Glansdorff and Jones (eds), *Liber amicorum Bernard Glansdorff* (Bruylant 2008) 465-494.

[20]   See also the contribution by *Poulou* in this volume as well as Lenaerts, van Nuffel and Corthaut (eds), *EU Constitutional Law* (OUP 2021) at para. 18.001 at 565.

[21]   Lenaerts, van Nuffel and Corthaut, (2021) *supra* note 20, 13.001 at 442.

[22]   ECJ, Case C-50/00 P, *Unión de Pequeños Agricultores v Council,* EU:C:2002:462, para. 44.

[23]   Petersen and Chatziathanasiou, *Primacy's Twilight? On the Legal Consequences of the Ruling of the Federal Constitutional Court of 5 May 2020 for the Primacy of EU Law* (European Parliament 2021), PE 692.276 at 33.

national court may make reference for a preliminary ruling on the interpretation of the Treaties or on the validity or interpretation of acts of the Union. Once the CJEU issues its preliminary ruling, it is for national courts to apply it to the disputes pending before them (decentralised enforcement). The procedure serves to assure the uniform application of Union law in the Member States.[24] The EU has millions of citizens and companies, but there are only 81 judges in the Court of Justice and the General Court in Luxembourg. The Court of Justice of the European Union has no jurisdiction to decide national disputes.[25] Consequently, it can only be the national judges that have to uphold and apply EU law in daily practice. It is the national judges that have to turn EU law into reality.[26]

After the rulings by the ECJ of *Costa v E.N.E.L.* and *Internationale Handelsgesellschaft*,[27] no Member State took the opportunity to raise the issue during an Intergovernmental conference, asking for a clause limiting "precedence" of Community law: not while negotiating the Merger Treaty of 1965, nor on the occasion of the Single European Act in 1986, the Maastricht Treaty in 1992, the Treaty of Amsterdam in 1997 or the Treaty of Nice in 2001.

The *Costa v E.N.E.L.* judgment does not state that Community law prevails over domestic law; it states that domestic law cannot prevail over EU law: that there is no primacy of domestic law, even posterior.[28] Similar, in *Internationale Handelsgesellschaft* in 1970, the ECJ held that the validity of EU measures cannot be challenged on grounds of national law rules or concepts, even if that is a violation of fundamental human rights provisions in a Member State's constitution. The ECJ claims that EU law has absolute primacy over the domestic legal order of the Member States, including the Member States' constitutions:[29]

> Recourse to the legal rules ... of national law in order to judge the validity of measures adopted by the institutions of the Community would have an adverse effect on the uniformity and efficacy of Community law. The validity of such measures can only be judged in the light of Community law... the law stemming from the treaty, an independent source of law, cannot because of its very nature be overridden by rules of national law, ... without being deprived of its character as Community

---

[24] Lenaerts, van Nuffel and Corthaut, (2021) *supra* note 20, 13.005 at 443.

[25] Pech, *The European Court of Justice's jurisdiction over national judiciary-related measures* (European Parliament 2023), PE 747.368 at 25.

[26] Cuyvers, 'Preliminary References under EU Law' in Ugirashebuja et al. (eds), *East African Community Law: Institutional, Substantive and Comparative EU Aspects* (Brill 2017), 275-284 at 275.

[27] ECJ, Case 11/70, *Internationale Handelsgesellschaft*, EU:C:1970:114.

[28] ECJ, Case 6/64, *Flaminio Costa v E.N.E.L.*, EU:C:1964:66 at 594.

[29] ECJ, Case 11/70, *supra* note 27 at para. 3.

law and without the legal basis of the Community itself being called in question. Therefore the validity of a Community measure or its effect within a member State cannot be affected by allegations that it runs counter to either fundamental rights as formulated by the constitution of that state or the principles of a national constitutional structure.

The year is 1970, no directly elected European Parliament exists, no Charter of Fundamental Rights, no accession of the Communities to the European Convention of Human Rights (ECHR). *Internationale Handelsgesellschaft* is a judgment after a procedure for a preliminary ruling with two questions by a German administrative court to the ECJ, expressing some worries about the legality of Community acts of the Common Agricultural Policy and their compliance with fundamental rights. The Court answered in general terms, that EC law did, of course, respect fundamental rights, in a manner akin to Member State legal systems. In this particular case, there was no fundamental right violation by the Commission regulation.

The ECJ's position was reiterated in 1978 in *Simmenthal*. The ECJ was asked for a preliminary ruling by an Italian court which had to decide on an action brought by a company. The referring court wanted to know whether it should wait for the legislature to amend Italian law or for the Constitutional Court to declare the unconstitutionality of certain fees, or whether it could immediately order their refund. The Italian government took the view that the request for a preliminary ruling was seeking to obtain an answer from the ECJ on a question of Italian law, which was not its role. The Court replied with reference to "any provision of a national legal system and any legislative, administrative or judicial practice which might impair the effectiveness of Community law". This wording therefore includes not only laws and all inferior regulatory provisions, but also the constitution, which is superior to laws.[30]

3.   ATTEMPTS TO CODIFY THE PRINCIPLE OF PRIMACY

Several years later, the draft Treaty establishing the European Union,[31] which was adopted by the European Parliament in 1984 and not followed up by the Heads of State and Government, marked by the inaugural endeavour to codify the principle of primacy, but employed the word 'precedence' in Article 42,

---

[30]   ECJ, Case 106/77, *Simmenthal*, EU:C:1978:49, para. 21.

[31]   Resolution on the draft Treaty establishing the European Union [1984] OJ C 77/33; Publications Office of the EU, *Draft Treaty establishing the European Union* (1984) <https://op.europa.eu/en/publication-detail/-/publication/52f9545f -202d-40c6-96a6-5a896a46ad70>.

which stated: "The law of the Union shall be directly applicable in the Member States. It shall take precedence over national law."

It is safe to say that ever since *Costa v E.N.E.L.* and up to the European Convention of 2002–2003, governments of the Member States implicitly accepted the case-law of the ECJ, and subsequently explicitly accepted this case-law when they signed the Constitutional Treaty of 2004 (which did not enter into force). The draft Treaty establishing a Constitution for Europe[32] of 29 October 2004 had proposed Article I-6, stating: "The Constitution and law adopted by the institutions of the Union in exercising competences conferred on it shall have primacy over the law of the Member States."

However, the British and Dutch governments requested that the provision on primacy not be included in the future new treaty ('constitution') because this could jeopardise ratification of what became the Treaty of Lisbon. At the occasion of the signing of the Treaty of Lisbon in 2007, Member States instead agreed on Declaration No. 17 concerning primacy. Annexed to this text is an opinion of the Council Legal Service of 22 June 2007[33] which stipulates that primacy resulted from the case-law of the Court of Justice and that it was a cornerstone principle of Community law. The fact that it would not be included in the future treaty should not in any way change the existence of the principle. While declarations, unlike protocols, are not binding in themselves, they nonetheless have substantial legal effect, as such declarations are formal evidence of the legal opinion of the signatory states (i.e. the EU Member States).[34]

Declaration 17 also establishes a uniform terminology: the terms 'primacy', 'primauté', 'primacía', 'Vorrang' and so forth. In particular, in English the term supremacy had often been used, but which was too much of an implicit reference to the wording of Article VI (2) of the U.S. Constitution.

4.   SELECTED NATIONAL JURISPRUDENCE QUESTIONING THE PRIMACY OF UNION LAW

At the 2007 Intergovernmental conference, a number of governments had felt that not including an article on primacy posed a risk, particularly if apex courts were to interpret this absence as if Member States did not recognise the primacy of EU law. Indeed, certain apex courts, since the 1970s onwards, expressed reservations about the application of the principle of primacy. National constitutional courts have also interpreted Article 4(2) TEU as a safeguard against the absolute supremacy of EU law over national constitutional

---

[32]   [2004] OJ C 310/1.
[33]   See also the contribution by *Bauerschmidt* in this volume.
[34]   Ziller, (2022) *supra* note 13 at 14.

law.[35] The issues that have led to clashes with constitutional or supreme courts have concerned either domestic legislative provisions or constitutional provisions. In a small number of high-profile and highly mediatised cases, the constitutional or supreme courts of Germany, Denmark, Hungary, Poland and France have openly defied the ECJ by expressly refusing to apply its decisions to them.

4.1   Poland

The Polish Constitutional Tribunal (PCT) has developed quite a rich case law on the relationship between EU law and domestic Polish law – dating back mostly to the time before the start of the judicial reforms in 2016. In particular, judgment K 18/04[36] is of major importance. It has been characterized as generally introducing a union-friendly interpretation of the Polish constitution, resulting in the general acceptance of the primacy of EU law.[37]

In its judgment of 27 April 2005 on the compatibility of the European arrest warrant with the constitutional ban on the extradition of nationals,[38] the PCT explained that, given the contradiction between the Polish Constitution and the requirements of Council Framework Decision 2002/584/JHA, which can provide for a Polish citizen to be handed over to another Member State, there were four steps to be taken: 1. The Tribunal should check whether an interpretation in conformity with EU law was possible. 2. If that were not possible, the government should ask for the Framework Decision to be amended. 3. If that were not possible, Poland should amend its Constitution. 4. And if that were not possible, the only remaining option was to implement Article 50 TEU and leave the EU.

Although an interpretation in conformity with EU law was not possible, the Tribunal did set a time-limit within which it considered that the handover would be possible, although in theory contrary to the Constitution, in order to allow the constituent power the time to adopt the necessary amendment. Some commentators see in this judgment a refusal of primacy, but that was not the case, as it underlined the link between primacy and the *pacta sunt servanda* principle by finding that the article of the Polish Code of Penal Procedure intended to implement the Framework Decision should continue to apply.

---

[35]   See also the contribution by *Poulou* in this volume.

[36]   Judgment of 11 May 2005, K 18/04.

[37]   Zoll, Południak-Gierz and Bańczyk, *Primacy of EU law and jurisprudence of Polish Constitutional Tribunal* (European Parliament 2022), PE 732.475 at 10.

[38]   Judgment of 27 April 2005, P 1/05 (OTK-A 2005/4, pos. 42). N P 1/05 <https://trybunal.gov.pl/fileadmin/content/omowienia/P_1_05_full_GB.pdf>.

Following the judgment K 18/04, the PCT added the concept of the protection of constitutional identity as another limitation of the primacy of EU law in judgment K 32/09.[39] This concept went beyond the concept of the sovereign and democratic functioning of the Polish state as it required that certain values and legal institutions of the Polish domestic order remained unaltered within the process of EU legal integration. The PCT assumed priority of the Polish Constitution but in the general framework of the loyalty to the EU institutions and to find a way to ensure practical primacy of the EU law.

On 7 October 2021, the PCT issued an assessment of the conformity to the Polish Constitution of selected provisions of the EU Treaty.[40] In this judgment, it declared that several provisions of the EU treaties violated the Polish Constitution and were thus inapplicable in Poland. The PCT found in particular three violations of the Polish Constitution caused by several provisions of the TEU:[41]

- Firstly, the Constitutional Tribunal found that an understanding of Article 1 read in conjunction with Article 4(3) TEU which required or authorised Polish bodies to issue decisions which disregarded the Polish Constitution or to apply laws which contravened the Polish Constitution to be in breach of Articles 2, 7, 8(1) in conjunction with 8(2), 90(1) and 91(2), as well as 178(1) of the Polish Constitution.
- Secondly, the Constitutional Tribunal interpreted Article 19 (1), second subparagraph, read in conjunction with Article 4 (3) TEU to require or authorise Polish bodies to apply laws which were previously declared unconstitutional by the Constitutional Tribunal. The PCT held that the mentioned provisions of the TEU violate Articles 2, 7, 8 (1) in conjunction with 8(2) and 91(2), 90(1), 178(1) as well as 190(1) of the Polish Constitution.
- Thirdly, the PCT considered Article 19(1), second subparagraph, read in conjunction with Article 2 TEU, which allow Polish courts to review the independence of judges appointed directly by the President of the Republic to be incompatible with Articles 8(1) in conjunction with 8(2), 90(1), 91(2), 144(3) (17) as well as 186 (1) of the Polish Constitution.[42]

---

[39] Judgment of 24 November 2010, PCT, Sprawa K 32/09.
[40] Ref. No. K 3/21.
[41] Petersen and Wasilczyk, *The Primacy of EU Law and the Polish Constitutional Law Judgment* (European Parlaiment 2022), PE 734.568 at 7.
[42] Ibid. at 11.

Future governments will have a difficult task to deal with the consequences of the activity of the PCT in the last years. According to some authors, this case law of the PCT will remain without long-lasting effects.[43]

4.2   France

Primacy of EU law is limited, because the *Conseil constitutionnel* expressly reserves itself the right to conduct a constitutional identity review since a landmark decision in 2006.[44] According to the *Conseil constitutionnel*, the "transposition of a Directive cannot run counter to a rule or principle inherent in the constitutional identity of France unless the Constituent power has agreed to the same." The *Conseil constitutionnel* is not the only French court that engaged in delimiting the applicability of EU law:[45] the *Conseil d'Etat* had, in its jurisprudence on *Daniel Cohn-Bendit's* expulsion, precluded in 1978 the reliance on European Community directives in administrative procedures, despite the ECJ's case law to the contrary. Looking at the *Cour de Cassation* (another French apex court) it expressed due respect with the ECJ[46] using exactly the wording in the ECJ case law referring to the specific nature of the EU's legal system, and thus accepting the same basis for the consequences of primacy as the ECJ.[47]

4.3   Czech Republic

The Czech Constitutional Court acknowledges the wide political discretion of the legislature and the primacy of EU law in principle, but also reserved for itself the right to review whether EU law conflicted with the 'fundamental core' of the Czech Constitution and State (*Sugar Quotas III*[48]). Only if the

---

[43]   Zoll, Południak-Gierz and Bańczyk, (2022) *supra* note 37 at 27.

[44]   Decision no. 2006-540 DC of 27 July 2006, para. 20, Copyright and related rights in the information Society, <https://www.conseil-constitutionnel.fr/ en/decision/2006/2006540DC.htm>; Petersen and Chatziathanasiou, (2022) *supra* note 23 at 34.

[45]   Conseil d'Etat, Ass, 22 December 1978, No. 11604, https://www.legifrance .gouv .fr/ ceta/ id/ C ETATEXT000 007666522/ ; Petersen and Chatziathanasiou, (2021) *supra* note 23 at 35.

[46]   Judgment of the French Court of Cassation, 24 May 1975, <https://www .legifrance.gouv.fr/juri/id/JURITEXT000006994625/>.

[47]   Ziller, (2021) *supra* note 13 at 29.

[48]   Decision of 8 March 2006, case No. P. OS 50/04, Sugar Quotas III (English translation available at <https://www.usoud.cz/en/decisions/2006-03-08-pl-us-50 -04-sugar-quotas-iii>).

scope of this discretion was clearly exceeded, the Court would intervene as an ultima ratio.[49] In *Lisbon Treaty I* of November 2008, the Court referred to the FCC decisions in *Solange II* and *Maastricht*.[50] In 2012, the Czech Constitutional Court was the first apex court of a Member State to declare an EU legal act *ultra vires* in its judgment of 31 January 2012 in the *Slovak pensions* case.[51] The judgment is considered an exception to the rule as the Czech Constitutional Court seemed to change course with its *Slovak Pensions* judgment, it found the decision of the CJEU in case *Landtová*[52] to be *ultra vires*, as in its opinion the CJEU had ignored the specific historic circumstances of the case. The refusal came in response to a judgment after request for a preliminary ruling made by the Czech Supreme Administrative Court with which it was in deep disagreement within the national judicial system. Due to this peculiar background, the judgment is usually regarded as not representative for the Court's approach to EU law, as it concerns the "battle over Slovak pensions" after the dissolution of Czechoslovakia.[53]

4.4   Germany

The German FCC is one of the most respected apex courts in the EU, and its doctrinal inventions are notably intricate and have exerted considerable influence on the approaches adopted by the courts of other Member States. For example, the *ultra vires* doctrine has inspired other courts to adopt similar doctrines. The Czech Constitutional Court referred in its *Slovak pensions* judgment to the German FCC and also the Polish Tribunal made reference to it. Of course, the PSPP judgment of 5 May 2020 did not come out of the blue and was just another chapter of the 'ups and downs' in the 'dialogue' between the CJEU and the FCC – dating back to the 1970s. In *Internationale Handelsgesellschaft*,[54] as the case was a preliminary ruling, the matter returned to the German Administrative Court in Frankfurt which was not satisfied by this somewhat apodictic sentence: in one paragraph the ECJ noted that Community law (even an act by the Commission in the field of agriculture policy), by its very nature, was to overrule even the *Grundgesetz* (the German

---

[49]   Petersen and Chatziathanasiou, (2021) *supra* note 23 at 29.
[50]   Decision of 26 November 2008, case No. Pl. ÚS 19/08, para 109, *Lisbon Treaty I*.
[51]   Judgment of 31 January 2012, Pl. ÚS 5/12, English translation at <https://www.usoud.cz/en/decisions/2012-01-31-pl-us-5->.
[52]   ECJ, Case C-399/09, *Landtová*, EU:C:2011:415.
[53]   Petersen and Chatziathanasiou, (2021) *supra* note 23 at 30.
[54]   Case 11/70, *Internationale Handelsgesellschaft*, EU:C:1970:114.

constitution). The national court, after having received the ECJ's answer, itself sensed the conflict this potentially faced, and had, in 1971 as follow up, now requested a preliminary ruling from the FCC on the legality of the Community decision originally in question (the Commission CAP measure).

In this preliminary ruling of the FCC[55] on the same case, it held in 1974 that, scrutinising the Community measure by the FCC was admissible. But, as long as ("*solange*") fundamental rights protection by the Community was evident, it would refrain from scrutiny of EU action in detail. This implied that the principle of primacy of secondary EU law would find its limits in the national fundamental rights of the *Grundgesetz* – at least in extreme cases of violation of those fundamental rights.

In 1986, in the *Solange II* judgment, the FCC[56] revised this approach partially. It held that because, since 1974, the CJEU had developed protection for fundamental rights and declarations on rights and democracy had been made by the Community institutions, and all EC Member States had acceded to the European Convention on Human Rights, it would no longer scrutinise EU law in every case. That meant that individual constitutional complaints ('*Verfassungsbeschwerde*') would simply not be admissible before the FCC anymore.

In its *Maastricht* decision[57] in 1993, the FCC ruled that "the Federal Constitutional Court and the European Court of Justice stand in a co-operative relationship which ensures the protection of fundamental rights and which allows them to complement one another." Peace lasted until 2010: In *Honeywell*,[58] the FCC was presented with its first real opportunity after the Lisbon Treaty to review an EU act. Any doubt as to whether the FCC would actually invoke its earlier jurisdiction to examine the validity of an EU act was amplified by the "Honeywell" case. It reiterated that it was "empowered and obliged" to review the validity of EU acts.[59] Already then, it invoked *ultra vires* jurisdiction[60] and explicitly clarified the conditions under which it would hold an EU law to be outside the powers of the EU. But luckily, the EU

---

[55] German FCC, 2 BvL 52/712, Order of the Second Senate of 29 May 1974 = BVerfGE 37, 271.

[56] German FCC, 2 BvR 197/83, Order of the Second Senate of 22 October 1986 = BVerfGE 73, 339.

[57] German FCC, 2 BvR 2134/92, 2 BvR 2159/92, Judgment of the Second Senate of 12 October 1993, point B. 2 c5), BVerfG 89, 155 (177 f.).

[58] German FCC, 2BvR 2661/09, Order of the Second Senate of 6 July 2010 = BVerfGE 126, 268. Available at <https://www.bundesverfassungsgericht.de/SharedDocs/Entscheidungen/EN/2010/07/rs20100706_2bvr266106en.html>.

[59] Ibid. point C.I.1.c) aa).

[60] Ibid. headnotes 1a), 1b).

action in *Honeywell* was not found to be *ultra vires*. The real importance of Honeywell lies in the standard enunciated as to when the FCC would actually hold an EU act *ultra vires*. As an initial procedural hurdle, the FCC stated that the CJEU must have first had the opportunity to "deliver its legal opinion by means of a preliminary ruling", meaning that the FCC will not invalidate an EU action unless the CJEU itself has specifically failed to act in that regard. It clarified that only those EU acts that are "manifestly" beyond the "transferred competences" and "highly significant in the structure of competences between the Member States and the Union with regard to the principle of conferral and to the binding nature of the statute under the rule of law" will be considered *ultra vires*.[61]

In the summer of 2012, Europe faced investors' dwindling confidence in whether the European currency, the Euro, could survive. The financial situation of various Member States of the euro area was becoming unsustainable as a result of the apparently unstoppable increases in the risk primes applied to their government bonds. Return to national currencies seemed possible. After the meeting of its Governing Council on 5–6 September 2012, the European Central Bank (ECB) issued a press release with details of a decision outlining a programme for the purchase of government bonds issued by States of the euro area — the Outright Monetary Transactions (OMT) programme. In the following weeks, plaintiffs, law professors and euro-sceptic politicians lodged an individual constitutional complaint (violation of fundamental rights of the *Grundgesetz*) against the alleged failure of the Federal Government and the Parliament to act with regard to those decision allowing participation of the Bundesbank in the announced programs of the ECB.

The FCC paused the proceedings in January 2014 and lodged a request for a preliminary ruling with the CJEU.[62] In the FCC's view, the announced measures could not be covered by the mandate of the ECB because they "no longer represent monetary policy measures, but primarily economic policy measures" and in so far as there was a violation of Article 119 and Article 127 paragraphs 1 and 2 TFEU. Such a violation could constitute an *ultra vires* act which would have the consequence that German authorities were no longer allowed to participate. In particular, alluding to the principle of conferral of powers provided for in Article 5(1) and (2) TEU, that the mandate assigned to the ESCB must be strictly limited in order to meet democratic requirements and that compliance with the limits concerned must be subject to comprehensive judicial review.

---

[61]   Ibid. point 61.

[62]   German FCC, Order of the Second Senate of 14 January 2014, 2 BvR 2728/13, available at <https:// www .bverfg .de/ e/ rs20140114 _2bvr272813en .html>.

On 16 June 2015, the ECJ ruled that[63] Articles 119, 123(1) and 127(1) and (2) TFEU and Articles 17 to 24 of the ESCB Protocol "must be interpreted as permitting the ESCB to adopt a programme for the purchase of government bonds on secondary markets, such as the programme announced in the press release to which reference is made in the minutes of the 340th meeting of the Governing Council of the European ECB on 5 and 6 September 2012." The judgment of 16 June 2015 was commonly perceived as a certain success for the German plaintiffs as the ECJ had accepted to scrutinize decisions of the ECB. The Irish, Greek, Spanish, French, Italian, Dutch, Portuguese and Finnish Governments, the European Parliament, the European Commission, and the ECB itself had challenged the admissibility of the request for a preliminary ruling.

Concerning proportionality the ECJ concluded from Articles 119(2) and 127(1) TFEU, read in conjunction with Article 5(4) TEU, "that a bond-buying programme forming part of monetary policy may be validly adopted and implemented only in so far as the measures that it entails are proportionate to the objectives of that policy... according to the settled case-law of the Court, the principle of proportionality requires that acts of the EU institutions be appropriate for attaining the legitimate objectives."[64]

Following that answer by the ECJ, on 21 June 2016 the FCC delivered its judgment on the OMT programme.[65] Loyally, it held that the programme did not violate the German Constitution and that the Bundesbank was allowed to participate in the programme, as long as the programme complied with the conditions under EU law, as pronounced by the ECJ. Again it stressed, a "cooperative relationship" between the FCC and the ECJ in matters of *ultra vires review*, whereby the ECJ "decides upon the validity and interpretation of an act", whereas the FCC on the other hand "must ensure that acts of institutions, bodies, offices, and agencies of the EU do not exceed the European integration agenda in a manifest and structurally significant way and thereby violate Article 38 sec. 1 sentence 1 in conjunction with Article 23 sec. 1 sentence 2, Article 20 sec. 2 sentence 1, and Article 79 sec. 3 *Grundgesetz* (GG)."[66]

The plaintiffs were satisfied: in their view, the FCC had drawn clear boundaries, the exceeding of which the Federal Government and the Bundestag would have to act. If these do not intervene, they announced the possibility to take legal action again.

---

[63] ECJ, Case C-62/14, *Gauweiler and Others*, EU:C:2015:400.

[64] Ibid. para. 66.

[65] German FCC, Judgment of the Second Senate of 21 June 2016, 2 BvR 27 28/13, available at <https://www.bverfg.de/e/rs20140114_2bvr272813en.html>.

[66] Ibid. para. 114-119 and 157.

But the apotheosis was still about to come: Meanwhile, the ECB enacted the PSPP, another secondary markets public sector asset purchase programme, on 9 March 2015, and of course, the FCC had been seized again of this new programme. By means of this programme, the ECB and the national central banks of the euro zone have been buying securities from issuers of the public sector on the secondary markets, up to today amounting to EUR 2.6 billion. Those decisions were attacked again in the context of a series of constitutional complaints by more than 1,700 individuals concerning the applicability, in Germany, of various decisions of the ECB.

In the spirit of continuing the dialogue with the CJEU, the FCC once again requested a preliminary ruling according to Article 267 TFEU in proceedings seeking to establish that an act of the ECB is manifestly *ultra vires* and is not compatible with German constitutional identity. By order of 18 July 2017, the Second Senate suspended the proceedings and requested fast track procedure as the nature of the case requires that it be dealt with within a short time (which was not given a follow up by the ECJ).[67] The FCC had asked five questions to the ECJ, stating that the constitutional complaints were to be complied with if the PSPP went beyond the mandate of the ECB or violated the ban on monetary financing.

The ECJ handed down its judgment in December 2018;[68] by that time the ECB programme had already been implemented for nearly four years. The ECJ ruled that question 5 was not admissible, because it saw "no relation to the actual facts of the main action or its purpose".[69] As for the other four questions, the ECJ held that the programme did not go beyond the mandate of the ECB, falling within the area of monetary policy in which the Union has exclusive competence for the euro countries and respects the principle of proportionality. Concerning proportionality,[70] the PSPP did not obviously go beyond what is necessary to increase the inflation rate. The ESCB had weighed up the various interests involved in such a way that disadvantages in the implementation of the PSPP that were obviously out of proportion to the objectives pursued were avoided. In particular, it duly took into account the risks to which the substantial volume of PSPP securities purchases that the central banks of the Member States may have been exposed.[71]

---

[67]   German FCC, Order of the Second Senate of 18 July 2017, 2 BvR 859/15, request for a preliminary ruling, available at <https://www.bverfg.de/e/rs20170718_2bvr085915en.html>.

[68]   ECJ, Case C-493/17, *Weiss and Others*, EU:C:2018:1000.

[69]   Ibid. para. 155.

[70]   Ibid. para. 80.

[71]   Ibid. para. 81.

Following the preliminary ruling by the ECJ, the Second Senate of the FCC passed the judgment[72] by 7 votes to 1 and held that (note that in the wording, it is as if it was "addressing" both to the ECJ and the ECB):

- The PSPP of the ESCB is an *ultra vires* act of the ECB "in so far as the ECB has not demonstrated its proportionality".[73]
- Since the ECJ has misjudged this limit of competence, its decision is simply not comprehensible and is therefore itself an *ultra vires* act. In the opinion of the FCC, the competence of the Court of Justice to interpret EU law also ends where "the interpretation undertaken by the [ECJ] is not comprehensible from a methodological perspective"– for whomever, but at any rate for the Constitutional Court itself.[74]
- The ECJ "manifestly fails to give consideration to the importance and scope of the principle of proportionality". The ECJ's view therefore "is no longer tenable from a methodological perspective given that it completely disregards the actual effects of the PSPP".[75]
- In light of the aforementioned considerations, the FCC "cannot rely on the *Weiss* Judgment" by the ECJ and must therefore conduct its own review to determine whether the ESBC's decisions on the adoption and implementation of the PSPP remain within the competences conferred upon it under EU primary law.[76]
- The Federal Government and the German Bundestag have a duty to take active steps against the PSPP in its current form (headnote 9). In this respect, the Federal Government and the Bundestag also have a duty to continue monitoring the decisions of the ESBC on the purchases of government bonds under the PSPP and use the means at their disposal to ensure that the ESCB stays within its mandate.

The case was settled one year later, when on 29 April 2021, the same Second Senate of the FCC found that the Federal Government had adequately implemented its ruling of 5 May 2020. The decision rejected the plaintiffs' application to order enforcement.[77] Now, the FCC downplayed the matter

---

[72] German FCC, Judgment of the Second Senate of 5 May 2020, 2 BvR 859/15, para. 80, available at <https://www.bverfg.de/e/rs20200505_2bvr085915en.html>.

[73] Ibid. para. 232.

[74] Ibid. para. 153.

[75] Ibid. para. 119.

[76] Cf. ibid. para. 164.

[77] German FCC, decision of the Second Senate of 29 April 2021, 2 BvR 1651/15 and 2 BvR 2006/15, available at <https://www.bverfg.de/e/rs20210429_2bvr165115en.html>.

somewhat, by stating that the Federal Government and the *Bundestag* (the federal parliament) had a broad margin of (political) appreciation, assessment and manoeuvre when taking measures in response to the judgment of 5 May 2020 and in exercise of their "responsibility with regard to European integration".[78] Concerning proportionality of the ECB Governing Council measures, not all individual steps might necessarily be documented in detail, the numerous activities undertaken by the Federal Government and the *Bundestag* in response to the judgment of 5 May 2020, which were in part carried out via or with the assistance of the *Bundesbank*, have led to the ECB Governing Council demonstrating that it indeed conducted a proportionality assessment.[79] Concerning *ultra vires* acts of EU institutions, the FCC concedes that, to ensure conformity with the integration agenda, the constitutional organs may even provide retroactive legitimation.[80] Also, the European Commission was satisfied with it and closed the infringement procedure against Germany on 2 December 2021.[81]

5.　　CONCLUSION

In general, Member States' constitutional or supreme courts do not all the time defy the CJEU, primacy is a well-accepted principle by Member State courts.[82] The number of requests for a preliminary ruling in which a court has asked the ECJ whether an EU legal rule prohibits the application of a national rule in a specific case demonstrates substantial deference: over the thousands of requests for a preliminary ruling in five decades, there have been only a small number of cases in which a court has refused to draw the consequences.

In 2022, there have been 806 cases brought before the CJEU, of which 564 preliminary rulings;[83] similar numbers occurred in previous years (2021: 567 preliminary rulings; 2020: 534; 2019: 641; 2018: 568). And even in the recently and highly mediatised case, the PSPP judgment of 5 May 2020, the

---

[78]　Ibid. para. 108.

[79]　Ibid. para. 109.

[80]　Ibid. para. 91.

[81]　Europäische Kommission, Vertretung in Deutschland, 'Vertragsverletzungsverfahren im Dezember: EU-Kommission stellt Verfahren gegen Deutschland wegen EZB-Urteil ein und fällt eine Reihe weiterer Beschlüsse' (2 December 2021) , <https://germany.representation.ec.europa.eu/news/vertragsverletzungsverfahren-im-dezember-eu-kommission-stellt-verfahren-gegen-deutschland-wegen-ezb-2021-12-02_de> accessed 1 December 2023.

[82]　Ziller, (2021) *supra* note 13 at 29.

[83]　CJEU Annual report 2022, p. 27, <https://curia.europa.eu/jcms/upload/docs/application/pdf/2023-04/qd-aq-23-001-en-n.pdf>.

FCC was keen to stress its respect for primacy. There is no evidence that there would be a proliferation of cases of requests for a preliminary ruling brought to the CJEU because of a deterioration of the rule of law situation in the EU. The annual average growth rate of preliminary references in the period between 1961 and 1998 was 16%.[84] Already in the period between 1992 and 1998, preliminary references had increased by 85%. The share of preliminary references in the total number of cases brought before the ECJ has also seen an increase from below 4% in 1961 to more than 64% in 1998. This notable upsurge in the case law may be a positive development. It could be attributed to the growth in the size of economic activity subject to EU legislation, to the increase in EU competence and legislation over the years and the enhanced awareness among courts regarding EU law.

The Member States from which the most requests for a preliminary ruling originated in 2022 are Germany (98), Italy (63), Bulgaria (43), Spain (41) and Poland (39).[85]

The Court of Justice has never explicitly renounced the absolute character of the primacy of EU law, but a closer analysis reveals that it has shown considerable flexibility when taking Member States' interests into account. It has recognized that fundamental principles of national constitutions must be taken into consideration in the justification analysis in the context of EU fundamental freedoms. It also afforded a margin of discretion to Member States' courts when applying abstract standards of EU law to concrete cases and often changed its jurisprudence in order to react to the concerns of Member States' apex courts.

---

[84] Tridimas, 'Knocking on heaven's door: fragmentation, efficiency and defiance in the preliminary reference procedure' (2003) 40 CMLRev. 1, 9-50 at 16.

[85] CJEU Annual report 2022, *supra* note 83 at 27.

9. Political Strategies to Overcome the Rule of Law Crisis Taking into Account National Political Discourses – The Case of East Central European EU Member States[1]

Astrid Lorenz, Jan Němec, Dietmar Müller, Madeleine Hartmann and Dorottya Víg[2]

1. INTRODUCTION

Over the last decade, the European Union has established a comprehensive rule of law framework and a range of legal instruments (commonly referred to as a "toolbox"[3]) to protect the rule of law in its Member States. In addition, the Court of Justice of the European Union has issued several essential and landmark judgments on shortcomings that explicitly or implicitly relate to the rule of law.[4] Nonetheless, the results have been mixed. The European Commission's 2023 Rule of Law Report highlighted numerous problems in the Member States. The Fidesz- and PiS-led governments of Hungary and Poland were particularly targeted for systematic attempts to curtail the judiciary and otherwise restrict the rule of law.[5] In this chapter, we advocate for more context-sensitive EU communication on issues surrounding the rule of

[1] Supported by Open Access funds of the University of Erfurt.

[2] This contribution is based on the research project "Rule of Law in East Central Europe", which is funded by the German Federal Ministry of Education and Research in the years 2021 to 2024 (project number 01UC2103).

[3] See the contribution by *Bauerschmidt* in this volume.

[4] Meier, Lorenz and Wendel (eds), *Rule of Law and the Judiciary* (Nomos 2023).

[5] European Commission, '2023 Rule of Law Report – the rule of law situation in the European Union', COM(2023) 800 final. For an overview see the Country Chapter Abstracts and Recommendations, available at https://commission.europa

law to enhance its efficacy. More precisely, it is argued that the connection to national parliamentary discourses concerning challenges to the rule of law should be strengthened.

Our analysis draws on original empirical research carried out during the three-year research project "Rule of Law in East Central Europe". In an international team, we analysed debates on the rule of law issues in the parliaments of Czechia, Hungary, Poland, Romania, and Slovakia since the early 1990s. This seems to be a promising approach because "(d)iscourses enacted in parliament not only reflect political, social, and cultural configurations in an ever-changing world, but they also contribute to shaping these configurations discursively, cross-rhetorically, and cross-culturally".[6] The five countries possess similar traits, including a shared experience of transition to democracy, the rule of law, and a market economy, as well as EU membership in or after 2004.[7] Nevertheless, our examination has demonstrated some disparities in discussions held in parliaments about challenges to the rule of law. Our qualitative content analysis combined deductive and inductive components to guarantee theoretical placement and awareness of contextual nuances. These involve covering speeches that refer to the rule of law and those that do not explicitly reference it but touch on the issue. Our study spans 30 years and enables us to detect the dynamics of parliamentarians addressing challenges to the rule of law as well as established narratives.

In what follows, we first theorise the relevance of context for effective policy and political communication. Subsequently, we provide a brief overview of how we mapped the narratives in the five countries under scrutiny regarding perceived challenges to the rule of law. Section 4 presents the results of our analysis of the narratives in the parliaments of these countries, and section 5 discusses how the European Union can better align its policies with national discourses to strengthen adherence to the rule of law.

2. THE RELEVANCE OF THE NATIONAL CONTEXT FOR MAKING THE RULE OF LAW WORK

Spreading and effectively implementing the rule of law is a challenging endeavour. Geographically, the liberal idea of the rule of law, paired with

---

.eu/system/files/2023-07/6.2_1_52666_count_chap_abstracts_and_recomm_en.pdf.

[6] Ilie, 'Parliamentary discourse', *The International Encyclopedia of Language and Social Interaction* (2015) 1.

[7] See also the chapter by *Küpper* in this volume.

democracy, initially emerged in the Global North West. Over time, Western nations have promoted the rule of law through multiple waves of action. Since the end of the 1980s and the beginning of the 1990s, this "institution based on Western, rational values" has been "backed by the authority of international organisations, and disseminated across the globe".[8] However, critics argue that the impact was limited despite the various methods employed to advance the rule of law, such as exporting legal models, instituting an impartial judiciary, and recent efforts focused on expanding the rule of law to encompass democratic civil and political rights.[9] The limited impact of the initiative can be attributed, in part, to the varying understanding of the concept of the rule of law,[10] but also – to some critics, primarily – to a lack of knowledge of the contexts of the recipient states, which differ from what the promoters know from their home countries.[11] Critics of the style of rule of law promotion have raised concerns about the widespread use of standard rule of law prescriptions based on Euro-American institutions, practices, and models instead of creating programmes tailored to the specific context.[12]

This challenge of effectively promoting and enforcing values and institutions also applies to Europe and the European Union. In numerous EU Member States today, including Czechia, Hungary, Poland, Romania, and Slovakia, the rule of law institutions were created during their post-1989 transition to democracy and a market economy based on the people's will. However, practical implementation proved challenging due to the need to rebuild the entire system within a limited timeframe, resulting in discrepancies between old and new legal systems, and the necessity to maintain effective governance with a significant portion of the personnel in the judiciary and public administration (but also economy) that had previously served the authoritarian regime. Dealing with issues such as moral responsibility for the repressive abuse of

---

[8] Schimmelfennig, 'A Comparison of the Rule of Law Promotion Policies of Major Western Powers' in Zürn, Nollkaemper and Peerenboom (eds), *Rule of Law Dynamics: In an Era of International and Transnational Governance* (CUP 2012) 111-132.

[9] Peerenboom, Zürn and Nöllkaemper, 'Conclusion: From Rule of Law Promotion to Rule of Law Dynamics' in Zürn, Nollkaemper and Peerenboom (eds), *Rule of Law Dynamics: In an Era of International and Transnational Governance* (CUP 2012) 305-324.

[10] Magen and Morlino, 'Hybrid regimes, the rule of law, and external influence on domestic change' in Magen and Morlino (eds), *International Actors, Democratization, and the Rule of Law. Anchoring Democracy?* (Routledge 2009) 1 ff at 7-8; Tamanaha, *On the Rule of Law. History, Politics, Theory* (CUP 2004) at 1.

[11] Peerenboom, Zürn and Nöllkaemper, (2012) *supra* note 8 at 309.

[12] Ibid. at 310-311.

power by the old regime was problematic under the new rule of law system, which prohibits retroactive legislation and protects the rights of individuals, including those of the former communist elite. The same applied to earlier expropriations of property and its subsequent restitutions. Various actors with diverse intentions used the rule of law to follow particular interests in the controversy over such problematic issues.

With the establishment of the 'Copenhagen criteria' for accession, the EU has made the implementation of a functioning rule of law and the adoption of its entire legal framework ('acquis') prerequisites for joining the Union. It has been argued[13] that candidate countries' desire to join the EU and their required commitment to EU principles would keep actors on track even in difficult phases of system change. The transposition of EU norms and laws was thus expected to impact national legal cultures and judicial practices[14] – similar to the general strategy of promoting the rule of law worldwide. Conditionality was maintained as a tool of the EU even after accessions, for example in the form of the Control and Verification Mechanism for Bulgaria and Romania as well as the latest conditionality mechanism governing financial transfers to all Member States.[15]

---

[13]   Whitehead, 'The International Dimensions of Democratization' in Whitehead (ed), *The international dimensions of democratization: Europe and the Americas* (OUP 1996) 3-25 at 19; Dimitrova and Pridham, 'International Actors and Democracy Promotion in Central and Eastern Europe. The Integration Model and its Limits' (2004) 11 Democratization 5, 91-112; Sadurski, 'Accession's Democracy Dividend: The Impact of the EU Enlargement upon Democracy in the New Member States of Central and Eastern Europe' (2004) 10 European Law Journal 4, 371-401; Schimmelfennig and Sedelmeier, 'Governance by conditionality: EU rule transfer to the candidate countries of Central and Eastern Europe' (2004) 11 Journal of European Public Policy 4, 661-679 at 678; Börzel and Sedelmeier, 'Larger and more law abiding? The impact of enlargement on compliance in the European Union' (2017) 24 Journal of European Public Policy 2, 197-215; Buzogány, 'Beyond Balkan exceptionalism. Assessing compliance with EU law in Bulgaria and Romania' (2021) 22 European Politics and Society 2, 185-202.

[14]   Cserne, 'Formalism in Judicial Reasoning: Is Central and Eastern Europe a Special Case?' in Bobek (ed), *Central European Judges under the European Influence: The Transformative Power of the EU Revisited* (Hart 2017) 23-42 at 40.

[15]   Priebus and Anders, 'Fundamental Change Beneath the Surface: The Supranationalisation of Rule of Law Protection in the European Union' (2023) Journal of Common Market Studies, <https://doi.org/10.1111/jcms.13489> accessed 1 December 2023; Baraggia and Bonelli, 'Linking Money to Values: The New Rule of Law Conditionality Regulation and Its Constitutional Challenges' (2022) 23 German Law Journal, 131-156.

However, backlashes against "elements of the post-1989 consensus",[16] as well as ongoing conflicts between the EU and some governments in the region, suggest that conditionality was most effective in the pre-accession phase when the countries were strongly motivated to become EU members, ensuring rapid formal institutional change, but less effective after accession. Early on, observers[17] identified various contextual factors that influence the adoption and outcomes of formal institutions, such as customary norms, established procedures, and specific challenges and circumstances in the region related, for instance, to minorities or lustration, i.e. the "systematic vetting of public officials for links to the communist-era security services".[18] Furthermore, some scholars emphasise the interconnection between promoting the rule of law and other pertinent issues. *Bâli* and *Rana*[19] argue that "the attachment of the model of constitutionalism to prescriptions of privatization and market liberalization produced a Beltway consensus that tied liberalism to what many Eastern Europeans experienced as rapacious forms of capitalism". Such problems may have affected the general rule of law narratives. In addition, increased awareness of the intricacies of the rule of law developments may have arisen as the new institutions were implemented, impacting further the discourse surrounding the rule of law.

Stepping back from scholarly research on the promotion of the rule of law, and specifically on the rule of law within the European Union, to more general research on institutions, it is evident that there is a common assumption that

---

[16] Lach and Sadurski, 'Constitutional Courts of Central and Eastern Europe: Between Adolescence and Maturity' (2008) 3 Journal of Comparative Law 2, 212-233 at 215.

[17] See e.g. Elgie and Zielonka, 'Constitutions and Constitution-Building: A Comparative Perspective' in Zielonka (ed), *Democratic Consolidation in Eastern Europe, Volume 1: Institutional Engineering* (OUP 2001) 47; Krygier, 'The Rule of Law' in Palombella and Walker (eds), *Relocating the Rule of Law* (Hart Publishing 2009) 45-70; Blokker, 'EU Democratic Oversight and Domestic Deviation from the Rule of Law. Sociological Reflections' in Closa and Kochenov (eds), *Reinforcing rule of law oversight in the European Union* (CUP 2016) 249-269 at 250; Pridham, *Designing democracy: EU enlargement and regime change in post-communist Europe* (Palgrave Macmillan 2005); Micklitz, 'Prologue: The Westernisation of the East and the Easternisation of the West' in Bobek (ed), *Central European Judges Under the European Influence. The Transformative Power of the EU Revisited* (Hart 2017) 1-12 at 10 ff.

[18] Williams, Fowler and Szczerbiak, 'Explaining lustration in Central Europe: a "post-communist politics" approach' (2005) 12 Democratization 1, 22-43 at 23.

[19] Bâli and Rana, 'Constitutionalism and the American Imperial Imagination' (2018) 85 The University of Chicago Law Review 2, 257-292 at 278.

institutions and concepts (such as the rule of law in our case) are situated within contexts that shape their organisation, perception, and functionality. Historical and sociological institutionalisms strongly support this assumption. From this perspective, diverse views, practices, and narratives are associated with varying development paths[20] and legal and constitutional cultures.[21] Institutions are "embedded in structures of meaning and resources that are relatively invariant in the face of turnover of individuals and relatively resilient to the idiosyncratic preferences and expectations of individuals and changing external circumstances".[22] This means that formally establishing the rule of law does not guarantee that it is universally applied or that it carries the same values. Although all countries under our examination implemented institutions of the rule of law and share some contextual similarities, there may be national differences in the specific concepts, narratives, and practices relevant to the challenges of the rule of law.[23]

When discussing the concept of the rule of law, political and other actors should refer to issues, narratives, events, problems, and conflicts familiar to their target audience to develop effective communication. The audience expects them to do so. Addressing well-known narratives of the target group is essential, as audiences tend to select messages that align with their existing views and values – a phenomenon captured by the term "confirmation bias".[24] Furthermore, people seek coherence in their worldviews, making them more likely to accept lessons they have learned earlier than new ones.[25] Messages not connected to local narratives may appear irrelevant or unfamiliar to the target audience and create the perception that the issues discussed are uninformed and disconnected from their country and concerns. Actors seeking to discredit the European rule of law framework and strategy may also exploit such a perception.

---

[20] Mahoney, 'Path Dependence in Historical Sociology' (2000) 29 Theory and Society, 507-548; Thelen, 'How Institutions Evolve. Insight from Comparative-Historical Analysis' in Mahoney and Rueschemeyer (eds), *Comparative Historical Analysis in the Social Sciences* (CUP 2003) 208-240.

[21] Vorländer, 'Constitutions as Symbolic Orders: The Cultural Analysis of Constitutionalism' in Blokker and Thornhill (eds), *Sociological Constitutionalism* (CUP 2017) 209-240.

[22] March and Olsen, 'Elaborating the "New Institutionalism"' in Binder, Rhodes and Rockman (eds), *The Oxford Handbook of Political Institutions* (OUP 2008), 3-20 at 3.

[23] Ilie, (2015) *supra* note 5.

[24] Nickerson, 'Confirmation Bias: A Ubiquitous Phenomenon in Many Guises' (1998) 2 Review of General Psychology 2, 175-220.

[25] Festinger, *A theory of cognitive dissonance* (Stanford University Press 1957).

3. MAPPING NARRATIVES ON CHALLENGES TO THE RULE OF LAW METHODOLOGY

In order to identify patterns of narratives surrounding challenges to the rule of law in selected EU Member States, we analysed parliamentary debates in five East Central European countries. The study covered about 30 years, beginning in 1990 for Hungary, Poland, and Romania, and in 1992 for Czechia and Slovakia, where the point of departure coincided with the adoption of their constitutions and the dissolution of the joint federal state.

We have collected official archival records of parliamentary debates on key legislation that invoked the rule of law, as defined by the relevant rule of law indices[26] (partial indices of the Freedom House Index, Worldwide Governance Indicators, Varieties of Democracy Index, the Democracy Barometer, and the Bertelsmann Transformation Index or the rule of law index developed by the World Justice Project) and discussed in the academic literature. Given the vast amount of empirical material, we could not analyse all speech acts. The collection encompasses discussions surrounding new constitutions, laws that regulate the judiciary, public prosecution, or public administration, and laws on specific issues connected to the democratic transition, like lustration or restitution. Additionally, we included plenary debates explicitly mentioning the term 'rule of law' three or more times, regardless of the matter of the respective parliamentary discussion. By combining deductive and inductive approaches in the way we collected and analysed our empirical data, we aim to produce results consistent with current comparative research on the rule of law, yet sensitive to national actors' rule of law concerns and contexts.

As statements on challenges to the rule of law, we coded all speech acts that referred to threats, problems, and risks for the rule of law or its elements. We *interpreted* the relevant parts of the plenary debates to identify such statements, i.e. speakers did not have to explicitly address debated issues as challenges to the rule of law (e.g. "xy threatens the rule of law"). However, the context or speech act should clearly indicate that a phenomenon was declared to challenge the rule of law. Subsequently, we sorted the statements based on the type of alleged challenge and assigned them to corresponding codes. These codes were initially developed deductively, based on existing research on the rule of law, and then refined and expanded following our pretest analysis of the empirical material.[27] All team members participated in ongoing discussions to ensure the interpretation of the cases and examples was consistent. Chosen

---

[26] On these indices see also the contribution by *Lewkowicz et al.* in this volume.
[27] These codes correspond to the thematic areas listed in Table 9.1 below.

debates were translated and regularly coded by the whole team to verify inter-coder reliability and ensure overall interpretation similarity.

Not all verbalised claims regarding challenges to the rule of law constitute narratives. Our starting point is the concept of a 'social narrative', defined as "a narrative embraced by a group that also tells, in one way or another, something about that group".[28] In concrete terms, we understand a narrative as a way of talking about an issue and relating it to other issues, used by multiple actors in a range of speech acts in different situations. The basic assumption for us is that in their speeches, members of parliament represent not only their personal positions but also those of their parties. However, our objective is not to capture particular policy positions or networks[29] but to identify statements beyond specific legislative plans or policies.

In the following section, we first describe the categories of issues to which the narratives referred. These thematic areas were operationalised by codes from our qualitative content analysis. This analysis of *what* was generally addressed in the narratives facilitates case comparison. Using a more inductive technique, we subsequently present paraphrased arguments from parliamentary debates that illustrate *how* actors approach perceived challenges to the rule of law in their narratives. These paraphrases provide a more detailed insight into country and group specifics.

Our study concentrates on 'overlapping' and 'diverging' narratives for analytical purposes. Overlapping narratives refer to those employed by representatives of various political parties, regardless of their competitive or cooperative relationships or individual ideological or programmatic backgrounds. Although there may be slight differences in nuances between the overlapping narratives, their core messages are identical. Therefore, there is no substantive conflict between the speakers, even though, depending on the circumstances of the debate, particularly the relations between the government and opposition camps, these narratives can serve ad hoc political struggles. Diverging narratives, on the other hand, represent divergent rhetoric positions, generally not hinged on the current political scenario but rather aligned with party ideology, agenda, or long-term inter-party competition. Counter-narratives used by other actors can mirror this conflict. For the purposes of this chapter and because of limited space, we also include one-sided narratives under the term 'diverging narratives', based on the fact that the respective statements are not overlap-

---

[28] Shenhav, *Analyzing Social Narratives* (Routledge 2015), 19.
[29] See e.g. Granat, 'The parliamentary politics of the rule of law crisis in the EU' (2023) 45 Journal of European Integration 7, 1017-1034; Buzogany and Varga, 'Illiberal thought collectives and policy networks in Hungary and Poland' (2021) 24 European Politics and Society 1, 40-58.

ping. One-sided narratives are only used by one party or a block of like-minded parties without their counterparts taking an explicit position on them in favour of focusing on other issues.

Four aspects are relevant for understanding the patterns revealed by our analysis. First, "(t)he rationale of parliamentary debate lies in the existence of opposite political camps and, implicitly, in the confrontation between different, and sometimes contradictory, standpoints and representations of reality".[30] The MPs address the public and their political competitors; therefore, they can use narratives strategically for their own political goals. Opposition parties are especially interested in attacking the government and presenting themselves as the better alternative.[31] Thus, their narratives do not necessarily represent their perceptions and beliefs or neutrally reflect reality.

Second, given the usually imposed time limits of parliamentary speeches, MPs most likely do not address many issues that the audience already knows or opinions that it widely shares, as such statements would not enhance their profile. Therefore, the findings should not be viewed as a reflection of all the narratives used by national actors during the investigated period. There are other influential platforms beyond parliamentary debates where politicians can disseminate their narratives. Therefore, the absence of a specific narrative in our chosen material does not imply its non-existence.

Third, in a democratic system, opposition parties seek to win the next election. Therefore, regardless of their ideological stances, they are motivated to criticise the executive also on unresolved rule of law issues (emphasising in this way the need to replace the current government) rather than highlighting areas of agreement with the ruling parties. Still, narratives addressing challenges to the rule of law used by opposition parties may overlap with those of parties in government, even if they are not used simultaneously, but only when speakers from the government bloc move to the opposition. To detect such similarities, one must examine and compare distinct legislative terms, as was done in our study.

Fourth, while our analysis includes hundreds of parliamentary debates, it is essential to remember the diversity of conditions of MPs' actions within individual national parliaments. These conditions include varying provisions for the length of speeches, distinct power relations, and varying governing styles reflected either in frequent legal amendments, providing the opposition with more opportunities for rhetoric interventions, or sparse legal change that may result in fewer speeches. Moreover, as mentioned, we had to select

---

[30] Ilie, (2015) *supra* note 5 at 7.
[31] Whitaker and Martin, 'Divide to conquer? Strategic parliamentary opposition and coalition government' (2022) 28 Party Politics 6, 999-1011.

documents for our qualitative analysis to ensure equal weight for all examined cases in our data corpus.[32] Therefore, counting or ranking narratives based on the frequency of their use in our material would not yield meaningful results.

4.   NARRATIVES ON CHALLENGES TO THE RULE OF LAW

This section presents our qualitative content analysis results from a comparative perspective. Firstly, we will outline the principal topics (in our methodological terminology: categories) of the narratives before delving into a refined insight into their contents.

Table 9.1 provides an overview of the main thematic areas to which the identified narratives on the rule of law challenges in each of the five countries referred to. If a narrative was related to different thematic areas, we chose the one which was more common. The selection is based on the significance (in qualitative terms) of a particular theme for a country. A checkmark in the column for a particular country means we have identified relevant MPs' narratives that fall into the respective category. Narratives falling under a particular category are well-established and used over a longer time, often several electoral periods.[33]

Politicisation or restriction of the public prosecution and other law enforcement bodies has been highlighted as challenging the rule of law in all five countries. The same problems concerning the judiciary[34] have been the subject of narratives in all countries except for Czechia, where similar challenges were also addressed but always together and with a stronger emphasis on public prosecution. Furthermore, members of all parliaments widely criticised rules being stretched, violated, or not complied with. The above thematic areas can be seen as the most prominent in the parliamentary narratives on challenges to the rule of law in the examined countries. Another highly relevant area was the functioning of the judiciary, public prosecution, and law enforcement.

---

[32] For instance, we found significantly more discussions featuring the expression 'rule of law' in Hungary, Poland, and Slovakia than in the Czech Republic and Romania. To counterbalance the potential over-representation of those three countries in our overall data set, we have limited our analysis of debates in these countries to a set that is comparable to the other countries included in the study.

[33] We targeted not only narratives dealing with current challenges, but also those that have been relevant for a certain timeframe. The temporality of narratives is discussed in more detail later in this section.

[34] Depending on the national context, under this category are included interventions in constitutional, administrative, and ordinary courts or in institutions in charge of judicial self-administration (judicial councils).

Table 9.1   Topics of relevant narratives on challenges to the rule of law since the 1990s

	CZ	HU	PL	RO	SK
Politicisation/restriction of public prosecution and law enforcement	✓	✓	✓	✓	✓
Rule overstretch or violation/non-compliance	✓	✓	✓	✓	✓
Functioning of the judiciary, public prosecution, and law enforcement		✓	✓	✓	✓
Lack of trust	✓		✓	✓	✓
Politicisation/restriction of the judiciary		✓	✓	✓	
Post-1989 transformation*	✓	✓	✓	✓	
Corruption/clientelism		✓	✓		
Politicisation of administration/independent institutions		✓	✓		
Sovereignty	✓				
Economic and other interest groups					✓
Juridification	✓				
Challenges pre-1989					

Notes: * Our analysis examines the political, social, and economic transformation after 1989 in connection with typical issues such as lustration, restitution, and privatisation. Our focus extends beyond the early transition period, encompassing related narratives throughout the years under study. In practice, we consider a story relevant to the post-1989 transformation if it addresses issues typically associated with democratisation and economic liberalisation, and not just those related to the transition period itself.
Source: Own compilation based on our empirical inquiry.

Corresponding narratives were typically linked to criticism of these institutions' low performance, often due to their supposed underfunding and understaffing. Also, a lack of trust in the rule of law and its institutions in the country and problems related to the post-1989 system change from an authoritarian regime to a democratic state were frequently discussed as challenges to the rule of law, albeit in very different ways (see below). Another thematic category relevant for at least three out of the five countries under study were problems with corruption and clientelism.

Further examination of our cases, however, reveals notable differences. Table 9.2 shows that the concrete narratives varied significantly between countries, indicating the influence of local developments and broader political discourse. Additionally, the table offers a clear breakdown of the narrative content by type. As noted in section 3, for the purpose of this chapter, we classify narratives as overlapping or diverging. As mentioned, overlapping narratives are used by different actors, but not necessarily simultaneously. The group of diverging narratives includes one-sided narratives. If statements formed a complex narrative on a particular issue, we condensed them into one bullet point. However, we separated them into different bullet points – even if they referred to the same thematic category – if speakers did not usually present them as a coherent set of sequences or causalities.[35]

Observers following media coverage and academic research from Western Europe may be surprised to learn that criticism of the EU encroaching on national sovereignty is a narrative present in the Czech Republic (and Poland) but not in Hungary. It is also noteworthy that narratives regarding the politicisation of the judiciary and governments manipulating the rule of law for their personal advantage are not limited to Poland and Hungary but have also circulated in Romania and Slovakia. In Romania, the narrative that the country offers only a façade-like rule of law but is characterised in practice by endemic rule violation overlaps across parties. In Slovakia, members of parliament commonly provided a narrative of undermining the separation of powers. Representatives from diverse parties in Czechia used a narrative regarding the government eroding public trust in the rule of law. All this suggests that the EU and other political actors must consistently evaluate whether their understanding of the domestic debates surrounding the rule of law is appropriate.

In all five countries, the overlapping narratives include strong criticism of the government. However, the reasons for this criticism vary. Concerns are expressed about the dominance of the executive, particularly in Hungary and Poland, its interfering in investigations (in Czechia, Romania, and Slovakia),

---

[35]   Because of limited space, we do not mention here the whole narrative with causes and effects of a given phenomenon.

Table 9.2   Type and content of narratives on challenges to the rule of law

	Overlapping narratives	Diverging narratives
CZ	• unconstitutional legislative proposals by the government • government's interference in investigations and prosecution • government undermining public trust in the rule of law	• activist Constitutional Court compromising separation of powers • interference in national sovereignty by international bodies, like the ECHR or the EU • lustration practice in contradiction with the rule of law principles
HU	• government undermining the separation of powers and democratic values • predominance of the executive • police violence in 2006 • erosion of opposition rights • slow court proceedings and excessive workload • too weak lustration law (target group defined too narrowly*)	• eroding independence of courts and (constitutional) judges • insufficient separation of powers • the Prosecutor General not independent • politicised media, State Audit Office, and professional chambers • distorted relationship between politics and business, influence of politics on the market economy • little or no debate with civil society or professional/specialised organisations in the legislative process

	Overlapping narratives	Diverging narratives
PL	• slow court proceedings, ineffective crime prosecution, not enough staff, underfunded, poorly equipped – also due to bad legislation • poorly functioning prosecution service/lengthy court proceedings undermining trust in the right to access courts, bad lawmaking /legislation infringing rights or legal certainty • corruption/clientelism, especially in post-1989 transition period • subjugating the civil service by ruling majority, filling administrative positions with 'their own people'	• post-1989 processes resulted in a lack of accountability of the judiciary and public prosecution • lack of decommunization/lustration/vetting, especially in the judiciary, old personnel remained; socialist influence/legacy in transformation period hindering the establishment of a just state • corruption/clientelism tied with the lack of lustration/decommunization and independence/impartiality of the judiciary, 'corrupt judges' • political instrumentalization of the fight against corruption by the PiS-led government (in 2006) • interference in national sovereignty/national legislation/basic law based on Polish traditions/values – mostly by EU institutions • interference in the judiciary by the ruling majority (compromising separation of powers)** • misuse/instrumentalization of the law by parliamentary majorities and authorities affiliated with the ruling parties** • politicisation of the public prosecution service (especially involvement of Minister of Justice)**

	Overlapping narratives	Diverging narratives
RO	• insufficient separation of powers – weak independence of the judiciary • politicised public prosecution • façade-like state under rule of law – endemic rule violation • slow court proceedings • lack of trust in the judiciary undermining public trust in the rule of law	• instrumentalised fight against corruption • weak lustration • slow and weak property restitution
SK	• unconstitutional legislative proposals and abuse of extraordinary "fast-track" law-making proceedings by the government • erosion of the separation of powers • low public trust in the rule of law • slow court proceedings, weak law enforcement	• lack of accountability of the judiciary and public prosecution • justice sector as part of a network of political and economic interests*** • instrumental reforms of the judiciary and public prosecution

Notes: For Hungary, the diverging and one-sided narratives were found predominantly after Fidesz came to power in 2010. * The Constitutional Court sanctioned a broader definition of target groups for lustration measures. ** Discussed with high intensity by the opposition after PiS came to power in 2015. *** Although the narratives on the justice sector in Slovakia include allegations of corruption and clientelism, these issues are not featured as distinct categories in Table 9.1. The reason for this is that corruption and clientelism were not identified as isolated problems affecting the rule of law. Instead, the narratives focused on politicisation and restriction of the judiciary and an excessive influence of economic groups as prominent challenges.

Source: Own compilation based on our empirical inquiry.

introducing unconstitutional legislative proposals (in Czechia and Slovakia), and undermining the separation of powers (in Hungary, Romania, and Slovakia). In Poland and Romania, various political parties have portrayed a story of limited judicial independence from politics. Slow court proceedings have been a significant theme shared among all countries except for Czechia, where it was an occasional topic of parliamentary debates until around 2010. Complaints about understaffing in Hungary and Poland, the recurring criticism of MPs from different parties in Poland that the ruling majorities frequently tried to fill positions in the public administration with 'their people', and complaints about poor law enforcement in Slovakia were also associated with this issue.

Intriguing differences between the cases can be observed in the issue of the lustration of public officials. Lustration laws differed by country. Whilst mild lustration was argued to be a challenge to the rule of law in Hungary across political parties, the supposedly insufficient lustration in Romania and the 'lack of decommunization' narrative in Poland did not constitute overlapping narratives presented in the parliament. In contrast to these countries, some political parties in Czechia denounced the established practice of lustration as contradicting the principles of the rule of law. For Slovak MPs, the issue was not a prominent challenge to the rule of law in the country.

As already touched on in connection with a critique of the length of judicial proceedings in Czechia, some important narratives were time-based. They may indicate that a matter was no longer of interest or relevance to parliamentary debate. However, in this scenario, the narratives may still be deemed relevant considering the institutional memory of parliaments, as there is potential for their future revival.

We also identified substantial dynamics of narratives in two cases – Hungary and Poland – that went beyond the usual patterns of opposition criticising the government. Here, additional narratives have emerged since Fidesz returned to power in 2010 and PiS entered government for the second time in 2015. They were related to the respective government's political strategy and the response of the opposition to measures taken by the executive. These new, predominantly diverging narratives were crucial to the specific case.

In Poland, for instance, PiS MPs strengthened their criticism of a perceived lack of accountability among judges and the prosecution service and insufficient efforts towards decommunization in the past, particularly concerning the judiciary. They contended that the socialist legacy hampered the establishment of a lawful state and that there were many 'corrupt judges' due to the lack of lustration/decommunization and judicial independence (impartiality). According to them, their reforms sought to address these challenges to the rule of law. Conversely, opposition parties accused PiS of interfering in the judiciary. They also criticised the misuse and instrumentalization of the law by the parliamentary majority and authorities associated with the ruling parties. Besides, the opposition parties highlighted the government's politicisation of the public prosecution by combining the position of the Minister of Justice with the General Prosecutor. Given the diverging character of these narratives, it is difficult to find a common ground.

The situation in Hungary was similar. Since the Fidesz–KDNP government launched its programme of 'renewing' the system, criticism of it has focused on deficiencies in the separation of powers, the erosion of the independence of courts, (constitutional) judges, and the Prosecutor General, the purging of the judiciary by lowering the retirement age, the extension of the term of office for new constitutional judges, and the politicisation of the media, the State Audit Office, and professional chambers.

Like in Poland, even if these issues were resolved after a potential alteration of parties in power, older established narratives on challenges to the rule of law coming from the executive would persist. It is worth noting that there is a rooted tradition of criticism of the state of the rule of law in both countries. Narratives critical of the government(s) and entrenched structural problems that are difficult to overcome have become firmly established. Since 1990, various parties in Hungary have criticised what they perceived as the erosion of democratic values and the separation of powers, a preponderance of executive power, a weakening of opposition rights, slow court proceedings, excessive workloads, and a weak lustration law that has allowed many supporters of the pre-1989 authoritarian regime to remain in office. Similarly, in Poland, several narratives overlapped before 2015. Corruption and clientelism, particularly during the post-1989 transition period, sluggish court proceedings, inadequate prosecution of crimes, insufficient funding and staffing of courts, issues with the prosecution service, low confidence in the right to access courts, and faulty law-making or legislation that undermines legal certainty and rights were all contributing factors.

The pattern of diverging narratives in the other three countries was slightly different. Our analysis of parliamentary debates in Czechia showed that non-overlapping narratives were predominantly one-sided. Consequently, we cannot conclude their potential for conflict. These narratives addressed perceived excessive activism of the Constitutional Court, mentioned by social democratic and communist MPs, took a position against supposed external interference in national sovereignty by the EU and the Council of Europe (ECHR), typically connected with speakers from the conservative Civic Democratic Party (ODS), or, as already mentioned, concerned lustration practice, a rather temporal issue addressed by Social Democrats and Communists.

In Romania, there were three established one-sided narratives voiced by one block of parties against another block. Two referred to the system change after 1989 – weak lustration and slow and weak property restitution – and, as an accusation, they were directed against the post-communist Social Democratic Party (PSD). Another narrative emerged after 2004. It concerned the alleged instrumentalization of the fight against corruption at the hands of special public prosecution agencies founded or reinforced under the presidency of *Traian Băsescu.*

In Slovakia, the diverging narratives related to the judiciary and public prosecution. On the one hand, there was a perception shared by MPs from the liberal-conservative bloc (for instance KDH, SDKU-DS, SaS) that these institutions and their personnel lack accountability and are linked to particular political and economic interests. On the other hand, left-wing and nationalist MPs spread a counter-narrative claiming that the liberal-conservative government(s) instrumentalise reforms of the judiciary and the prosecution to subordinate and use these institutions for their own political goals. However, the arguments on both sides were not ideological but rather stemmed from long-standing rivalries between political parties.

5. FINE-TUNING THE EU's COMMUNICATION AND COOPERATION STRATEGY

In order to develop an effective communication strategy and partnerships, it is crucial to understand the patterns of discourse on the rule of law challenges in the parliaments of EU Member States. As noted in section 2, effective communication requires themes and narratives relevant to the intended audience. The main narratives that should be invoked, or at least acknowledged, have been identified in our analysis above. Based on this analysis, we offer three recommendations.

First, we suggest that the EU actors improve their communication with the members of national parliaments, the "second pillar of representative democracy in the EU according to Article 10 TEU, alongside the EP".[36] Although the national parliaments play an increased role "in controlling, scrutinising, and debating EU issues"[37] and the EU has broadened its dialogue on the rule of law to domestic stakeholders like judges and NGOs, there is still room for more

---

[36] Nicolaidis, von Ondarza and Russack, 'The Radicality of Sunlight. Five Pathways to a More Democratic Europe.' (2023) Report of the CEPS-SWP High-Level Group on Bolstering EU Democracy, CEPS & SWP, at 32, <https://www.ceps.eu/ceps-publications/the-radicality-of-sunlight/> accessed 1 December 2023.

[37] Neuhold and Rosén, 'Introduction to "Out of the Shadows, Into the Limelight: Parliaments and Politicisation"' (2019) 7 Politics and Governance 3, 220-226 at 222 f.

intensive communication with parliaments. For example, the Rule of Law Reports 2023 on Czechia, Poland, Romania, and Slovakia did not mention any meetings with members of parliament as a source of information.[38] The Commission solely engaged with executive and judicial authorities, multiple non-governmental organisations, and occasionally the administration of parliament. Productive communication with MPs can enhance the effectiveness of legislative policymaking on the rule of law. Additionally, MPs can help to resolve "conflicting interests and expectations of different groups and communities through the democratic means of dialogue and compromise".[39] Last but not least, improving communication with national parliaments could increase their visibility and reputation, while at the same time empowering them vis-à-vis the government. This measure responds to a rule of law challenge mentioned across party lines in all five countries: the fear of executive dominance.

Current disputes over the rule of law and other aspects of liberalism focus on the relationship between legitimacy through elections (by elected officials) and legitimacy through law (by non-majoritarian agencies interpreting and enforcing the law). Strengthening legitimacy could involve engaging with parliaments and referencing narratives presented by elected representatives (MPs) who have all received a popular mandate. This approach would underscore that many of the challenges to the rule of law addressed by EU actors are also subject to criticism by domestic actors across party lines within their respective countries. References to narratives that overlap – how they were articulated and by whom – would garner such criticism greater acceptance than relying solely on references to EU actors, executive branches, judicial bodies, or non-governmental organisations. This dynamic is particularly relevant in the cases of Czechia and Poland, where some MPs expressed concerns about EU policies affecting national sovereignty. It also applies to Hungary, where the government, outside of parliamentary proceedings, engaged in anti-Brussels campaigns and emphasised the importance of the popular vote.[40]

---

[38] European Commission, '2023 Rule of Law Report. Country Chapter on the rule of law situation in Czechia', SWD(2023) 803 final at 29 f.; European Commission, '2023 Rule of Law Report. Country Chapter on the rule of law situation in Poland', SWD(2023) 821 final at 45 f.; European Commission, '2023 Rule of Law Report. Country Chapter on the rule of law situation in Romania', SWD(2023) 823 final at 35 f.; European Commission, '2023 Rule of Law Report. Country Chapter on the rule of law situation in Slovakia', SWD(2023) 825 final at 35 f.

[39] Ilie, (2015) *supra* note 5 at 1.

[40] The recommendation to strengthen communication with the parliaments corresponds with ideas elaborated by a CEPS-SWP expert group composed of 23 politicians, officials, diplomats, and scholars from different Member States and

Second, to enhance communication effectiveness on the rule of law issues, it is necessary to publicly acknowledge the existence of entrenched narratives across party lines that underpin deep structural issues beyond the usual differences in political positions observed in democracies. In the case of the countries under study, they consist of accounts of a politicised judiciary, governments utilising the rule of law measures for their interests, and endemic rule violations. National parliamentarians also claimed that public trust in the rule of law was low. The optimism associated with the transition to democracy and the rule of law seems to have disappeared. This can be partly explained by the fact that in the 1990s, there were examples of politicians who claimed to be committed to the rule of law but abused their powers, restricted the rule of law, or at least neglected to develop it, and engaged in transformation-related corruption. However, such a mismatch between political rhetoric and practice can also be traced in the post-transition period. Even if the challenges to the rule of law are resolved in the future, the established narratives that the rule of law is compromised and that politicians can manipulate regulations will endure for an extended period, making the systems vulnerable to distrust and instability.

While there are discussions on resolving these issues in several European institutions and judicial networks, organising debates with MPs from different Member States could potentially aid in problem-solving. This approach may enable the sharing of successful strategies from other countries and provide a platform to contemplate their transferability within different national contexts. Such a horizontal discourse can also refer to the challenges around the illiberal backlash in Poland and Hungary and how to cope with it. Evidently, any future changes to the judiciary following a change in power – even if they only intend to restore the status quo ante – can perpetuate narratives of elites undermining judicial independence, resulting in an infinite regress. However, the more nuanced patterns of concrete narratives presented above suggest that this is not the only challenge to the rule of law, and we do not need one communication for all but must tailor it to the respective national discourses.

Third, communication with and by parliaments is crucial for supporting initiatives and projects to mainstream the rule of law as a vital issue for the functioning of pluralistic societies and as a shared fundamental value of the European Union. It is not only in the countries covered by our study that a significant part of society perceives the rule of law as an overly abstract concept that mainly concerns the functioning of the judiciary and does not affect

---

institutions to "bolster national parliaments' link with 'Europe'". They highlight the need to enhance parliaments' role in "actively contributing to the good functioning of the Union" (Article 12 TEU). See Nicolaidis, von Ondarza and Russack, (2015) *supra* note 35 at 32-35.

their everyday lives. As politicians and judges from the five countries argued frequently in interviews for our research project, tackling the problems of the rule of law is rarely a priority for society. They are usually overshadowed by issues considered more pressing, such as the deteriorating economic or security situation. This underestimation of the crucial importance of the rule of law and its institutions for everyday life is also the reason for the lack of interest in these challenges among the general public in the EU Member States. Public mobilisation often occurs only during major crises when it may be too late to repair the damage already done to the rule of law.

In such an environment, communication to a broader public by MPs and projects prepared by them based on their knowledge of local specificities, problems, and means of communication could, in the long term, strengthen awareness and the rule of law in the European Union as a shared value, but also as an efficient tool for everyday life. Such a mainstreaming is difficult to reach from the EU level (alone). It needs to include a variety of national actors, like media, the academic sphere, the education sector in general, and NGOs. Overlapping narratives can provide a sound basis for building a rhetorical or even political consensus on challenges to the rule of law and their viable solutions.[41] EU actors could stimulate such initiatives, participate, and learn from them how EU rule of law issues are perceived in the European societies to find the "right language" for their own communication.

To sum up, it would benefit EU stakeholders to connect their communication to narratives in national parliamentary settings and to strengthen cooperation with national MPs. This would also support the European Union's constitutional approach. In the preamble to the Treaty on European Union, the signatories outlined that the Union "draws inspiration from the cultural, religious and humanist inheritance of Europe, from which have developed the universal values of the inviolable and inalienable rights of the human person, freedom, democracy, equality and the rule of law". Therefore, it is essential to merge a pan-European narrative of challenges to the rule of law with context-specific language and examples and to cooperate with a wide range of national partners, such as MPs.

---

[41] The need for a consensus-seeking dialogue on the rule of law issues was raised by our interlocutors from political and judicial ranks we interviewed. Moreover, in their perspective, the rule of law cannot and should not be understood and presented as an abstract value only, but rather as a practical instrument to protect citizens' rights. The rule of law is only strong if it is widely accepted, trusted, and supported. Therefore, it is necessary for as many members of society as possible to have a positive experience, whether their own or mediated.

6.   CONCLUSION

In this chapter, we aimed to contribute to the debate on suitable strategies to overcome disputes over the rule of law within the European Union, particularly between its institutions and Member States. Following ongoing discussions that delve into the essence of European integration and its core values, we provided recommendations for communication strategies of EU actors, drawing on empirical findings from our comparative research in five countries of East Central Europe.

In this research, we analysed parliamentary debates in Czechia, Hungary, Poland, Romania, and Slovakia, focusing on how challenges to the rule of law are approached from the perspective of members of parliament. While our approach departed from established conceptions of the rule of law, we emphasised specific national contexts. In this aspect, we identified the main shortcoming in the current communication between EU actors and member states. Specifically, EU institutions address the rule of law issues in the Member States according to a uniform pattern, an approach that some influential national actors perceive as a lack of understanding of local specificities.

In the empirical material covering the thirty years from the beginning of the democratisation in the early 1990s, we identified two basic types of narratives. Firstly, the overlapping narratives used across political parties, meaning there is a consensus on the core message, although individual parties may use them as needed to criticise the current government. The key point is that the problems identified in these narratives are acknowledged as critical issues by relevant actors regardless of their mutual political rivalries. Typically, these are long-term structural problems in the functioning of the rule of law in a given country. The second group of narratives is not used across political parties but instead reflects and often sustains conflict between ideologically or programmatically defined party blocs. There is no inter-party agreement on the content of these diverging narratives.

Building upon these findings, presented in a comparative perspective for all five countries in our study, we have formulated three recommendations. The common denominator of these recommendations is greater involvement of actors from the national parliaments in discussions on the rule of law in the European Union. The overlapping narratives used across political parties should serve as common thematic points. This approach would achieve a more substantial consideration of national specifics. Simultaneously, the involvement of members of national parliaments would deepen the democratic legitimacy of such a dialogue, whose alleged absence is currently exploited by Euro-critical political currents. An integral part of the communication strategy of the European Union should be to support the mainstreaming of the rule of law in Member States based on local needs, knowledge, and experiences.

We are aware that narratives on challenges to the rule of law are not only formulated and spread by members of parliament in parliamentary discussions. For this reason, further research should focus on the influence of other actors, such as the media, civil society organisations, or relevant professional associations. For the dimension of debates between EU institutions and national states, exploring the possibly overlapping narratives between these two levels is crucial. This way, areas that are factually undisputed in their content can be identified, even though certain actors may present them as conflicting at a particular time. Lastly, if the recommendations we have formulated are implemented, it would be desirable to conduct a follow-up inquiry on how they were implemented and the effect they produced. Such findings can be used to enhance communication strategies towards countries aspiring to join the EU or more broadly in dialogue with external partners of the European Union.

10. The Rule of Law in the European Union and the Toolbox to Defend it: Article 7 TEU, Rule of Law Report and Dialogue, Budgetary Conditionality

Jonathan Bauerschmidt[1]

1.   INTRODUCTION

The rule of law in the European Union is under threat. A founding value which forms part of the EU's constitutional identity risks being eroded by undermining judicial independence, not pursuing corruption cases and disregarding judgments of the Court of Justice. This threat calls all Union institutions and Member States to action.

The rule of law is of fundamental importance for any constitutional order. *Ralf Dahrendorf*, former Commissioner and later director of the London School of Economics, already emphasized this in 1990 when reflecting about the events that brought down the iron curtain and ended the division of Europe in two parts. Writing in the tradition of Edmund Burke,[2] *Dahrendorf's* 'Reflections on the Revolution in Europe' set out the challenges ahead for ensuring lasting democracy through law: 'The rule of law is not just about having legal texts to refer to; it is about the effective substance of these texts. This in turn can ultimately be guaranteed only by an independent judiciary which is seen to be incorruptible and fair, and which includes those who guard the constitution itself and its principles.'[3]

---

[1]   The views expressed by the author are strictly personal and do not engage the institution for which he works.

[2]   Edmund Burke, *Reflections on the Revolution in France* (Penguin [1790] 1986).

[3]   Ralf Dahrendorf, *Reflections on the Revolution in Europe* (Chatto & Windus 1990) 81.

This advice has lost little of its importance and faces particular challenges in the EU. Although a founding value, the rule of law remains a contested concept. It is only through a deeper understanding of its origins that the transformation from a Community of law to a Union based on the rule of law will be understood (section 2). This allows to group the vast case-law around formal and substantive elements of the rule of law (section 3). In addition to the Court of Justice, which is indispensable in defending the rule of law, there is a (growing) number of instruments in the EU's toolbox.[4] The following will focus on the Article 7 TEU procedures (section 4), still evolving soft-law instruments by the Commission and the Council (section 5) as well as the Conditionality Regulation adopted by the European Parliament and the Council (section 6). It will be argued that the European Union is not only developing a more comprehensive understanding of the rule of law, the various instruments also are complementary in how they safeguard the rule of law.

2. THE RULE OF LAW AS A CONTESTED CONCEPT

The rule of law as a founding value of the Union is explicitly enshrined in primary law since the Treaty of Lisbon. Previously, it was mentioned in the Recitals of the Treaty of Maastricht[5] and became part of the Articles in the Treaty of Amsterdam as a principle.[6] Subsequently, the draft Constitutional Treaty foresaw in Article 2 founding values including the 'rule of law'[7] which

---

[4] See for a recent overview Clemens Ladenburger, Yona Marinova and Jonathan Tomkin, 'Institutional Report' in Alexander Kornezov (ed) *Mutual Trust, Mutual Recognition and the Rule of Law – FIDE 2023 Vol 1* (Ciela Norma 2023) 67, 95–110. Apart from the tools explored here, also the so-called horizontal enabling conditions in Article 15 and Annex III of the Common Provisions Regulation 2021/1060 [2021] OJ L 231/159, and the Recovery and Resilience Facility (RRF) in Regulation 2021/241 [2021] OJ L 63/1 may contain certain rule of law related conditions or milestones whose fulfillment is necessary to receive EU funding.

[5] The contracting parties 'CONFIRMING their attachment to the principles of liberty, democracy and respect for human rights and fundamental freedoms and of the rule of law.'

[6] Article F TEU: 'The Union is founded on the principles of liberty, democracy, respect for human rights and fundamental freedoms, and the rule of law, principles which are common to the Member States.'

[7] CONV 528/03 of 6.2.2003.

was not changed during the negotiations.[8] This was taken over in the Treaty of Lisbon and Article 2 TEU now reads:

> The Union is founded on the values of respect for human dignity, freedom, democracy, equality, the rule of law and respect for human rights, including the rights of persons belonging to minorities. These values are common to the Member States in a society in which pluralism, non-discrimination, tolerance, justice, solidarity and equality between women and men prevail.

The rule of law forms part of the constitutional traditions common to the Member States, a notion used by the Court of Justice to draw inspiration and to further flesh out fundamental concepts in Union law.[9] By taking a closer look at three language traditions (2.1) it will become clear how this concept evolved from the Community of law to a Union based on the rule of law (2.2).

2.1   Origins: Rule of Law, *État de droit* and *Rechtsstaat*

In the English language, rule of law is a broad concept which applies to any association of human beings where authoritative rules have to be established and recognised.[10] Jurisprudence and literature in the United Kingdom (and similarly in the United States) distinguish[11] between a formal understanding of the rule of law, which encompasses the method of promulgation of laws, the clarity of the resulting laws and the temporal dimension of the rules

---

[8]   An overview of all the suggested amendments to Article 2 can be found in CONV 574/1/03 of 26 February 2003, 17–23.

[9]   Sabino Cassese, 'The "Constitutional Traditions Common to the Member States" of the European Union' (2017) Rivista Trimestrale di Diritto Pubblico 939–48. See also the chapter by *Raitio* in this volume.

[10]   On this fundamental role see Michael Oakeshott, 'The Rule of Law', in *On History and Other Essays* (Blackwell 1983) 119, 136: '[the rule of law] stands for a mode of moral association exclusively in terms of the recognition of the authority of known, noninstrumental rules (that is, laws) which impose obligations to subscribe to adverbial conditions in the performance of the self-chosen actions of all who fall within their jurisdiction.' See also Martin Loughlin, *Foundations of Public Law* (OUP 2010) 324–31.

[11]   See only *Entick v Carrington* (1765) 19 Howell's State Trials 1029 cited in Boyd v United States 116 U.S. 616, 626 (1886). Overview of English case-law at Colin Turpin, Adam Tomkins, *British Government and the Constitution* (CUP 2011) 96 f., and for the U.S. Constitution in the context of the due process clause Erwin Chemerinsky, *Constitutional Law* (7th edn, Wolters Kluwer 2023) chapter 7.

(non-retroactivity).[12] However, such a formal understanding of the rule of law does not say whether the laws are 'good' or 'bad'. Therefore, a substantive understanding goes beyond formal elements and also protects certain substantive rights,[13] such as moral and political rights,[14] fundamental rights,[15] justice and freedom.[16] Nevertheless, the rule of law remains an essentially contested concept,[17] whose precise contours and meaning are only revealed in the exchange of legal arguments.[18]

In the French language, the term *État de droit* is closely linked to *Raymond Carré de Malberg*, who distinguished between the *État légal* and the *État de droit*. The former relates mainly to the law of administration and is equivalent to a formal conception of the rule of law. The latter is to ensure that a polity is acting solely in the interests and protection of its citizens. As a result, the (substantive) *État de droit* goes beyond the (formal) *État légal* to also protect fundamental rights even where the legislator formulates the *volonté générale*.[19] For some public law scholars the *État de droit* is an expression that political power is not only linked to social solidarity, but is also subject to the law itself.[20] Others see the particular function of the *État de droit* to secure indi-

---

[12] Albert Venn Dicey, *Introduction to the Study of the Law of the Constitution* (10th edn, Macmillan Press [1959] 1979) 202 f.; Lon Fuller, *The Morality of Law* (Yale University Press 1969) 38 f.; Joseph Raz, 'The Rule of Law and its Virtue' in *The Authority of Law* (OUP 2009) 214–218.

[13] On this classic distinction Paul Craig, 'Formal and Substantive Conceptions of the Rule of Law' (1997) Public Law 467; Brian Tamanaha, *On the Rule of Law* (CUP 2004) 91–113.

[14] Ronald Dworkin, *A Matter of Principle* (Harvard University Press 1985) 11 f.

[15] Trevor Allan, *Law, Liberty, and Justice: The Legal Foundations of British Constitutionalism* (OUP 1993) 28–34; Tom Bingham, *The Rule of Law* (Penguin 2010) 66–84.

[16] John Rawls, *A Theory of Justice* (Harvard University Press 1999) 207 f.

[17] Jeremy Waldron, 'Is the Rule of Law an Essentially Contested Concept (in Florida)?' (2002) 21 Law and Philosophy 137, 153–159.

[18] Neil MacCormick, *Rhetoric and The Rule of Law* (OUP 2005) 14 f., 26–28.

[19] Raymond Carré de Malberg, *Contribution à la Théorie générale de l'État t. I* (Dalloz [1920] 2004) 488–493. For an overview see only Marie-Joëlle Redor, *De l'État légal à l'État de droit – L'évolution des conceptions de la doctrine publiciste française 1879–1914* (Economica 1992) 294–316.

[20] Léon Duguit, *L'État, le droit objectif et la loi positive* (Dalloz [1901] 2003) 256: 'si le pouvoir politique n'est jamais légitime par son origine, s'il est en soi un fait étranger au droit, il peut devenir légitime par son exercise; il peut devenir un *Rechtsstaat*.' On Duguit's *État de droit* see Luc Heuschling, *État de droit, Rechtsstaat, Rule of law* (Dalloz 2002) 387–95.

vidual and political freedom.[21] As a result, like the rule of law *État de droit* distinguishes between formal and substantive elements. And although the *État de droit* is developed for the state,[22] it is not limited to the state, but can also apply in relation to other political communities.

In the German language, the *Rechtsstaat* is closely linked to the emergence of the liberal constitutional state in the 19th century and originally meant a special kind of state, which ensures that people live together in accordance with the principles of common sense, while respecting the freedom and security of the person and the property.[23] In particular, some scholars reduced the *Rechtsstaat* to a mere formal concept,[24] according to which the rule of law only deals with the relationship between legal entities under objective law[25] and is limited to the judicial review of the administration.[26] This closely resembles the formal rule of law and the *État légal*. Conversely, other scholars interpret *Rechtsstaat* as meaning that the state is not above the law, but rather established and governed by the law.[27] In its jurisprudence, the German Constitutional Court uses 'the principle of the rule of law' which comprises

---

[21] Maurice Hauriou, *Précis élémentaire de droit constitutionnel* (2nd edn, Sirey 1930) 26: 'La garantie des libertés individuelles, aussi bien que celle de la liberté politique, demandent, comme première condition, que les différents pouvoirs de l'Etat, pouvoir administratif, pouvoir judiciaire, pouvoir législatif, soient astreints à l'observation soit des lois ordinaires, soit des lois constitutionnelles'.

[22] Jacques Chevallier, *L'État de droit* (6th edn, LGDJ 2017) 23 f.; Jean-Pierre Henry, 'Vers la fin de l'État de droit?' (1977) Revue de droit publique 1207–35; Éric Millard, 'L'État de droit' (2004) Boletin Mexicano de Derecho Comparado 111–40; Michel Troper, 'Le concept d'État de droit' (1992) 15 Droits 51–63.

[23] Karl Theodor Welcker, *Die letzten Gründe von Recht, Staat und Strafe* (Heyer 1813) 80–108; Johann Christoph von Aretin, *Staatsrecht der konstitutionellen Monarchie* (Literatur-Comptoir 1824) 163; Robert von Mohl, *Die deutsche Polizeiwissenschaft nach den Grundsätzen des Rechtsstaates I* (Laupp 1833) 6–8; *Das Staatsrecht des Königreichs Württemberg* (Laupp 1829) 8. See on the Kantian influences Ernst-Wolfgang Böckenförde, 'Entstehung und Wandel des Rechtsstaatsbegriffs' in *Recht, Staat, Freiheit* (Suhrkamp 1991) 146 f.

[24] In line with the programme formulated by Carl Friedrich von Gerber, *Über öffentliche Rechte* (Laupp & Siebeck 1852) 27, that 'political and state philosophic reasoning' should not be substituted for the legal construction.

[25] Paul Laband, 'Besprechung von Otto Mayer, Theorie des französischen Verwaltungsrechts' (1887) 2 Archiv des öffentlichen Rechts 149–162, 152 & 161.

[26] Otto Mayer, *Deutsches Verwaltungsrecht I* (3rd edn, Duncker & Humblot 1924) 58, 62 f.

[27] Otto von Gierke, *Genossenschaftsrecht I* (Weidmannsche Buchhandlung 1868) 831; Hugo Preuß, *Gemeinde, Staat, Reich als Gebietskörperschaft* (Springer 1889) 230 f.

formal elements such as legal certainty as well as substantive elements such a separation of powers and proportionality.[28] Legal literature has taken this constitutional principle to be a 'generator of subtopoi'[29] and groups them around elements such as access to justice, administrative procedures, organisation as well as scope of judicial review.[30] In conclusion, it is clear that rule of law, *État de droit* and *Rechtsstaat* all distinguish between formal and substantive elements. However, only the German concept seems to be so closely linked to the state that it underwent a linguistic transformation when entering into the EU Treaties.

2.2   From Community of Law to Union Founded on the Rule of Law

The English and French language versions of Article 2 TEU refer to the rule of law and *État de droit* respectively without any linguistic transformation as both concepts are not dependent on a state. Conversely, since the German *Rechtsstaat* is closely related to the state, the German version of the Treaty uses *Rechtsstaatlichkeit* which, first, turns the word into an adjective (*rechtsstaatlich*) to describe a condition or a property and, second, adds a suffix to create a noun. No other language version of Article 2 TEU undergoes comparable linguistic transformations.[31]

---

[28]   See recently German Constitutional Court, Order of the Second Senate of 15 December 2015, 2 BvL 1/12 – Treaty override (= BVerfGE 141, 1), para. 78, available at <https://www.bverfg.de/e/ls20151215_2bvl000112en.html>: "The relevant principles include the principle of the rule of law, which derives from an integrated assessment of the stipulations in Article 20(3) GG, specifying the binding effect on the three branches of government, and those in Articles 1(3), 19(4), and 28(1) first sentence GG, as well as from the Basic Law's overall concept."

[29]   Philip Kunig, *Rechtsstaatsprinzip* (Mohr Siebeck 1986) 256 f.

[30]   Eberhard Schmidt-Aßmann, 'Der Rechtsstaat' in *Handbuch des Staatsrechts II* (3rd edn, CF Müller 2004) § 26 paras. 69 f. Katharina Sobota, *Prinzip Rechtsstaat* (Mohr Siebeck 1997) 27 f. identifies 25 rule of law elements.

[31]   The Bulgarian правовата държава (prawotawa držawa), Danish retsstaten, Estonian õigusriik, Finnish oikeusvaltio, Greek κράτος δικαίου (krátos dikaíou), Italian Stato di diritto, Croatian vladavine prava, Lithuanian teisine valstybe, Maltese l-istat taddritt, Dutch rechtsstaat, Polish państwo prawne, Portuguese Estado de direito, Romanian statul de drept, Swedish rättsstaten, Spanish Estado de Derecho, Slovak právneho štátu, Slovenian pravne države and Czech právního státu are translated to État de droit/Rechtsstaat (without any linguistic morphology). The Gaelic smacht reachta, Latvian tiesiskumu and Hungarian jogállamiság are translated similar to rule of law. For an overview see Robert Ullerich, *Rechtsstaat und Rechtsgemeinschaft im Europarecht* (Nomos 2011) 225.

Apart from this linguistic change, there are also important transformations in the case law of the Court of Justice which started using the term 'rule of law' only in its more recent jurisprudence. This is at least partly due to the closely connected concept of 'Community of law'. Coined by *Walter Hallstein* who tries to avoid the term of *Rechtsstaat*,[32] community of law seeks to clarify that '[t]he European Economic Community is a phenomenon of law in three respects: it is the creation of law, it is the source of law and it is the legal order."[33] The Court of Justice took up this term in the famous *Les Verts* judgment when it held that the European Economic Community 'is a Community based on the rule of law'.[34] Subsequently, the Court started incorporating the notion of the 'Community based on the rule of law' into its jurisprudence.[35] At the same time the Court developed general principles such as legal certainty, the protection of legitimate expectation, the prohibition of retroactivity, legal certainty and effective judicial protection which were linked to the Community based on the rule of law comprising formal elements. Conversely, principles relating to a substantive understanding of the rule of law – such as fundamental rights and proportionality – were also developed by the Court but not linked to the Community of law.

Interestingly, the rule of law has been explicitly included only in the more recent case-law.[36] Originally, with reference to the system of judicial protection under the Treaties,[37] and then in the external relations context, if sanctions

---

[32]　Walter Hallstein, 'Die EWG – eine Rechtsgemeinschaft' in *Europäische Reden* (Deutsche Verlags-Anstalt 1979) 341; 'Rede auf dem Kongress Europäischer Föderalisten' ibid 109.

[33]　Walter Hallstein, *Der unvollendete Bundesstaat* (Econ-Verlag 1969) 33:'Die Europäische Wirtschaftsgemeinschaft ist in dreifacher Hinsicht ein Phänomen des Rechts: Sie ist Schöpfung des Rechts, sie ist Rechtsquelle und sie ist Rechtsordnung.' See also Franz Mayer, 'Europa als Rechtsgemeinschaft' in *Europawissenschaften* (Nomos 2005) 429–87; Ingolf Pernice, 'Begründung und Konsolidierung der Euro-päischen Gemeinschaft als Rechtsgemeinschaft' in *Der Beitrag Walter Hallsteins zur Zukunft Europas* (Nomos 2003) 56–70; Antoine Vauchez, *L'Union par le droit* (Presses de Sciences Po 2013) 47 ff.

[34]　Case 294/83 *Les Verts* EU:C:1986:166, para. 23.

[35]　Case 222/84 *Johnston v Chief Constable* EU:C:1986:206, paras. 18 f.; Case 222/86 *Unectef v Heylens* EU:C:1987:442, para. 14; Case T-461/08 *Evropaïki Dynamiki v EIB* EU:T:2011:494, para. 118.

[36]　Previous uses are confined to submissions of the parties and opinion of Advocates-General, see Ullerich (2011) *supra* note 31 at 162–4.

[37]　Case C-354/04 P *Gestoras per Amnistía v Council* EU:C:2007:115, para. 51; Case C-355/04 *Segi v Council* EU:C:2007:116, para. 51; Case C-303/05 *Advocaten voor de Wereld* EU:C:2007:261, para. 45.

are linked to the violation of the 'rule of law' in third countries.[38] Drawing inspiration from the Venice Commission's rule of law checklist,[39] the General Court for the first time formulated a non-exhaustive list of formal and substantive rule of law elements: 'the principles of legality and legal certainty and the prohibition of arbitrary exercise of power by the executive; independent and impartial courts; effective judicial review, extending to respect for fundamental rights and equality before the law'.[40] Subsequently, the Court referred for the first time to the rule of law in relation to Member States when it ordered Poland to comply with interim measures in the context of Article 260 TFEU and imposed periodic penalty payments whose purpose 'is to guarantee the effective application of EU law, such application being an essential component of the rule of law, a value enshrined in Article 2 TEU and on which the European Union is founded.'[41]

While the case law originally developed formal elements of the rule of law by finding general principles and relying on the concepts of legal certainty and community based on the rule of law, the Court has started giving Article 2 TEU and the founding value of rule of law further contours and meaning. This still emerging transition from a Community of law towards a Union founded on the rule of law is marked by three changes: First, formal rule of law elements are accompanied by substantive elements, such as the protection of fundamental rights and equality before the law. Second, the rule of law referred to in Article 2 TEU does not apply solely to the Union, but also to the Member States themselves as a value 'common to the Member States' in accordance with Article 2 TEU. Third, the Union is not only a Community of law and therefore creation of the law, legal source and legal order, but at the same time a political union comprised of the European Union and its Member States. This marks the constitutional character of the rule of law, where the Union is founded on the values of respect for human dignity, freedom, democracy, equality, the rule of law and respect for human rights, which requires an inclusive interpretation of all the founding values enshrined in Article 2 TEU.

---

[38] Without definition Case T-190/12 *Tomana v Council and Commission* EU:T:2015:222, paras. 93 f.

[39] Adopted by the European Commission for Democracy through Law at its 106th Plenary Session in Venice, 11-12 March 2016.

[40] Case T-340/14 *Klyuyev* EU:T:2016:496, paras. 87 f.; Case T-346/14 *Yanukovych* EU:T:2016:497, paras. 97 f.

[41] Order in Case C-441/17 R *Commission v Poland* EU:C:2017:877, para. 102. See also Case C-64/16 *Associação Sindical dos Juízes Portugueses* EU:C:2018:117, paras. 30 f.

3.   ELEMENTS OF THE RULE OF LAW

Rule of law as a founding value of the Union is by now not only enshrined in Article 2 TEU but also starting to be used in the jurisprudence of the Court of Justice. While the exact contours will continue to be contested, one can already extract a number of elements. In this respect the Venice Commission's rule of law checklist is used by the courts[42] and the Union legislator[43] to better understand the contours of the rule of law which can be grouped around formal (3.1) and substantive elements (3.2).

3.1   Formal Elements

The first group of formal elements concerns the *principle of legality*. This principle has been acknowledged by the Court of Justice as an element of the rule of law.[44] It comprises the supremacy of law meaning that state action must be authorized by and be in accordance with the law.[45] Moreover, legality concerns the relationship between international and domestic law and seeks to ensure compliance with human rights law, including binding decisions of international courts.[46] As regards law-making, the principle of legality seeks to ensure the supremacy of legislature, limits the law-making powers of the executive and asks whether the process for enacting laws is transparent, accountable, inclusive and democratic. A review of draft legislation makes restrictions to fundamental rights easier to justify.[47] Finally, legality also requires that exceptions in emergency situations are provided for by law.[48]

The second group of formal elements concerns the *principle of legal certainty*. This principle has been acknowledged by the Court of Justice in its early jurisprudence[49] and requires rules to be clear and precise, so that

---

[42]   See only Case T-340/14 *Klyuyev* EU:T:2016:496, paras. 87 f.; Case T-346/14 *Yanukovych* EU:T:2016:497, paras. 97 f.; Case C-156/21 *Hungary v EP and Council* EU:C:2022:97, paras. 230; Case C-157/21 *Poland v EP and Council* EU:C:2022:98, para. 325.

[43]   See only Recital (16) of the Conditionality Regulation.

[44]   Case C-496/99 P *Commission v CAS Succhi di Frutta* EU:C:2004:236, para. 63.

[45]   Venice Commission, Rule of Law Checklist adopted in March 2016, paras. 44 f.

[46]   Ibid paras. 47 f.

[47]   ECtHR, App no 48876/08, *Animal Defenders International v UK* (22 April 2013) paras. 106 ff.

[48]   Venice Commission (2016) *supra* note 45, paras. 51 f.

[49]   Joined Cases 42 & 49/59 *S.N.U.P.A.T.* EU:C:1961:5, page 97; Case 265/78 *Ferwerda* EU:C:1980:66, paras. 15–17.

individuals may ascertain unequivocally their rights and obligations.[50] Legal certainty comprises public accessibility of legislation and court decisions[51] and requires that the effects of laws are foreseeable.[52] Moreover, legal certainty comprises the principles of legitimate expectations[53] as well as non-retroactivity.[54] Finally, it comprises the principles of *res judicata* as well as *ne bis in idem* regarding the protection of final judgments and the strict limits to reopen them.[55]

A third group concerns the prevention of abuse or misuses of powers (*détournement de pouvoir*).[56]

A fourth group concerns *access to justice* which can be further divided. On the one hand, *independence and impartiality* starts with the independence of the judiciary and ask whether there are sufficient constitutional and legal guarantees for judicial independence and impartiality. In this regard, the European Court of Human Rights (ECtHR) identified four elements of judicial independence concerning the manner of appointment, the term of office, the existence of outside pressure and whether the judiciary appears as independent and impartial.[57] The Court of Justice has taken up this jurisprudence and assesses whether the rules on composition of the body, its appointment, length of service and grounds for abstention, rejection and dismissal of its members are such as 'to dispel any reasonable doubts in the minds of the individuals as to the imperviousness of that body to external factors and its neutrality

---

[50] Case 169/80 *Gondrand and Garancini* EU:C:1981:171, para. 17; Case C-344/04 *IATA and ELFAA* EU:C:2006:10, para. 68. See also more recently Case C-72/15 *Rosneft* EU:C:2017:236, para. 161.

[51] Venice Commission (2016) *supra* note 45, para. 57.

[52] ECtHR, App no 6538/74, *Sunday Times v UK* (26 April 1979) paras. 46 ff.

[53] Case 14/81 *Alpha Steel v Commission* EU:C:1982:76, paras. 10–12, 28–30; Case C-90/95 P *De Compte v Parliament* EU:C:1997:198, paras. 35–43; ECtHR, App no 73049/01, *Anhaeuser-Busch v Portugal* (11 January 2007), para. 65.

[54] Case 98/78 *Racke v Hauptzollamt Mainz* EU:C:1979:69, paras. 19 f.; Joined Cases C-143/88 and C-92/89 *Zuckerfabrik Süderdithmarschen* EU:C:1991:65, para. 49.

[55] Joined Cases 97/86, 193/86 and 215/86 *Asteris v Commission* EU:C:1988:199, paras. 27–30 (without yet calling it res judicata); Case C-281/89 *Italy v Commission* EU:C:1991:59, para. 14; ECtHR, App no 75/07, *Duca v Moldova* (3 March 2009) paras. 32 f.

[56] Joined Cases 46/87 and 227/88 *Hoechst v Commission* EU:C:1989:337, para. 19; Case C-94/00 *Roquette Frères* EU:C:2002:603, para. 47; ECtHR, App no 7511/13, *Husayn v Poland* (24 July 2014), paras. 521 ff.

[57] ECtHR, App nos 7819/77 and 7878/77, *Campbell and Fell v UK* (28 June 2014) para. 78. See also Venice Commission (2016) *supra* note 45 paras. 74–90.

with respect to the interests before it.'[58] These requirements for independence are also relevant for public prosecutors when they are involved in issuing European Arrest Warrants.[59]

On the other hand, access to justice also encompasses *effective judicial protection* and *fair trial*. Inspired by Article 6 ECHR, this has been recognized as a general principle of Union law and ensures that everyone is entitled to a fair trial and public hearing within a reasonable time by an independent and impartial tribunal established by law[60] and is now also enshrined in Article 47 of the EU Charter of Fundamental Rights. Effective judicial protection is at the heart of the most recent case-law on the interpretation of Article 19(1) TEU which requires that Member States 'shall provide remedies sufficient to ensure effective legal protection in the fields covered by Union law.' The Court held that the 'fields covered' is broader than the implementation of Union law in Article 51(1) of the Charter and it is sufficient that a national court could rule on questions concerning the application or interpretation of Union law.[61] This has given rise to important judgments to safeguard judicial independence.[62]

3.2   Substantive Elements

A first group of substantive rule of law elements concerns the protection of *fundamental rights*. While those rights were originally developed without reference to the rule of law,[63] the Charter now makes prominent reference to it in its Preamble.

---

[58] Case C-506/04 *Wilson* EU:C:2006:587, para. 53; Case C-896/19 *Repubblika* EU:C:2021:311, para. 53. See in more detail on appointment procedures and judicial independence the chapter by *Mikuli*, *Fox* and *Puchta* in this volume.

[59] Joined Cases C-508/18 and C-82/19 PPU *OG & PI* EU:C:2019:456, para. 74; Case C-509/18 *PF* EU:C:2019:457, para. 52.

[60] Case C-185/95 P *Baustahlgewebe v Commission* EU:C:1998:608, paras. 20 f.; Case C-174/98 P *Netherlands and Van der Wal v Commission* EU:C:2000:1, para. 17; Case C-385/07 P *Der Grüne Punkt v Commission* EU:C:2009:456, para. 177. See also ECtHR, App no 4451/70, *Golder v UK* (21 January 1975) paras. 26 ff.

[61] Case C-619/18 *Commission v Poland* EU:C:2019:531, paras. 50 f. referring to Case C-64/16 *Associação Sindical dos Juízes Portugueses* EU:C:2018:117, paras. 29 f.

[62] Case C-791/19 *Commission v Poland* EU:C:2021:596, paras. 52 f.; Case C-204/21 *Commission v Poland* EU:C:2023:442, paras. 69 f.

[63] Case 29/69 *Stauder* EU:C:1969:57, para. 7; Case 11/70 *Internationale Handelsgesellschaft* EU:C:1970:114, paras. 3 f.

A second substantive element is the principle of *proportionality*. First developed in case-law[64] it is now enshrined in Article 5(4) TEU.

A third group concerns the *equality before the law* and the principle of *non-discrimination*. Both have been acknowledged as fundamental principles by the Court of Justice[65] and are now enshrined in Articles 20 and 21 of the Charter. Equal treatment requires that comparable situations must not be treated differently and that different situations must not be treated in the same way unless such treatment is objectively justified.[66]

A particular emanation is 'the equality of Member States before the Treaties' which is now enshrined in Article 4(2) TEU. This substantive element of the rule of law is intrinsically linked to the primacy of EU law over the law of the Member States[67] for three reasons: First, only the principle of primacy can ensure the uniform interpretation and application of EU law. Second, the uniform interpretation and application of EU law is crucial for guaranteeing the equality of Member States. Third, the uniform interpretation of EU law may only be ensured by one court and that is the Court of Justice of the European Union. Primacy thus ensures that both the Member States and their citizens are equal before the law. And without primacy, there would be no uniformity and thus, no equality. Hence, the judicial enforcement of the uniform interpretation and application through the principle of primacy by the Court of Justice ensures that all Member States – regardless of their size, political interests, or economic power – and their citizens are treated equally before the law.[68] From this also follows that the principle of primacy forms an integral part of the rule of law enshrined in Article 2 TEU.

---

[64] Case 114/76 *Bela Mühle* EU:C:1977:116, paras. 5–7; Case 266/84 *Denkavit France* EU:C:1986:23, para. 17; Case 265/87 *Schräder* EU:C:1989:303, para. 21.

[65] Joined Cases 117/76 and 16/77 *Ruckdeschel* EU:C:1977:160, para. 7; Case C-127/07 *Arcelor Atlantique and Lorraine* EU:C:2008:728, para. 23.

[66] Case C-390/06 *Nuova Agricast* EU:C:2008:224, para. 66; Case C-550/07 P *Akzo Nobel Chemicals* EU:C:2010:512, para. 55.

[67] See Declaration 17 to the Intergovernmental Conference which adopted the Treaty of Lisbon. See also the contribution by *Bux* in this volume.

[68] Koen Lenaerts, José A. Gutiérrez-Fons, Stanislas Adam, 'Exploring the Auto-nomy of the European Union Legal Order' (2021) 81 Zeitschrift für ausländisches öffentliches Recht und Völkerrecht 47–88, 70 f. See also Opinion of AG Tanchev in Case C-824/18 *A.B. and Others* EU:C:2020:1053, para. 82.

4.   ARTICLE 7 TEU

Article 7 TEU is a crucial tool for defending the founding values in Article 2 TEU such as the rule of law. It finds its origin in the Treaty of Amsterdam[69] and since the Treaty of Nice[70] has two arms (4.1). The Article 7 TEU proceedings are an imminently political tool not least due to the limited jurisdiction of the Court of Justice (4.2).

4.1   Two Arms of Article 7 TEU

Article 7 TEU foresees two types of procedures. Under the 'preventive arm' in Article 7(1) TEU the Council may determine that there is 'a clear risk of a serious breach' of the founding values. A breach of Article 2 TEU is thus not necessary, but it suffices that there is such a qualified threat. This procedure can be triggered by the broadest range of actors upon a reasoned proposal by one third of the Member States, the European Parliament or the Commission. Subsequently the Council acts, after obtaining the consent of the Parliament, by four fifths of its members excluding the Member State concerned.[71] The Council may determine that there is a clear risk of a serious breach and may also issue recommendations in accordance with the same procedure. The legal effect of both the determination and the recommendation are limited, which distinguishes the preventive arm from the suspensive arm. Before any action is taken, the Council must also hear the Member State in question to safeguard its procedural 'right to be heard'.

Currently, there are two Article 7(1) TEU proceedings ongoing. In December 2017, the Commission adopted a reasoned proposal regarding the rule of law in Poland, which focuses on the Constitutional Tribunal and judicial independence.[72] In September 2018, the European Parliament adopted a reasoned proposal regarding founding values in Hungary, which covers a broad range of topics ranging from the functioning of the constitutional and electoral system, the independence of the judiciary all the way to fundamental rights of migrants as well as economic and social rights.[73] In order to organise the hearings, the Council adopted standard modalities which set out the sequence of the hear-

---

[69] Article 6 TEC, now Article 7(2)–(4) TEU.
[70] Now Article 7(1) TEU.
[71] Article 354(1) TFEU, i.e. 21 out of 26 members. See also Rule 89 of the EP's Rules of Procedure.
[72] Commission Reasoned Proposal of 20 December 2017, COM(2017) 835 final.
[73] EP Resolution of 12 September 2018, P8_TA(2018)0340.

ings at the Council and allow Coreper to set the scope ahead of each hearing.[74] In accordance with these rules, the General Affairs Council organises regular hearings of both Member States and the General Secretariat of the Council produces a report.[75]

Article 7(2)–(4) TEU contains the 'suspensive arm' which enables the European Council to determine the 'existence of a serious and persistent breach' of the founding values. In contrast to the preventive arm, a mere threat to Article 2 TEU is not sufficient. Rather, the violation must be sufficiently severe which has been interpreted as systemic deficiencies by scholars.[76] This procedure may only be initiated by one third of the Member States or the Commission. While the European Parliament therefore cannot initiate this part of the Article 7 TEU procedure, it is still involved because it must give its consent before any action is taken by the European Council. The latter must also invite the Member State in question to submit its observation which safeguards its 'right to be heard'. Once the European Council has made a determination under Article 7(2) TEU, the Council, acting by (reinforced) qualified majority,[77] may suspend certain rights deriving from the Treaties. The Council has a broad margin of discretion choosing a suitable course of action which can target economic rights, such as suspending access to EU funds, or non-economic rights, such as suspending the voting rights. Since the sanctions are aimed at Member States, the Council must take into account the possible effects on natural and legal persons. In any case, the possibility to suspend rights does not go so far as ending membership in the EU, a right which pursuant to Article 50 TEU remains with each Member State to be exercised in accordance with its own constitutional requirement.[78]

4.2 The Political Nature of Article 7 TEU and Limited Judicial Review

Throughout the Article 7 TEU proceedings, the Court of Justice's jurisdiction is considerably limited. In accordance with Article 269 TFEU the Court may only review the European Council's and Council's acts under Article 7 TEU

---

[74] Standard modalities for hearings referred to in Article 7(1) TEU, ST 10641/19 REV 2.

[75] See for example report on the hearings of 30 May 2023 for Poland (ST 10100/23) and Hungary (ST 10101/23).

[76] Armin von Bogdandy and Michael Ioannidis, 'Systemic Deficiency in the Rule of Law' (2014) 51 Common Market Law Review 59–96, 65 ff.

[77] Articles 283(3)(b) and 354(2) TFEU.

[78] See on this Case C-621/18 *Wightman* EU:C:2018:999, paras. 45 ff.

as regards procedural aspects and solely upon request of the Member State concerned. In particular, the Court may review whether all the voting require- ments set out in Article 354 TFEU are complied with. In the summer of 2021, the Court did just that when it examined whether the European Parliament had acted with the required two-thirds majority of the votes cast, representing the majority of its members, when it adopted the reasoned proposal starting the Article 7(1) TEU proceedings vis-à-vis Hungary.

Hungary argued that the European Parliament had committed an error when calculating the two-thirds majority because it excluded abstentions. Had those abstentions been taken into account, the two-thirds majority would not have been met. However, the European Parliament's Rules of Procedure stipulate that when calculating whether a text has been adopted or rejected, account is to be taken only of the votes cast for and against excluding abstentions.[79] In its judgment, the Court of Justice not only asserted its jurisdiction and interpreted narrowly Article 269 TFEU to preserve the principle that the EU is a union based on the rule of law with a complete system of legal remedies.[80] The Court also ruled on the procedural question and held that the concept of 'votes cast' must be interpreted as precluding the taking into account of abstentions.[81] Moreover, since the Members of Parliament were informed beforehand that abstentions would not be counted as votes cast, there was also no violation of the principle of democracy or the principle of equal treatment.[82]

From this it is clear that the Court takes its jurisdiction to review procedural aspects very seriously. At the same time, the lack of substantive legal review allows to qualify the Article 7 TEU proceedings as imminently political with broad margins of discretion for the involved Union institutions. This also entails that activating Article 7 TEU comes at a high political price since attaining a four fifths majority in the Council or unanimity in the European Council is very difficult. Moreover, the unanimity requirement in Article 7(2) TEU gives any voting Member State a veto position even if they have them- selves issues complying with the rule of law. And although Article 7(1) TEU avoids such veto positions, it suffers from a paradox: on the one hand, it is still politically difficult to attain the four fifths majority and, on the other hand, the Council's determination or recommendations carry only a limited legal effect.

---

[79] Rule 187(3) of the EP's Rules of Procedure: 'In calculating whether a text has been adopted or rejected, account shall be taken only of votes cast for and against, except in those cases for which the Treaties lay down a specific majority.'
[80] Case C-650/18 *Hungary v European Parliament* EU:C:2021:426, para. 34.
[81] Ibid para. 93.
[82] Ibid paras. 99 f.

This may explain why in the two ongoing Article 7(1) TEU proceedings it has so far not been possible to muster the political support to take action.

Finally, this inaction led some to suggest limiting political discretion and strengthening the role of the Court by tasking it to assess whether Article 2 TEU is breached. However, it may not only be difficult to agree on the necessary Treaty change. This also risks juridifying the Article 7 TEU proceedings for all founding values (not only the rule of law) while at the same time politicising the Court and may, thus, entail unwanted 'side effects'.

5.   SOFT-LAW INSTRUMENTS BY THE COMMISSION AND THE COUNCIL

Apart from Article 7 TEU procedures, the Union institutions also created soft-law instruments to address new challenges posed for the rule of law. In this context soft law can be defined as rules of conduct that are laid down in instruments which have not been attributed legally binding force as such, but nevertheless may have certain (indirect) legal effects.[83] Particularly noteworthy are the Commission's Rule of Law Reports (5.1) and the Council's Rule of Law Dialogue (5.2).

5.1   Commission Rule of Law Report

Ever since the challenges for the rule of law arose, the Commission showed initiative to establish mechanisms to protect the rule of law. Already in 2014 the Commission sent a communication announcing its intention to establish a framework to strengthen the rule of law before Article 7 TEU procedures are triggered.[84] In addition, the Commission announced further initiatives to promote the rule of law in 2019.[85] At the core is a Rule of Law Review Cycle which brings together Union institutions, Member States as well as civil society and other stakeholders and feeds into the Annual Rule of Law Report. Based on broad consultations and a variety of sources, the Commission pro-

---

[83] Linda Senden, *Soft Law in European Community Law* (Hart 2004) 113; Karel C. Wellens, Gustaaf M. Borchardt, 'Soft Law in European Community Law' (1989) 14 European Law Review 267–321, 285.

[84] Commission Communication, *A new EU Framework to strengthen the Rule of Law*, COM(2014) 158 final. See in more detail Dimitry Kochenov, Laurent Pech, 'Better Late than Never? On the European Commission's Rule of Law Framework and its First Activation' (2016) 54 Journal of Common Market Studies 1062–74.

[85] Commission Communication, *Strengthening the rule of law within the Union*, COM(2019) 343 final.

vides a synthesis of significant developments in the area of rule of law both at national and EU level. The Rule of Law Report highlights best practices, but also identifies recurrent problems and negative developments. In order to focus the Report, it covers four pillars: the justice system, the anti-corruption framework, media pluralism, and other institutional issues related to checks and balances.

Since 2020, the reports have been issued annually by the Commission.[86] They contain a general overview of all developments in a given year as well as 27 country specific chapters with more detailed information about each Member State. All Member States may provide information through a questionnaire, which is supplemented by exchanges during country visits and other information from stakeholders. Also, the methodology for the assessment is discussed with Member States, but the assessment itself ultimately remains the Commission's responsibility. Moreover, the country chapters also refer to opinions from the Council of Europe, including the Venice Commission.

Since 2022, the reports include recommendations to Member States which can be more general to 'continue measures to provide adequate human and financial resources for the justice system' or more specific to 'establish a robust track record for hight level corruption cases' in the case of Hungary or to 'separate the function of the Minister of Justice from that of the Prosecutor-General' in the case of Poland. When the Commission presented its 2023 Rule of Law Report it noted that 65% of its recommendations have already been followed up; with full or significant progress for 25%, some progress for 40% and no progress for the remaining 35% of the recommendations.[87] Thus, the Commission's recommendations are a typical example of soft law, which although legally non-binding, are having effects in Member States. In this vein, some Member States have used the Rule of Law Report as an incentive to start national initiatives such as Pact for the Rule of Law in Germany[88] or the State Commission on the Rule of Law in the Netherlands.[89] However, the Rule of Law Report's most important impact is not of an

---

[86]   See Commission Communications COM(2020) 580 final; COM(2021) 700 final; COM(2022) 500 final; COM(2023) 800 final as well as the accompanying Staff Working Documents (SWD) containing the country chapters.

[87]   COM(2023) 800 final, p. 1.

[88]   It seeks to increase funding the judiciary and new posts for judges, but implementation is lagging behind: Hasso Suliak, 'Marco Buschmann lässt Bundesländer abblitzen' (2022) Legal Tribune Online 17 September, <https://www.lto.de/recht/justiz/j/streit-pakt-fuer-rechtsstaat-digitalpakt-marco-buschmann-bund-laender-gallina-eisenreich/> accessed 1 December 2023.

[89]   Decree of 10 February 2023, No 2023000264 establishing a State Commission on the Rule of Law.

(immediate) legal nature: its comprehensive scope and uniform methodology closes a significant gap by providing politicians, researchers and citizens much needed reliable information. Thus, the reports give an impartial overview on rule of law developments and can feed into further discussion, as the Council's Rule of Law Dialogue shows.

5.2   Council Rule of Law Dialogue

In December 2014, the General Affairs Council and the Member States established an annual Rule of Law Dialogue.[90] Partly a response to the Commission's rule of law communication of the same year, this Dialogue aims to promote and safeguard the rule of law in the framework of the Treaties. The Dialogue is based on the principles of objectivity, non-discrimination and equal treatment of all Member States and is conducted on a non-partisan and evidence-based approach (para. 2). This approach emphasises the principle of conferral and the respect of national identities of Member States inherent in their fundamental political and constitutional structures (para. 4). The Dialogue also is aimed to be complementary avoiding duplication and taking into account existing instruments (para. 5). The Dialogues are held in the General Affairs Council and are prepared directly by the Committee of Permanent Representatives (Coreper) without the involvement of a specialised Working Party as the rule of law is considered too important and too horizontal to task a single Working Party of the Council.

While a change of the original Conclusion was politically difficult to reach,[91] in 2020 the then German Presidency suggested to give the Rule of Law Dialogue a new structure comprising two types of regular discussions:[92] on the one hand, there is a horizontal discussion covering general rule of law developments in the EU usually held in the fall semester. On the other hand, there are country-specific discussions addressing key developments one by one in each Member State following the protocol order one in the fall semester and another in the spring semester. This new structure fits into the established framework of 2014 without changing it, since it pertains to the prerogatives of the Council

---

[90]   Conclusions of the Council of the EU and the Member States of 16 December 2014, Council doc. ST 17014/14.

[91]   See Presidency Conclusions of 19 November 2019 (supported by 26 of 28 Cou-ncil members), Council doc. ST 14173/19.

[92]   See Presidency Note of 28 September 2020, Council doc. ST 11094/20. Sub- sequently continued during the Portuguese (ST 7379/21), Slovenian (ST 12467/21), French (ST 6705/22), Czech (ST 11510/22), Swedish (ST 6826/23) and Spanish (ST 11839/23) presidencies.

Presidency to organise the discussions on the Rule of Law Dialogue.[93] And although an evaluation in December 2023 again failed to find consensus,[94] the Rule of Law Dialogue will take place even more frequently in the future, with four debates per year.

At the same time, the Rule of Law Dialogue can also make use of the Commission's Rule of Law Report in line with its ambition to use all the expertise in this area. Since its first publication in 2020, the Rule of Law report has become an important source and is often referred to during discussions in the Council. Thus, the Council's Dialogue evolved together with the Commission's Report and the discussions in the Council feed back into the Commission's Rule of Law cycle. And although the Council has been criticised for inaction,[95] this underestimates the Dialogue's importance in putting matters related to the rule of law regularly and consistently on the agenda of ministers' discussions.[96] Thus, the added value of the Council Rule of Law Dialogue consists in continuously addressing challenges for the rule of law. These (sometimes frank) exchanges can help build trust and allow to discuss matters which would have been unthinkable more than a decade ago.

6.   CONDITIONALITY REGULATION

The possibly most far-reaching new tool is the introduction of budgetary conditionality. The Conditionality Regulation (EU, Euratom) 2020/2092 creates a general regime for the protection of the Union budget.[97] In case of breaches of the rule of law in a Member State which affect or seriously risk affecting the sound financial management or the financial interests of the Union in a sufficiently direct way, payments may be interrupted, reduced, terminated or suspended and new budget commitments can be prohibited. The conformity of the Conditionality Regulation has been questioned before the Court of Justice (6.1) and there is currently one ongoing case (6.2).

---

[93] See Council doc. ST 17014/14, para. 6, and Article 3(1) and (7) of the Council's Rules of Procedure [2009] OJ L325/35.

[94] See Presidency Conclusions of 12 December 2023, Council doc. ST 16547/23, supported by 25 of 27 members of the Council. Subsequently, the new Polish government indicated its support.

[95] Peter Olivier, Justine Stefanelli, 'Strengthening the Rule of Law in the EU: The Council's Inaction' (2016) 54 Journal of Common Market Studies 1075–1084.

[96] See on the importance of discussing even difficult matters Christoph Möllers, Linda Schneider, *Demokratiesicherung in der EU* (Mohr Siebeck 2018) 144.

[97] Regulation 2020/2092 on a general regime of conditionality for the protection of the Union budget [2020] OJ L 433I/1.

6.1   Conformity with the Treaties

In two actions for annulment, Hungary and Poland questioned whether the Conditionality Regulation could be adopted on the basis of Article 322(1) TFEU claiming it circumvented the special procedure foreseen in Article 7 TEU for the protection of the founding values such as the rule of law.

In response, the Court found that sound financial management is a principle enshrined in Article 310(5) TFEU which is spelled out in the financial rules for establishing and implementing the budget based on Article 322(1) TFEU. Moreover, respect of the founding values is not only a condition for accession under Article 49 TEU. The continued compliance with Article 2 TEU is a condition for benefitting from all the rights under the Treaties. And since these values are shared by all Member States, the Union must be able to defend those values. Thus, in accordance with the principles of conferral (Article 5(2) TEU) and consistency (Article 7 TFEU), the rule of law is capable of constituting the basis for a conditionality mechanism.[98]

From this follows that an act of secondary law may establish procedures relating to the founding values such as the rule of law, provided those procedures are different from Article 7 TEU in both their aim and subject matter.[99] Whereas, Article 7 TEU seeks to penalise serious and persistent breaches of Article 2 TEU, the Conditionality Regulation seeks to protect the Union budget. Thus, the Union legislator rightfully introduced the requirement that there must be a 'genuine link' between rule of law breaches by a Member State and the effect or the serious risk of effecting the Union budget.[100] In other words, not just any rule of law breach by a Member State may lead to the application of the Conditionality Regulation, but it must be clear that there is a risk for the Union budget. In this regard, Article 4(2) of the Conditionality Regulation sets out a number of relevant rule of law breaches ranging from the functioning of the budgetary authorities, effective judicial review all the way to other situations that are relevant to sound financial management or the protection of the financial interest of the Union.

---

[98] Case C-156/21 *Hungary v European Parliament and Council* EU:C:2022: 97, paras. 126–128; Case C-157/21 *Poland v European Parliament and Council* EU:C:2022:98, paras. 144–146.

[99] Ibid paras. 168 and 207 respectively.

[100] Ibid paras. 147 & 176 and 165 & 179 respectively. See on this crucial condition Baraggia and Bonelli, 'Linking Money to Values: The New Rule of Law Conditionality Regulation and Its Constitutional Challenges' (2022) 23 German Law Journal 146 f.; Weber, 'Horizontale Unionsaufsicht und vertikale Werteentwicklung zum Schutz der unionalen Verfassungsidentität' (2022) Europarecht 788.

6.2   First Application regarding Hungary

Where the requirements for taking action are met and there are no other more effective procedures, the Commission is to initiate the procedure under Article 6 of the Conditionality Regulation. After setting out the grounds and exchanges with the Member State concerned, the Commission must submit a proposal to the Council if the remedial measures are not sufficient. The Council is in turn obliged to adopt an implementing decision on the appropriate measures within one month of receiving the Commission's proposal, which may exceptionally be extended by a maximum of two months. In theory, the Member State concerned may request the matter to be referred to the next European Council for discussion.[101] This 'emergency brake' procedure does not, however, render the consensus rule of Article 15(4) TEU applicable. Rather, after discussion by the Heads of State or Government, the Council continues to take its decision by qualified majority. This even applies where the Council amends the Commission proposal, as Article 6(11) of the Conditionality Regulation makes clear.[102]

In April 2022, the Commission launched for the first time a procedure with regard to Hungary and in September proposed to the Council to adopt measures.[103] On 15 December 2022, the Council adopted its implementing decision imposing measures for the protection of the Union budget against the consequences of breaches of the rule of law in Hungary, concerning public procurement, effectiveness of prosecutorial action and the fight against corruption. Although Hungary had adopted some remedial measures, they remained inadequate to address the significant weaknesses for the rule of law. Hence, 55% of the budgetary commitments under three programmes in Cohesion Policy amounting to about EUR 6.3 billion were suspended.[104] Although Hungary could have taken legal action against the Council's Implementing Decision, it chose not to. Instead, a number of Hungarian universities took legal action before the General Court.[105]

However these legal procedures end, the adoption of the Conditionality Regulation by the European Parliament and the Council and its first application by the Commission and the Council regarding Hungary shows the Union

---

[101]   Recital (26) Conditionality Regulation.

[102]   In the absence of this provision, the unanimity requirement under Article 293 TFEU would apply.

[103]   COM(2022) 485 final. See in more detail the chapter by *Symann* in this volume.

[104]   Council Implementing Decision 2022/2506 [2022] OJ L325/94.

[105]   Cases T-115/23, T-132/23, T-133/23, T-138/23, T-139/23 and T-140/23.

institutions' resolve to tackle challenges for the rule of law also through novel instruments. In this regard it is also noteworthy that Union legislator defined for the first time the concept of the rule of law. Pursuant to Article 2(a) Conditionality Regulation, the rule of law refers to the founding value in Article 2 TEU. It includes (formal elements) such as the principles of legality, legal certainty, prohibition of arbitrariness, effective judicial protection; but also (substantive elements) such as fundamental rights, separation of powers, non-discrimination and equality before the law. Moreover, and very important from a constitutional perspective, the rule of law must be understood not in isolation but by having regard to the other founding values of the Union.

7.   CONCLUSION

The rule of law is a founding value of the European Union enshrined in Article 2 TEU and shared by the Member States. These values not only define the very identity of the European Union as a common legal order, the European Union must also be able to defend those values as the Court of Justice rightly emphasised.[106] Although the rule of law remains a contested concept in the European Union, from the constitutional traditions of the Member States and the Court's case law emanate a broad range of formal and substantive elements which form the rule of law. The sheer breadth of these elements confirms an insight already expressed by *Ralf Dahrendorf* after the fall of the iron curtain: 'The rule of law is of course all-pervasive, at least so far as the rules of the democratic game are concerned.'[107] Thus, by protecting the rule of law also democracy and the other founding values enshrined in Article 2 TEU are strengthened.

The European Union disposes of a wide variety of instruments which are used to protect the rule of law. There are the largely political Article 7 TEU procedures with their broad scope of application encompassing all founding values enshrined in Article 2 TEU. While some bemoan that in two ongoing procedures vis-à-vis Poland and Hungary it has so far not been possible to muster the political support to take action, this may just show that rule of law matters remain politically divisive. And it is unlikely to change even if the Court of Justice were given the power to assess whether Article 2 TEU is breached by way of Treaty amendment. Rather than depoliticizing the task, this risks politicising the Court, a 'side effect' the Treaty framers sought to avoid when giving it limited jurisdiction in Article 269 TFEU.

---

[106] Case C-156/21 *Hungary v European Parliament and Council* EU:C:2022:97, para. 127; Case C-157/21 *Poland v European Parliament and Council* EU:C:2022: 98, para. 145.

[107] Dahrendorf (1990) *supra* note 3 at 82.

In addition, there are novel soft-law instruments specifically dedicated to the rule of law: the Commission's Rule of Law Report and the Council's Rule of Law Dialogue are not designed to have enforceable legal effects, but respectively seek to gather reliable information and provide a forum to discuss the rule of law. This does not mean they are not effective as new initiatives by Member States to protect the rule of law show. Rather, the added value of such soft-law instruments consists in continuously addressing challenges for the rule of law on matters and in a level of detail which would have been unthinkable more than a decade ago.

It is against this background that the Union legislator chose to adopt the Conditionality Regulation as an instrument to protect the Union budget if breaches of the rule of law affect or risk affecting the EU financial interests. The far-reaching powers to suspend payments and prohibit budgetary commitments can only be exercised if there is a 'genuine link' between rule of law breaches by a Member State and the risk for the Union budget. This shows that the Conditionality Regulation is not an instrument to be used for any issue related to the rule of law and can explain why it has only been applied once. Nevertheless, its mere existence allows to survey developments in Member States and may discourage them from adopting measures with an impact on the EU financial interests.

All these instruments in the European Union's toolbox have different objectives, scopes of application and procedures to be applied. They are far from perfect and have not resolved all the rule of law challenges the European Union and its Member States are facing. On the contrary, when focusing on the rule of law one discovers how pervasive and interconnected this founding value is. To address these complexities, the European Union's toolbox not only provides various instruments which are of a complementary nature. This toolbox has also evolved over time to address new challenges and is likely to be developed further in the future. This leaves beyond any doubt that safeguarding a founding value such as the rule of law is a continuous endeavour.

11. Article 7 TEU as 'Nuclear Option'? An Analysis of its Potential and its Shortcomings[1]

Robert Böttner and Nic Schröder

1. INTRODUCTION

In his State of the Union address in 2012, then President of the European Commission *José Manuel Barroso* spoke of the real threat to legal and democratic structures in some European states and thus to the Union's values. In this context he described Article 7 TEU as a 'nuclear option' in the fight for these very values,[2] insinuating that due to its impact, this Article 7 can only be used in extreme emergencies and is rather a procedure whose mere existence provides a disciplining effect.

This chapter will analyse if in fact Article 7 TEU serves as an instrument for safeguarding the values laid down in Article 2 TEU. Before the prevention and the sanction mechanisms are explained, the focus is placed on the principle of homogeneity and the rule of law principle in particular and the related question of why uniform respect for values is of great importance in the EU. Following that, the chapter will analyse the structure and characteristics of the Article 7 procedure.[3] Based on this analysis, we will evaluate the instrument and discuss potential reforms.

---

[1] Supported by Open Access funds of the University of Erfurt.

[2] President of the European Commission, State of the Union Address of 12 September 2012, <https:// ec .europa .eu/ commission/ presscorner/ detail/ en/ SPEECH_12_596> accessed 1 December 2023. It is interesting to note that the German version speaks of a *"radical* option".

[3] In addition to this 'hard-law' constitutional instrument of Article 7 TEU, there are other 'soft-law' and secondary law instruments such as the rule of law dialogue or the Conditionality Regulation, which will be dealt with elsewhere in this volume: See the contributions by *Bauerschmidt* and by *Symann* in this volume.

2. THE PRINCIPLE OF HOMOGENEITY AND THE RULE OF LAW

While sentence 1 of Article 2 TEU defines the values of the Union, sentence 2 states that these values are not limited to the Union but are also "common to the Member States in a society in which pluralism, non-discrimination, tolerance, justice, solidarity and equality between women and men prevail". This wording is an expression of the principle of homogeneity. The concept of homogeneity can be understood as sameness or likeness, but is not to be confused with the concept of uniformity.[4] The principle of homogeneity is mostly associated with the doctrine of federal States, such as in Germany with the homogeneity clause in Article 28(1) of the German Constitution (Basic Law), which states that "the constitutional order in the Länder must conform to the principles of a republican, democratic and social state governed by the rule of law within the meaning of this Basic Law". While the *Länder* (the German states) enjoy constitutional autonomy, the Basic Law aims to bring about a certain homogeneity (not conformity or uniformity) by binding the *Länder* to the guiding principles.[5] The *Länder* are thus "committed to a constitutional order that is structurally consistent - homogeneous - with that of the federal level".[6] This idea can be applied *mutatis mutandis* also to the supranational organisation of the European Union. As *F. Schorkopf* puts it: "Homogeneity is therefore a principle of order which has as its content the similarity of certain characteristics of related associations."[7]

Homogeneity can be understood as an organizing principle of the European Union and is characterised by the similarity of the values mentioned in Article 2 TEU (horizontally) between the individual Member States on the one hand

---

See also Diel-Gligor, 'Sicherungsinstrumente für die Rechtsstaatlichkeit in der EU' (2021) Zeitschrift für Rechtspolitik, 63-66.

[4]   Cf. Hilf and Schorkopf, 'Artikel 2 EUV' in Grabitz, Hilf and Nettesheim (eds), *Das Recht der Europäischen Union* (C.H.Beck May 2020) para. 9.

[5]   German Federal Constitutional Court, judgment of the Second Senate of 27 April 1959, 2 BvF 2/58, BVerfGE 9, 268 (279); judgment of the Second Senate of 22 July 1969, 2 BvK 1/67, BVerfGE 27, 44 (56). See further Mehde, 'Artikel 28 GG' in Dürig/Herzog/Scholz, Grundgesetz-Kommentar (C.H.Beck May 2023), para. 1 ff.

[6]   German Federal Constitutional Court, judgment of 12 October 1989, 2 BvF 2/89, BVerfGE 81, 53 (55) (our translation).

[7]   Schorkopf, *Homogenität in der Europäischen Union* (Duncker & Humblot 2000) at 34 (our translation).

and, on the other hand, between the Union and the Member States (vertically).[8] This equality of values is of central importance for European integration. The Member States can only form and maintain a supranational organisation if there is a minimum of common consensus in the achievement of its goals and the preservation of its values. In addition, the common values serve to secure the basis of legitimacy of Union legal acts. Furthermore, in addition to the consensus and legitimacy function, homogeneity is also said to have an integration function. Only through the commonality of structural and substantive values can a framework of orientation be created for the Member States and the EU, "which forms the essence of a common European legal culture".[9] Since Article 2 TEU expresses the EU's 'constitutional core',[10] homogeneity also has a safeguarding effect by ensuring the functioning of the Union.[11]

In the EU context, homogeneity originally meant *horizontal* homogeneity. The founding states needed guiding principles for their union, which result from their respective national constitutions. Accordingly, the states had an interest in the homogeneity of their guiding principles in order to found a community.[12] With the creation of the European Union in its present form, one can also identify a sort of *vertical* homogeneity between the European level and the Member States. For if one were to assume that the Member States do not uphold the homogeneity of the values of Article 2 TEU, then the existence of the European Union itself would be in danger. By emphasizing that the Union is founded on these values, Article 2(1) TEU creates a "linguistic link between the legal structures of the Member States and of the Union [and] corresponds to the concept of vertical homogeneity."[13] With the ratification of the Treaty of Lisbon in 2009, the treaty makers introduced Article 2 TEU in its current version. Formulated here are "classical structural features of a liberal constitutional state".[14] With Article 2 TEU, the European Union claims to be seen as a union of values.[15]

---

[8] Cf. ibid., p. 68 (our translation). See also Mangiameli and Saputelli, 'Article 7 TEU', in Blanke and Mangiameli (eds), *The Treaty on European Union (TEU)* (Springer 2013) para. 1.

[9] Schorkopf, (2000) *supra* note 6 at 41 (our translation).

[10] Calliess, 'Artikel 2 EUV', in Calliess and Ruffert (eds), *EUV/AEUV* (6th edn. C.H.Beck 2022) para. 7.

[11] Cf. Hau, *Sanktionen und Vorfeldmaßnahmen zur Absicherung der europäischen Grundwerte* (Nomos 2002) at 27.

[12] Schorkopf, (2000) *supra* note 6 at 43.

[13] Schorkopf, (2000) *supra* note 6 at 102 (our translation).

[14] Calliess, (2022) *supra* note 9 at para. 10 (our translation).

[15] Cf. ibid. at para. 10.

As early as 1974, the first President of the Commission of the European Economic Community, *Walter Hallstein* dubbed the EEC a 'community based on the rule of law'.[16] On closer examination, it becomes clear that the rule of law was one of the fundamental values in the history of the European Union from its very beginnings. Particularly through the Treaties of Maastricht, Amsterdam, and Lisbon, one can observe an increasing anchoring of the rule of law principle in the EU context. After the Member States committed themselves to the rule of law in the preamble to the Maastricht Treaty in 1992, the rule of law was then enshrined in Article 6 TEU during the negotiations in Amsterdam in 1997 and was also considered a prerequisite for accession in accordance with Article 49 TEU.[17]

There is, however, no legal definition of this term and concept, which remains ambiguous against the background of different *national* rule of law concepts.[18] For the European Commission, "the rule of law is the backbone of any modern constitutional democracy."[19] In the course of establishing a new Rule of Law Mechanism, the European Commission elaborated a definition of the rule of law. In its Communication on a new EU framework to strengthen the rule of law the Commission declares as principles of the rule of law: "legality, which implies a transparent, accountable, democratic and pluralistic process for enacting laws; legal certainty; prohibition of arbitrariness of the executive powers; independent and impartial courts; effective judicial review including respect for fundamental rights; and equality before the law."[20] It is noticeable that the Commission has taken its cue from the principles of the so-called 'Venice Commission'.[21] After examining the understanding of the rule of law in numerous national and international legal texts, the Venice Commission published a report on the rule of law on 4 April 2011.[22] This report created the basis for a common consensus among the individual EU institutions on the understanding of the rule of law. It becomes apparent that the rule of law does

---

[16]   Hallstein, *Die Europäische Gemeinschaft* (2nd edn. Econ-Verlag 1974) at 51 (our translation).

[17]   Cf. Pech, 'The Rule of Law as a Constitutional Principle of the European Union' (2009) Jean Monnet Working Paper No. 04/09 at 17-19.

[18]   See on this inter alia the contributions by *Rautio* and by *Bauerschmidt* in this volume.

[19]   Commission Communication, 'A new EU Framework to strengthen the Rule of Law', COM(2014) 158 final, p. 2.

[20]   COM(2014) 158 final, p. 4.

[21]   See on this the contribution by *Rautio* in this volume.

[22]   Cf. Venice Commission, Report on the Rule of Law (4 April 2011), CDL-AD (2011) 003 rev, Study no. 512/2009.

not boil down to a simple definition but must be seen in a discursive context with its constitutive elements.

In order to guarantee the rule of law in the European Union from the outset, the values in Article 2 TEU are a prerequisite for accession. Article 49(1) sentence 1 TEU states that any European State which respects the Union's values and is committed to promoting them may apply to become a member of the European Union. The states are required to make their legal order and constitution compatible with the Union's values. In particular, it is a matter of actively standing up for these values. In view of the constitutional autonomy of the Member States (see Article 4(2) TEU), they are free to choose how they implement the structural requirements of Article 2 TEU.[23] In addition to the values mentioned in Article 49(1) sentence 1 TEU, the criteria of the European Council must also be taken into account (Article 49(1) sentence 4 TEU), which covers the so-called Copenhagen criteria adopted in 1993. These include, *inter alia*, "achieved stability of institutions guaranteeing democracy, the rule of law, human rights and respect for and protection of minorities".[24] Furthermore, the adaption of the candidate state's legal order to the *acquis communautaire* includes a chapter on 'Justice and Fundamental Rights'. Due to current developments in Europe, the European Commission gives priority to this chapter and only continues accession negotiations when the candidate country takes measures to remedy the deficiencies regarding the rule of law, justice and fundamental rights.[25]

Member States are also required *after* accession to respect and promote the Union's values.[26] As Article 4(3) TEU underlines, in accordance with the principle of sincere cooperation, Member States must fulfil their treaty obligations uniformly and without restriction. The states therefore have a duty to act as well as a duty to refrain from detrimental action. The Member States must refrain from all measures that jeopardise the realisation of the EU's

---

[23] See Ohler, 'Artikel 49 EUV' in Grabitz, Hilf and Nettesheim (eds), *Das Recht der Europäischen Union* (C.H.Beck July 2017) para. 15.

[24] European Council in Copenhagen, 21-22 June 1993, Conclusions of the Presidency, SN 180/1/93, p. 13, available at <https://www.consilium.europa.eu/media/21225/72921.pdf>.

[25] Cf. Šelih, Bond and Dolan, 'Can EU funds promote the rule of law in Europe? (21 November 2017) Centre for European Reform Policy Brief, <https://www.cer.eu/publications/archive/policy-brief/2017/can-eu-funds-promote-rule-law-europe> accessed 1 December 2023. On pre-accession experience, see also the chapter by *Usvatov* and *Muharemovic* in this volume.

[26] On post-accession experience, see the chapter by *Küpper* in this volume.

objectives.[27] While accession candidates such as Albania or Montenegro are expected to fulfil the Copenhagen criteria,[28] states that are already members of the Union violate these criteria, a discrepancy that is referred to as the 'Copenhagen Dilemma'.[29]

3.   STRUCTURE AND CHARACTERISTICS OF THE ARTICLE 7 PROCEDURE

Support by the Member States for the Union's values is decisive "for trust between all intuitions, it legitimises EU decision-making, and it confirms Europe's understanding as a union of liberal democracies."[30] What happens, however, when the violation of values occurs in a continuity of great magnitude, i.e. when there is a 'systemic deficit' in a Member State?[31] In order to counter this systemic deficit in individual areas, the treaty makers put Article 7 TEU at the disposal of the EU institutions (and the Member States). It provides for a differentiated sanctions procedure aimed at safeguarding the fundamental values of the Union. The procedure gives the EU institutions the possibility to ensure that each Member State respects the values mentioned in Article 2 TEU. For many years, Article 7 TEU was associated with the expectation that the mere existence of this article in the Treaties would have a "deterrent effect to prevent retrogression in the rule of law and democracy".[32] This assumption was further confirmed by the characterisation of Article 7 TEU as a 'nuclear option'.[33]

---

[27]   See Franzius, 'Artikel 4 EUV', in Pechstein, Nowak and Häde (eds), *Frankfurter Kommentar zu EUV, GRC und AEUV* (Mohr Siebeck 2017) para. 105.

[28]   European Commission, 'EU enlargement', <https://commission.europa.eu/strat egy-and-policy/policies/eu-enlargement_en> accessed 1 December 2023.

[29]   Cf. Philipp, 'Art. 7 EUV als Rettung für den Rechtsstaat?' (2021) Europäische Zeitschrift für Wirtschaftsrecht, 697-698.

[30]   von Bogdandy and Ioannidis, 'Das systemische Defizit - Merkmale, Instrumente und Probleme am Beispiel der Rechtsstaatlichkeit und des Rechtsstaatlichkeit-saufsichtsverfahrens' (2014) Heidelberg Journal of International Law, 283 ff. at 284 (our translation).

[31]   Cf. ibid. at 284f.

[32]   Boysen, 'Das geeinte Europa der »ever closer union« und ein neues Narrativ differenzierter Integration?' in Franzius, Mayer and Neyer (eds), *Die Neuerfindung Europas: Bedeutung und Gehalte von Narrativen für die europäische Integration* (Nomos 2019), 147 ff. at 168.

[33]   Ibid.

The preventive mechanism of Article 7(1) TEU has so far been activated twice.[34] With regard to the situation in Poland concerning the Constitutional Tribunal and judicial independence in general, the Commission adopted a reasoned proposal in December 2017.[35] Nine months later, in September 2018, the European Parliament adopted a reasoned proposal with regard to Hungary, which covers a variety of issues including the constitutional and electoral system, the independence of the judiciary, fundamental rights of migrants as well as economic and social rights.[36] So far, however, neither of the two procedures has yielded any tangible progress.

3.1   Preventive Mechanism under Article 7(1) TEU

Article 7(1) TEU serves to identify the risk of a serious breach and can also be understood as a preventive mechanism. On the one hand, it functions as an early warning to the affected Member State to make it clear that the current situation is serious, and on the other hand, it prevents premature and hasty action by the Union.[37]

The preventive mechanism leads to the determination of "a clear risk of a serious breach by a Member State of the values referred to in Article 2". Determining a danger or risk requires a prognosis and thus a forward-looking view. A danger is identifiable if it causes "a serious breach if events continue unchecked".[38] This prognosis must be based on concrete indications that make a danger recognisable, but it cannot solely rely on breaches of the values in the past. There is, however, no clear definition of when an actual 'risk' exists, as

---

[34]   In 2000, 14 of the then 15 Member States of the Union agreed on a "common reaction" against Austria when a right-wing party joined the Austrian government. This, however, was no formal application of Article 7. See Schorkopf, 'Artikel 7 EUV' in Grabitz, Hilf and Nettesheim (eds), *Das Recht der Europäischen Union* (C.H.Beck April 2017) para. 58 f.

[35]   European Commission, 'Proposal for a Council Decision on the determination of a clear risk of a serious breach by the Republic of Poland of the rule of law', COM(2017) 835 final.

[36]   European Parliament, 'proposal calling on the Council to determine, pursuant to Article 7(1) of the Treaty on European Union, the existence of a clear risk of a serious breach by Hungary of the values on which the Union is founded (2017/2131(INL))', resolution of 12 September 2018, P8_TA(2018)0340.

[37]   Cf. Nowak, 'Artikel 7 EUV' in Pechstein, Nowak and Häde (eds), *Frankfurter Kommentar zu EUV, GRC und AEUV* (Mohr Siebeck 2017) para. 6.

[38]   Träbert, *Sanktionen der Europäischen Union gegen ihre Mitgliedstaaten: die Sanktionsverfahren nach Art. 228 Abs. 2 EGV und Art. 7 EUV* (Peter Lang 2010) at 249.

the term is rather vague and leaves a margin of appreciation.[39] The European Commission clarifies its understanding of a clear risk with a concrete example. Thus, the *adoption* of a law that would suspend procedural guarantees in case of war would be a clear danger and the *application* of this law would then be the serious breach.[40] This idea is contested by the European Parliament. It sees a danger already in a government programme with a corresponding declaration of intent and thus defines the clear risk with a lower threshold than the European Commission.[41] This different understanding of 'risk' may be detrimental to the effective application of Article 7(1) TEU.

A further criterion is the serious violation of the values mentioned in Article 2 TEU. In order to determine a violation of the rule of law, a comparison of the actual state with the target state is to be used. "If the Member State concerned itself, i.e. through the actions of its organs or subordinate units, deviates negatively from the content of the values",[42] a violation or breach exists. This deviation can occur both through positive action and omission. The situation is different with the additional adjective 'serious', for which no concrete definition can be found. Against the background that Article 2 TEU is the foundation of the values of the European Union, a particular seriousness can already be presumed for every established violation. For this reason, the literature speaks of a "targeted impairment"[43] of the values of Article 2 TEU in the context of a serious breach.

There are three routes through which the preventive mechanism of Article 7(1) TEU may be initiated. One third of the Member States (currently nine),[44] the European Parliament[45] or the European Commission are entitled to issue

---

[39]   Ibid. at 248 f.

[40]   European Commission, 'Communication on Article 7 of the Treaty on European Union. Respect for and promotion of the values on which the Union is based', COM(2003) 606 final, p. 8.

[41]   See European Parliament, 'Commission communication on Article 7 of the Treaty on European Union: Respect for and promotion of the values on which the Union is based (COM(2003) 606 – C5-0594/2003 – 2003/2249(INI))', legislative resolution of 20 April 2004, para. 2, in conjunction with the explanatory statement to the Report of the Committee on Constitutional Affairs of 1 April 2004, A5-0227/2004.

[42]   Schorkopf, (2017) *supra* note 33 at para. 30.

[43]   Cf. Schorkopf, (2000) *supra* note 6 at 150.

[44]   In accordance with Article 354(1) TFEU, the member of the Council representing the Member State concerned shall not be counted in the calculation of the one third of Member States.

[45]   In accordance with Article 354(4) TFEU, the European Parliament shall act by a two-thirds majority of the votes cast, representing the majority of its compo-

a reasoned proposal on why there is a "a clear risk of a serious breach" of one of the Union's values by the Member State concerned. The requirement to justify the proposals aims to rationalize the procedure and to prevent it from being used too light-heartedly.[46]

On the basis of that reasoned proposal, the Council, with a four-fifths majority of its members (currently 21) and the consent of the European Parliament (acting on a committee proposal), can *determine* a clear risk of a serious breach of the values of Article 2 TEU. It is remarkable that it is the Council, i.e. the Member States' representation at the level of ministers, and not the European Council, i.e. the meeting of the Heads of State or Government of the Member States, that makes this determination.[47] Before deciding on such a finding, the Council must hear the Member State concerned, either in writing or orally. The arguments expressed by the Member State concerned must be taken into account by the Council and require a substantive discussion. Furthermore, the Council can make recommendations to the Member State concerned. Although these recommendations must be decided in accordance with the procedure described in the first sentence, they are not legally binding. The regular review of the findings referred to in the second subparagraph is also not explained in more detail. Apart from the recommendation, which is not binding, the Member State concerned does not have to fear any further legal consequences under Article 7(1) TEU.[48]

3.2 Sanction Mechanism under Article 7(2) TEU

Whereas paragraph 1 has a preventive or warning character, paragraph 2 of Article 7 TEU is reactive in nature and allows sanctioning breaches that have already occurred. Even though the structure of Article 7 TEU suggests a step-by-step approach, the sanction mechanism according to paragraph 2 is independent of the preventive mechanism regulated in paragraph 1.[49] The aim of Article 7(2) TEU is to ensure effective action by the Union in the event of a serious and persistent breach of the values set out in Article 2 TEU. At the

---

nent Members.

[46] Cf. Dashwood, 'The Constitution of the European Union after Nice: Law-making Procedures' (2001) 26 European Law Review, 215 ff. at 233.

[47] Schorkopf, (2017) *supra* note 33 at para. 22.

[48] Nowak, (2017) *supra* note 36, para. 12-14.

[49] Pechstein, 'Artikel 7 EUV' in Streinz (ed), *EUV/AEUV* (3rd edn C.H.Beck 2018) para. 10.

same time, a situation is to be re-established in which the promotion of and respect for the values is guaranteed.[50]

In contrast to paragraph 1, the mere risk of a serious violation is no longer sufficient. There must be an actual serious and also persistent breach. The temporal criterion of a 'persistent' breach presupposes that the measures contrary to the treaty by the Member State concerned take place over a longer period of time and will continue in the future. A single (even serious) violation of one of the Union's values does not suffice to impose sanctions via the Article 7 procedure.[51]

The procedure for initiating the sanction mechanism differs from the previous preventive mechanism. This time, only one third of the Member States (again, not counting the Member State concerned) and the Commission have the right of initiative. The European Parliament has no right to initiate the procedure, which may be due to the fact that this procedure is similar to the infringement action before the Court of Justice under Articles 258 f. TFEU.[52] Still, the European Parliament has to approve the initiative (by a two-thirds majority of the votes cast and by a majority of its members). The Member State concerned must be given the chance to react to the allegations. Whether the state makes use of this possibility is up to it.

The European Council decides by unanimity on the actual existence of a serious and persistent violation of values (without the vote of the Member State concerned). The determination by the European Council has no immediate consequences. However, its decision is a prerequisite for the suspension of certain rights under paragraph 3.[53] The Council alone has both the power of initiative and the power to take decisions on sanctions. A renewed statement by the Member State is no longer required, as the investigation has already been concluded with the procedure under paragraph 2. Sanctions are decided on by qualified majority in the Council, which requires at least 72% of the members of the Council (currently 20) comprising at least 65% of the population, in accordance with Articles 354(2) and 238 (3)(b) TFEU.

3.2.1   Suspension of Rights

In case of a "serious and persistent breach" and a determination to this end, the Council may adopt sanctions in the form of the suspension of rights stemming from the Treaties. Specifically, Article 7(3) TEU mentions the withdrawal of the sanctioned state's voting rights in the Council, but it may also exclude it

---

50   Nowak, (2017) *supra* note 36, para. 15.
51   Cf. Schorkopf, (2017) *supra* note 33 at para. 34.
52   Cf. ibid., para. 29.
53   Pechstein, (2018) *supra* note 48 at paras. 15-16.

from the European Council's decision-making. The consequence is that henceforth decisions can be taken in the Council without any influence by the state concerned. On the other hand, members of other institutions not representing the Member State itself, i.e. the Commissioner with the nationality of the Member State concerned or MEPs from that country, may not be deprived of their rights.[54]

The Council may only suspend rights of the Member State concerned, not obligations. The decision under paragraph 3 is intended to deprive the Member State of specific benefits and advantages from the Treaties. Whether this may also include funding is disputed among scholars,[55] but has lost its relevance with the introduction of the so-called conditionality mechanism.[56] As the suspension concerns only *rights*, the decisions taken by the Union are still binding on the Member State concerned, which is spelled out by subparagraph 2 of the provision, stating that "obligations of the Member State … shall in any case continue to be binding".

The extent of the sanctions is determined by the Council without, of course, considering the vote of the sanctioned state. While the Council has a wide margin of appreciation, it must observe the principle of proportionality (Article 5(4) TEU) when choosing sanction measures. According to this, the decisions must be necessary and appropriate for the goal, i.e. the restoration of compliance with the Union's values and thus the homogeneity within the EU. To this end, there must be no milder means besides the sanctions decided upon.[57] Sanctions under Article 7 TEU are not a penalty and a means in itself, but instead an injunction aimed at restoring compliance with the Union's values and preventing new infringements.[58]

The imposition of sanctions is further limited by the so-called 'Union citizen protection clause' as a manifestation of the principle of proportionality. According to this, the Council "shall take into account the possible consequences of such a suspension on the rights and obligations of natural and

---

[54] With a different view Peers, 'Can a Member State be expelled or suspended from the EU? Updated overview of Article 7 TEU' (4 April 2022) EU Law Analysis, <https://eulawanalysis.blogspot.com/2022/04/can-member-state-be-expelled-or.html> accessed 1 December 2023.

[55] For this possibility, see Ruffert, 'Artikel 7 EUV' in Calliess and Ruffert (eds), *EUV/AEUV* (6th edn. C.H.Beck 2022) para. 29; against: Schorkopf, (2017) *supra* note 33 at para. 43.

[56] See on this the contribution by *Symann* in this volume.

[57] Cf. Nowak, (2017) *supra* note 36, para. 19.

[58] Cf. with a critical view, Kassner, *Die Unionsaufsicht, Ausmaß und Bedeutung des Überwachungsmechanismus nach Art. 7 des Vertrages über die Europäische Union* (Peter Lang 2003) at 138.

legal persons", which, with regard to Article 18 TFEU, covers mostly (but not exclusively) Union citizens. The interpretation of 'take into account' is crucial here. If it were a question of *not affecting* the rights of Union citizens, then sanctions could almost never be imposed under Article 7 TEU. Rather, it is a question of weighing up the EU's interest in restoring homogeneity and the rights and duties of the Union's citizens against each other. In doing so, it must be assumed that the individual shares the Union's interests with regard to the preservation of and respect for values. The ratification requirement of certain decisions represents a further restriction of the content of sanction measures. Since decisions, such as treaty amendments according to Article 48 TEU or the accession of a new Member States according to Article 49 TEU, are dependent on the ratification of all Member States, the sanctioned Member State may not be excluded.[59]

3.2.2   Expulsion

The sanctions discussed so far only include the suspension of membership rights or cutting other advantages stemming from membership in the Union. However, what about membership itself? A frequently discussed question is whether the suspension of certain rights mentioned in Article 7(3) TEU also includes a complete exclusion from the European Union. One could assume that Article 7 TEU can only be called a 'nuclear option' if it would also include the most definitive sanction, i.e. result in the expulsion of a Member State.

Article 7 TEU itself gives no indication that a possible sanction could be the expulsion of a state. Rather, Article 7(3) TEU, in providing that the affected Member State continues to be bound by the obligations arising from the Treaty, insinuates that an expulsion is no possible sanction at all. If exclusion were possible, the described continuation of the binding effect would make no sense. Specifically, the wording "in any case" should be pointed out. It shows that in all cases the contractual obligation to the European Union continues to exist and thus cannot simply be dissolved.[60]

Moreover, an exclusion would also contradict the fundamental idea of the European Union, which the preamble and Article 1 of the TEU describe as "creating an ever closer union among the peoples of Europe".[61] For Article 7 TEU is not about excluding a state from European integration, but rather about demanding compliance with the values in Article 2 TEU. Exclusion as

---

[59]   Pechstein, (2018) *supra* note 48 at para. 19.

[60]   Cf. Träbert, (2010) *supra* note 37 at 327.

[61]   See on this Blanke, 'Article 1 TEU', in Blanke and Mangiameli (eds), *The Treaty on European Union (TEU)* (Springer 2013) para. 24 ff.

a sanction is therefore alien to the system in the European Union.[62] Another argument against exclusion is the principle of reversibility. According to Article 7 (4) TEU, the Council may amend or repeal sanctions. This means that sanctions can be removed at any time and the Member State is re-granted its original rights. The exclusion is an irreversible measure and membership can only be reinstated through a (lengthy) accession procedure in accordance with Article 49 TEU. Thus, the principle of reversibility of sanctions speaks against the possibility of exclusion.[63]

While clearly Article 7 itself does not allow for expulsion, some scholars discuss exclusion from the European Union on the basis of general international law. Article 60 of the Vienna Convention on the Law of Treaties provides in its paragraph 2(a)(i) that "a material breach of a multilateral treaty by one of the parties entitles the other parties by unanimous agreement to suspend the operation of the treaty in whole or in part or to terminate it ... in the relations between themselves and the defaulting State". Clearly, any situation amounting to a 'serious and persistent breach' under Article 7 TEU would constitute a 'material breach' under Article 60 VCLT, thus generally opening the way for an expulsion of a treaty member. However, Article 50 VCLT stipulates in its paragraph 4 that this provision is "without prejudice to any provision in the treaty applicable in the event of a breach", thus codifying the general principle of *lex specialis derogat legi generali.*[64]

Thus, it boils down to the question of general and specific treaty / international law provision. Proponents of the possibility to expel a Member State argue that Article 7 TEU is not a comprehensive provision. They argue that the European Treaties only require having recourse to the Article 7 procedure before any other action is taken. Thus, expulsion under Article 60 VCLT would not be excluded, but could be used as a last resort.[65] Others argue that the European Union is a self-contained regime, thus barring recourse to general norms of international law on sanctioning members.[66] In fact, the system of

---

[62] Cf. Mangiameli and Saputelli, (2013) *supra* note 7 at para. 40.

[63] Hau, (2002) *supra* note 10 at 72-73.

[64] See Giegerich, 'Article 60 VCLT' in Dörr and Schmalenbach (eds), *Vienna Convention on the Law of Treaties - A Commentary* (2nd edn. Springer 2018) para. 68; Villiger, *Commentary on the 1969 Vienna Convention on the Law of Treaties* (Nijhoff 2009), Article 60 para. 22 with reference to the case law of the ICJ.

[65] Nettesheim, 'Ein Ausschluss aus der EU ist als Ultima-Ratio-Maßnahme möglich' (2 November 2021), Verfassungsblog, <https://verfassungsblog.de/ein-ausschluss-aus-der-eu-ist-als-ultima-ratio-masnahme-moglich/> accessed 1 December 2023.

[66] Schorkopf, (2017) *supra* note 33 at para. 54; Giegerich, (2018) *supra* note 63 at para. 70.

rights and obligations that the EU Treaties establish is comprehensive. If the treaty-makers had wished to include the right to exclude a member from the Union, they could (and should) have written in into the Union's constitution. There is no constitutional basis for the arguments that "in every social or legal community, there are exclusion or termination mechanisms with which this community protects itself from the damage that an individual member can cause" and that "there is no evidence to suggest that the founding states of an international organisation such as the EU would have waived this fundamental and elementary right".[67] If the EU Member States *meant* to include this option, they probably would have done so, as for example the Council of Europe's Statute does in its Article 8 (which the treaty-makers must have been aware of). In the end, there is currently no possibility to force a member out of the Union unless that member decides for itself to leave the club (Article 50 TEU).

3.3   Criticism

Events – or better yet: inaction – since the initiation of the two Article 7 procedures show the weaknesses of this instrument. The reasons for this vary.

First of all, the initiation of any stage of the Article 7 procedure is political in nature. It does not come as a surprise that neither of the two cases were initiated by a group of Member States, but instead by the European Commission and the European Parliament as *European* institutions. Still, hesitance on the part of the Council – and further enhanced by the rotating Council presidency[68] – or the European Council has a backlash on the other institutions' likeliness to initiate an Article 7 procedure. This was the case with Poland: One reason for the hesitant behaviour in Brussels was and is the fact that neither the Council nor the European Council actively supported an activation of Article 7.[69] Moreover, the European Commission was aware that the required four-fifths majority of Member States in the Council for a finding of clear risk was not secured. In particular, the Visegrád group around Poland, Hungary, the Czech Republic and Slovakia, but also countries like Austria and Slovenia, which are close to the Visegrád states, can prevent the necessary majority.[70]

---

[67]   Nettesheim, (2021) *supra* note 64.

[68]   Hernández, 'The Powers of the Presidency of the Council of the EU to Shape the Rule of Law Enforcement Agenda: The Article 7 Case' (2023) Journal of Common Market Studies, doi: 10.1111/jcms.13551.

[69]   Coli, 'Article 7 TEU - From a Dormant Provision to an Active Enforcement Tool?' (2018) 10 Perspectives of Federalism, 272-302 at 291.

[70]   Hummer, 'Nutzlose "rote Karte" der Kommission gegen Polen?' (8 January 2018) EU-Infothek <https://www.eu-infothek.com/nutzlose-rote-karte-der-kommission

Secondly, the procedure cannot take effect because the actors involved do not agree on the concrete steps to be taken. In most cases, their own political interests prevail. It must also be clearly stated that the Member States lack the political will to continue the procedure.[71] An indication of this is the lack of hearings regarding Poland between 2019 and 2021. While the Romanian Council Presidency itself had to struggle with constitutional deficits and thus did not hold any hearings, the Finnish Council Presidency did not want to initiate hearings during the Polish parliamentary elections. Furthermore, it was often argued by the governments of the Member States that one must first wait for the judgments by the ECJ in potential parallel infringement proceedings and the Member States' reaction to them.[72]

Practice proved that the procedure mentioned in Article 7 TEU is primarily a political procedure, which allows for a great deal of influence behind the scenes.[73] This is also shown by the (lack of) jurisdiction of the European Court of Justice within the framework of Article 7 TEU, for the ECJ is only competent for procedural matters. Article 7 TEU as a legal procedure thus becomes a mixture of law and politics.[74] Moreover, the ECJ's lack of a clear definition of the concept of the rule of law has ensured that the assessment of a violation of the rule of law in Article 7 TEU is decided according to political rather than legal criteria.[75]

Another point of criticism is the question as to what extent Article 7 TEU can actually contribute to solving the situation in a particular Member State.[76] If there is a finding of a clear risk of a serious breach of the values mentioned in Article 2, it is questionable what impact this would have on the Member

---

-gegen -polen -erstmalige -einleitung -des -sanktionsverfahrens -gem -art -7 -euv -wegen -systemischer-gefaehrdung-des-rechtsstaatsprinz/> accessed 1 December 2023.

[71] Kochenov 'Article 7: A Commentary on a Much Talked-About "Dead" Provision' (2019) University of Groningen Faculty of Law Research Paper No. 21/2019 at 4.

[72] Ibid. at 17.

[73] Closa, Kochenov and Weiler, 'Reinforcing Rule of Law Oversight in the Eur-opean Union' (2014) EUI Working Paper RSCAS 2014/25 at 7.

[74] Kochenov, 'Busting the myths nuclear: A commentary on Article 7 TEU' (2017) EUI Working Paper LAW 2017/10 at 6 f.

[75] Grzeszczak and Karolewski, 'Mind the Gap! Schwierigkeiten der Rech-tssta-atlichkeit in der EU' (26 September 2017) Verfassungsblog, <https://verfassungsblog.de/mind-the-gap-schwierigkeiten-der-rechtsstaatlichkeit-in-der-eu/> accessed 1 December 2023; Serini, *Sanktionen der Europäischen Union bei Verstoß eines Mit-gliedstaats gegen das Demokratie- und Rechtsstaatsprinzip* (Duncker & Humblot 2009) at 196.

[76] Kochenov, (2019) *supra* note 70 at 17.

State's government and its behaviour. Even the 'naming and shaming' effect linked to the findings in Article7 is hardly able to prevent the government from continuing to implement its plans and policies. It can therefore be assumed that a declaratory decision under Article 7 (1) TEU would not have much effect. Due to the lack of possible consequences, the claim that Article 7 TEU is 'nuclear' is greatly exaggerated with regard to paragraph 1.

Furthermore, as explained above, the preventive mechanism in paragraph 1 is no prerequisite to the sanctions procedure under paragraph 2. In both of the current cases it is clear that we are no longer dealing with a 'risk', but actual breaches. Why the European Commission did not immediately initiate the sanction mechanism is, however, both regrettable and equally obvious and understandable. Due to the unanimity requirement in the Council for the declaratory decision, the European Commission faces a major hurdle. The political situation in the EU makes unanimity seem impossible. As explained above, there is close support between the Visegrád states. In the case of Poland, Hungarian Prime Minister *Viktor Orbán* pledged his support to the Polish government. As long as Hungary lays its protective hand over Poland, the country does not have to fear sanctions under Article 7.[77] This, of course, holds true for the other way around. Economic or political interests of individual Member States thus determine the entire action of the European Union in this procedure. In case of more than one disobedient state, the situation is clear: There's honour among thieves. With Hungary's announcement to boycott the vote for any sanctions under Article 7 against Poland, the sanctions procedure, too, is deprived of its effect as a 'nuclear option'. Thus, a collusion of two Member States can completely undermine and nullify the potential effects of Article 7. Historically, however, it can be assumed that the treaty-makers did not foresee that there would ever be such a serious violation of the Union's values in several states at the same time. But there is no guarantee for the application of sanctions with a reduced majority requirement either, as the case (non-application) of the EMU's deficit procedures in the early 2000s excellently proved.

There have been several suggestions to overcome this situation. In the political arena, some argue that the existence of a breach of values and possible sanctions in several Member States should be decided on together, which would exclude all Member States in question from the vote. Some specify this idea by establishing some prerequisites for a common procedure.

---

[77] Scheppele. 'Can Poland be Sanctioned by the EU? Not Unless Hungary is Sanctioned Too' (24 October 2016) Verfassungsblog, <https:// verfassungsblog .de/can-poland-be-sanctioned-by-the-eu-not-unless-hungary-is-sanctioned-too/> accessed 1 December 2023.

On the one hand, there must be materially similar violations of the values of Article 2 TEU by both Member States. Secondly, it must be shown that there is a "well-founded suspicion of collusive behaviour by the Member States concerned with a view to preventing a unanimity decision by the European Council".[78] However, the wording of Article 7 TEU (in conjunction with Article 354 TFEU) is clear: The procedure is directed against a single Member State. If two or more Member States are affected, individual proceedings have to be initiated.[79] This result can also be derived from the consequences for the calculation of the qualified majority, which would lead to considerable shifts if several Member States were affected.[80]

Another idea is to extend the restriction of voting rights in own cases contained in Article 354(1) TFEU to all pending Article 7 procedures. In other words, "no state that has already been warned under Article 7(1) should be able to vote against sanctions raised against any other state under Article 7(2)".[81] This, too, however, would hardly be covered by the provision's wording, which is designed for a single procedure against a single Member State. Furthermore, even with a common procedure, neither the four-fifths majority nor unanimity is guaranteed. In the current cases, there are still countries in Eastern and South-Eastern Europe which do not take a clear position against Poland and Hungary. The danger of an even deeper division of the EU would be too great with such a procedure.[82]

4. CONCLUSIONS AND OUTLOOK

It is not without cause when former Polish Foreign Minister *Jacek Czaputowicz* considered that "Article 7 is dead; the European Commission has lost"[83] or when Vice-President of the EU Commission *Margaritis Schinas* held that

---

[78] Thiele, 'Art. 7 EUV im Quadrat? Zur Möglichkeit von Rechtsstaats-Verfahren gegen mehrere Mitgliedsstaaten' (24 July 2017) Verfassungsblog, <https://verfassungsblog.de/art-7-euv-im-quadrat-zur-moeglichkeit-von-rechtsstaats-verfahren-gegen-mehrere-mitgliedsstaaten/> accessed 1 December 2023 (our translation).

[79] Symann, *Schutz der Rechtsstaatlichkeit durch europäisches Haushaltsrecht: Plädoyer für einen neuen Sanktionsmechanismus* (Mohr Siebeck 2021) at 47.

[80] Schorkopf, (2017) *supra* note 33 at para. 21.

[81] Scheppele, (2019) *supra* note 76.

[82] Okonska, Debatte: Artikel 7 gegen Ungarn und Polen gleichzeitig?' (8 August 2017), <https://www.treffpunkteuropa.de/debatte-artikel-7-gegen-ungarn-und-polen-gleichzeitig?lang=fr> accessed 1 December 2023 .

[83] Polska, "Artykuł 7 jest martwy; Komisja Europejska przegrała" (11 December 2018), <https://www.polsatnews.pl/wiadomosc/2018-12-11/czaputowicz-kosiniak-kamysz-goscmi-wydarzen-i-opinii-transmisja/> accessed 1 December 2023.

a continuation of the Article 7 procedure made no sense.[84] Article 7 does in fact *not* work as a 'nuclear option'. The procedure has so far not proved to be a suitable means of resolving systemic deficits in Member States and the tensions between Brussels and the capitals. On the contrary, the fronts appear to be even more hardened and the scope for solutions within *this* procedure is becoming smaller and smaller. Political alliances paralyse the procedure and make it a 'blunt sword'.[85] This formulation seems very appropriate in the current situation. A sword can be used to deter opponents, to defend oneself, but also to win battles. A blunt sword, however, does not pose a direct threat to the opponent. And this is also the case with Article 7 TEU.

Against this background, other instruments have been considered and implemented, which tackle the issue of non-compliance with the Union's values at other angles.[86] One is the less formal rule of law dialogue that the European Commission designed as a sort of pre-Article 7 instrument. Practice shows, however, that there is no real effect in this either. This is why ways have been sought to grab the 'rouge states' by the purse. The conditionality mechanism links EU funding to compliance with rule of law standards.[87] This, as opposed to other instruments and approaches, seems to have an actual effect on states' behaviour. However, it was designed against the background of the current situation and does not mean that it could work as a universal tool to defend other EU values (if need be).

Nonetheless, it does not mean that Article 7 is a dead letter provision *per se*. The *approach* contained in Article 7 TEU is a unique procedure in the European Treaties to identify a (imminent) violation of the Union's values and to re-establish compliance with these values while at the same time keeping the state in question within the community. But the 'blunt sword' needs to be sharpened.

One aspect is to remove the *political* momentum from the procedure, which at the same time could (and should) make it faster and more expedient. In order to make the initiation of Article 7 TEU less dependent on and less vulnerable to political motives, the establishment of an expert committee has been suggest-

---

[84]   Brzozowski, 'Schinas: EU approach to Poland eyes results, "nuclear option" not on the table' (10 December 2021), <https:// www .euractiv .com/ section/ politics/ short _news/ schinas -eu -approach -to -poland -eyes -results -nuclear -option -not -on -the -table/ ? _ga = 2 .187596975 .646415762 .1642931461 -1032481223 .1642931461> accessed 1 December 2023.

[85]   As referred to by Träbert, (2010) *supra* note 37 at 95.

[86]   See on these other instruments the contribution by *Bauerschmidt* in this volume. See further Germelmann, 'Alternativen zum Rechtsstaatsverfahren nach Art. 7 EUV?' (2021) Die Öffentliche Verwaltung, 193-204 at 196 ff.

[87]   See in more detail the contribution by *Symann* in this volume.

ed.[88] The committee, composed of one expert per Member State, could send an 'early warning' to the Member State. Should the state fail to take satisfactory measures within a specified deadline, Article 7(1) TEU would automatically be activated, which would prevent a deadlock in the institutions (especially the Council). Furthermore, a role could be foreseen for the European Court of Justice, for example for the decision on sanctions. However, this change in procedure is possible only with a treaty amendment.

Meanwhile, the European Parliament, as a response to the recent Conference on the Future of Europe, has adopted a proposal for a comprehensive treaty revision.[89] The rule of law is one of the explicit areas for which Parliament suggests adaptions in the light of past shortcoming, namely "to strengthen and reform the procedure in Article 7 TEU with regard to the protection of the rule of law by ending unanimity, introducing a clear timeframe, and by making the Court of Justice the arbiter of violations".[90] More specifically, it proposes Article 7 TEU in the following form:[91]

1. On a reasoned proposal by one third of the Member States, by the European Parliament or by the European Commission, the Council, acting by a *qualified* majority after obtaining the consent of the European Parliament, *shall* determine *within six months of receiving a proposal whether* there is a clear risk of a serious breach by a Member State of the values referred to in Article 2. Before making such a determination, the Council shall hear the Member State in question and may address recommendations to it, acting in accordance with the same procedure.

    The Council shall regularly verify that the grounds on which such a determination was made continue to apply.

2. The Council, acting by *a qualified majority within six months of receiving* a proposal by one third of the Member States, *by the European Parliament, acting by a majority of its component Members, or by the Commission,* may *submit an application to the Court of Justice on* the existence of a serious and persistent breach by a Member State of the values referred to in Article 2.

> *The Court of Justice shall decide on the application after inviting the Member State in question to submit its observations.*

3.   Where a determination under paragraph 2 has been made, the Council, acting by a qualified majority, *shall* decide *within six months thereof to take appropriate measures. Such measures may include the suspension of commitments and payments from the Union's budget, or the suspension of* certain of the rights deriving from the application of the Treaties to the Member State in question, including the voting rights of the representative of the government of that Member State in the Council *and the right of the Member State in question to hold the Presidency of the Council.* In doing so, the Council shall take into account the possible consequences of such a suspension on the rights and obligations of natural and legal persons.

   The obligations of the Member State in question under the Treaties shall in any case continue to be binding on that State.

4.   The Council, acting by a qualified majority, may decide subsequently to vary or revoke measures taken under paragraph 3 in response to changes in the situation which led to their being imposed.

5.   The voting arrangements applying to the European Parliament, the European Council and the Council for the purposes of this Article are laid down in Article 354 of the Treaty on the Functioning of the European Union.

The reform of the Article 7 procedure is but one of many proposals the European Parliament makes.[92] The suggested amendments take account of the deficiencies and shortcomings that this procedure has seen in the past. If amended in this sense, Article 7 TEU (new) could indeed become a 'sharp sword', maybe even the 'nuclear option' that it was said to be in the beginning.

---

[92]   The resolution counts 245 amendments in total, some formal and minor, others fundamental in nature.

12. Financial Sanctions as a Remedy to Enforce the Rule of Law in Poland and Hungary

Malte Symann[1]

1. RULE OF LAW BACKSLIDING IN THE EU

Over the last years, the rule of law and other fundamental pillars of our European democracy came increasingly under threat in Hungary and Poland – as the most prominent examples – but also in other EU Member States. In these Member States, as well as other countries worldwide, we can observe that it is often the same types of fundamental rights that are dismantled first, i.e., the independency of the judiciary and media and election laws. In the EU, these types of laws are indeed, and for good reasons, to a large extent regulated at national level – and that should not change. However, being member of the value-based EU comes not only with benefits but also with important obligations. There are certain boundaries for these fundamental pillars of a democratic society which must be observed in all Member States to ensure the proper functioning of the EU and, more importantly, the fundamental rights of each and every EU citizen.[2]

1.1 Poland, Hungary and Other Member States

For Hungary, the backsliding began when Prime Minister *Viktor Orbán* – notably once a strong supporter of European and democratic values – came into power again in 2010. Ever since, he has tightened his grip on the media, judiciary, and his own party to promote and strengthen his project of an

[1] The views expressed in this chapter are the author's own. The author would like to thank *Freya Schramm* and *Ferdinand Schmidt-Feuerheerd* for their valuable support on this contribution.

[2] On the notion of the rule of law see also the chapters by *Raitio* and by *Bauerschmidt* in this volume.

'illiberal democracy'.[3] In Poland, the ruling PiS party – promoting itself as a defender of 'Law and Justice' – came into power in 2005 and again in 2015.[4] Under the rule of *Jarosław Kaczyński*, the party leader, PiS and the government became increasingly hostile towards the independent judiciary and independent media.[5]

But while these two Member States have suffered by far the most from rule of law backsliding, the rule of law is under threat in other Member States, too. For instance, reforms of the judiciary and a high level of corruption in Bulgaria and Romania have raised concerns in Brussels and other European capitals.[6] Also the most recent election results in Slovakia remind us of several severe corruption scandals and, more generally, threats against independent media under former Prime Minister *Fico*.[7] These breaches of rule of law are serious in themselves and any further backsliding should be avoided. However, on a global perspective, the rule of law deficiencies which can be observed in these countries are, at least currently, less challenging (and dangerous) for the EU than the Hungarian and Polish deficiencies.

---

[3] Kelemen, 'Europe's Other Democratic Deficit: National Authoritarianism in Eur-ope's Democratic Union' (2017) 52 Government and Opposition 2, 211 ff. at 221 f.

[4] Symann, *Schutz der Rechtsstaatlichkeit durch europäisches Haushaltsrecht* (Mohr Siebeck 2021) at 25 f.

[5] For an overview see e.g. Blanke and Sander, 'Die europäische Rechtsstaatlichkeit und ihre Widersacher – Anmerkungen zur Situation in Polen mit einem Seitenblick auf Ungarn' (2023) 54 Europarecht, 62 ff.; Symann, (2021) *supra* note 4 at 31 f.

[6] The developments relating to the Rule of Law in European Member States are monitored by the European Commission and subject to the annual Rule of Law Report accessible on the Commission Website <https://commission.europa.eu/strategy-and-policy/policies/justice-and-fundamental-rights/upholding-rule-law/rule-law/rule-law-mechanism_en> accessed 23 October 2023; for Bulgaria and Romania, the Commission also published several progress reports under the Cooperation and Verification Mechanism on its website <https://commission.europa.eu/strategy-and-policy/policies/justice-and-fundamental-rights/upholding-rule-law/rule-law/assistance-bulgaria-and-romania-under-cvm/reports-progress-bulgaria-and-romania_en> accessed 29 October 2023; Symann, (2021) *supra* note 4 at 38 f.

[7] Lopatka and Hovet, 'Pro-Russion ex-PM wins Slovak election, needs allies for government' (2023), Reuters, <https://www.reuters.com/world/europe/slovaks-choose-between-pro-russian-ex-pm-fico-pro-western-liberals-2023-09-29/> accessed 23 October 2023. See the chapter "Slovakia" in Liebich, *The Politics of a Disillusioned Europe* (Palgrave Macmillen 2021) at 67 ff.

1.2 Judiciary, Media, and Elections Laws – Always the Same Type of Targets?

When taking a closer look at these countries, one can observe that the main challenges for the rule of law mostly revolve around three main topics: undermining the independency of the judiciary,[8] putting independent media on the leash, and fiddling with election laws. The main objective is always to keep the ruling party in power and protect its supporters against investigations by the judiciary and independent media. This 'cocktail' allows corruption to flourish, often supporting the members of the ruling party(ies) and their near ones financially and otherwise.[9]

For instance, in its decision to recommend financial sanctions against Hungary, the Commission noted "an increase in concentration of awards in public procurement [and] an increase in the odds of winning for actors of the Hungarian ruling party", which the Commission corroborated with a "statistical empirical analysis" as well as reports by media and stakeholders.[10] This describes only superficially that many indicators show that Hungary indeed has a significant corruption problem.[11] Also for Poland, indicators and various reports show that corruption, and thus the risk that Polish and EU funds are not utilized efficiently, is on the rise.[12]

1.3 Why Should the EU – and We All – Care About This?

These shortcomings are most problematic for the Member State, i.e., its society and economy, itself as they suffer from any rule of law backsliding directly. However, also for the EU at a broader level, this is deeply concerning.

The rule of law is enshrined in Article 2 TEU as a fundamental value of the EU:[13] Apart from its importance for all European citizens it is also a fundamental pillar for the functioning of the EU. Without rule of law, European rules and values as well as decisions taken by the EU's democratically elected representatives in the European Parliament and the Council can ultimately not be

---

[8] See also the chapter by *Mikuli, Fox* and *Puchta* in this volume.

[9] For an overview of corruption mechanisms see Bernatt and Jones, 'Populism and public procurement: an EU response to increased corruption and collusion risks in Hungary and Poland' (2022) 41 Yearbook of European Law, 11 ff. at 14 f.

[10] European Commission, 'Proposal for a Council Implementing Decision on measures for the protection of the Union budget breaches of the principles of the rule of law in Hungary', COM(2022) 485 final, Recital 13.

[11] For an overview see Bernatt and Jones, (2022) *supra* note 9 at 25 f.

[12] Ibid. at 28 f.

[13] See also the chapter by *Raitio* in this volume.

enforced throughout the EU. Undermining the rule of law in one Member State is therefore a threat to the EU's functioning as a whole: it is the very essence of the EU that diverging interests of Member States are debated and resolved by European institutions and such solutions are adhered to in the entire EU. If that principle cannot be upheld, the EU loses trust first and foremost among its citizens but also as a global actor which it aspires to be.

Moreover, the cooperation of Member States, i.e., of the Member States' judiciaries and administrations, cannot be upheld if serious rule of law deficiencies persists in certain Member States: national (constitutional) courts like the German *Bundesverfassungsgericht* may intervene (even more forcefully) and demand to suspend the cooperation with certain Member States, e.g., with regard to the European arrest warrant, if the protection of fundamental rights cannot be ensured in all Member States.[14] This would have serious consequences for the EU, and its citizens, as a whole. Moreover, having a strong and efficient rule of law, capable of fighting corruption and ensuring a predictable investment climate, is a precondition for a sustainable economic development benefiting the Member State itself but also the EU as a whole.[15]

The EU therefore has a strong interest in protecting its values and the rule of law. Already before the new Conditionality Mechanism was introduced, the EU had several tools at its disposal to take action against Member States breaching the European rule of law and European rules more generally. This included, inter alia, the Article 7 TEU proceeding and the infringement procedure according to Articles 258 f. TFEU.[16]

However, the developments in Poland and Hungary in particular proved that these tools are not sufficient to ensure the universal application of the rule of law in the EU.[17] In fact, the many infringement proceedings against Poland

---

[14]   This is also acknowledged in ECJ, Case C-216/18 PPU, *Minister for Justice and Equality (Deficiencies in the system of justice)*, EU:C:2018:586, paras. 60 f.; Symann, (2021) *supra* note 4 at 16 f.; Wendel, 'Mutual Trust, Essence and Federalism – Between Consolidating and Fragmenting the Area of Freedom, Security and Justice after LM' (2019) 15 EuConst 1, 17 ff.

[15]   Candela and Piano, 'Rule of Law' in Marciano and Ramello (eds.), *Encyclopedia on Law and Economics* (Springer 2017); Kazai, 'Economic Interests and the Rule of Law Crisis in the EU' (2020), Verfassungsblog, <https://verfassungsblog .de/ economic -interests -and -the -rule -of -law -crisis -in -the -eu/ > accessed 23 October 2023.

[16]   On the Article 7 TEU proceeding see the chapters by *Bauerschmidt* and by *Böttner* and *Schröder* in this volume.

[17]   Blanke and Sander, 'Enforcing the Rule of Law in the EU: The case of Poland and Hungary' (2023) 26 Zeitschrift für Europarechtliche Studien 2, 239 ff.; Symann, (2021) *supra* note 4 at 42 f.

and Hungary may have been helpful to 'correct' certain individual reforms at least prima facie. But overall, these changes were rather cosmetic and did not fundamentally improve the situation in Poland and Hungary.[18] In the eyes of many academics and, ultimately, the European legislator, a more forceful tool is needed to protect European values and the rule of law.

2.   FINANCIAL SANCTIONS FOR POLAND AND HUNGARY

Therefore, another more powerful sanction mechanism which can (i) actually be enforced and (ii) has significant consequences for the Member State concerned was deemed necessary. After years of academic discussions and political debates, the EU finally agreed on a "general regime of conditionality for the protection of the Union budget".[19] This Conditionality Mechanism entered into force on 1 January 2021[20] but, following a controversial political compromise with Poland and Hungary, the Commission started implementing this mechanism only after the ECJ had declared its conformity with EU treaties on 16 February 2022.[21]

Next to the Conditionality Mechanism, the European institutions also use the Recovery and Resilience Facility (RRF), which was initially introduced in response to the economic turbulences caused by the Covid-19 pandemic,[22] as a means to strengthen the rule of law in various countries through financial pressure. The RRF allows the EU to set certain milestones for the respective Member State to achieve before any payments are made,[23] which the Commission uses in particular in the case of Hungary and Poland. A third option for the Commission to seek financial sanctions in the case of rule of law backsliding is to bring an infringement proceeding to the ECJ and to seek penalty payments according to Article 260(2) TFEU. While the Commission previously often counted on Member States' willingness to comply with judg-

---

[18]   Kelemen, (2017) *supra* note 3 at 223 f. concludes that the Commission has "won the battle but lost the war".

[19]   Parliament and Council, Regulation (EU, Euratom) 2020/2092 on a general regime of conditionality for the protection of the Union budget [2020] OJ L 433I/1 (hereafter 'Conditionality Mechanism Regulation').

[20]   Ibid., Article 10.

[21]   ECJ, Case C-156/21, *Hungary v Parliament and Council,* EU:C:2022:97 and ECJ, Case C-157/21, *Poland v Parliament and Council,* EU:C:2022:97. See also the chapter by *Bauerschmidt* in this volume.

[22]   Parliament and Council, Regulation (EU) 2021/241 establishing the Recovery and Resilience Facility [2021] OJ L 57, p. 17 f. (hereafter "RRF Regulation").

[23]   Articles 20 (5) and 24 RRF Regulation.

ments rendered by the highest court in the EU without such financial sanctions, it has started using this option more, in particular in the case of Poland.

2.1 Hungary

The Commission applied the Conditionality Mechanism for the first time against Hungary: On 18 September 2022, the Commission recommended to essentially block the payment of approximately EUR 7.5 billion to Hungary.[24] In its decision, the Commission listed in particular "systemic irregularities, deficiencies and weakness in public procurement", and noted inter alia "a systemic inability, failure or unwillingness, on the part of the Hungarian authorities, to prevent decisions that are in breach of the applicable law, as regards public procurement and conflicts of interest, and thus to adequately tackle risks of corruption. They constitute breaches of the principle of the rule of law, in particular the principles of legal certainty and prohibition of arbitrariness of the executive powers and raise concerns as regards the separation of powers".[25] The Commission further noted "additional issues as regard limitations to effective investigation and prosecution of alleged criminal activity, the organisation of the prosecution services, and the absence of a functioning and effective anti-corruption network".[26]

To avoid financial sanctions for these severe infringements of the rule of law, the Hungarian government had previously submitted 17 remedial measures to address the Commission's concerns. These included inter alia a newly established Integrity Authority, an Anti-Corruption Task Force, closer cooperation with the European anti-fraud office OLAF and several administrative measures.[27] The Commission acknowledged that these remedial measures would in principle address the concerns if implemented correctly. In essence, however, the Commission – given the history of breaches of rule of law in Hungary probably rightly so – wanted to confirm a change in practices 'on the ground' before financial sanctions are withdrawn.[28] Therefore, the

---

[24] European Commission, 'Proposal for a Council Implementing Decision on mea-sures for the protection of the Union budget against breaches of the principles of the rule of law in Hungary", COM(2022), 485 final, Article 2. See also the chapter by *Bauerschmidt* in this volume, and Blanke and Sander, (2023) *supra* note 5, 78 f.

[25] COM(2022) 485 final, Recital 11.

[26] Ibid., Recital 12.

[27] Ibid., Recitals 26 f.

[28] Ibid., Recitals 27 f.

Commission initially recommended that 65% of the budgetary commitments under three cohesion programs should be suspended.[29]

To show implementation progress, Hungary further provided the Commission with an overview of the remedial measures taken already in November 2022. The Commission examined these measures and published its assessment on 30 November 2022,[30] with a further update on 9 December 2022.[31] The Commission again acknowledged the importance of the remedial measures but, overall, came to the conclusion that the steps taken by Hungary thus far would in fact "put an end to the relevant breaches of the principles of the rule of law [and] risks to the sound financial management of the Union's budget", but in particular referred to the "ensuing uncertainty about their application in practice".[32]

Following debates and a compromise in the Coreper on 12 December 2022, the Council adopted its final implementing decision on 15 December 2022:[33] the Council acknowledged the remedial measures announced by Hungary to address the Commission's concerns and noted that some of these measures had been implemented or were in the process of being implemented already.[34] However, the Council noted that "important weaknesses, risks and shortcomings" remained and that the measures taken so far would "not put an end to the identified breaches of the principles of the rule of law".[35]

Accordingly, the Council decided to suspend 55% of the budgetary commitments of the EU under three operational programmes of the EU's Cohesion

---

[29]   The three operational programmes concerned are the Environmental and Energy Efficiency Operational Programme Plus, the Integrated Transport Operational Programme Plus, and the Territorial and Settlement Development Operational Programme Plus. Ibid., Article 2.

[30]   European Commission, 'On the remedial measures notified by Hungary under Regulation (EU, Euroatom) 2020/2092 for the protection of the Union budget', COM(2022) 687 final.

[31]   European Commission, Letter on the Council Implementing Decision on measures for the protection of the Union budget against breaches of the principles of the rule of law in Hungary, 9 December 2022, Council doc. 15890/22.

[32]   COM(2022) 687 final, in particular para. 155.

[33]   Council Implementing Decision (EU) 2022/2506 of 15 December 2022 on measures for the protection of the Union budget against breaches of the principles of the rule of law in Hungary, [2022] OJ L 325/94.

[34]   Ibid., Recitals 34 f.

[35]   Ibid., Recitals 55 f.

Policy,[36] which amounts to approximately EUR 6.3 billion.[37] Notably, the spending cut is 10 percentage points lower than suggested by the Commission in September 2022 to acknowledge the efforts taken by Hungary already.[38] In addition, the Council obligated Hungary to inform the Commission regularly about the implementation of the remedial measures.[39] So far, the Hungarian government did not file for an annulment action against the decision taken by the European institutions but is still debating remediation actions with the Commission.

Interestingly, instead of the Hungarian government, six Hungarian universities have appealed to the General Court.[40] These universities claim, inter alia, that the Council decision would discriminate against universities maintained by public-interest trusts vis-à-vis those operating under another maintenance model, would interfere with the Member States' competences in education and scientific research and, more generally, would violate the principle of proportionality. In particular, the interests of those ultimately suffering from the financial sanctions mechanism have not been taken into account and that their right to be heard during had been violated. Moreover, in its proceedings against the Council, the university *Debreceni Egyetem* also applied for interim measures to suspend the application of the Article 2(2) of the Council decision, i.e., to effectively suspend the financial sanction against Hungary. The President of the General Court rejected the application of interim measures mainly on the grounds that the university did not prove in detail that its eco-

---

[36] The three operational programmes concerned are the Environmental and Energy Efficiency Operational Programme Plus, the Integrated Transport Operational Programme Plus, and the Territorial and Settlement Development Operational Programme Plus. Council Implementing Decision (EU) 2022/2506, Article 2.

[37] Council, Press release, 'Rule of law conditionality mechanism: Council decides to suspend €6.3 billion given only partial remedial action taken by Hungary', 12 December 2022, <https:// www .consilium .europa .eu/ en/ press/ press-releases/ 2022/ 12/ 12/ rule-of-law-conditionality-mechanism/> accessed 23 October 2023.

[38] Council Implementing Decision (EU) 2022/2506, Recital 60.

[39] Ibid., Article 3.

[40] GC, Case T-115/23, *Debreceni Egyetem v Council*, EU:T:2023:297; GC, Case T-132/23, *Óbudai Egyetem v Council*, pending; GC, Case T-133/23, *Állatorvostudamányi Egyetem v Council*, pending; GC, Case T-138/23, *Semmelweis Egyetem v Council*, pending; GC, Case T-139/23, *Miskolci Egyetem v Council*, pending; GC, Case T-140/23, *Dunaújvárosi Egyetem v Council*, pending.

nomic situation was in fact seriously endangered by the financial sanction of the EU against Hungary.[41]

The General Court is likely to render its final judgment late 2024 and the Hungarian government will certainly follow these proceedings closely. Overall, it seems less likely that the General Court will ultimately render a decision in favour of the universities and annul the Council's decision. One may question already whether the universities have standing according to Article 263(4) TFEU, as they are not the addressees of the Council's decision. In fact, the Conditionality Mechanism only suspends the EU's budgetary commitment to refund the Member States for their disbursements made in accordance with an applied EU programme.[42] In theory, final beneficiaries of existing programmes are therefore protected and should not suffer from a financial sanction against a Member State.

Also in the contested decision, the Council stated that Hungary can still implement the relevant EU programmes so that the rights of the final beneficiaries "are preserved".[43] However, it is questionable, whether this holds true in practice as Hungarian students and researchers may in fact loose access to EU funds as a consequence of the Council's decision, in particular with regards to new programmes and disbursements.[44] Also the Commission acknowledged this.[45] Nevertheless, giving all potentially affected final beneficiaries the right to challenge decisions by the Council under the Conditionality Mechanism would (over-)stretch the requirement of standing.

On substance, the Court has to consider that the applicants as universities benefit from academic freedom, which his enshrined in Article 13 of the EU Charter of Fundamental Rights, and that the Treaties bind the EU to promote its scientific bases (Article 3(3) TEU and Article 179(1) TFEU). Arguably, the EU's financial sanctions against Hungary could undermine this goal and the

---

[41]   GC, Case T-115/23 R, *Debreceni Egyetem v Council*, pending; GC, Case T-115/23, *Debreceni Egyetem v Council*, EU:T:2023:297, paras. 12 f.

[42]   Conditionality Mechanism Regulation, Articles 5 (2), (4) and (5).

[43]   Council Implementing Decision (EU) 2022/2506, Recital 61.

[44]   Ceran and Guerra, 'The Council's Conditionality Decision as a Violation of Academic Freedom?' (2023) Verfassungsblog, <https://verfassungsblog.de/the-coun cils-conditionality-decision-as-a-violation-of-academic-freedom/> accessed 23 October 2023.

[45]   Joint statement by Commissioners Hahn and Gabriel on the application of Council Implementing Decision of 15 December 2022 in relation to Hungarian public interest trusts, 26 January 2023, <https://commission.europa.eu/news/joint -statement -commissioners -hahn -and -gabriel -application -council -implementing -decision-15-december-2023-01-26_en> accessed 23 October 2023.

protection of the Hungarian universities' basic freedoms.[46] However, the protection of universities under Article 13 EUCFR and the Treaties is not absolute and must be balanced against the objectives of the Conditionality Mechanism. Protecting the proper implementation of the EU's budget and, as a broader goal, the rule of law and the fundamental values of the EU as enshrined in Article 2 TEU is of particular importance for the EU's functioning and, one should add, the EU's existence in its current form. Moreover, enforcing the rule of law across the EU also helps to protect universities from undue influence. In this context, the consequences for the universities, however severe they may be for individual students and researchers, are therefore not disproportionate.

When the ECJ rendered its judgment to confirm the lawfulness of the sanction mechanism in general, it also briefly touched upon the protection of final beneficiaries. The ECJ noted that the Member States remain obliged to adhere to pre-existing obligations but that no new obligations are imposed on Member States.[47] As a consequence, the ECJ implicitly admitted that (new) final beneficiaries who would benefit from new disbursements co-financed by the EU may indeed be affected by the Conditionality Mechanism. In light of the important objectives of the Conditionality Mechanism and if the respective decision is proportionate, such consequences on (new) final beneficiaries are, albeit regrettable from a policy perspective, inevitable and acceptable. It is therefore unlikely that the General Court will concur with the Hungarian universities on substance and block the implementation of the sanction against Hungary. However, this legal action reminds the Commission that, both under its legal obligation according to Article 5 (2), (4) and (5) Conditionality Mechanism Regulation and from a broader policy perspective to ensure continued support for its measures to protect the rule of law, it must ensure that final beneficiaries are protected as much as possible.

Next to the Conditionality Mechanism, the European institutions also use the RRF as leverage in its battle for the rule of law in Hungary: The RRF for Hungary foresees an overall allocation of approximately EUR 5.8 billion of EU funds for investments in Hungary in particular to strengthen its sustainable development and digital transition.[48] On 13 December 2022, the Council in

---

[46] See also the debate on this issue in Ceran and Guerra, (2023) *supra* note 44.

[47] See above and ECJ, Case C-156/21 *Hungary v Parliament and Council,* EU: C:2022:97 and ECJ, Case C-157/21, *Poland v Parliament and Council,* EU:C:2022:97, paras. 115, 150, 310 f., in particular 312.

[48] Council Implementing Decision on the approval of the assessment of the recovery and resilience plan for Hungary, Council doc. 15447/22, Article 2. For an overview of measures planned for Hungary, see Hungary's recovery and resilience plan <https://commission.europa.eu/business-economy-euro/economic-recovery/

principle approved the Commission's assessment of the Hungarian Recovery and Resilience Programme.[49] However, for Hungary, the Commission suggested – and the Council adopted – 27 "super milestones" to strengthen its rule of law by, inter alia, various institutional reforms such as establishing an Integrity Authority, an Anti-Corruption Task Force and monitoring and control systems as well as strengthening the independence of the Hungarian Supreme Court.[50] These "super milestones" to a large extent overlap with the requirements addressed under the Conditionality Mechanism, as discussed above, and address the same recommendations which the Commission had already given earlier as part of the European Semester process.[51]

At several occasions, the implementing act strengthens the need that "those measures are effectively implemented before the submission of the first payment request", which the Commission will assess according to Article 24 RRF Regulation. In essence, the RRF programme for Hungary is effectively blocked until the reforms to ensure the protection of the Unions budget and, more broadly, fight corruption and strengthen the rule of law are implemented. Together with the sanctions under the Conditionality Mechanism, Hungary has no access to overall approximately EUR 12 billion.

Given the size of the Hungarian economy and its overall economic situation, this financial sanction, next to debates and other judicial and political pressure, seems to start bearing fruits as Hungary has already taken several steps to address the European institutions' concerns. In particular, it has

---

recovery-and-resilience-facility/country-pages/hungarys-recovery-and-resilience-plan_en> accessed 23 October 2023.

[49] Council, Communication (EU) CM 5860/22 on written procedure of 15 December 2022. Only recently and in light of the energy crisis, Hungary has suggested to amend its plan to increase spendings. See Commission, Daily News MEX/23/4321 (EU) (1 September 2023) <https://ec.europa.eu/commission/presscorner/detail/en/mex_23_4321> accessed 23 October 2023.

[50] Recitals 56 et seq. of and Annex to the proposed Council Implementing Decision, *supra* note 48. See also Parliament and Policy Department for Budgetary Affairs, Briefing (EU), PE 741.581 on Rule of law-related 'super milestones' in the recovery and resilience plans of Hungary and Poland, <https://www.europarl.europa.eu/ RegData/ etudes/ BRIE/ 2023/ 741581/ IPOL _BRI(2023)741581 _EN.pdf> accessed 23 October 2023, at 2 f.

[51] Council, Recommendation (EU) 2019/C 301/17 on the 2019 National Reform Programme of Hungary and delivering a Council Opinion on the 2019 Convergence Programme of Hungary [2019] OJ C 301, p. 17, Recommendation 4; Council Reco-mmendation (EU) 2020/C 282/17 on the 2020 National Reform Programme of Hungary and delivering a Council Opinion on the 2020 Convergence Programme of Hungary [2020] OJ C 282, p. 17, Recommendation 4.

strengthened the role of the National Judicial Council and the independence of the Supreme Court Curia and is introducing various anti-corruption measures.[52] Nevertheless, it remains to be seen how effective these reforms will be and whether and when Hungary will also implement the remaining important reforms to strengthen the rule of law. In fact, several important concerns expressed in the Commission's decision on the Conditionality Mechanism, milestones for the RRF programme as well as in the rule of law report for Hungary remain unaddressed.[53]

In addition, the Commission continues to use infringement proceedings for rule of law deficiencies. While the Commission is generally successful before the ECJ with these proceedings, the implementation of the ECJ's rulings in Hungary, i.e., changes and tangible improvements to the rule of law situation on the ground is a different matter.[54] Most recently, the Commission initiated infringement proceedings with a view to an Hungarian law which, according to the Commission, violates basic rights of sexual minorities[55] and with a view to a decision of the Hungarian Media Council's decision to reject an application for the use of radio spectrum on "highly questionable grounds".[56] However, unlike for Poland as outlined below, infringement proceedings against Hungary for its rule of law backsliding have not yet resulted in significant direct financial consequences.

---

[52] European Commission, '2023 Rule of Law Report - Country Chapter on the rule of law situation in Hungary', COM(2023) 817 final, p. 3 f. and 10 f.

[53] Ibid., p. 2. Hungarian civil society organization equally see certain progress but overall remain sceptical of the Hungarian steps to address the concerns. See Amnesty International, Eötvös Károly Institute, TASZ, Hungarian Helsinki Committee and Monitor and Transparency International, 'Assessment of the Compliance of Hungary with conditions to access European Union funds' (2023), <https://transparency.hu/wp-content/uploads/2023/04/HU_EU_funds_assessment _Q1_2023.pdf> accessed 23 October 2023.

[54] For an overview, Symann, (2021) *supra* note 4 at 30 f.

[55] ECJ, Case C-769/22, *Commission v Hungary*, pending; European Commission, Press release IP 22/2689, 'Commission refers Hungary to the Court of Justice of the EU for violation of LGTBTIQ rights' (15 July 2022) <https://ec .europa.eu/commission/presscorner/detail/en/ip_22_2689> accessed 23 October 2023.

[56] ECJ, Case C-92/23, *Commission v Hungary*, pending; European Commission, Press release IP 22/2689, (2022) *supra* note 55.-

2.2   Poland

Next to Hungary, Poland is the other Member State which raises most rule of law concerns. However, the Commission has not yet applied the Conditionality Mechanism against Poland. This may partly also be due to political reasons – i.e. the Commission acknowledging Poland's role in the EU's reaction to the Russian war against Ukraine, including the fact that Poland has welcomed more than 1.5 million refugees,[57] to keep more room for discussion with Poland and to have an additional means of escalation in reserve.

But, as with Hungary, the Commission uses the RRF for Poland as a means to put financial pressure on Poland to improve the rule of law. Overall, Poland is entitled to support of approximately EUR 22.5 billion in grants and approximately EUR 11.5 billion in loans.[58] Before any payments are made, however, Poland must meet milestones "for a reform strengthening the independence and impartiality of courts, a reform to remedy the situation of judges affected by the decisions of the Disciplinary Chamber of the Supreme Court [...] and a reform ensuring an effected audit and control of Poland's Recovery and Resiliency Program, including protection of the financial interests of the Union".[59]

Regarding the independence of the judiciary, the Council implementing decision requests that all disciplinary cases relating to judges should be transferred to "another chamber [...] meeting the requirements of independence, impartiality, and being established by law" and that any judge should be able to "initiate a verification of whether a court meets the requirements of independence, impartiality, and being established by law". In doing so, the Council Implementing Decision specifically 'targets' the Polish Disciplinary chamber which, as discussed below, has also been the object of infringement proceedings. However, the Council Implementing Decision does not address all country-specific recommendations for Poland's judiciary system[60] and requirements set by the Court of Justice which led to legal actions against the

---

[57] For more statistics see the UNHCR data on the Ukraine Refugee Situation: <https://data.unhcr.org/en/situations/ukraine>.

[58] Council Implementing Decision (EU) 9728/22 on the approval of the assessment of the recovery and plan for Poland, Council doc. 9728/22, Articles 2 and 3.

[59] Ibid., Recital 45.

[60] Council Recommendation of 20 July 2020 on the 2020 National Reform Programme of Poland and delivering a Council opinion on the 2020 Convergence Programme of Poland [2020] OJ C 282/135, Recommendation 4; Council Recommendation of 9 July 2019 on the 2019 National Reform Programme of Poland and delivering a Council opinion on the 2019 Convergence Programme of Poland [2019] OJ C 301/123, Recital 19.

Council Implementing Decision[61] and the Commission's financing and loan agreements.[62] In any event, Poland has not yet implemented all these milestones but has only taken initial steps to remedy the situation, in particular by reforming the disciplinary systems for judges (see also below).[63] Therefore, the disbursement of these funds is effectively blocked. Poland has not appealed this decision yet but seems to continue to engage in discussions with the Commission – which may be more fruitful under a new government following the elections in October 2023.

The Commission has made use of its powers to initiate infringement proceedings against Poland for its rule of law deficiencies.[64] Most importantly, following unsuccessful discussions on the judicial reform of 2019, the Commission launched an infringement proceeding with a view to the newly established Disciplinary Chamber for judges as well as other provisions which were widely understood as undermining the judicial independence. With an interim order, the ECJ required Poland to immediately suspend the application of the relevant laws and, in effect, the work of the Disciplinary Chamber in July 2021.[65] In October 2021, the ECJ dismissed the application of Poland seeking to cancel the interim order[66] and, at the request of the Commission, ordered a periodic penalty payment of 1m Euros for each day the Disciplinary Chamber would remain effective.[67] In response to this unprecedented penalty payment order, Poland implemented several changes to its disciplinary system for judges and, in particular, abolished the Disciplinary Chamber by law.[68] However, other provisions as well as decisions taken by the Disciplinary Chamber remained (partially) in effect, so that the ECJ only reduced the periodic penalty payment to EUR 500,000 per day.[69]

In June 2023, the ECJ rendered its final judgment and found that main parts of the Polish judicial reform of 2019 conflict with EU law, in particular the introduction of the Disciplinary Chamber and other rules affecting the independence of Polish judges.[70] It remains to be seen if and how Poland will implement this judgment and if the Commission will seek new penalty pay-

---

[61] GC, Case T-530/22, *Medel v Council*, pending; GC, Case T-533/22, *Rechters voor Rechters v Council*, pending.

[62] GC, Case T-116/23, *Medel v Commission*, pending.

[63] Blanke and Sander, (2023) *supra* note 5 at 73 f.

[64] For an overview see also Symann, (2021) *supra* note 4 at 36 f.

[65] ECJ, Case C-204/21 R, *Commission v Poland*, EU:C:2021:593.

[66] ECJ, Case C-204/21 R, *Commission v Poland*, EU:C:2021:834.

[67] ECJ, Case C-204/21 R, *Commission v Poland*, EU:C:2021:878.

[68] ECJ, Case C/204/21 R, *Commission v Poland*, EU:C:2023:334, paras. 25 f.

[69] ECJ, Case C-204/21 R, *Commission v Poland*, EU:C:2023:334.

[70] ECJ, Case C-204/21, *Commission v Poland*, EU:C:2023:442.

ments for non-compliance. In any event, Poland continues to be obliged to pay the penalty payments accrued during the interim proceedings. As it is unlikely that the Polish government will indeed transfer this amount, also given the political signals this would entail, the Commission may deduct this amount from any future payments to Poland.[71]

3.   DO FINANCIAL SANCTIONS LIVE UP TO THEIR EXPECTATIONS?

Overall, financial sanctions for rule of law violators are a welcome step in the right direction as they prove that the EU is willing to defend its core values more forcefully than before. This is not only an important sign to politicians who may have dreams about building an 'illiberal democracy' but also all European citizens who rightfully expect the EU to live up to its expectations and to be strong when it needs to defend its core values.

As shown above, this sharper sword in the Commission's hand, i.e., seeking severe financial sanctions, is not only based on the new Conditionality Mechanism but also the RRP as well as penalty payments in infringement proceedings. The introduction of the Conditionality Mechanism ensuring the protection of the Union's budget was an important sign, not only because of the new tools at the Commissions and Council's disposal but also because all Member States, albeit some less enthusiastically, accepted that violations of the rule of law which impact the Union's budget can have severe financial consequences. But the last months have shown that the RRF may play an equally important role in protection the rule of law; it may also serve as a blueprint for other European programmes to follow. Combined with infringement proceedings, which may lead to penalty payments, the Commission has now several tools that can be effectively implemented. As the examples of Hungary and Poland show, the Commission uses these tools and combines them in different ways for different Member States.

It also appears that these financial sanctions start to bear, albeit still minimal, fruits: For the first time in years, the Polish and Hungarian governments are

---

[71] Parliament and Council, Regulation (EU) 2018/1046 on the financial rules applicable to the general budget of the Union [2018] OJ L 193/1, Articles 100 f. ('Financial Regulation'). See also Pohjankoski, 'Contesting the Ultimate Leverage to Enforce EU Law' (2023) Verfassungsblog, <https://verfassungsblog .de/ contesting -the -ultimate -leverage -to -enforce -eu -law/> accessed 23 October 2023, and the recent cases GC, Case T-200/22, *Poland v Commission*, pending; GC, Case T-314/22, *Poland v Commission*, pending; GC, Case T-830/22, *Poland v Commission*, pending, and GC, Case T-156/23, *Poland v Commission*, pending.

engaging in, what at least appear from the outside to be somewhat serious, discussions on the status of the rule of law and their recent reforms with the European institutions. Compared to their former position, where both countries always claimed that the EU had no say in their rule of law reforms, this is a step in the right direction. In recent months, we have not seen significant additional rule of law backsliding in both countries either. While it is difficult to decipher the real motivation for the Polish and Hungarian governments it is likely that the financial sanctions imposed, and the threat of additional sanctions have motivated both governments to engage in these discussions with the Commission and to take first small steps to restore the rule of law in their countries.

But, as these initial steps are far from sufficient, it remains to be seen if and how these financial sanctions will indeed prove to be fully successful on the long run. Much will depend on the Commission's and other European institutions' handling of these financial sanctions against Poland and Hungary as the first major cases. And there are of course political implications and other dossiers which have to be considered at the same time. In particular with regard to the current economic and geopolitical environment, the Commission and Council may be inclined to make compromises also in rule of law proceedings in order to obtain the necessary support for other dossiers. Poland and Hungary are certainly betting on this by threatening to block decisions by the EU which require unanimity among Member States.

However, more generally, the support for more stringent measures has risen in Brussels and national capitals and across major political parties. Also European politicians, in particular politicians of the European People's Party who partly defended *Viktor Orbán* or generally argued for more dialogue instead of sanctions in previous years,[72] have lost patience with Hungary and Poland. In addition, the most recent election results in Poland of October 2023 are a sign of hope that societies do not accept politicians dismantling the rule of law on the long run. Also the broader political picture, i.e., the brutal attack by the Russian Federation on Ukraine, shows that modern societies are willing to defend their freedom and reminds us all of the importance of the EU and its core values. There are therefore good reasons to believe that the EU will be able to defend its core values and restore the rule of law, at least to a significant extent, over the next years.

Nevertheless, introducing and having to enforce a sanction mechanism is only the second-best option and a sign of deeper political divides: apparently, and contrary to what many European politicians and large(r) parts of the European society had hoped for, not all EU Member States, important

---

[72] Kelemen, (2017) *supra* note 3 at 225 f.

European and national politicians share the same basic values and concepts to build (or at least not demolish) a common European future. Also the fact that the Hungarian and Polish governments were elected and re-elected in free, albeit arguably not entirely fair, elections with strong results, shows that large parts of the constituency in Hungary and Poland, but also other Member States do not rank the rule of law as high as other parts of the EU. Working on a common European understanding of the rule of law and other basic European values, which the society at large is able and willing to defend against any attacks is one of the most important tasks for the next years. Only an EU which – despite any reasonable democratic debates on future policies – shares common values can be as a strong political actor.

Such support from the society for the protection of the rule of law is all the more important as these financial sanctions will be the most powerful tools for the Commission and the Council in the coming years. Other powerful options, in particular proceedings under Article 7 EUV, have proven to be too difficult to implement in practice.[73] And it is unlikely that the Commission and the Council will be awarded with additional sanction mechanisms in the years to come – apart from the fact that it is also unclear how they should look like. If the European institutions fail to solve the rule of law crisis even with these financial sanctions and other tools at their disposal, they are running out of options.

---

[73] For an overview of the Article 7 proceedings see the chapters by *Bauerschmidt* and by *Böttner* and *Schröder* in this volume.

Index

2020 Rule of Law Index of the World
    Justice Project 54
2023 Rule of Law Report by European
    Commission 173, 191

abstract (systemic) trust 152
    described 136–7
    rebuttal 137–8
accelerated integration 79
acquis communautaire 83, 144, 223
advocates 50
Albania
    Constitutional Court judges 122
    ignoring rule of law debate 82
    vetting process 97
Amsterdam Treaty *see* Treaty of
    Amsterdam
Annual Rule of Law Report 211
appointment commission model 102
Appointments Clause (US Constitution)
    103
Argentina 105
Aristotle 99
Article 7 procedure 62–4, 198, 235–8
    preventive mechanism under Article
        7(1) TEU
        clear risk of serious breach
            226–7
        danger 225–6
        serious violation 226
    restriction of voting rights 235
    sanction mechanism under Article
        7(2) TEU
        expulsion 230–32
        'persistent' breach 227
        procedure for initiation 228
        serious and persistent violation
            of values 228
        suspension of rights 228–30
    structure and characteristics 224–5
    criticism 232–5

preventive mechanism
    under Article 7(1)
    208–9, 225–7
sanction mechanism under
    Article 7(2) 208–9,
    227–32
Article F TEU 197
asylum procedures 61
Austria 118–19
authoritarian judge 51

blind trust 12–13
Bosnia and Herzegovina (BiH)
    ignoring rule of law debate 83
    "rule of the cartel" 91
Brazil
    Constitution 104
    judicial appointments 112
bribery in WB countries 90
budgetary conditionality 214
    see also Conditionality Regulation
Bulgaria
    Constitutional Court judges 121
    court systems, structural problems
        of 45
Bundesrat (Federal Council, Germany)
    119–20
Bundesverfassungsgericht (Germany)
    119–20

challenges to rule of law
    narratives 195
        counter-narratives 180
        diverging narratives 180, 184,
            190
        lustration laws 188
        one-sided narratives 180–81,
            184, 189–90
        overlapping narratives 180,
            184, 188, 193

parliamentary debates analysis
179–82
slow court proceedings 188
social narrative 180
substantial dynamics in
Hungary and Poland
188–9
topics of relevant narratives
182, 183
type and content 184–7
Chamber of "Professional Liability" 11
communication and cooperation strategy
of EU
actors communication with members
of national parliaments
190–91
consensus-seeking dialogue on rule
of law issues 193
legitimacy 191
overlapping narratives 193
with and by parliaments 192–3
productive communication with
MPs 191
rule of law issues, enhancement on
192
stakeholders 193
Community of law concept 202
conditionality mechanism 176–7, 229,
243
Article 2 of EU Treaty 69
Cohesion Funds 74
Commission's Delegated Regulation
(EU) No 240/2014 72
Common Provisions Regulation
(EU) 1303/2013 71
Conditionality Regulation 72–3
EU cohesion funds 67
EU funds
fundamental rights and values
68
in Hungary 66–8
EU money distribution 72
financial sanctions 64–5, 243
Hungary 244–8
Union's budget 253
governmental corruption 66
Hungary 244–8
political conditions against EU
treaties 71
refugees, issue of 65

RRF 73–4
veto, threat of 72–3
Conditionality Regulation 4–5, 214, 218
conformity with treaties 215
first application regarding Hungary
216–17
confirmation bias 178
Conseil constitutionnel 164
Constitutional Court judges 115–23, 131
Albania 122
Austria 118–19
Bulgaria 121
composition and appointment
method of 124–30
Croatia 121
Czech Republic 122
disadvantages of models 122
France 120
Germany 119–21
Hungary 121
Italy 117, 120
model 115–16
Romania 121–2
Slovenia 121
Spain 118, 120
term of office, duration of 120–21
Turkey 120–21
Constitutional courts of the Member
States
Czech Republic 164–5
FCC *see* German Federal
Constitutional Court (FCC)
see also Constitutional Court judges
co-option model 102
Copenhagen criteria 2, 32–3, 176, 223–4
Copenhagen Dilemma 224
copy-and-paste approach 95
corruption 17, 90
Corte Costituzionale jurisprudence
(Italy) 117
counter-narratives 180
courts
Constitutional Court judges *see*
Constitutional Court judges
Constitutional courts of the Member
States *see* Constitutional
courts of the Member States
New Member States: courts and
judges
Czech constitutional justices 39

Hungarian court 38–9
Polish court 39
public administration 40
Slovenian counterpart 39
role of 100
structural problems
Bulgaria 45
inner independence 50–51
outer independence 46–50
Romania 46
Croatia
Constitutional Court judges 121
feudalizing effects of judicial
councils 48
Czech Constitutional Court 164–5
Czech Republic 182
administration of courts 49
challenges to rule of law *see*
challenges to rule of law
Constitutional Court judges 122
democratic backsliding 77
length of judicial proceedings 188
national sovereignty 184
non-overlapping narratives 189
primacy of EU law 164–5

Declaration No. 17 concerning primacy
161
de facto rule of law 20
de jure vs. 76
de facto veto power 111
de jure rule of law
de facto vs. 76
democracy 2, 5
illiberal 253
surveys of questions about rule of
law and 26
discourse 5, 174, 192
political *see* primacy of EU law
rule of law challenges in parliaments
of EU Member States
see communication and
cooperation strategy of EU
diverging narratives 180, 184, 190
Domarnämnden (Judges Proposals
Board) 111

English Rule of Law 5–7
Enlargement Strategy (2011) 77

European Arrest Warrants 206
European Commission's 2023 Rule of
Law Report 173
European Council 210, 216, 223, 227,
228, 232, 234, 238
Article 7(2)–(4) TEU: suspensive
arm 209
rule of law as value in 1–5
European Court of Human Rights
(ECtHR) 4, 12, 42, 77, 83, 101,
109, 205
European Economic Community 8, 202,
221
European law
enforcement of 148
fully harmonized areas 145–6
non-harmonized (or partly
harmonized) areas 146
secondary 147
European public policy clause based on
Article 2 TEU 143–4
European Union (EU)
rule of law challenge in EU
enlargement 76–8
democratic backsliding 77
safeguard clauses 77–8
WB countries 77–8
rule of law as value in 1–5
European values
future: mutual trust 11–13
homogeneity 222–3
mutual trust principle 133–5
non-regression principle 139
ex-ante conditionality mechanism 142
expulsion 230–32

Fidesz leadership 41–2, 55–6
Curia 42
electoral system 41–2
intimidation 43
PiS *vs.* 45
power to transfer pending cases
42–3
financial sanctions
conditionality mechanism 243
Hungary 244–8
Union's budget 253
Hungary 244–50
conditionality mechanism
244–8

economy and economic
situation 249–50
government 253–5
implementation progress 245
interim measures 246–7
operational programmes EU's
Cohesion Policy 245–6
remedial measures to address
Commission's concerns
244–5
rights of final beneficiaries 247
RRF 248–50
universities benefit from
academic freedom 247–8
illiberal democracy 253
infringement proceeding and penalty
payments 243–4
Poland
government 253–5
independence of judiciary
251–2
infringement proceeding 252
penalty payments 252–3
RRF 251
RRF 243
Hungary 248–50
Poland 251
Framework Decision on the European
Arrest Warrant 142–3
France
Constitutional Court judges 120
Supreme Council of Judiciary
(*Conseil supérieur de la
magistrature*) 107–8

genuine judicial council 47
German Federal Constitutional Court
(FCC) 154–5
financial situation of various
Member States 167
Honeywell case 166–7
Internationale Handelsgesellschaft
case 165–6
Maastricht decision 166
OMT programme 168
PSPP 169
purchase of government bonds
167–8
Solange II judgment 166
ultra vires act 167

Germany
Basic Law 220
Constitutional Court judges 119–21
FCC *see* German Federal
Constitutional Court (FCC)
judicial appointments 110–11
primacy of EU law 165–71
Germany Rule of Law 7

homogeneity
Article 2(1) TEU 221
Basic Law (Germany) 220
concept described 220
Copenhagen criteria 223–4
horizontal 220, 221
rule of law 221–2
Union's values 222–3
vertical 220, 221
human rights 2, 5, 12–13
Hungarian Recovery and Resilience
Programme 249
Hungary 53–4, 74–5
challenges to rule of law *see*
challenges to rule of law
conditionality mechanism *see*
conditionality mechanism
Constitutional Court judges 121
courts 38–9, 49
criminalization of homelessness 40
current state of affairs 54
EU's traditional tools to cope with
rule of law situation
Sargentini report: Article 7
TEU 62–4
Tavares report 57–61
Fidesz leadership *see* Fidesz
leadership
financial sanctions *see* financial
sanctions
judicial independence *see* judicial
independence: Hungary and
Poland
liberalism 54–5
rule of law backsliding 239–40
rule of law 'counter-revolution' of
2010
cardinal or super-majority laws
55
Fidesz party 55–6
Fourth Amendment 56

Transitory Provision to the
Fundamental Law 56
substantial dynamics of narratives
188–9
value conditionality 64–74

idealists 6
impartiality of court system 10
independence of courts 4, 10
judicial councils 46–7
genuine judicial council 47
loyalty from judges 48
New Member States 47
Northern new Member States
48
phoney judicial council 47
presidents, domination by 47–8
Slovenia 48–9
outer independence
administration of courts 49
career decisions 49
genuine judicial council 47
judicial councils 46–8
loyalty 48
phoney judicial council 47
rule-of-law ethos 49–50
socialist systems 46
see also judicial independence:
Hungary and Poland
independence of judges
inner independence
advocates 50
authoritarian judge 51
see also judicial independence:
Hungary and Poland
informal institutions 88–91
inter alia 15, 31, 34, 35, 40, 41, 48, 101,
122, 223, 242, 244, 246
Italian High Council of Judiciary 108–9
Italy
Constitutional Court judges 117,
120

Japan
judicial appointments 111–12
judges
appointment of *see* judicial
appointments

Constitutional Court 115–23, 131
Albania 122
Austria 118–19
Bulgaria 121
composition and appointment
method of 124–30
Croatia 121
Czech Republic 122
disadvantages of models 122
France 120
Germany 119–21
Hungary 121
Italy 117, 120
model 115–16
Romania 121–2
Slovenia 121
Spain 118, 120
term of office, duration of
120–21
Turkey 120–21
in courts of ordinary jurisdiction
101–14
described 100
hallmark of actions 100
New Member States: courts and
judges
Czech constitutional justices 39
Hungarian court 38–9
Polish court 39
public administration 40
Slovenian counterpart 39
judicial appointments 101–2, 123
appointment commission model 102
Argentina: presidents of the republic
and parliaments cooperation
105
Brazil 112
Brazilian Constitution 104
co-option model 102
Japan 111–12
South Korea 112
Germany 110–11
Japan 111–12
judicial council 107–9
Italian judges appointment
by competitive
examinations 108–9
model 102

Supreme Council of Judiciary
(*Conseil supérieur de la
magistrature*) (France)
107–8
models of 113–14
monarch, by 102–3
Poland 109–10
political model 102
presidential discretion in superior
courts 105
single-body appointment mechanism
103
South Korea 112
transitional model 102
UK
Judicial Appointments
Commission for England
and Wales 105–6
Lord Chancellor guidelines to
selection commission
107
selection commission 105–7
Supreme Court 106–7
US constitutional mechanism
applied at federal courts
103–4
Judicial Appointments Commission for
England and Wales 105–6
judicial council model 102
judicial independence: Hungary and
Poland
Fidesz leadership
Curia 42
electoral system 41–2
intimidation 43
PiS *vs.* 45
power to transfer pending cases
42–3
PiS leadership 41
elements 44
European Court of Human
Rights and 44
Fidesz *vs.* 45
Polish laws, control of 44–5
judicial recruitment *see* judges
judiciary
independence and impartiality of
100
law-making role of 100

legal certainty principle 10, 204–5
legality principle 3, 204
legitimate expectations principle 10
Les Verts case 8
Lisbon Treaty *see* Treaty of Lisbon
lustration laws 188, 189

Maastricht Treaty (1992) 83, 159, 222
Merger Treaty (1965) 159
Montenegro
ignoring rule of law debate 82–3
Montesquieu 100
mutatis mutandis 220
mutual trust principle 132–3, 152–3
characteristics
abstract (systemic) trust *see*
abstract (systemic) trust
cooperation relationships,
reducing complexity in
137
rebuttal 137–8
risk, level of 137
specific trust *see* specific trust
tripartite structure, distinguish
by 136
definition 138–9
EU secondary law, exceptions under
147
EU values (Article 2 TEU) 133–5
ex-ante conditionality mechanism
142
general suspension towards Member
State 143
human rights protection 12–13
legal basis in EU primary law
Article 2 TEU 139
Article 4(2) TEU 140
Article 4(3) TEU 140–42
limitations
Article 7(2) TEU 142–3
European public policy clause
based on Article 2 TEU
143–4
national constitutional identity
clause 144–6
Opinion 2/13 11–12
principle of sincere cooperation and
140–41
rule of law crisis 147–9
mutual trust crisis, as 149

systemic deficiencies doctrine
149–52
systemic deficiencies doctrine
149–52

narratives
counter-narratives 180
diverging 180, 184, 190
one-sided 180–81, 184, 189–90
overlapping 180, 184, 188, 193
social 180
see also challenges to rule of law
national constitutional identity clause
144–6
New Member States
court systems, structural problems of
Bulgaria 45
inner independence 50–51
outer independence 46–50
Romania 46
inner independence of judges 50–51
law in
EU law 38
inter alia 35
legal nihilism concept 36
populations' value system 38
Rechtsstaat doctrine 37
rule of law: courts and judges 38–41
Czech constitutional justices 39
Hungarian court 38–9
Polish court 39
public administration 40
Slovenian counterpart 39
non-regression principle 139, 144
non-retroactivity principle 10
North Macedonia
ignoring rule of law debate 82–3

one-sided narratives 180–81, 184,
189–90
Outright Monetary Transactions (OMT)
programme 167, 168
overlapping narratives 180, 184, 188,
193

pacta sunt servanda principle 156, 162
parliamentary debate analysis 179–82,
194–5
Czechia 189

MPs' actions within individual
national parliaments 181–2
narratives
counter-narratives 180
diverging 180, 184, 190
one-sided 180–81, 184, 189–90
overlapping 180
social 180
opposition parties criticizing
executive 181
plenary debates 179
rationale 181
speech acts, coding of 179–80
time limits of speeches 181
personal communication 80
'phasing-in' approach 79
phoney judicial council 47
PiS leadership 41, 240
elements 44
European Court of Human Rights
and 44
Fidesz *vs.* 45
Polish laws, control of 44–5
Poland
challenges to rule of law *see*
challenges to rule of law
financial sanctions *see* financial
sanctions
judicial appointments 109–10
judicial independence *see* judicial
independence: Hungary and
Poland
PiS leadership *see* PiS leadership
primacy of EU law 162–4
constitutional identity
protection: K 32/09
judgment 163
K 18/04 judgment 162
PCT violations of Polish
Constitution 163–4
rule of law backsliding 240
substantial dynamics of narratives
188–9
Poland's Recovery and Resiliency
Program 251
Polish Constitutional Tribunal (PCT)
162–4
Polish National Council of Judiciary 109
political model 102
politics

judges *see* judges
strategies to overcome rule of law
crisis 173–95
Präsidialrat (judicial appointment
council of the court) 111
precedence of EU law *see* primacy of
EU law
primacy of EU law 154–5, 171–2
codify, attempts to 160–61
courts, enforcement by 158–60
Costa v E.N.E.L. judgment
158–9
*Internationale
Handelsgesellschaft* case
159–60
Simmenthal case 160
decentralised enforcement of union
law 157–8
Declaration 17 161
national jurisprudence questioning
161–2
Czech Republic 164–5
France 164
Germany 165–71
Poland 162–4
origins and sources
courts, enforcement by 158–60
decentralised enforcement of
union law 157–8
no uniform terminology 157
pacta sunt servanda principle
156
pacta sunt servanda principle 156
terminology 157, 161
principle of accountability 24
principle of proportionality *see*
proportionality principle
principle of sincere cooperation 12,
140–41, 223
proportionality principle 145, 207
public administration 40

quantitative methods 15–16

Rechtsstaat concept 7, 37, 39
recovery and resilience facility (RRF)
73–4, 243
Hungary 248–50
Poland 251

red judges 43
Reflections on the Revolution in Europe
196
Romania
challenges to rule of law *see*
challenges to rule of law
Constitutional Court judges 121–2
one-sided narratives 189–90
rule of law 30–31, 196–7
access to justice
effective judicial protection and
fair trial 206
independence and impartiality
205–6
advantages and disadvantages 14
à la Européenne 34–5
backsliding in EU
cooperation of Member States
242
developments in Poland and
Hungary 242–3
judiciary, media, and elections
laws 241
Poland, Hungary and other
Member States 239–40
values 242
case law of European Court of
Justice 8–11
Ajos case 9
Conditionality Regulation
2020/2092 10
European Economic
Community 8
independence and impartiality
of national courts 10
judicial review 9–10
Kadi case 8
Les Verts case 8
muzzle laws 11
challenges *see* challenges to rule
of law
community of law to union founded
on, from 201–3
comparison of indices
derivation methodology,
reproducibility and
description of 28
dissimilarities 28–9
indicators due to changes,
robustness of 28

information availability 26
interpretation 26–7
subcomponents 25–6
surveys of questions about
democracy and rule of
law 26
conditionality mechanism 141–2
Conditionality Regulation 4–5
consensus-seeking dialogue on
issues 193
contested concept, as 197–8
community of law to union
founded, from 201–3
État de droit and *Rechtsstaat*
198–201
contrat social 34
Copenhagen criteria 2
de jure and *de facto* 16
elements 2–3
formal 204–6
substantive 206–7
English and German concept 5–7
EU enlargement, challenge in 76–8
European values future: mutual trust
11–13
ex-ante conditionality mechanism
142
formal elements
access to justice 205–6
effective judicial protection and
fair trial 206
legal certainty principle 204–5
legality principle 204
prevention of abuse or misuses
of powers 205
indices 179
comparison of 25–9
V-Dem *see* Varieties of
Democracy (V-Dem)
rule of law index
WGI *see* Worldwide
Governance Indicators
(WGI) rule of law index
WJP *see* World Justice Project
(WJP) rule of law index
judicial independence: Hungary
and Poland *see* judicial
independence: Hungary and
Poland
legal interpretation 3

measuring 14–15
mutual trust principle, crisis in
147–9
mutual trust crisis, as 149
systemic deficiencies doctrine
149–52
national context 174–5
conditionality mechanism
176–7
confirmation bias 178
Copenhagen criteria 176
critics 175
institutions 175, 177–8
limited impacts 175
moral responsibility for
repressive abuse of
power 175–6
narratives of target group 178
research on institutions 177–8
objectives 2–3
Rechtsstaat 33–4
sub-principles 4
substantive elements
equality before the law and
non-discrimination
principle 207
equality of Member States
before the Treaties 207
fundamental rights, protection
of 206
proportionality principle 207
Venice Commission 3–4
Western Balkans, debate 79–81
(re)definition of term and
misappropriation of
acquis 83–6
ignoring debate 81–3
institutions as agents 86–93
Rule of Law Dialogue 213–14
"Rule of Law in East Central Europe"
project 173, 174
Rule of Law Report 211–13
Rule of Law Review Cycle 74, 211
"rule of the cartel" 91

sanctions
financial *see* financial sanctions
under Article 7(2) TEU
expulsion 230–32
'persistent' breach 227

procedure for initiation 228
  serious and persistent violation
    of values 228
  suspension of rights 228–30
Sargentini report: Article 7 TEU 62–4
self-restraint mechanism
  judges appointment 111
separation of powers doctrine 99–100,
  103
Serbia
  ignoring rule of law debate 83
single-body appointment mechanism 103
Single European Act (1986) 159
Slovakia
  challenges to rule of law *see*
    challenges to rule of law
  diverging narratives 190
Slovenia
  Constitutional Court judges 121
  democratic backsliding 77
  judicial councils 48–9
social narrative, defined 180
soft-law instruments
  Commission Rule of Law Report
    211–13
  Council Rule of Law Dialogue
    213–14
  soft law defined 211
Solange jurisprudence 165, 166
South Korea
  judicial appointments 112
Spain
  Constitutional Court judges 118,
    120
specific trust 152
  described 137
  rebuttal 137
state capture 91–2
supremacy of EU law *see* primacy of
  EU law
Supreme Council of Judiciary (*Conseil
  supérieur de la magistrature*)
  (France) 107–8
systemic deficiencies doctrine 152–3
  defined 150
  EU vis-à-vis the Member States,
    relationship of 151
  Member States, relationship of 151
  negative effects 151–2
  rule of law, relation to 150–52

Tavares report
  anti-European and anti-rule of law
    immigration laws 60–61
  asylum procedures 61
  Charter as treaty obligation in
    Hoffmeister 61–2
  death penalty and anti-migration
    political campaign 60
  Fundamental Law, changes in 58
  infringement actions 59
  new EU framework 58–60
  Resolution 69/2013 on "the equal
    treatment due to Hungary" 57
  Rule of Law Framework 60–61
transitional model 102
Treaty of Amsterdam 159, 197, 208, 222
Treaty of Lisbon 156, 158, 161, 197,
  198, 222
Treaty of Maastricht 197
Treaty of Nice 159, 208
trust from sociology concept 136
Turkey
  Constitutional Court judges 120–21

ultra vires doctrine 165–7
Union citizen protection clause 229
United Kingdom (UK)
  judicial appointments
    Judicial Appointments
      Commission for England
      and Wales 105–6
    Lord Chancellor guidelines to
      selection commission
      107
    selection commission 105–7
    Supreme Court 106–7
United States (US)
  judicial appointments 103–4

values 222–3, 228
  see also European values
Varieties of Democracy (V-Dem) rule of
  law index 14, 16–17
  Bayesian approach 18
  categories 17
  compliance and independence 17
  corruption 17
  dataset 17
    advantage 18

excerpt of 19
government and administration 17
WJP's and WGI's indices compared
25–9
V-Dem *see* Varieties of Democracy
(V-Dem) rule of law index
Venice Commission 3–4, 56, 212, 222
factors included in rule of law 3–4
rule of law checklist 203

Western Balkan (WB) countries 77–8
bribery 90
corruption 90
economic impact 90–91
ignoring rule of law debate
Albania 82
Bosnia and Herzegovina 83
North Macedonia and
Montenegro 82–3
reasons for 81–2
Serbia 83
institutions as agents of rule of law
debate 86–7
administrative capacity 87
captured and extractive
institutions 91–2
informal institutions rule 88–91
low trust problem 92–3
public administration reform 87
materiality as consequence for
accession process
civil society 97–8
copy-and-paste approach 95
public services to be
democratised 97
reforms against informal
networks and institutions
97
regulations and institutions,
comprehensive analysis
of 97
Slovenia 95–6

substantive implementation of
acquis 94–5
rule of law debate
decision-makers 79–80
(re)definition of term and
misappropriation of
acquis 83–6
ignoring debate 81–3
"improper conduct" 84
institutions as agents 86–93
media 79
population 79
WGI *see* Worldwide Governance
Indicators (WGI) rule of law
index
'what-aboutism' 82
WJP *see* World Justice Project (WJP)
rule of law index
World Justice Project (WJP) rule of law
index 14, 23–5
composite factors 23
cross-country comparisons 25
excerpt of 24–5
General Population Poll 23–4
Qualified Respondent's
Questionnaire 24
V-Dem's and WGI's indices
compared 25–9
Worldwide Governance Indicators
(WGI) rule of law index 14,
19–23
confidence intervals 22
cross-country comparisons 23
dataset 20, 21
disadvantage 20
Hungary, analysis of perception in
22–3
subcomponents 20–21
unobserved component model 20–21
updated versions of dataset 20
V-Dem's and WJP's indices
compared 25–9